TWO CENTURIES OF
ROMAN PROSE

Also available in BCP series:

Two Centuries of Roman Poetry, E.C. Kennedy & A.R. Davis
Four Greek Authors, E.C. Kennedy

TWO CENTURIES OF ROMAN PROSE

EXTRACTS FROM
CICERO, NEPOS, SALLUST, LIVY, PETRONIUS,
SENECA, PLINY AND TACITUS

Edited with Introduction,
Notes and Vocabulary by
E.C. KENNEDY
and
A.R. DAVIS

Bristol Classical Press

First published by Macmillan Education Ltd in 1972

This edition published in 1996 by
Bristol Classical Press
an imprint of
Gerald Duckworth & Co. Ltd
The Old Piano Factory
48 Hoxton Square, London N1 6PB

A catalogue record for this book is available
from the British Library

ISBN 1-85399-495-2

Available in USA and Canada from:
Focus Information Group
PO Box 369
Newburyport
MA 01950

Printed in Great Britain by
The Cromwell Press, Melksham, Wilts.

PREFACE

In 1964 we edited *Two Centuries of Roman Poetry*, which provided extracts from seven Latin poets for reading in the middle forms of schools, thus giving boys and girls a much wider acquaintance with Latin poetry than is possible when they are confined to reading part of one author only. The kind reception given to that book has encouraged us to follow it up with a similar book of Latin Prose, this time containing extracts from eight authors, four living in the first century B.C., four in the first century A.D., a total of about 520 lines in each of the two parts. The four Silver Latin authors are some way off the beaten track of Latin usually read in schools — and perhaps may be the more welcome for that very reason — but Pliny, Petronius, and Seneca are no harder than Caesar or Livy. Tacitus is rather more difficult, but the extract about Britain is of special interest to English readers and they should find the story of Nero's collapsible ship exciting, and we think that the help given in the notes brings them well within the range of middle-school pupils.

The author conspicuous by his absence from this book is Julius Caesar. We have omitted him, not because we think that his *Gallic War* is not suitable for our purpose — far from it — , but merely because almost every Examining Board has prescribed part of a book of Caesar every year, so that there is no need for us to include him here too. There is also a natural tendency, especially at girls' schools, to regard 'military' Latin as being unsuitable and even dull; we therefore hope that this book of almost entirely 'non-military' Latin will be a welcome change that will stimulate

the interest of its readers.   We believe that practically none
of the Latin extracts contained here have been made available
for middle forms before.

There have been important changes in the approach to and
the teaching of Latin during the last few years, with a growing
tendency to concentrate on the translation, closer under-
standing, and appreciation of Latin authors at the expense of
formal syntax and the turning of English into Latin.   We
hope that our attempts, begun seven years ago and continued
in this book, to broaden the range of authors available and
thus make Latin more interesting to the average pupil will be
regarded as being in keeping with the new trends in the
study of Latin.   At the same time we must mention that we
have thought it necessary to define and when required to
explain the various uses of cases, moods, and tenses.   Such
knowledge may no longer be considered essential in our
classrooms, but those who want to understand the Latin will
find the explanations here, perhaps not for examination
purposes but because they are of an enquiring turn of
mind.

As in the preparation of *Two Centuries of Roman Poetry*
we owe much to the fine collection of scholarly and readable
books which have been part cause, part effect of the cautious
renaissance in Latin studies in the two decades or so since
the war.   We would mention in particular the *Studies in Latin
Literature* series edited by T. A. Dorey, of which the volumes
on Cicero, Latin Historians and (for Cornelius Nepos) Latin
Biography have been a great help and inspiration; also, from
the same publisher (Routledge and Kegan Paul) the
stimulating essay on Tacitus in Professor Quinn's *Latin
Explorations*.   Other books of special value to us have been
Professor Michael Grant's *The Ancient Historians*, Stephen
Usher's *The Historians of Greece and Rome*, Sir Ronald Syme's
books on Sallust and Tacitus, P. G. Walsh's *Livy: his*

historical aims and methods, the pamphlet on Cicero by
A. E. Douglas published by *Greece and Rome,* and L. P.
Wilkinson's, *Golden Latin Artistry* (C.U.P.) Though few
recent commentaries have appeared which include our
selected passages we have been fortunate with those that do.
We gratefully acknowledge a debt too obvious to need under-
lining to the edition of Tacitus *Agricola* by the late Professor
I. A. Richmond and R. M. Ogilvie and the latter's Livy
I–V; A. N. Sherwin-White's *Fifty Letters of Pliny* and his
large commentary on the Letters of Pliny have also been
invaluable. No less important, in a different way, has been
the mushroom growth of *Penguin Classics* translations
including most of the passages we have selected. The help
we have received from these *as translations* is considerable,
and will no doubt be shared with alacrity by our young
readers. But we would emphasise also the lively and
authoritative background reading they provide for a deeper
appreciation of the authors studied; our debt here to all the
volumes concerned with our authors is extensive. But we
would mention in particular *The Letters of the Younger Pliny*
by Mrs. Betty Radice, to whom we are specially grateful also
for her generous assistance with information and advice about
the spring at the Villa Pliniana which complemented our
own observations.

We owe much to the books mentioned above. In addition
we have consulted general works such as *The Oxford Classical
Dictionary* and, for historical matters, *The Cambridge Ancient
History*, Professor H. H. Scullard's *From the Gracchi to Nero*
and Sir Ronald Syme's *The Roman Revolution.* Our debt to
other books on more general aspects of Roman civilisation
will be obvious, but is too vast to specify. In the realm of
visual aids we give pride of place to the two Nelson illustrated
Classical Atlases, the large one by Van Der Heyden and
Scullard and the smaller one, containing many new and

entirely different illustrations, by Professor Scullard. We
have used the editions of Cicero by Denniston and Peskett
(*Philippic* II), Holden (*De Officiis*), and, for the *Letters*,
Tyrrell and Purser and, when they included the letters in our
selection, Tyrrell and Duff/Lacey. In this and in a more
general way we owe much to R. G. C. Levens' *A Book of
Latin Letters*, S. J. Wilson's *The Thought of Cicero*, and
N. Fullwood's *Cicero on Himself*. For the other authors we
have used, as well as the recent editions mentioned above,
those of Sallust by Capes; of Livy by Freeman, Edwards,
Dimsdale, and Pyper; of Petronius by Sedgwick; of Seneca
by Summers; of Pliny by Allen, and Prichard and Bernard;
and of Tacitus (*Annals* XIV) by Professor Woodcock,
Pitman and Furneaux. The *Loeb Classical Library* volumes
covering our authors have been invaluable. Our suggestions
on 'How to read Latin' are based on the I.A.A.M.'s handbook on *The Teaching of Classics* and on Professor Allen's
Vox Latina; and our marking of 'hidden quantities' in the
vocabulary mainly on S. A. Handford's excellent little
Latin Dictionary published by Langenscheidt and Methuen.
We have followed the *Oxford Classical Texts* (by kind permission of the publishers) where these exist, with a few
minor alterations and the change of the third declension
accusative plural -*is* to -*es*. For Cicero *De Officiis* and
Tusculan Disputations we have used the text of the *Loeb
Classical Library*, and for Petronius the text in Sedgwick's
revised edition (Oxford University Press) with minor
changes, including, in Part II, No. 13(46,5), the emendation
venit abit. scit quidem litteras, which we owe to the *Penguin
Classics* Petronius of John Sullivan (page 189, Note 30).
The use of these texts we again owe to the kind permission
of the publishers.

Though we have collaborated closely throughout, the first
drafts of the Introductions and Notes in Part I were made

by E. C. Kennedy, of those in Part II by A. R. Davis. The biographical and other essays were divided between us, but the whole work had been revised by us both. We are grateful to Nicolas Lowton, Vaughan Irons, Tim Lake and David Lewinson, of the Classical Upper Sixth at Merchant Taylors' School, for doing a final proof check and offering some valuable suggestions.

E. C. KENNEDY

A. R. DAVIS

CONTENTS

LIST OF PLATES

xiii

THE COVER

From a photograph, by one of the editors, of the Arch of Titus
erected in the Forum at Rome by the emperor Titus to com-
memorate his capture of Jerusalem in A.D. 70.

ILLUSTRATIONS, MAPS AND PLANS
IN THE TEXT

HOW TO READ LATIN

All Latin, both prose and poetry, was generally intended to be read aloud, and in order to be able to read any kind of Latin correctly we must have some knowledge of (I) the length, or 'quantity', of vowels and how they are pronounced; (II) the correct division of words into syllables; and (III) the stress accent with which words were spoken in Latin.

(I) THE QUANTITY OF VOWELS

The quantity, or length, of vowels in a word and their pronunciation must be learned from teachers who speak and read Latin correctly in school, by practice and experience, and by paying careful attention to the 'long' marks placed over long vowels in modern grammars and dictionaries. In the vocabulary of this book all the known long vowels are marked, except diphthongs, which are always long, so that all unmarked vowels are short.

(II) SYLLABLE DIVISION

The Romans pronounced every syllable separately and distinctly, and divided words into syllables in the following way.

(i) When a vowel or a diphthong (i.e. vowels pronounced together, like -ae in *mensae*) is followed either by another vowel or diphthong or by a single consonant, the syllable division comes after the first vowel or diphthong, e.g. *a-ni-mō, flē-mus, au-fe-rat*.

(ii) When there are two or more consonants between two vowels or diphthongs, the syllable division usually comes after the first consonant, e.g. *dē-lec-tat, car-ce-rem, aes-ti-mā-tis*. An exception to this rule is that when the two consonants that come together in the middle of a word are such that can begin a Latin word (*b, c, d, f, g, p, t* followed by *l* or *r*), the syllable division usually comes after the vowel, as in Rule (i), e.g. *pa-trī, a-grō*. But the division in poetry can come after the first consonant, as in Rule (ii), e.g. *pat-rī, ag-rō*. The poets were thus able to make such syllables either short or long, to suit the metre; but in reading prose aloud Rule (i) should be followed. When three consonants come together, a syllable must begin with a combination that can begin a Latin word, so that e.g. *planc-tus* is thus divided. A word with a preposition-prefix is divided after the prefix, e.g. *cōn-strā-vit, ab-rum-pit*, unless there is only one consonant in the prefix, when the division comes after the first vowel, e.g. *a-be-ō, su-bi-gō*. *x* and *z* are 'double consonants' and are pronounced *cs* and *ds*; hence *exeō* is pronounced *ec-se-ō*.

The letter which is usually printed *v* in Latin was spelt and pronounced *u* by the Romans, who used *V* as the capital form for both the vowel *u* and the consonantal *u* (*v*). Thus *vīs* is really *uīs*, pronounced originally *oo-īs*, which when spoken quickly becomes *wīs* (like the French *oui*): so too *amāvit* (originally written *amāuit*), is pronounced *amāwit*. In most books, including this one, the consonantal *u* is printed *v*. Consonantal *u* (*v*) and vowel *u* sometimes come together in a word, as in *vult*, originally written *uult* and pronounced *wult*; the spelling in capital letters was *VVLT*. *u* before a vowel in words like *suāvis* and *lingua* is the consonantal *u*, pronounced like our *w*.

There is also a vowel *i* and a consonantal *i*. The latter used to be (wrongly) printed or written *j* (but not by the Romans), and should be pronounced as *y* when it occurs before a vowel at the beginning of a word, e.g. *iam, iēci, iocus, iuvenis*, or in compounds of such words, e.g. *iniciō* (pronounced *inyiciō*), or between two vowels inside a word,

e.g. *māior* (*mā-yor*). *qu* is treated as a single consonant, e.g.
a-qua, qui-dem; and the enclitic *-que* is one short syllable.

Until the beginning of the third century B.C. the capital
letter *C* was used for both *C* and *G*. This explains why the
abbreviations *C.* and *Cn.* were used for the names *Gāius* and
Gnaeus even after *G* was brought into the alphabet. It is
worth noting that *Gā-i-us* is a word of three syllables, with a
long *a*, as we know from its scansion in Latin poetry;
Gnae-us has two syllables.

(III) STRESS ACCENT

In English reading and conversation many monosyllables
are stressed, and nearly all words of more than one syllable
are pronounced with a slight stress or accent on one or more
of their syllables; some words vary their accent according to
whether they are nouns or verbs, e.g. 'We must concért a
plan to make the cóncert a success', or 'To accént this word
correctly you must put the áccent on the first syllable'.
Latin words also are accented, but the rules for stress accent
are much simpler, and are as follows:

(i) Words of two syllables are accented on the first syllable,
e.g. *vírum, ámās, déa, áudīs*, no matter what the length of
either syllable is.

(ii) Words of more than two syllables are accented on the
last syllable but one (the penultimate) if that syllable is long,
e.g. *amáre, pugnándum*; and on the last syllable but two (the
antepenultimate) if the penultimate syllable is short, e.g.
fácere, interéā, cónficit.

Monosyllables are accented when they are emphatic, and
very long words have a secondary accent, which is found by
working backwards from the last accented syllable and

applying again the rules just given, e.g. *cŏnstituērunt*, *exposcēbant*. The enclitics *-que* and *-ve* alter the stress of the word to which they are attached, e.g. *virum*, but *virumque*. It will be seen that the words of the old song, 'Amo, amas, I love a lass', get the stress of both Latin words and the quantity of the second word quite wrong; they should be pronounced *amō*, *amās*.

PUTTING LATIN PROSE TO WORK

Mr Jourdain: What? When I say 'Nicole, bring me my slippers and give my my nightcap', that's prose?

Philosophy Master: Yes, sir.

Mr Jourdain: Gracious me! I've been talking prose for the last forty years and have never known it. (Molière, *Le Bourgeois Gentilhomme*, II, iv).[1]

This snatch of dialogue, though often referred to, is less often studied in its context. What it says is that we often do things without realising it; what it implies is that when we do, we are apt to do them badly, and this is certainly true of that inescapable chore, writing prose. Whether it is a letter, or a school essay, or whatever, we all have to do it. If you are satisfied that you could not do it better, this is not for you. But most of us can learn something from Latin prose to improve our own.

First, the sound of it. Most Latin was written to be heard in public readings (*recitationes*), and aims therefore to please

---

[1] M. Jourdain: Quoi? quand je dis: 'Nicole, apportez moi mes pantoufles, et me donnez mon bonnet de nuit', c'est de la prose?
Le Maître de Philosophie: Oui, monsieur.
M. Jourdain: Par ma foi! il y a plus de quarante ans que je dis de la prose sans que j'en susse rien.

the ear rather than the eye. It is a mistake to say that because Latin is a 'dead language' and you are not required to speak it, you need not bother to read it aloud. It was meant to be and deserves to be. As you listen to it notice the care the Romans, especially Cicero, Seneca and Tacitus, took with the sound of what they wrote. What sounds well reads well. Can you learn something from this — perhaps by reading aloud some of that essay or letter you are working on before you inflict it on somebody else? If you find there is nothing you want to strike out, shift or rephrase, you surprise us.

Then, and arising from this, the order of words. Latin, being an inflected language, enjoys much more freedom here than we do because meaning is determined by the endings of words, rather than by their order, which thus remains free to be manipulated for subtle emphasis or sound. The poet Gerard Manley Hopkins, who tried to do this with English, lapsed at times into obscurity. You need not go that far, but words and phrases *can* be moved around in English without altering the sense and frequently, by giving a different emphasis, can make it clearer or more forceful. Study what Tacitus does in Part II, No. 16; you cannot go all the way with him, but going some of the way could improve your English strikingly.

What about your choice of words? Television interviews with 'the man in the street' often produce answers of traffic-light predictability. At the moment what is liked is 'smashing' or 'fabulous' or 'fab', what is disliked is 'disgusting' or 'diabolical', while 'no comment' is the smoke-screen of ignorance (much more impressive than an honest admission). By the time this is printed the reflex words will no doubt have changed with fashion; but the latest favourites will be just as mercilessly overworked. The Romans were more fastidious; the words chosen had both to be right and sound right. Their language was rich in synonyms and subtleties; but so is English. Shakespeare's vocabulary is the largest in English literature and probably unsurpassed anywhere. Since his time we have multiplied our verbal coinage, but how much of it, archaisms apart, lies buried away in leather-bound retirement, never taken out for an airing? Skimming through a dictionary (even a pocket one) is a chastening experience: buried treasure that too few can be bothered to disinter.

Restricted though many of us are in our range of vocabulary, we are nevertheless prone to extravagance with the little we have. Inflation afflicts language also, and too many words chase too few ideas. Latin, by contrast, is an economical language. Inflexions eliminate many trivial, mostly monosyllabic, prepositions, verbs do not need subject pronouns; and their insertion, or a change of order, avoids the clumsy devices English is obliged to use for emphasis. Latin gives wonderful value for space in an epitaph or motto. Take, for instance, a sentence from Sallust (Part II, No. 11, near the end), who says of Cato: *esse quam videri bonus malebat*. One translation (*Penguin Classics*) has 'he was more concerned to be a good man than to be thought one'; another (*Loeb*) 'he preferred to be, rather than seem, virtuous'. The first has nearly three times as many words as the Latin (14 against 5), the second (9 words) nearly twice as many, and loses in naturalness (especially the word 'virtuous', which does not quite meet *bonus* here) what it saves in words. This is in no sense a criticism of either translation; both, in their different ways, could scarcely be bettered. But the point is this: if English expends words at about twice or three times the rate of Latin, can we really afford to waste them on saying nothing, or very little, or merely repeating ourselves? Given something to write, especially in an examination, we abhor the blank sheet as nature abhors a vacuum, and all too easily become word wasters. Then is the moment to remember word-thrifty Latin, and the timely warning of Pope:

Words are like leaves; and where they most abound
Much fruit of sense beneath is rarely found.

(*Essay on Criticism*, 309)

To sum up, in a slightly different sequence:

P ick your words with care;
R eshape their
O rder;
S ound it out;
E liminate word waste.

This formula, rigorously applied, should give you a much-improved product of its initial letters, with the important proviso that you have something to say and a fairly clear idea of what it is. Our aim, in this book, is to help you enjoy Roman prose, not to provide you with 'Roman Prose for Profit'. But if your enjoyment brings a little bonus that overflows into all your other studies, so much the better.

TABLE OF DATES

Here are the dates of some of the more important events that took place in Italy and Britain during the 'two centuries' of this book. Many that occurred outside Italy, especially under the Empire, have been omitted. Those that concern our eight authors are in italics.

B.C. 106, *Birth of Cicero.*
102–101, Marius defeats the Teutones and Cimbri.
c. 100, Birth of Julius Caesar.
100, *Birth of Cornelius Nepos.*

B.C. 91–88,   Social War in Italy.

86,   *Birth of Sallust.*

82–77,   Supremacy of Sulla (d. 78).

81,   *Cicero's first speech,* PRO QUINCTIO.

73–71,   Rebellion of Spartacus.

70,   First consulship of Pompey and Crassus. Cicero's SPEECHES AGAINST VERRES.

66,   *Cicero's Lex Manilia gives Pompey command in the East.*

63,   *Consulship of Cicero.* Conspiracy of Catiline. Cicero's SPEECHES AGAINST CATILINE. Birth of Octavius (later the emperor Augustus).

60,   First Triumvirate (Caesar, Pompey, Crassus).

59,   First consulship of Caesar.

c. 59,   *Birth of Livy.*

58–57,   *Banishment of Cicero.*

58–51,   Caesar's campaigns in Gaul.

56,   First Triumvirate renewed at Luca.

55,   Caesar's First Invasion of Britain.

54,   Caesar's Second Invasion of Britain.

53,   Defeat and death of Crassus at Carrhae.

52,   *Cicero's speech* PRO MILONE (written but not delivered). Pompey sole consul.

51,   *Cicero's governorship of Cilicia.*

49–45,   Civil War between Caesar and the Senate.

48,   Defeat of Pompey at Pharsalus; his murder in Egypt.

46–45,   Battles of Thapsus and Munda. Supremacy of Caesar.

45–44,   *Publication of Cicero's* TUSCULAN DISPUTATIONS.

44,   Murder of Caesar.

44–43,   *Cicero's* SPEECHES AGAINST ANTONY (PHILIPPICS).

B.C. 43, Second Triumvirate (Antony, Octavian, Lepidus).
Murder of Cicero.

42, Antony and Octavian defeat Brutus and Cassius at Philippi.

35, *Death of Sallust.*

31, Agrippa and Octavian defeat Antony and Cleopatra at Actium.

B.C. 27–A.D. 14, Principate of Augustus (Octavian).

B.C. c. 25, *Death of Nepos.*

c. 4, *Birth of Seneca and Petronius.*

A.D. 14–37, Principate of Tiberius.

17, *Death of Livy.*

37–41, Principate of Gaius (Caligula).

41–54, Principate of Claudius.

43, Invasion of Britain by Aulus Plautius.

49, *Seneca becomes tutor to Nero.*

51, Defeat of Caratacus in Britain by Ostorius Scapula.

54–68, Principate of Nero.

c. 54, *Birth of Tacitus.*

61, Rebellion of Boudicca, queen of the Iceni, in Britain, put down by Suetonius Paulinus.

c. 61, *Birth of the Younger Pliny.*

62, *Withdrawal of Seneca from the court of Nero.*

64, Great Fire at Rome. Persecution of the Christians.

65, Conspiracy of Piso. *Death of Seneca.*

66, *Death of Petronius.*

68–69, Principates of Galba, Otho, Vitellius.

69–79, Principate of Vespasian.

70, Capture of Jerusalem by Titus.

78–84, Agricola's governorship of Britain.

79–81, Principate of Titus.

A.D. 79,   Destruction of Pompeii and Herculaneum in eruption of Vesuvius.

81–96,   Principate of Domitian.

96–98,   Principate of Nerva.

98,   *Publication of Tacitus'* LIFE OF AGRICOLA.

98–117,   Principate of Trajan.

111,   *Pliny's governorship of Bithynia.*

113,   *Death of Pliny.*

117–138, Principate of Hadrian.

117,   *Death of Tacitus.*

122–127, Building of Hadrian's Wall in Britain.

When Octavian became supreme at Rome he took the name of Augustus and the title of *Princeps*, 'leader', which was used by all succeeding emperors; 'Principate' therefore means 'imperial reign'.

Of the eight authors included in this book, Seneca was a Spaniard, Nepos and Livy natives of Cisalpine Gaul (later northern Italy), and the remaining five were born in Italy but not in Rome itself, though all eight lived most of their lives there.

The period 80–40 B.C. is called the 'Ciceronian Age', during which Cicero, Nepos, Sallust (and Julius Caesar) lived. Then came the 'Augustan' or 'Golden Age', 40 B.C.– A.D. 14, the time of Livy and the greatest of the Roman poets. This was followed by the 'Silver Age' in the first century A.D., during which Seneca, Petronius, Tacitus, and Pliny lived. It is so called because Latin literature was then beginning to show a decline from the highest standards of poetry and prose which were reached in the previous century.

PART I

CICERO

Marcus Tullius Cicero (106–43 B.C.) was born at Arpinum, in the Volscian mountains of central Italy. In a long life which embraced four careers — politician, orator, philosopher, and man of letters — we can only cover the chief events. Son of a business man (*eques*), and therefore a 'new man' (*novus homo*) who had to earn entry to the Senate, he studied oratory and philosophy at Rome and made his mark in his first surviving speech in 81 by opposing the distinguished orator Hortensius and showed courage in his second by attacking a powerful agent of Sulla. We can review his career in four stages, which might be called *advancement, achievement, setback* and *come-back*.

Advancement came steadily. After further study at Athens and Rhodes he married Terentia, a lady of good family but domineering disposition, and in 75 was quaestor in Sicily. In 70 he championed the cause of the Sicilians against their rapacious governor, Verres, and secured his exile. An admirer of Pompey, he pleaded eloquently and successfully, as praetor in 66 in his speech *On the Command of Cn. Pompeius*, that the distinguished general should be given a command against Mithridates in the East.

His name was made, and in 63, his year of *achievement*, he was elected consul. This was the year of Catiline's conspiracy to overthrow the government and set up a revolutionary regime (see Introduction to Sallust in Part II, No. 11). In his four speeches *Against Catiline* he uncovered the plot, secured the arrest and summary execution of the other ringleaders and organised the defeat of Catiline and his army near Florence. It was a fine achievement, but it went to his head. Cicero's consulship, 'justly but endlessly praised' (*non sine causa sed sine fine laudatus*, Seneca, *De Brevitate Vitae* 5, 1) distorted his sense of proportion and antagonised potential friends. He dreamed of a 'harmony of the classes' (*concordia ordinum*) at Rome, with himself, no doubt, as *maestro*, and when, in 60, he received overtures from the First Triumvirate (Caesar, Pompey, and the wealthy Crassus) he set his terms too high.

Now began more than a decade and a half of *setback*. Clodius, Caesar's political agent and no friend of Cicero, who had prosecuted him for sacrilege in 62, was set loose on him and secured his exile in 58 on a charge of executing Roman citizens (the Catilinarian conspirators) without right of appeal. He returned in 57 by grace of Caesar but apparently unchastened, for he defended enemies of Clodius like Sestius and Caelius Rufus and even attacked a land bill of Caesar's. In 55 he smelt danger sufficiently to support, in his speech *On the Consular Provinces*, the extension of Caesar's command in Gaul. In January 52 the murder of Clodius by Pompey's agent, Milo, tempted him to 'divide and rule' Pompey and Caesar by defending Milo, but the over-hasty disappearance of the defendant into exile and the 'rent a crowd' activities of Clodius' supporters prevented the speech *For Milo* being delivered, though it was afterwards published as a pamphlet. In 51, reluctantly and belatedly, he became governor of the province of Cilicia in southern Asia Minor, where he governed fairly and even achieved some military success (he was saluted *imperator* by his troops — *imperatores appellati sumus*, *Ad Att.* V, 20) but returned in 49 to find Rome on the brink of civil war between Caesar and Pompey. After long hesitation he joined Pompey's camp at Pharsalus in 48 as a gloomy non-combatant. But on Pompey's death and with hopes (encouraged by a letter of Caesar promising a policy of mercy —

it is preserved in the Atticus correspondence IX, 7c) that Caesar would restore the republic he spoke in praise of him in the speech *For Marcellus* in 46. Once more he overreached himself with a speech in praise of Cato after his suicide at Utica in 46 (see note on Part II, No. 11 (Sallust), 7) which provoked a counterblast from Caesar, the *Anticato*. Retiring despondently from public life he found little comfort in the domestic scene. In 46 he divorced Terentia and married his former ward, Publilia, only to divorce her for her lack of sympathy when his beloved daughter Tullia died in 45. But he found refuge in writing, and this was the most productive period of his life. Turning night into day through insomnia he wrote, speeches and letters apart, over 30 books on rhetorical and philosophical subjects including the five *Tusculan Disputations* and three books *On Duties* (*De Officiis*) from which extracts appear in this book. He approved of the assassination of Julius Caesar in 44; his only regret, he tells Cassius in a letter written in 43 (and Trebonius in similar terms, *ad Fam.* X, 28), was that he had not been invited to the working-dinner to plan it — had he been there would have been no 'leavings' (i.e. Mark Antony) (*vellem Idibus Martiis me ad cenam invitasses; reliquiarum nihil fuisset*, *Ad Fam.* XII, 4).

Cicero's own attempt to deal with the 'leavings' was his *come-back*. In his fourteen *Philippics* (so called after the speeches of that name by Demosthenes against Philip of Macedon, a political vendetta like Cicero's own against Antony) he attacked Mark Antony relentlessly. Some of these were delivered in the Senate or Forum but the greatest, of which the last few lines appear in this selection (Part II, 9(*a*)), was published as a pamphlet and is a scathing attack on Antony's whole career. Cicero supported the young Octavian, Caesar's heir and the future emperor Augustus, against Antony and even achieved some success in the defeat of Antony at Mutina in 43. But Octavian joined Antony and Lepidus to form the Second Triumvirate and supported Antony's demand that Cicero must be silenced. He was murdered by Antony's soldiers on 7 December 43 and his head and hands were displayed on the *rostra* (speakers' platform) in the Forum. Whether or not, in raising up Caesar's heir against Antony, 'the last year of Cicero's life, full of glory and eloquence no doubt, was ruinous to the Roman people' (Syme, *The Roman Revolution*, p. 4) depends on an ultimate assessment of Octavian helped by hindsight denied to Cicero. The emperor himself was more magnanimous: finding a work of Cicero in the hands of one of his grand-nephews he observed, so Plutarch tells us, 'An eloquent man, my child, and a lover of his country'.

Cicero's literary output was phenomenal. To list it here would be neither possible not profitable. A selection has been made under four headings including those you are most likely to meet in advanced Latin studies (the names are given in English as a clue to their content):

(a) Speeches: *For Roscius Amerinus* (80); *Against Verres* (70); *On the Command of Cn. Pompeius* (66); *For Cluentius* (a defence against a charge of poisoning, 66); *Against Catiline* (63); *For Murena* (a defence against bribery with an amusing attack on Cato's extreme stoicism, 63); *For Archias* (a defence of the right of a Greek poet to Roman citizenship, and containing a fine passage in praise of literature, 62); *For Caelius* (a defence against a charge of attempted poisoning brought by Clodia, the 'Lesbia' of Catullus, 56): *Philippics* (44–43).
(b) Letters: *To Atticus*, 16 books (63–43); *To his Friends*, 16 books (62–43); *To his Brother Quintus*, 3 books (60–54).
(c) Treatises on Oratory: *On the Orator* (55); *Brutus* (?46); *The Orator* (containing an interesting digression on the

role of the historian, with special stress on truthfulness, 46).
(d) Philosophical Works: *On the Republic* (before 51); *On the Laws* (?52); *Academics* (a discussion of the doctrines of various philosophical schools, 45); *On the Highest Degrees of Good and Evil* (a discussion on the ethics of the Stoic and Epicurean schools and the Old Academy, 45); *On the Nature of the Gods* (45); *Tusculan Disputations* (conversations on the condition of happiness reaching in the main the Stoic conclusion that the wise and good man is happy always, 45); *On Old Age* (45–44); *On Friendship* (44); *On Duties* (in the form of a letter to his son Marcus dealing with the four cardinal virtues, Wisdom, Justice, Courage, and Temperance and their practical application to life, seen as a problem of reconciling personal interest with honourable conduct, 44–43). A good overall picture of Cicero's philosophical ideas can be gained from the extracts in *The Thought of Cicero* by S. J. Wilson (Bell).

Mention should also be made of Cicero's poetry, most of it far better than the jingling line quoted by Juvenal (see page 16) and playing an important part in the growth of Roman verse; and of his work as a translator, catching the spirit of the original without being over-literal, of which a sample appears in Part I, No. 1. Those studying Greek will find a comparison with the original in Plato's *Apology* instructive.

Until the nineteenth century Cicero, commonly known as 'Tully', enjoyed an enviable reputation, but since then he has met with a decline from which he has yet to recover. He suffers from having four reputations at stake, those of politician, orator, writer, and man who has revealed himself without inhibitions in his published private correspondence. It is all too easy to judge one reputation by the criteria of another, and the whole man by his failures in each or all. Our concern is with him as a writer, but we must first clear

away prejudice arising from his other rôles. As a politician
he indeed had his failures: it was not easy to move through
the corridors of power in the last century of the Roman
Republic, and even Julius Caesar felt obliged to find his
way armed with purse and sword only to be met, at the end,
by his assassins' daggers. As an orator Cicero is judged
on written versions of his speeches, and not always the best
speeches at that. A speech, to do it justice, needs atmosphere, the speaker's own voice and gestures, the occasion.
Some of Sir Winston Churchill's wartime speeches make
poor *reading* for those of us who heard them delivered.
Cicero might have fared better had the tape-recorder been
invented 2000 years ago. Again how many reputations
could stand up, as Cicero's is required to do, to public
scrutiny of his most intimate hopes and fears as disclosed
in his private correspondence? And then there is his vanity
pilloried by Juvenal (*o fortunatam natam me consule Romam*,
see *Two Centuries of Roman Poetry*, page 219) and never
forgiven since. Yet even this can be explained, if not
condoned. The British cult of exaggerated modesty is not
everywhere observed. As a *novus homo* Cicero felt his place
in senatorial circles far from secure and needed the reinforce-
ment of a little self-advertisement. Also this self-advertisement is applied almost exclusively to his consulship;
elsewhere, in his letters, he can be quite self-depreciating.
It has been suggested that he had a conscience about the
summary execution of the Catilinarian conspirators (as
Caesar had none about the executions of convenience that
punctuated his 'clemency') and whistled ever after to keep
his courage up. Cicero himself wrote a treatise (lost) *De
Gloria* (See Part II, 9 (*f*)); as a specialist in the field he can
perhaps be excused for being concerned about his own.

This is not to exonerate Cicero, but merely an attempt to
clear away extraneous prejudice before we assess him as a

writer. Here his achievement is so vast that it is difficult to visualise the near vacuum in Latin resources of expression and even vocabulary which he filled. A passage from a speech by the elder Cato (234–149 B.C.) can help. We have not translated it because it is important to concentrate attention on the Latin words and their order:

Scio solere hominibus in rebus secundis atque prolixis atque prosperis animum excellere, superbiam atque ferociam augescere atque crescere. quod mihi nunc magnae curae est, quod haec res tam secunde processerit, ne quid advorsi eveniat, quod nostras secundas res confutet, neve haec laetitia nimis luxuriosa eveniat. advorsae res edomant, et docent quid opus sit facto. secundae res transvorsum trudere solent a recte consulendo atque intellegendo. (Aulus Gellius, *Noctes Atticae* VI, 3, 14)

The passage makes its point (the need not to have one's head turned by success) after a fashion. But it lacks shape and elegance. There is little variety of expression or sound. Synonyms pile up — *secundis atque prolixis atque prosperis, augescere atque crescere, consulendo atque intellegendo* — and jingle with like endings. *atque* (four times in the first sentence) and *quod* (three times in the second) are overworked. There is no concern for rhythm. Cato's motto was *rem tene, verba sequentur*, 'concentrate on the subject, the words will follow'; and so they do, with the mechanical dullness of cartons on a conveyor-belt. Contrast this with the passage from Cicero's *Second Philippic* (Part II, No. 9 (*a*)), and the difference in sound, structure, sentence lengths, variety and interest will be obvious.

But Cicero's achievement is not in oratory alone. He suffers by being read first, and sometimes exclusively, in speeches, and this book attempts to redress the balance. In philosophy he had a whole new vocabulary to invent, and did it with a taste and discretion that makes his words seem natural and very Latin. His prose here is clear, precise and workmanlike and dispels the false impression that he wrote only in long 'periods' (in his speeches, too, there are terse, incisive passages of narrative complete with historic infinitives). In his *Letters*, again, the style is matched to the medium. Letter writing, he says, is conversation (*in epistula tecum loquor*), but without the embarrassment of personal confrontation, for 'a letter does not blush' (*epistula non erubescit*). The Latin of the *Letters* is everyday Latin employing diminutives, colloquialisms, short sentences darting about with the mercurial inconsequence of actual talk. Those who know the Cicero of the *Letters*, calling himself an 'utter ass' (*germanum asinum, Ad Att*. IV, 5, 3) for backing the senators instead of the triumvirate, confessing to fright, indecision, grief, pride or whatever mood of the moment, begin to forget the 'commercials' for his consulship. This is as it should be, and if our selection from him helps you to do this, we shall be well satisfied.

1. 'Brave Men Despise Death.'   (*Tusculan Disputations* I, 96–102)

Tusculanae Disputationes is the name given to the five books of philosophical conversations whose imaginary scene was Cicero's villa at Tusculum, five miles south-east of Rome. They were written in 45 B.C., at a sad period in Cicero's life, when he had divorced his first wife Terentia, had lost his beloved daughter Tullia, and had now married again, but unhappily; he had retired in despair from the political scene and disapproved of Julius Caesar's despotism, though he remained on good terms with him.

Cicero spent his retirement in literary work, translating and adapting for Roman readers for the first time the books of Greek philosophers, not as an independent thinker himself but doing good service to future generations by expressing the thoughts of others in elegant Latin that has survived when most of the original writings in Greek have been lost. He had studied all forms of Greek philosophy and at first followed the teachings of the 'New Academy' (derived from the writings of Plato, 427–348, who taught in a grove at Athens sacred to the hero Academus), which rejected positive definitions and balanced the arguments on both sides of a question to obtain a probable result; but in ethics he inclined to Stoicism (the school of Zeno, c. 460, who taught in the *Stoa Poekile*, a painted colonnade at Athens), a belief in the existence of God and of free-will, and that a life of virtue in harmony with nature was God's will and could produce happiness. The books of the *Disputations* deal with the Stoic view of the wise man's contempt of death, with his endurance of pain and insensibility to sorrow, and with the proof that virtue alone can bring happiness. Seneca too was a Stoic philosopher, and refers to some of the Stoic doctrines in a letter (No. 6) in this book.

This extract from Book I describes the heroic deaths of Theramenes, Socrates, and (80 years earlier) the Three Hundred Spartans under Leonidas at Thermopylae, which is mentioned on page 24. We begin with a later stage in the history of Athens, the first part of which is summarised on pages 27–28. By the middle of the fifth century the Confederacy of Delos, originally intended for the defence of Greece against a Persian invasion, had become an Athenian maritime empire in the Aegean. Now followed the period of the greatest expansion of Athenian power in what is called the Age of Pericles, a statesman who lived from c. 500 to 429 and gained almost complete ascendancy over the democracy of Athens. In the thirty years of his leadership most of the great temples on the citadel of the Acropolis were built and decorated under the general supervision of the famous sculptor Phidias, and Sophocles and Euripides brought to perfection Greek tragedy, of which Aeschylus had been the forerunner. In Pericles' last years the Peloponnesian War (431–404) broke out between the democratic 'Ionian' sea-power of Athens, with its Aegean island empire, and the oligarchic 'Dorian' land-power of Sparta (in southern Greece), whose allies were the other Peloponnesian states and Thebes, a neighbour of Athens. The turning-point of the war was the unsuccessful invasion of Sicily by Athens in 415–413, which ended in total disaster for the Athenians and led to their ultimate capitulation in 404, after the Persians had joined the Spartans and Athens had fallen for a while under oligarchic rule. Theramenes, whose noble death is here described by Cicero, supported a moderate policy, midway between oligarchy and democracy, at the time of the oligarchic revolution in 411, a policy which earned for him the nickname of 'Cothurnus', a loosely fitting boot, used for hunting and on the stage, that could be worn on either foot. He commanded a warship at the battle of Arginusae in 406 and became one of the Thirty appointed to draw up a new constitution after the submission of Athens to Sparta in 404, but his opposition to the extreme oligarchical methods of his rival Critias led to his downfall and death in the same year.

Five years later the great Athenian thinker, Socrates, suffered the same fate. Born in 469, Socrates left no writings of his own but profoundly influenced all later philosophy. He fought bravely in two battles in the Peloponnesian War, and later first opposed an unjust decision of the democracy and then defied an equally unjust order of the oligarchic Thirty. He was a man of ugly exterior but great charm of manner, and though loved by his friends he aroused the hostility of those who professed to be wise by cross-examining them and gradually leading them on to admit that though claiming knowledge they were in fact just as ignorant as he himself always declared that he was; he was also bold enough to criticise some weaknesses in the democratic constitution. This way of life eventually led to his being accused of introducing new deities and of corrupting the youth, charges of which he was most unjustly found guilty and was put to death in 399 by being made to drink in prison a poison called hemlock, in the same way as Theramenes.

Socrates was a rebel against authority when it was not supported by knowledge and truth, which he held must be correctly defined. He did not believe in the many deities of Greek religion but in one Divine Spirit, and claimed that he received warnings on certain occasions from an inspired voice that he called his 'daemon'. He seems to have believed that the soul is immortal and would receive judgement after death. His influence on the young men who were his pupils was always morally good, for he taught them that virtue is knowledge and that the good is the useful. The chief authorities for our knowledge of Socrates are the historian Xenophon and especially Plato, who wrote many books in which he expanded the views of Socrates into his own philosophical doctrines. Plato describes the trial of Socrates in his *Apology*, part of which is here translated into Latin by Cicero, and his heroic death in his *Phaedo*.

1 (I, 96–97). *What a noble death Theramenes died, when he jested with his last breath and drank the poison to the health of his bitterest enemy. Soon afterwards Socrates met a similar and equally unjust death in the same prison. His last words have been preserved by Plato.*

1 Quam me delectat Theramenes! quam elato animo est! etsi enim flemus, cum legimus, tamen non miserabiliter

vir clarus emoritur: qui cum coniectus in carcerem triginta iussu tyrannorum venenum ut sitiens obduxisset, reliquum sic e poculo eiecit ut id resonaret; quo sonitu reddito adridens, 'propino' inquit 'hoc pulchro Critiae', qui in eum fuerat taeterrimus; Graeci enim in conviviis solent
2 nominare cui poculum tradituri sint. lusit vir egregius extremo spiritu, cum iam praecordiis conceptam mortem contineret, vereque ei cui venenum praebiberat mortem
3 eam est auguratus quae brevi consecuta est. quis hanc maximi animi aequitatem in ipsa morte laudaret, si mortem malum iudicaret? vadit in eundem carcerem atque in eundem paucis post annis scyphum Socrates, eodem scelere iudicum quo tyrannorum Theramenes. quae est igitur eius oratio, qua facit eum Plato usum apud iudices iam morte multatum?

2 (97–99). *'I believe,' said Socrates, 'that death is a good thing, for it is either the endless and dreamless sleep of non-existence or a migration to another place where I shall meet my real judges and converse with the great poets and heroes of antiquity. So I bear no grudge against my accusers or against those who have condemned me.'*

1 'Magna me' inquit 'spes tenet, iudices, bene mihi evenire quod mittar ad mortem; necesse est enim sit alterum de duobus, ut aut sensus omnino omnes mors auferat aut in
2 alium quendam locum ex his locis morte migretur. quam ob rem sive sensus exstinguitur morsque ei somno similis est qui nonnumquam etiam sine visis somniorum placatissimam quietem adfert, di boni, quid lucri est emori! aut quam multi dies reperiri possunt qui tali nocti anteponantur? cui si similis futura est perpetuitas omnis consequentis
3 temporis, quis me beatior? sin vera sunt quae dicuntur, migrationem esse mortem in eas oras quas qui e vita

excesserunt incolunt, id multo iam beatius est. tene, cum
ab iis qui se iudicum numero haberi volunt evaseris, ad eos
venire qui vere iudices appellentur, Minoem, Rhadaman-
thum, Aeacum, Triptolemum, convenireque eos qui iuste
et cum fide vixerint — haec peregrinatio mediocris vobis
4 videri potest? ut vero colloqui cum Orpheo, Musaeo,
Homero, Hesiodo liceat, quanti tandem aestimetis? equidem
saepe emori, si fieri posset, vellem, ut ea quae dico mihi
liceat invenire. quanta delectatione autem adficerer cum
Palamedem, cum Aiacem, cum alios iudicio iniquo circum-
5 ventos convenirem! temptarem etiam summi regis, qui
maximas copias duxit ad Troiam, et Ulixi Sisyphique
prudentiam, nec ob eam rem, cum haec exquirerem, sicut
6 hic faciebam, capite damnarer. ne vos quidem, iudices ii
qui me absolvistis, mortem timueritis. nec enim cuiquam
bono mali quicquam evenire potest nec vivo nec mortuo,
nec umquam eius res a dis immortalibus neglegentur, nec

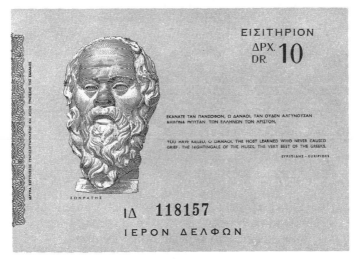

HEAD OF SOCRATES
from an entrance ticket to the precinct at Delphi

mihi ipsi hoc accidit fortuito. nec vere ego iis a quibus
accusatus aut a quibus condemnatus sum habeo quod
7 succenseam, nisi quod mihi nocere se crediderunt.' et haec
quidem hoc modo; nihil autem melius extremo: 'sed tempus
est' inquit 'iam hinc abire, me ut moriar, vos ut vitam agatis.
utrum autem sit melius, di immortales sciunt: hominem
quidem scire arbitror neminem.'

3 (100–102). *A Spartan whose name is unknown had a
similar contempt for death, and our own Roman soldiers were
willing to advance into a hopeless position. The epitaph of
the Three Hundred Spartans who fell at Thermopylae is well
known. Spartan women too did not grudge the loss of their
sons in defence of their country.*

1 Sed quid ego Socratem aut Theramenem, praestantes
viri virtutis et sapientiae gloria, commemoro? cum
Lacedaemonius quidam, cuius ne nomen quidem proditum
est, mortem tanto opere contempserit ut, cum ad eam
duceretur damnatus ab ephoris et esset vultu hilari atque
laeto, dixissetque ei quidam inimicus 'contemnisne leges
2 Lycurgi?' responderit 'ego vero illi maximam gratiam
habeo, qui me ea poena multaverit quam sine mutuatione
et sine versura possem dissolvere'. o virum Sparta dignum!
ut mihi quidem qui tam magno animo fuerit innocens
3 damnatus esse videatur. tales innumerabiles nostra civitas
tulit. sed quid duces et principes nominem, cum legiones
scribat Cato saepe alacres in eum locum profectas unde
4 redituras se non arbitrarentur? pari animo Lacedaemonii
in Thermopylis occiderunt, in quos Simonides:

'dic, hospes, Spartae, nos te hic vidisse iacentes,
    dum sanctis patriae legibus obsequimur.'

e quibus unus, cum Perses hostis in colloquio dixisset

glorians 'solem prae iaculorum multitudine et sagittarum
5 non videbitis', 'in umbra igitur' inquit 'pugnabimus.' viros
commemoro: qualis tandem Lacaena? quae cum filium
in proelium misisset et interfectum audisset, 'idcirco' inquit
'genueram, ut esset qui pro patria mortem non dubitaret
occumbere.' esto, fortes et duri Spartiatae, magnam habet
vim rei publicae disciplina.

CORNELIUS NEPOS

Cornelius Nepos (*c.* 100–25 B.C.) was a native of Cisalpine
Gaul, now northern Italy, the homeland of Livy, Pliny, and
other famous writers (see the Introduction to Livy). He
was born probably at Pavia or Ticinum but spent most of
his life at Rome, where he was friendly with the poet
Catullus (also born in Cisalpine Gaul), Cicero, and Cicero's
closest friend Atticus. He lived all through the civil wars
of that troubled era but kept aloof from politics and war,
for he possessed ample means that allowed him to live a
retired life devoted to the writing of his numerous historical
works. These included a history of the world (*Chronica*),
extracts from Roman history (*Exempla*), lives of Cato and
Cicero, and sixteen books *De Viris Illustribus*; of these books
twenty-four biographies survive, of which nineteen are of
famous Greek generals, three of 'barbarians', including
Hannibal, one of various kings, a brief life of Cato, and a
longer one of Atticus, of whom he wrote from personal
knowledge, as also he did in his (lost) life of Cicero.

In his 'Lives' Nepos is successful in bringing out the chief
characteristics of his subjects by means of straightforward
narrative and anecdote, though as a scientific historian he is
sadly deficient in accuracy and critical research. He lays
stress on the qualities of honour, patriotism, and dignity in
his accounts of Hannibal and the famous generals of Greece.

Cicero speaks of Nepos as being 'immortal', and Catullus
addresses his first epigram to him, mentioning his *Chronica*,
which he calls 'learned and full of hard work' and likely to
live for many years; it is probable that the later writings of
Nepos were superior to those that survive, since they were
so highly praised by his literary contemporaries. The style
of Nepos is on the whole clear and simple, though with an
occasional lapse into obscurity. His 'Lives' was a popular
school book in England for 400 years but are less often read
nowadays, so that the present time seems a good opportunity
to introduce him to boys and girls of today.

2. The Life of Aristides

Aristides was born in about 520 B.C. and fought with
distinction in three great battles against the Persians. He
was a citizen of Athens and was renowned for his justice,
uprightness, and good sense, and won great fame for his
organisation of the Confederacy of Delos in 477, when he
was appointed to decide what contributions each member
should make to the common fund. He died in 468 after a
lifetime of service to Athens, with a unique reputation for
integrity, though his rivalry with Themistocles for the
leadership of the city caused him to be 'ostracised', i.e.
banished by popular vote for ten years without loss of
property; Aristides however was recalled after only two
years, just before the second Persian invasion in 480.

This Life of Aristides is the shortest of the biographies
written by Nepos. It deals with a critical period in the
history of the western world, when the Persians threatened
to overthrow Greece and its civilisation. At the beginning
of the fifth century B.C. Hellas, as the Greeks called (and
still call) their country, consisted of a number of independent
city-states, each one controlled either by an 'oligarchy'

(rule by a few of the leading citizens) or by a 'democracy' (rule by the people or by representatives appointed by the people); these states found it difficult to combine with one another except in times of extreme danger, and not always even then. For most of the fifth century Athens, the capital of the small country of Attica, was a democracy that not only played a leading part in repelling the two Persian invasions but also produced masterpieces of art, especially in architecture and sculpture, and of literature of nearly every kind that have never been surpassed by any other community in so short a space of time.

In 490 the Persian invaders sent by King Darius were defeated by a small Athenian army at Marathon, 26 miles from Athens, in a battle in which Aristides took part as one of the ten generals. Ten years later Xerxes, son of Darius, himself brought an enormous fleet and army against Greece. The Spartan king, Leonidas, with only 6000 Greeks held up the Persian army for three days in the narrow pass of Thermopylae in northern Greece, until his rear was turned by treachery; the well-known epitaph on Leonidas and his 300 Spartans, who fought to the last man, is quoted (in Latin) by Cicero on page 24. The invaders then marched south and destroyed Athens, after which the Athenian Themistocles persuaded Eurybiades, the Spartan commander of the allied fleet, to await the Persian naval attack between the mainland of Attica and the little island of Salamis, from which the great battle took its name. Aristides held a command at Salamis, having returned home after only two years' 'ostracism', as related by Nepos.

In the following year, 479, the Persians were defeated on land at Plataea by a combined Greek army under the Spartan regent, Pausanias, in which the Athenian contingent was commanded by Aristides. They returned to Persia, but the danger of a Persian invasion remained and was met by the establishment of the Confederacy of Delos, a maritime league headed by Athens (after Pausanias and the Spartans had withdrawn from naval operations in the Aegean). The Confederacy consisted of Athens, many of the Aegean islands, and some of the Ionian cities on the west coast of Asia Minor. The members agreed to provide ships or to contribute towards a total of 460 talents annually to the Treasury of the Confederacy at Delos out of which ships were to be built for a combined fleet; the fund was to be administered and the ships built by the Athenians, but in 454 they transferred the Treasury to Athens and used the money provided by the annual contributions of nearly all the members to establish an Athenian empire in the Aegean, reducing the member-states to the position of subject-allies. One of Aristides' several claims to fame was the absolute integrity with which he 'rated' the contributions which were to be made by each member of the Confederacy in 477; he would surely have opposed the action of the Athenians (taken after his death) in using the common fund for their own purposes.

1. *Aristides, nicknamed The Just, was the chief rival of Themistocles as leader of the Athenian democracy. He was banished by 'ostracism' for ten years (in 482) but was recalled from exile when Xerxes invaded Greece (in 480).*

1   Aristides, Lysimachi filius, Atheniensis, aequalis fere fuit Themistocli, itaque cum eo de principatu contendit:
2   namque obtrectarunt inter se. ᐧ in his autem cognitum est quanto antestaret eloquentia innocentiae. quamquam enim adeo excellebat Aristides abstinentia ut unus post hominum memoriam, quem quidem nos audierimus, cognomine Iustus sit appellatus, tamen a Themistocle collabefactus
3   testula illa exsilio decem annorum multatus est. qui quidem

cum intellegeret reprimi concitatam multitudinem non posse
cedensque animadverteret quendam scribentem ut patria
pelleretur, quaesisse ab eo dicitur quare id faceret aut quid
Aristides commisisset cur tanta poena dignus duceretur.
4 cui ille respondit se ignorare Aristiden, sed sibi non placere
quod tam cupide elaborasset ut praeter ceteros Iustus
5 appellaretur.   hic x annorum legitimam poenam non
pertulit.   nam postquam Xerxes in Graeciam descendit,
sexto fere anno quam erat expulsus populi scito in patriam
restitutus est.

POTSHERD USED TO OSTRACISE ARISTIDES

2. *Aristides fought at Salamis and Plataea, and showed
such integrity and justice that when the leadership of the
combined Greek fleets was transferred from Sparta to Athens
(in 478) nearly all the city-states of Greece joined the naval
alliance (the Confederacy of Delos) led by Athens to oppose the
Persians.*

1   Interfuit autem pugnae navali apud Salamina, quae
facta est prius quam poena liberaretur.   idem praetor fuit
Atheniensium apud Plataeas in proelio quo Mardonius
2 fusus barbarorumque exercitus interfectus est.   neque aliud
est ullum huius in re militari illustre factum quam huius

imperii memoria, iustitiae vero et aequitatis et innocentiae multa, in primis quod eius aequitate factum est, cum in communi classe esset Graeciae simul cum Pausania, quo duce Mardonius erat fugatus, ut summa imperii maritimi ab Lacedaemoniis transferretur ad Athenienses: namque ante id tempus et mari et terra duces erant Lacedaemonii.

3 tum autem et intemperantia Pausaniae et iustitia factum est Aristidis ut omnes fere civitates Graeciae ad Atheniensium societatem se applicarent et adversus barbaros hos duces deligerent sibi.

3. *Aristides was appointed to assess the contributions of money to be made annually by each state in the Confederacy to the Treasury kept at Delos and later transferred to Athens. Although he was responsible for dealing with large sums of money he died a poor man (in 468) and his daughters were brought up and given a dowry for their marriage at the public expense.*

1   Quos quo facilius repellerent, si forte bellum renovare conarentur, ad classes aedificandas exercitusque comparandos quantum pecuniae quaeque civitas daret, Aristides delectus est qui constitueret, eiusque arbitrio quadringena et sexagena talenta quotannis Delon sunt collata: id enim

2 commune aerarium esse voluerunt. quae omnis pecunia postero tempore Athenas translata est. hic qua fuerit abstinentia nullum est certius indicium quam quod, cum tantis rebus praefuisset, in tanta paupertate decessit ut qui

3 efferretur vix reliquerit. quo factum est ut filiae eius publice alerentur et de communi aerario dotibus datis collocarentur. decessit autem fere post annum quartum quam Themistocles Athenis erat expulsus.

SALLUST

The little we know of the life of Gaius Sallustius Crispus (86–35 B.C.) suggests that, unlike Cicero, he was content to leave his reputation in the hands of his enemies. Born at Amiternum, in the Sabine hills, he joined the democratic party (*populares*) and became perhaps a quaestor in 55, certainly a tribune in 52, when he tried to secure the condemnation of Milo for the murder of Clodius (see page 12). It was said that Sallust had earlier been horsewhipped by Milo for misconduct with his wife, daughter of the conservative statesman Sulla, and that for this and a previous act of sacrilege he was expelled from the Senate by the censors in 50. But this story, a little too neatly tailored to what the enemies of Julius Caesar and the democratic party would have liked to believe, may be merely the scandal of their own invention. When civil war broke out between Caesar and Pompey in 49 he joined Caesar, at first without much success (he failed to relieve the beleaguered Antonius in Illyricum and to quell a mutiny in Campania), but later, as praetor in 46, he showed a talent for collecting supplies for Caesar, and was made proconsular governor of the newly-created province of Africa Nova (Numidia). Here he seems to have shown excessive zeal in supply-collection on his own account, and returned with a fortune so vast that, despite Caesar's habit of turning a blind eye in these cases, his enemies dared to prefer charges. These were dismissed, reputedly at the cost to Sallust of a handsome commission to Caesar, but there was still enough left from the plundered royal residences and treasures of Numidia for Sallust to build himself a villa and landscape the renowned Sallustian Gardens below the Quirinal, later the haunt of emperors. There he retired, disillusioned (he tells us) with the frustrations of public life, to tell in a posture of lofty disdain the story of the degeneration of Rome from the gallant little city of the seven hills into the 'city for sale' (*urbem venalem* as Jugurtha called it), the imperial capital of intrigue and corruption that had enriched and soured him.

On the face of it literary survival has dealt no more kindly with Sallust's writings than did his enemies with his reputation. His major work, the *Histories*, covering the period after the retirement of Sulla (78–67), survives only in fragments, mostly of speeches. Other works sometimes attributed to him, a miscellaneous assortment of political letters and personal attacks, e.g. on Cicero, are now generally regarded as spurious. He must be judged on his two historical monographs, the *War of Catiline* (published about 43) and the *War of Jugurtha* (about 41). The latter gives an account of the war (111–104) between Rome and the African prince Jugurtha, and contains much exciting narrative and incident with striking character sketches. But it is also an attack on the Roman nobles who were bribed by Jugurtha into allowing the war to drag on, and a glorification of the self-made general Marius, who brought it to a triumphant conclusion.[1] To be fair, however, Sallust does give due credit to the achievements of the aristocrat general, Metellus, whom Marius superseded, and to the debt of Marius, in his hour of victory, to the adroit diplomacy of Sulla. Of Sallust's other work, the *War of Catiline*, more will be said by way of historical background in the introduction to the extract from it in Part II. Briefly it is the story of the failure of a plot in 63 B.C. to overthrow the Roman government and establish a new, truly 'democratic order' by a group of conspirators led by Lucius Sergius

---

[1] It has also provided a motto for Merchant Taylors' School: *concordia parvae res crescunt*, *Jug.* 10. 6 ('small communities grow through harmony'); and some amusement to one of the editors when from time to time it is wrongly attributed to Virgil with bizarre attempts to make it scan.

Catilina, an aristocrat with a dubious past and a mass of debt. Sallust's treatment of the conspiracy, though lacking the furious indignation of Cicero, is hostile; and if it seems strange to find an avowed democrat condemning a democratic revolution, the reason is not far to seek. Its leader was a renegade aristocrat, and his very extremism damaged the more moderate popular cause of Caesar by playing into the hands of men like Cicero and Cato. Sallust's main theme, as in the *Jugurtha*, is the degeneration of Rome through the nobles, and Catiline, for all his belated conversion, is still one of 'them'. That is why, too, the extract below from the early history of Rome is 'a very shadowy outline' and names no names. Sallust is trying to establish a golden atmosphere of utopian dawn, and the hazier the dawn the sharper and starker the grim figures of present daylight would seem. Tarquin the Proud had no place in a rosy backcloth to the crimes of Catiline.

Sallust's style of writing is highly individual and contrasts sharply with Cicero's. The short, terse sentences, the archaisms of language, the contrived antitheses, the abruptness — all are part of a deliberate attempt to avoid the commonplace even at the risk of artificiality. His model was Thucydides, the Greek historian of the Peloponnesian War (431–404 B.C.), who, using a language which was by nature more antithetic than Latin, accentuated its character by seeing in history a world of contrasts: between theory and practice, between public and private, between alleged and true causes, between democrat and oligarch. With Sallust the style was father to the man. Striving for contrasts in his writing he contrived matching contrasts in his material; between nobles and democrats, between early and contemporary Rome, between the duplicity of the barbarian and the gullible greed of Roman aristocrats, and so on. It is this that explains the minor role of Cicero in the

War of Catiline. Passing compliments are paid to him: he is *optimus consul*, his first speech against Catiline 'brilliant and beneficial to the State'. But despite his execution of the conspirators, which Sallust does not condemn, he is a man of moderation, a *novus homo*, a middle-of-the-road man, neither patrician nor plebeian, for whom there can be no room in the centre of the stage. This is reserved for Caesar and Cato, and for them the contrasted character study (see No. 11) and the decisive speeches.

Sallust thinks and writes in extremes, and thereby presents a strangely modern image. He has much in common with those journalists and television interviewers who seek to trap their unwary victims into polarised positions of right and left, progressive and reactionary, 'for' and 'against', in quest of an eye-catching confrontation. For them, as for the Roman historian, there is little room in the centre. Sallust would be at home in Fleet Street or Lime Grove. But this approach had its positive side. Through his admiration of Thucydides and consequent revolutionary handling of the Latin language he somehow managed to graft Greek antithesis on to Ciceronian precision and amplification. Not that there is no antithesis in Cicero; but with him it is softened by balance and symmetry, often cushioned away in a 'period', while in Sallust it is stark and rugged, highlighted by the short sentences, the brevity, even the archaisms, asyndeta and historic infinitives. Cicero's is the art that conceals art; Sallust's parades itself to the point of mannerism, and mannerisms, as any teacher will tell you, get noticed — and imitated! After Sallust Latin prose was never quite the same again. Nor was the approach to history; and if at times Sallust looks at historical events and personalities through a magnifying glass or distorting mirror this at least was better than the blinkers of some of his contemporaries. It is worth recalling that

Tacitus, after toying with writing like Cicero, in the end
opted for Sallust; out of him he fashioned something
greater and far more memorable, but we could not have had
the one without the other.

3. The Early History of Rome (*Catiline*, 6, 7, 9)

Sallust here professes to give an outline of the early
history of Rome, but it is a very shadowy outline which
does not even mention Romulus, the legendary founder of
the city from which his name was derived, or any of the
leading figures of the early republic in the first two centuries
of its existence after the expulsion of the kings. The Greek
and Roman legends of the origin of the Romans and the
foundation of the city were invented in various forms in
the sixth, fifth and fourth centuries B.C., combined into one
story before the end of the third century, and finally established by the poets Virgil and Ovid and the historian Livy
in the time of Augustus. The stories are as follows.

Troy was captured by the Greeks in 1184 (the date
indicated by archaeology is about fifty years earlier) and a
Trojan prince, Aeneas, son of Anchises and the goddess
Venus, wandered over the Mediterranean to found a new
Troy until he reached Latium on the west coast of Italy,
where he killed a local prince called Turnus and married
Lavinia, daughter of Latinus, king of the aboriginal inhabitants. Aeneas lived for three years with his wife in a
new city called Lavinium and was succeeded by his son
(by a previous wife), Ascanius or Iulus, who ruled there for
thirty years and then transferred the capital of the united
Trojans and Latins to Alba Longa, where his descendants
lived for three hundred years.

The daughter of Numitor, the last king of Alba, was
Rhea Silvia or Ilia, a Vestal Virgin, with whom the god

Mars fell in love. When she gave birth to twins, Romulus and Remus, her usurping uncle ordered her to be killed and the twins to be thrown in the Tiber near the future site of Rome, but they were rescued and suckled by a she-wolf and brought up by a shepherd and his wife. On growing up they restored their grandfather to the throne and later decided to found a new city sixteen miles north-west of Alba, which was called Rome, but while building it on the Palatine Hill Romulus unwillingly caused the death of his brother. The traditional date of the foundation is 753. Romulus was succeeded by six kings, the story of one of whom is told in the extract from Livy that follows, until in 510 the tyranny of the seventh king caused his expulsion and the establishment of a republic governed by two annually elected consuls advised by a council of elders called the Senate.

This extract from Sallust sketches the history of Rome down to about 270 B.C., the time when the great foreign wars began, first of defence and then of aggression and conquest overseas. During these first five centuries the little settlement on the Tiber fourteen miles from the sea established itself against the attacks of its neighbours and then gradually overcame them until it became supreme over all Italy south of the River Rubicon. Sallust's tribute to the courage and victorious progress of the legions, which consisted of untrained citizens, not yet of professional soldiers, is fully justified, but he gives an entirely false picture of the social situation, which he describes as complete harmony between rich and poor, all men living virtuous and thrifty lives in concord with one another. In fact, the efforts of the rich land-owning patrician families to retain their wealth and power at the expense of the plebeians, who were oppressed by poverty and debt, led to constant friction and several 'secessions' (the first probably in 449), in which the plebeians withdrew *en masse* from Rome and threatened to form a separate community unless their demands for social justice were met. After a long struggle they obtained almost complete equality with the patricians by 287 B.C., which is the point at which we end Sallust's outline of the early history of Rome.

i (6). *Rome was founded by Aeneas and his Trojan followers, who combined with the aboriginal inhabitants to form a new community. They repelled attacks from their neighbours and helped their own allies. The first rulers were kings, advised by a Senate of elders, but when the kings became tyrants they were expelled and were replaced by two annually elected consuls (509 B.C.).*

1 Urbem Romam, sicuti ego acccpi, condidere atque habuere initio Troiani, qui Aenea duce profugi sedibus incertis vagabantur, cumque eis Aborigines, genus hominum agreste, sine legibus, sine imperio, liberum atque
2 solutum. hi postquam in una moenia convenere, dispari genere, dissimili lingua, alii alio more viventes, incredibile memoratu est quam facile coaluerint; ita brevi multitudo
3 dispersa atque vaga concordia civitas facta est. sed postquam res eorum civibus, moribus, agris aucta, satis prospera satisque pollens videbatur, sicuti pleraque mortalium
4 habentur, invidia ex opulentia orta est. igitur reges populique finitumi bello temptare, pauci ex amicis auxilio
5 esse: nam ceteri metu perculsi a periculis aberant. at Romani domi militiaeque intenti festinare, parare, alius alium hortari, hostibus obviam ire, libertatem, patriam parentesque armis tegere. post, ubi pericula virtute propulerant, sociis atque amicis auxilia portabant, magisque dandis quam accipiundis beneficiis amicitias parabant.
6 imperium legitumum, nomen imperi regium habebant.

delecti, quibus corpus annis infirmum, ingenium sapientia validum erat, rei publicae consultabant; ei vel aetate vel
7 curae similitudine patres appellabantur. post, ubi regium imperium, quod initio conservandae libertatis atque augendae rei publicae fuerat, in superbiam dominationemque se convortit, immutato more annua imperia binosque imperatores sibi fecere; eo modo minume posse putabant per licentiam insolescere animum humanum.

2 (7). *Now free from the tyranny of the kings, Rome began to extend her power, and her soldiers showed great courage in war, winning glory by defeating superior numbers and capturing strongly-fortified towns.*

1 Sed ea tempestate coepere se quisque magis extollere
2 magisque ingenium in promptu habere. nam regibus boni quam mali suspectiores sunt semperque eis aliena virtus
3 formidulosa est. sed civitas incredibile memoratu est adepta libertate quantum brevi creverit; tanta cupido
4 gloriae incesserat. iam primum iuventus, simul ac belli patiens erat, in castris per laborem usum militiae discebat magisque in decoris armis et militaribus equis quam in
5 scortis atque conviviis lubidinem habebant. igitur talibus viris non labor insolitus, non locus ullus asper aut arduus erat, non armatus hostis formidulosus; virtus omnia
6 domuerat. sed gloriae maxumum certamen inter ipsos erat; se quisque hostem ferire, murum ascendere, conspici dum tale facinus faceret, properabat; eas divitias, eam bonam famam magnamque nobilitatem putabant. laudis avidi, pecuniae liberales erant; gloriam ingentem, divitias
7 honestas volebant. memorare possem quibus in locis maxumas hostium copias populus Romanus parva manu fuderit, quas urbes natura munitas pugnando ceperit, ni ea res longius nos ab incepto traheret.

3 (9). There was complete harmony among all classes, and the only object of the citizens was to live a virtuous life. In war some eager young men were even punished for fighting contrary to orders, and in peace the state governed defeated peoples by kindness, not by fear.

1 Igitur domi militiaeque boni mores colebantur, concordia maxuma, minuma avaritia erat, ius bonumque apud
2 eos non legibus magis quam natura valebat. iurgia, discordias, simultates cum hostibus exercebant, cives cum civibus de virtute certabant. in suppliciis deorum magnifici,
3 domi parci, in amicos fideles erant. duabus his artibus, audacia in bello, ubi pax evenerat aequitate, seque remque
4 publicam curabant. quarum rerum ego maxuma documenta habeo, quod in bello saepius vindicatum est in eos qui contra imperium in hostem pugnaverunt quique tardius revocati proelio excesserunt, quam qui signa relinquere
5 aut pulsi loco cedere ausi erant; in pace vero, quod beneficiis magis quam metu imperium agitabant, et accepta iniuria ignoscere quam persequi malebant.

LIVY

Titus Livius was born in 59 (or perhaps 64) B.C. in Cisalpine Gaul, now northern Italy, a Roman province which was often called Italy even before it was incorporated into Italy proper in 42 B.C. It was the native land of several famous Roman authors besides Livy, e.g. Cornelius Nepos, Catullus, Virgil, and the Elder and the Younger Pliny. Livy's birthplace was Patavium, now Padua, and the literary critic Pollio (quoted by Quintilian) mentions a certain 'Patavinity' in his Latin, perhaps referring to some provincialisms of style which cannot now be detected, or possibly to the

eloquence of his language. He spent most of his adult life
at Rome and eventually returned to Patavium, where he
died in A.D. 17. He held no official post at Rome, and we
know little of his private life except that he joined the literary
circle of Augustus, who appreciated his talent despite the
fact that his history (in the part now lost) favoured the side
of Pompey and the Senate in his account of the Civil War,
instead of that of Julius Caesar, the great-uncle and pre-
decessor of Augustus. Livy is said to have encouraged the
future emperor Claudius to pursue the study of history as a
young man.

Livy wrote a history of Rome from 753 B.C. to A.D. 9 in
142 books, *ab urbe condita libri*, of which only 35 survive
(I–X, the early years, XXI–XLV, the Second Punic War
and the wars in Greece), with summaries of most of the
others. His sources were the works of the 'annalists', as the
first historians were called. The earliest were Fabius
Pictor, who fought in the Gallic War of 225, and Cinctius
Alimentus, who served in the Second Punic War (218–202),
both of whom wrote in Greek; others, in Latin, were Cato
the Censor (d. 149), who is quoted by Cicero on page 17,
Calpurnius Piso (consul in 133), and Coelius Antipater
(*c.* 120). For the Regal Period, which is hardly more than
legendary (described in Book I), Livy mainly followed
Licinius Macer (d. 66) and Valerius Antias (*c.* 90), using
their accounts one at a time and alternately, and for the
Second Punic War (Books XXI–XXX) Fabius Pictor and
especially the Greek historian Polybius (*c.* 202–120). But
he made almost no use of the scholarly researches of the
great antiquarian Varro (116–27), which would have greatly
increased the accuracy and value of the whole work.

Livy's defects as a writer of history include a lack of the
critical faculty required by scientific historians; a refusal to
make use of the original sources at his disposal and to weigh

up and collate the varying accounts of the annalists;
ignorance of geography, archaeology, and early Roman
institutions; and lack of knowledge of military tactics and
the art of war, which makes his account of battles confused
and difficult to follow. But his great virtues are his lofty
moral and political ideals, his skill in reconstructing historical
events and in depicting character (especially by means of
speeches, which were not of course delivered in Livy's
words but which reveal the character of the speakers with
great psychological insight), and the elaborate yet lucid style
of his language, which Quintilian (c. A.D. 90) called *mira
facundia*, 'marvellous eloquence', and *lactea ubertas*, 'milky
richness'. He uses many poetical words and expressions,
and his prose marks the beginning of the transition of the
Golden Age of Roman literature in the second half of
the first century B.C. to the Silver Age of Latin under the
Empire. His intention was to produce a history of Rome
that should be worthy of the greatness of the city and to
inspire in his readers a love of the old Roman virtues that
were beginning to disappear. Cicero calls the earlier
annalists *narratores rerum, non exornatores*, referring to the
dry, matter-of-fact style of their writing, but Livy is pre-
eminently an *exornator rerum* who adds a poetic elegance to
all his work. His fame was so great in his lifetime that it is
said that a Spaniard travelled from Cadiz to Rome just
to see the famous historian and then immediately returned
home.

4. How Servius Tullius became King of Rome (I, 39–41)

We have already described on pages 35–36 how, according
to a fusion of Greek and Roman legends, Aeneas came from
Troy to Latium and how his descendant Romulus four
centuries later founded Rome in 753. The fourth of the six

semi-legendary kings who succeeded him was Tarquinius Priscus (616–578), who was said to have been the son of a Corinthian exile settled at Tarquinii, a town in Etruria, the country north of Rome. He came to Rome with his Etruscan wife Tanaquil and on the death of King Ancus Martius seized the throne from Ancus' sons. In this extract Livy describes the rise to power of Servius Tullius, a boy of obscure origin, round whose head as he slept a mysterious fire played, which Tanaquil interpreted as foretelling high fortune for him. His mother was said to have been a slave, or (according to another story) Ocrisia, wife of a nobleman of Corniculum in Latium, who was captured and brought to Rome, where she was kindly treated by Tanaquil. The legend of fire playing around the head of a child, to signify originally that the father was the Fire god, was applied to several children favoured by fortune, including Ascanius (Iulus), son of Aeneas (*Aeneid* II, 680 *ff.*), and Lavinia, daughter of King Latinus and second wife of Aeneas, from whom Romulus was descended (*Aeneid* VII, 71 *ff.*). Servius Tullius was brought up after the incident of the divine fire as the son of the king and queen, and succeeded to the throne after the murder of Tarquin in 578. He had a long and prosperous reign until 534 (all these dates are merely traditional), when he was murdered by his own daughter Tullia, who had married a son of Tarquinius Priscus; this man became the seventh and last king of Rome as Tarquinius Superbus.

1 (I, 39), 1–4. *A flame begins to play round the head of a boy called Servius Tullius while he is asleep in the palace of Tarquin and Tanaquil. The queen lets him sleep on until the flame disappears, and tells Tarquin that they must adopt the boy as their son, for he is destined to defend the royal power in times of danger. Servius is brought up as a prince and turns*

*out to be of truly royal character, so that Tarquin gives him his
own daughter in marriage.*

1   Eo tempore in regia prodigium visu eventuque mirabile
fuit. puero dormienti, cui Servio Tullio fuit nomen, caput
2 arsisse ferunt multorum in conspectu; plurimo igitur
clamore inde ad tantae rei miraculum orto excitos reges, et
cum quidam familiarium aquam ad restinguendum ferret,
ab regina retentum, sedatoque eam tumultu moveri vetuisse
puerum donec sua sponte experrectus esset; mox cum
3 somno et flammam abisse. tum abducto in secretum viro
Tanaquil 'viden tu puerum hunc' inquit, 'quem tam humili
cultu educamus? scire licet hunc lumen quondam rebus
nostris dubiis futurum praesidiumque regiae adflictae;
proinde materiam ingentis publice privatimque decoris
4 omni indulgentia nostra nutriamus.' inde puerum liberum
loco coeptum haberi erudirique artibus quibus ingenia ad
magnae fortunae cultum excitantur. evenit facile quod
dis cordi esset; iuvenis evasit vere indolis regiae nec, cum
quaereretur gener Tarquinio, quisquam Romanae iuventutis ulla arte conferri potuit, filiamque ei suam rex despondit.

  1, 5–6. *Livy cannot believe the story that a person of such
ability was the son of a slave-woman; he thinks that Servius'
mother was the wife of a prince and was brought as a captive
from her home at Corniculum to Rome, where Tanaquil
rescued her from slavery and befriended her and her son.*

5   Hic quacumque de causa tantus illi honos habitus credere
prohibet serva natum eum parvumque ipsum servisse.
eorum magis sententiae sum qui Corniculo capto Ser.
Tulli, qui princeps in illa urbe fuerat, gravidam viro occiso
uxorem, cum inter reliquas captivas cognita esset, ob
unicam nobilitatem ab regina Romana prohibitam ferunt

servitio partum Romae edidisse Prisci Tarquini in domo;
6 inde tanto beneficio et inter mulieres familiaritatem auctam
et puerum, ut in domo a parvo eductum, in caritate atque
honore fuisse; fortunam matris, quod capta patria in
hostium manus venerit, ut serva natus crederetur fecisse.

2 (40), 1–3. *Servius is now universally held in honour, but
the two sons of the former king, Ancus Martius, are indignant
at the prospect of their father's throne passing from a foreign
usurper to a man of servile birth.*

Duodequadragesimo ferme anno ex quo regnare coeperat
Tarquinius, non apud regem modo sed apud patres ple-
2 bemque longe maximo honore Ser. Tullius erat. tum Anci
filii duo, etsi antea semper pro indignissimo habuerant se
patrio regno tutoris fraude pulsos, regnare Romae advenam
non modo vicinae sed ne Italicae quidem stirpis, tum
impensius iis indignitas crescere si ne ab Tarquinio quidem
3 ad se rediret regnum, sed praeceps inde porro ad servitia
caderet, ut in eadem civitate post centesimum fere annum
quam Romulus deo prognatus deus ipse tenuerit regnum
donec in terris fuerit, id servus serva natus possideat. cum
commune Romani nominis tum praecipue id domus suae
dedecus fore, si Anci virili stirpe salva non modo advenis
sed servis etiam regnum Romae pateret.

2, 4–7. *They therefore make a plot against Tarquin, who is
the real object of their resentment, and hire two shepherds, who
pretend to quarrel in the king's presence until he turns his
back on one of them; the other then strikes a deadly blow with
an axe at his head.*

4 Ferro igitur eam arcere contumeliam statuunt; sed et
iniuriae dolor in Tarquinium ipsum magis quam in Servium
eos stimulabat, et quia gravior ultor caedis, si superesset,

rex futurus erat quam privatus; tum Servio occiso, quemcumque alium generum delegisset, eundem regni heredem
5 facturus videbatur; ob haec ipsi regi insidiae parantur. ex
pastoribus duo ferocissimi delecti ad facinus, quibus
consueti erant uterque agrestibus ferramentis, in vestibulo
regiae quam potuere tumultuossime specie rixae in se omnes
apparitores regios convertunt; inde, cum ambo regem
appellarent clamorque eorum penitus in regiam pervenisset,
6 vocati ad regem pergunt. primo uterque vociferari et
certatim alter alteri obstrepere; coerciti ab lictore et iussi
in vicem dicere tandem obloqui desistunt; unus rem ex
7 composito orditur. cum intentus in eum se rex totus
averteret, alter clatam securim in caput deiecit, relictoque
in vulnere telo ambo se foras eiciunt.

3 (41), 1–3. *Tanaquil declares that her husband's wound is*
not serious, sends for Servius, and urges him to be a man and
seize the throne in accordance with the omen of the sacred fire
that once played round his head.

1   Tarquinium moribundum cum qui circa erant excepis-
sent, illos fugientes lictores comprehendunt. clamor inde
concursusque populi, mirantium quid rei esset. Tanaquil
inter tumultum claudi regiam iubet, arbitros eiecit. simul
quae curando vulneri opus sunt, tamquam spes subesset,
sedulo comparat, simul si destituat spes, alia praesidia
2 molitur. Servio propere accito cum paene exsanguem virum
ostendisset, dextram tenens orat ne inultam mortem soceri,
3 ne socrum inimicis ludibrio esse sinat. 'tuum est' inquit,
'Servi, si vir es, regnum, non eorum qui alienis manibus
pessimum facinus fecere. erige te deosque duces sequere
qui clarum hoc fore caput divino quondam circumfuso
igni portenderunt. nunc te illa caelestis excitet flamma;
nunc expergiscere vere. et nos peregrini regnavimus; qui

sis, non unde natus sis reputa.   si tua re subita torpent
consilia, at tu mea consilia sequere.'

3, 4–7. *She then tells the people that Tarquin's wound is
not serious and that until it is healed Servius will act as regent.
He does so for some days after the king's death, and when the
truth is revealed he is already established as king with the
approval of the Senate.   The sons of Ancus go into exile.*

4   Cum clamor impetusque multitudinis vix sustineri posset,
ex superiore parte aedium per fenestras in Novam Viam
versas — habitabat enim rex ad Iovis Statoris — populum
5   Tanaquil adloquitur. iubet bono animo esse; sopitum fuisse
regem subito ictu; ferrum haud alte in corpus descendisse;
iam ad se redisse; inspectum vulnus absterso cruore; omnia
salubria esse; confidere propediem ipsum eos visuros; interim Ser. Tullio iubere populum dicto audientem esse; eum
6   iura redditurum obiturumque alia regis munia esse. Servius
cum trabea et lictoribus prodit ac sede regia sedens alia
decernit, de aliis consulturum se regem esse simulat.
itaque per aliquot dies, cum iam exspirasset Tarquinius,
celata morte per speciem alienae fungendae vicis suas opes
firmavit, tum demum palam factum est comploratione in
regia orta.   Servius praesidio firmo munitus, primus
7   iniussu populi, voluntate patrum regnavit.   Anci liberi, iam
tum comprensis sceleris ministris, ut vivere regem et tantas
esse opes Servi nuntiatum est, Suessam Pometiam exsulatum ierant.

PETRONIUS

Gaius Petronius is generally agreed to have been the
author of the book called *Satyricon*.   All that we know about
his life and character comes from Tacitus (*Annals* XVI, 18),

who tells us that Petronius had served as proconsul (governor) of Bithynia and later as consul at Rome, showing himself to be an energetic and capable administrator though he had previously been a man of great indolence who was devoted to the pursuit of luxury. After holding these two official posts he became the intimate friend of the emperor Nero (A.D. 54–68) and his *Arbiter Elegantiae* (arbiter of elegance, or adviser on matters of taste), but Nero's favourite, Tigellinus, became jealous of Petronius and in 66 turned Nero against him by false accusations. While on his way to join the court in Campania Petronius was detained by Nero's orders at Cumae and decided to take his own life without waiting in suspense between hope and fear. He opened his veins and then had the wound bound up and opened again while he conversed with his friends, dined, slept, rewarded or punished his slaves, wrote a list of Nero's crimes in his will, which he sent to the emperor, broke his signet ring so that it should not be used to bring others into danger, and so eventually died.

The *Satyricon* belongs to the class of Roman literature called 'Menippean Satire'. The word satire is derived from *satura*, 'a medley', which was a mixture of prose and verse written on a variety of subjects. Earlier satirists were Lucilius (*c.* 120 B.C.) and Varro (118–28 B.C.), followed by Horace (65–8 B.C.), Persius (A.D. 34–62), and Juvenal (*c.* A.D. 100), all three of whom wrote their satires only in hexameters. Seneca (4 B.C.–A.D. 65), some of whose prose work is included in this book, probably wrote the *Apocolocyntosis* ('Pumpkinification', a parody of *Apotheosis*, 'deification') of the emperor Claudius, in prose interspersed with some poetry (see page 52), and the *Satyricon* of Petronius took the same form. It must have been a very long work if it is true that the surviving portions were part of the fifteenth and sixteenth books. It describes the adventures of two disreputable ex-slaves called Encolpius and Ascyltus, with their slave-boy Giton, in the half-Greek towns of Campania and southern Italy. The chief episode, probably set in Cumae, near Naples, is the 'Feast of Trimalchio', another ex-slave who had become enormously rich and was spending his money in tasteless luxury and extravagance. During the dinner one of the guests, Niceros, tells the story of the were-wolf, and another, Echion, boasts of the cleverness of his son. The story continues with the entrance of a depraved old poet, Eumolpus, who is shipwrecked with his three companions on their way to Crotona; among other things he recites some poetry of his own (i.e. written by Petronius) in criticism of contemporary epic poetry, probably aimed in particular at Lucan, a nephew of Seneca and author of an epic on the Civil War called *Pharsalia*. The *Satyricon*, as we have it, tails off into incoherent fragments.

The *Satyricon* is the first of what are called 'picaresque' novels and is the forerunner of all similar novels in later literature. The word is derived from the Spanish *picaro*, 'a rogue', and implies a description, without a formal plot, of the adventures of often disreputable characters. Smollet and Fielding are the leading writers of this kind of book in England. Petronius gives an extraordinarily vivid picture of life among the lower classes in the provincial towns of Italy during the first century A.D. It contains some good poetry, much intelligent literary criticism, many scenes of adventure and intrigue, and above all the actual words and phrases used at the time by the great mass of the uneducated people, which show the beginning of the debasement of classical Latin on its way to the transition to medieval and modern Italian. There are many colloquialisms, proverbial sayings, and irregularities of grammar and syntax, some of which appear in the two extracts given in this book; all of them are of course explained in the Notes.

5. The Werewolf (*Satyricon* 61, 6–62)

1, 1–3 (61, 6–9). *At Trimalchio's Dinner Party one of the guests, an ex-slave called Niceros, tells a story.* 'When I was still a slave here at Cumae I was in love with Melissa, the wife of Terentius, who was the innkeeper of an inn owned by our master in the country. Terentius died suddenly, and I decided to go and see if I could help Melissa in her trouble.'

1 Cum adhuc servirem, habitabamus in Vico Angusto; nunc Gavillae domus est. ibi, quomodo dii volunt, amare coepi uxorem Terentii cauponis: noveratis Melissam
2 Tarentinam, pulcherrimum bacciballum. si quid ab illa petii, numquam mihi negatum; fecit assem, semissem habui; quidquid habui, in illius sinum demandavi, nec
3 umquam fefellitus sum. huius contubernalis ad villam supremum diem obiit. itaque per scutum, per ocream, egi, aginavi, quemadmodum ad illam pervenirem; scitis autem, in angustiis amici apparent.

2 (62), 1–8. '*In my master's absence I set out for the inn, accompanied by a soldier who was staying in the house. When we reached a cemetery near the road, my companion took off his clothes, turned into a wolf, and went off howling into the woods, leaving his clothes turned to stone.*'

1 Forte dominus Capuam exierat ad scruta scita expedienda.
2 nactus ego occasionem persuadeo hospitem nostrum ut mecum ad quintum miliarium veniat. erat autem miles,
3 fortis tamquam Orcus. apoculamus nos circa gallicinia;
4 luna lucebat tamquam meridie. venimus intra monimenta; homo meus coepit ad stelas facere; sedeo ego cantabundus
5 et stelas numero. deinde ut respexi ad comitem, ille exuit se et omnia vestimenta secundum viam posuit. mihi

6 anima in naso esse; stabam tamquam mortuus. at ille
subito lupus factus est. nolite me iocari putare; ut mentiar,
7 nullius patrimonium tanti facio. sed, quod coeperam
dicere, postquam lupus factus est, ululare coepit et in silvas
8 fugit. ego primitus nesciebam ubi essem, deinde accessi
ut vestimenta eius tollerem: illa autem lapidea facta sunt.

2 (62), 9–14. *'On reaching Melissa's house half dead with
fright, I was told that a wolf had worried all the sheep but had
received a spear-wound in the neck. I hurried home at dawn,
finding on the way that the soldier's petrified clothes had turned
into a pool of blood, and when I arrived he was lying in bed,
with a doctor attending to a wound in his neck.'*

9 Qui mori timore nisi ego? gladium tamen strinxi et in
tota via umbras cecidi, donec ad villam amicae meae per-
10 venirem. ut larva intravi, paene animam ebullivi, sudor
mihi per bifurcium volabat, vix umquam refectus sum.
11 Melissa mea mirari coepit quod tam sero ambularem, et
'si ante' inquit 'venisses, saltem nobis adiutasses; lupus
enim villam intravit et omnia pecora perculit; tamquam
lanius sanguinem ille misit. nec tamen derisit, etiam si
12 fugit; servus enim noster lancea collum eius traiecit.' haec
ut audivi, operire oculos amplius non potui, sed luce clara
Gai nostri domum fugi tamquam caupo compilatus, et
postquam veni in illum locum in quo lapidea vestimenta
13 erant facta, nihil inveni nisi sanguinem. ut vero domum
veni, iacebat miles meus in lecto tamquam bovis, et collum
illius medicus curabat. intellexi illum versipellem esse,
nec postea cum illo panem gustare potui, non si me
14 occidisses. viderint alii quid de hoc exopinissent; ego si
mentior, genios vestros iratos habeam.

Lycanthropy, the belief that human beings can turn
themselves into wolves or other wild animals, has existed

in all parts of the world from the earliest times; in some parts of Asia and Africa even today men are believed to take the form of tigers, leopards, or hyenas. It is probably a kind of hysteria in which the sufferer desires to eat raw flesh or believes that he or she has been transformed into an animal. It was often combined with witchcraft and a belief in vampires and in the re-incarnation of the soul in wild animals, and it was thought that the werewolf, as the sufferer was called, could assume the animal-form at will. Until quite recently the superstition lingered on in remote parts of the British Isles, where certain old women were believed to turn into hares and to receive the same wound on their human bodies that the hares received if injured; in the eighteenth century a silver bullet shot from a gun was thought necessary to kill such an animal. Another form of the malady, according to popular belief, was that the body of the sufferer remained in a trance while his spirit entered the body of a wolf or other wild animal.

Seneca

Lucius Annaeus Seneca (4 B.C.–A.D. 65) was born at Corduba, the chief town of Roman Spain. His father, Marcus Annaeus Seneca (the Elder) was an authority on rhetoric, and his brother Novatus, later called Gallio, was the governor of Achaea who refused to hear the case of St Paul (*Acts* XVIII, 11–17). Seneca suffered all his life from asthma, and once only affection for his father saved him from suicide. He was educated at Rome and spent some of his early life in Egypt, where he studied the geography and ethnology of Egypt and India and developed an interest in natural science. After training for the bar he became quaestor and, on the accession of Caligula in A.D. 37, enjoyed such a reputation as a speaker that only assurance that the invalid's days were numbered saved him from execution by a jealous emperor.   In 41, when Claudius succeeded Caligula, he was again threatened with execution, this time commuted to banishment, allegedly for misconduct with Julia, the late emperor's sister, but probably through the influence of Messalina, Claudius' wife, who considered him dangerous and knew how to get her way.   His eight years' exile (41–49) in the island of Corsica were endured far from stoically, but nevertheless profitably, for he spent it composing tragedies and essays to friends which made his literary reputation.   This no doubt contributed to his recall by Agrippina (Claudius' second wife after the execution of Messalina) to be praetor and tutor to her son Lucius Domitius Ahenobarbus, then aged 12, the future emperor Nero.   Seneca was probably not involved in the poisoning of Claudius in 54.   But if his hands were clean his pen had not been idle; Tacitus tells us that he wrote the accession speech when Nero became emperor, aged seventeen, and he may well have been the author of the *Apocolocyntosis* or 'Pumpkinification' of Claudius (see page 47), an unkind skit showing the gods engaged in unfriendly debate on the late emperor's application to enter Heaven.

That the first five years of Nero's reign avoided the worst excesses of later years was largely due to Seneca and Burrus, an army officer and prefect of the praetorian guard, who tactfully kept the young emperor and his mother in the background while they set about various reforms in taxation, the checking of extortion by provincial governors and the prosecution of a successful war in Armenia.   But by 58 the emperor began to listen to other advisers who pointed out the inconsistency between Seneca's philosophy and practice and drew attention to his vast wealth and extravagance (he was said to be worth 300,000,000 sesterces).   Seneca could retort that wealth was the wise man's servant but the fool's master, something the true Stoic could dispense with; his plain diet, lifelong teetotalism, hard bed, cold baths and daily runs appeared to make his point and for the time being he came to no harm. The murder of Agrippina in 59 (see page 131) produced an aftermath which called for Seneca's statecraft once again. Though there is no proof, despite the innuendoes of Tacitus and Dio Cassius (author of a history of Rome in Greek, c. 200), that Burrus or Seneca had a hand in the matricide, the latter was obligingly ready to help pick up the pieces. He managed to persuade the Senate that Nero's foresight had narrowly forestalled his own murder, while perhaps dissuading Nero himself from a preventive massacre of suspects by saying 'However many people you slaughter you cannot kill your own successor'. When Burrus died, probably murdered, in 62, Seneca's influence with Nero declined, for the emperor's jealous temperament could easily be persuaded that his adviser's wealth, popularity and literary eminence outshone his own. Preferring honourable retirement to probable execution, Seneca managed to persuade the emperor to let him withdraw from public life and devoted his last three years to literary pursuits, including the writing of the *Moral Letters* to Lucilius Iunior. But despite the precaution of leaving his entire estate to the emperor and living on a simple diet of wild fruit and running water as a precaution against poison, there was no escape. In 65 Piso's abortive conspiracy, with associated rumours of a sub-plot to make Seneca himself emperor, led to the customary invitation from the palace to open his veins. Neither this nor poison could destroy his lean, tough old body; nothing less than suffocation in a vapour bath could compass the end, and Tacitus devoted five superb chapters (*Annals* XV, 60–64) to describing it.

The works of Seneca are: (1) Nine tragedies with plots based on Greek legends, including *Oedipus* and *Medea*; stagy without, apparently, ever being staged, they probably exercised more influence on Shakespeare and Elizabethan drama than all the Greek dramatists put together; (2) Twelve dialogues on philosophical subjects including such titles as *Providence*, *Anger*, *Clemency*, and *Consolations*; (3) *Problems of Natural Science* (*Naturales Quaestiones*), an examination of natural phenomena from the Stoic point of view; of little scientific value, they are nevertheless of interest for their digressions on such subjects as the source of the Nile and reflection and magnification; (4) The 124 *Letters to Lucilius*. Written between 62 and his death in 65 to his friend Lucilius Iunior, a native of Pompeii and governor of Sicily at the time, they deal with various aspects of life — happiness, riches, the terror of death — often using some personal experience as a starting point. Two examples are included in this selection (Nos. 6 and 14). All Seneca's works reflect his Stoic philosophy, whose aim, like that of the Epicureans (see *Two Centuries of Roman Poetry*, pages 29–30) was to secure contentment in troubled times, but by different beliefs and conduct (see page 19), most striking of which were the doctrine of the brotherhood of man, of a providence according to whose dictates man should strive to live, and an unshakeable resolve to meet the blows of fate.

Seneca's manner of writing contrasts sharply with Cicero's. Intended for public recitation to a bored yet sophisticated audience, which sought gladiatorial cut and thrust in the salon as the ordinary Roman sought it in the amphitheatre, his sentences are short, pithy, epigrammatic, designed to win applause by piecemeal impact rather than cumulative effect. Period gives place to point, the sonorous to the startling. This emerges most sharply, perhaps, in his plays, where characters in tragic situations pepper each other with epigrams with the profusion of Oscar Wilde but without the compensation of raising a chuckle. Fronto, tutor to the emperor Marcus Aurelius, compared Seneca to a diner who throws olives in the air and catches them in his mouth, and we have this opinion from Macaulay: 'I cannot bear Seneca . . . His works are made up of mottoes. There is hardly a sentence which might not be quoted; but to read him straightforward is like dining on nothing but anchovy sauce'. Montaigne[1] names him, with Plutarch, the author 'on whom I draw unceasingly'; Erasmus thus rounded off some advice to a friend: 'to study Plato and Seneca, love his wife, and disregard the world's opinion'. Queen Elizabeth I 'did much admire Seneca's wholesome advisings'.

'A favourite with all ages except our own.' Such was the judgement of an editor of Seneca some forty years ago (R. G. C. Levens, *A Book of Latin Letters*, page 144). More recently the translator of the *Letters to Lucilius* in the *Penguin Classics* (1969) called him a forgotten author. Yet in an age that values a good headline more than good news he is surely due for a revival. None of the many who read Caesar's *Gallic Wars* will actually experience being a linkman in a *testudo* or help shove a battering-ram under a mantlet; but most of us have had thoughts of a sort in a tunnel or been distracted by an infernal din outside the window. To compare notes with Seneca is a worthwhile exercise and may even tempt us, at the risk of a surfeit of anchovy sauce, to read on.

[1] Sir Kenneth Clark, in his admirable book (and television series) *Civilisation*, page 163, credits Montaigne with inventing the essay, 'the accepted form of humanist communication for three centuries, from Bacon to Hazlitt'. Bacon himself had other ideas: 'the word (essay) is late but the thing is ancient. For Seneca's Epistles . . . are but Essays'; and a contemporary of Montaigne called him 'the French Seneca'.

6. Thoughts in a Tunnel (*Epistulae Morales* 57)

Seneca was not fond of travel, and in a previous letter (53) he describes a sea-voyage from Puteoli to Naples that ended in a storm and sea-sickness.   In this letter he describes the journey by road from Baiae to Naples, which was about twelve miles by the coast road but three miles shorter by the inland road and the Naples Tunnel, the route taken by Seneca on this occasion.   This tunnel, then called the *Crypta Neapolitana* and now the *Grotta Vecchia*, was constructed by the orders of Agrippa and Octavian (afterwards the Emperor Augustus) in about 30 B.C. under the hill of Posilipo.   It was about 775 yards long, seven yards wide, and up to seven yards high, dimly lighted at intervals by torches but full of clouds of dust thrown up by the wheels of carriages passing through it.   Seneca evidently did not think that the mental and physical discomfort was worth the time saved by avoiding the longer road along the promontory of Posilipo.   Petronius (fr. 16) says that travellers in the tunnel (presumably sitting in carriages) had to stoop down in some places to avoid striking their heads on the roof.

The tunnel was enlarged in the fifteenth and again in the eighteenth century and was closed in 1885, when the *Grotta Nuova* was completed, first for carriages and trams and now for the underground railway.   The English diarist, John Evelyn, passed through the *Grotta Vecchia* on 7 February, 1645, after its first enlargement, and described it in his Diary as follows:

'After we were advanced into this noble and altogether wonderful crypt, consisting of a passage spacious enough for two coaches to go abreast, cut through a rocky mountain near three-quarters of a mile (. . . by L. Cocceius, who employed a hundred thousand men on it), we came to the midway, where there is a hole bored through the diameter of this vast mountain . . . The way is paved underfoot, but it does not hinder the dust, which rises so excessively in this much-frequented passage, that we were forced at intervals to use a torch. At length we were delivered from the bowels of the earth into one of the most delicious plains in the world.'

1–2. *To avoid another sea-trip, I returned from Baiae to Naples by land, but the journey began with wet mud on the road and ended with dry dust in the tunnel, where the dim light of the torches was made even dimmer by the dust that we stirred up on our way through.*

SENECA LVCILIO SVO SALVTEM

1 Cum a Bais deberem Neapolim repetere, facile credidi tempestatem esse, ne iterum navem experirer; et tantum luti tota via fuit ut possim videri nihilominus navigasse. totum athletarum fatum mihi illo die perpetiendum fuit: a ceromate nos haphe excepit in crypta Neapolitana. nihil illo carcere longius, nihil illis facibus obscurius, quae nobis praestant, non ut per tenebras videamus, sed ut ipsas. ceterum etiam si locus haberet lucem, pulvis auferret, in aperto quoque res gravis et molesta: quid illic, ubi in se volutatur et, cum sine ullo spiramento sit inclusus, in ipsos a quibus excitatus est recidit? duo incommoda inter se contraria simul pertulimus: eadem via, eodem die et luto et pulvere laboravimus.

3–5. *The darkness in the tunnel gave me a thrill, but not of fear, for even a 'perfect' man can be startled or feel dizzy. This is not fear, for some brave men cannot bear the sight of another's blood, though they are willing to shed their own in battle.*

3 Aliquid tamen mihi illa obscuritas quod cogitarem dedit:
sensi quendam ictum animi et sine metu mutationem quam
insolitae rei novitas simul ac foeditas fecerat. non de me
nunc tecum loquor, qui multum ab homine tolerabili,
nedum a perfecto, absum, sed de illo in quem fortuna ius
perdidit; huius quoque ferietur animus, mutabitur color.
4 quaedam enim, mi Lucili, nulla effugere virtus potest;
admonet illam natura mortalitatis suae. itaque et vultum
adducet ad tristia et inhorrescet ad subita et caligabit si
vastam altitudinem in crepidine eius constitutus despexerit;
non est hoc timor sed naturalis adfectio inexpugnabilis
5 rationi. itaque fortes quidam et paratissimi fundere suum
sanguinem alienum videre non possunt; quidam ad vulneris
novi, quidam ad veteris et purulenti tractationem inspectionemque succidunt et linquuntur animo, alii gladium facilius
recipiunt quam vident.

6–7. *My good spirits returned at the first glimpse of daylight.*
How foolish we are to feel degrees of fear, for it is no worse to be
killed by a mountain than by a falling tower. Some people
believe that a man's soul is crushed and utterly destroyed by a
great weight, but in fact the soul is immortal and cannot perish.

6 Sensi ergo, ut dicebam, quandam non quidem perturbationem sed mutationem; rursus ad primum conspectum
redditae lucis alacritas rediit incognita et iniussa. illud
deinde mecum loqui coepi, quam inepte quaedam magis
aut minus timeremus, cum omnium idem finis esset. quid
enim interest utrum supra aliquem vigilarium ruat an mons?
nihil invenies. erunt tamen qui hanc ruinam magis timeant,
quamvis utraque mortifera aeque sit; adeo non effectus sed
7 efficientia timor spectat. nunc me putas de Stoicis dicere,
qui existimant animam hominis magno pondere extriti
permanere non posse et statim spargi, quia non fuerit illi

exitus liber? ego vero non facio; qui hoc dicunt videntur
mihi errare. itaque de illo quaerendum est, an possit
immortalis esse. hoc quidem certum habe: si superstes
est corpori, obteri illam nullo genere posse, quoniam nulla
immortalitas cum exceptione est, nec quicquam noxium
aeterno est. vale.

PLINY

Publius Caecilius Secundus, who on adoption by his uncle
took the names Gaius Plinius Caecilius Secundus, was born
in A.D. 61 or 62 at Novum Comum (Como) in Cisalpine
Gaul, the native land of Livy and other famous writers (see
the Introduction to Livy). His father's early death caused
him to become the ward of the famous soldier Verginius
Rufus, who twice refused the imperial crown offered by his
soldiers, but Pliny was adopted and brought up by his uncle,
the Elder Pliny, a man of equestrian rank (not a Senator),
who was an author of immense industry on a great number
of subjects, though only his *Natural History* now survives;
he died in the eruption of Vesuvius in 79, an event described
by his nephew in two famous letters written to Tacitus.
Pliny was educated at Comum and studied rhetoric under
Quintilian at Rome. On the death of his uncle he inherited
great wealth and began to practise at the bar, specialising
in the 'Hundred Court', which dealt with cases of inheritance
and disputed property. None of his speeches survive
except the non-forensic 'Panegyric on Trajan', but he took
part in several famous political trials and was evidently a
successful barrister. After military service in Syria he
passed through the usual political offices of quaestor,
tribune, praetor (he was the first of his family to become a
Senator), and consul *suffectus* (for a month or two), and

finally became governor of the province of Bithynia, in
Asia Minor, under Trajan in 110. He died in about 113,
possibly in Bithynia.

Pliny owned much property, including two villas on
Lake Como and one at Laurentum (near Rome) of which he
was very proud, and he was a man of great humanity whose
treatment of slaves showed a kindness unusual at that time.
He did much for his native town of Comum, both by gifts
and bequests. He married three times but had no children;
his third wife, Calpurnia, brought him great happiness.
His chief claim to fame rests on the nine books of letters to
his friends, which he collected and published himself, after
revising them and arranging them carefully to obtain
variety in their subject-matter. They deal with a large
number of subjects, including some ghost stories, the tale
of a pet dolphin (now proved to be perfectly possible),
descriptions of his villas and of his life at Rome and in the
country, accounts of the trials in which he took part and of
the eruption of Vesuvius, and many other matters of interest
to his correspondents and to modern readers. After his
death a tenth volume was published, consisting of his letters
from Bithynia addressed to the emperor Trajan, full of
detail of the administrative work of a provincial governor;
the most interesting is his report to Trajan of the behaviour
of Christians in the province and how he dealt with them,
together with Trajan's reply to Pliny's inquiry on how to
treat them.

Pliny's revision of his letters for publication cause them
to lack the complete spontaneity and unselfconsciousness of
Cicero's letters, which show him as he was without any
attempt on his part to impress his readers. But in spite of
this Pliny appeals to us as being a man of ability, charm, and
kindliness, though not without a certain naive vanity that
gives his letters an additional attraction. They paint a vivid

picture of the life and interests of a rich and cultured Roman in the time of the Early Empire, written in a polished blend of Ciceronian and Silver Latin.

7 (*a*). A Mysterious Spring (4, 30)

This letter is addressed to Licinius Sura, a Spaniard by birth, who was a lawyer and an intimate friend and adviser of the Emperor Trajan. He was consul in 98, 102, and 107, and was a scholar who took a deep interest in natural phenomena; his reply to this letter has unfortunately not survived.

The 'Larian Lake' is Lake Como in North Italy, on the eastern shore of which stands Como, the Novum Comum where Pliny was born and brought up. Six miles north of Como, on the Bay of Molina, is Torno, where this mysterious spring is still ebbing and flowing at regular intervals. In the sixteenth century a house called the *Villa Pliniana* was built adjoining the grotto that contains the spring; it is private property, but visitors can inspect it during the afternoon. The water emerges from an underground source into a small oval pool about six feet long, four feet wide, and three feet deep, which when full overflows and joins a magnificent cascade to the left of the grotto that falls with a loud roaring noise into the lake about a hundred feet below.

Pliny's uncle says (*Natural History* 2, 232) that the pool rose and fell every hour, but he had probably not visited it himself, for the Younger Pliny states definitely that this happened three times a day. If by 'a day' he meant the nearly eighteen hours of light of a summer's day, the working of the spring has not changed in 2000 years, for today it takes three hours to fill and three to empty. Exactly what happens behind the rock face cannot of course be seen, but it seems clear that there is a natural siphon caused by a fault in the rock that periodically draws water out of a hidden reservoir fed by underground springs and discharges it into the pool in the grotto. A siphon is a device for carrying water by atmospheric pressure up a slope and over an intervening obstruction by means of a narrow tube shaped like an inverted U or V with one limb shorter than the other. In this case the shorter limb starts near the bottom of the hidden reservoir and reaches its highest point (the top of the inverted U) outside and just below the level of the top of the reservoir. When the water reaches the level of the top of the siphon, it is forced up the shorter limb and over the bend of the U, from which it flows down the longer limb into the pool in the grotto, which it enters unseen below the lowest water-level.

The flow continues for three hours, until the water in the reservoir falls to the level of the lower limb of the siphon, after which it stops for another three hours until the reservoir fills up again. Meanwhile, the water first fills up the pool in the grotto and then overflows to join the cascade. When the siphon stops working, the water no longer overflows but gradually sinks in the pool, no doubt ebbing away through a very small outlet near the bottom that allows it to escape unseen under the floor of the grotto. There is an 'ebbing and flowing' well near Giggleswick-in-Craven, in Yorkshire, that must work on the same principle, but there the flow lasts for a very short time and is extremely irregular, often ceasing altogether for months or years on end. The remarkable thing about the spring at Torno is that the flow and the temperature of the water (cold but not ice-cold) apparently never varies in summer or winter, in times of drought or flood, presumably because the reservoir is large and situated deep in the rock. The great Italian artist, scientist, and inventor, Leonardo da Vinci, visited the

spring in about 1500 and described the six-hour cycle of rise
and fall, just as it was in Pliny's time and still is today.

*1–5. Here is a problem for you from my native country. A
spring flows down from the mountains into Lake Como, above
which it forms a pool in an artificial grotto. The water is very
cold and rises and falls in the pool at regular intervals three
times a day.*

C. PLINIVS LICINIO SVRAE SVO S.

1 Attuli tibi ex patria mea pro munusculo quaestionem
2 altissima ista eruditione dignissimam. fons oritur in monte,
per saxa decurrit, excipitur cenatiuncula manu facta; ibi
3 paulum retentus in Larium lacum decidit. huius mira
natura: ter in die statis auctibus ac diminutionibus crescit
decrescitque. cernitur id palam et cum summa voluptate
deprenditur. iuxta recumbis et vesceris, atque etiam ex
ipso fonte (nam est frigidissimus) potas; interim ille certis
4 dimensisque momentis vel subtrahitur vel adsurgit. anulum
seu quid aliud ponis in sicco, adluitur sensim ac novissime
operitur, detegitur rursus paulatimque deseritur. si diutius
observes, utrumque iterum ac tertio videas.

*5–11. There are five possible explanations of this pheno-
menon. 1. An air-current that opens and closes the outlet of
the spring. 2. The principle that causes tides in the sea.
3. Something that periodically blocks the flow of water.
4. A reservoir in the rock that is filled and emptied in turn
(i.e. a natural siphon). 5. A hidden force of water that causes
the rise and fall. Please consider the problem and let me know
your solution.*

5 Spiritusne aliquis occultior os fontis et fauces modo
laxat, modo includit, prout illatus occurrit aut decessit

6 cxpulsus? quod in ampullis ceterisque generis eiusdem
videmus accidere, quibus non hians nec statim patens
exitus. nam illa quoque, quamquam prona atque ver-
gentia, per quasdam obluctantis animae moras crebris
7 quasi singultibus sistunt quod effundunt. an, quae oceano
natura, fonti quoque, quaque ille ratione aut impellitur aut
resorbetur, hac modicus hic umor vicibus alternis suppri-
8 mitur vel egeritur? an ut flumina, quae in mare deferuntur,
adversantibus ventis obvioque aestu retorquentur, ita est
9 aliquid quod huius fontis excursum repercutiat? an
latentibus venis certa mensura, quae dum colligit quod
exhauserat, minor rivus et pigrior; cum collegit, agilior
10 maiorque profertur? an nescio quod libramentum abditum
et caecum, quod cum exinanitum est, suscitat et elicit
11 fontem; cum repletum, moratur et strangulat? scrutare
tu causas (potes enim), quae tantum miraculum efficiunt:
mihi abunde est, si satis expressi quod efficitur. vale.

7 (b). The Source of the Clitumnus (8, 8)

This letter was written to C. Licinius Voconius Romanus,
a Spaniard from Saguntum, interested in literature and one
of Pliny's closest friends, who had been a student with him.
He was of an equestrian family, and Pliny later petitioned
the Emperor Trajan to give him a seat in the Senate.

The river Clitumnus, now called the Clitunno, rises about
seven miles north of Spoleto in Umbria, near Trevi, and
flows into the Tinia, one of the tributaries of the Tiber.
The springs have been admired for at least two thousand
years. Virgil, Propertius, and Juvenal speak of the herds
of large white cattle in great demand as sacrificial victims
that pastured on the banks and bathed in the stream,
Poussin and Corot painted the scene, and Byron says (in
Childe Harold 4, 66):

But thou, Clitumnus! in thy sweetest wave
Of the most living crystal that was e'er
The haunt of river nymph . . .

                      thou dost rear
Thy grassy banks whereon the milk-white steer
Grazes; the purest god of gentle waters!
And most serene of aspect, and most clear.

Today the springs are as beautiful as ever. They consist
of several connected pools or small lakes into which the
water bubbles up from underground, never failing even in
the driest summer. Except for a few larger wells about
eight feet deep, the water is seldom more than a yard deep
and is constantly in motion from the hundreds of tiny
springs welling up in quivering jets with a soft whispering
sound through the beds of white sand and gravel. The
pools are surrounded by poplars and willows, and the cool,
clear water flows gently away to form the river Clitumnus
whose source seems to rise almost miraculously out of the
dry plain at the foot of the hills which extend eastwards.
The springs are now on private property, but the owner
allows interested visitors to walk about and see this remarkable and most beautiful sight.

*1–4. At the foot of a hill the spring gushes out of the ground
by several channels and forms a pool as clear as glass. Then it
broadens out into a river large enough to take boats, though the
stream is so strong that it is hard to row against it.*

C. PLINIVS ROMANO SVO S.

1   Vidistine aliquando Clitumnum fontem? si nondum
(et puto, nondum: alioqui narrasses mihi), vide; quem
2 ego (paenitet tarditatis) proxime vidi. modicus collis

adsurgit, antiqua cupressu nemorosus et opacus. hunc
subter exit fons et exprimitur pluribus venis sed imparibus,
eluctatusque quem facit gurgitem lato gremio patescit,
purus et vitreus, ut numerare iactas stipes et relucentes
3 calculos possis. inde non loci devexitate, sed ipsa sui copia
et quasi pondere impellitur, fons adhuc et iam amplissimum
flumen, atque etiam navium patiens; quas obvias quoque
et contrario nisu in diversa tendentes transmittit et perfert,
adeo validus ut illa qua properat ipse, quamquam per solum
planum, remis non adiuvetur, idem aegerrime remis con-
4 tisque superetur adversus. iucundum utrumque per iocum
ludumque fluitantibus, ut flexerint cursum, laborem otio
otium labore variare.

*4–6. Trees line the banks of the stream, near which is an
ancient temple and image of the god Clitumnus and smaller
shrines of other gods all around. A bridge separates the sacred
from the ordinary waters, and the people of Hispellum maintain
baths and an inn for visitors. You will admire most of the
inscriptions that honour the spring and its god, and you are too
kind-hearted to smile at any of them.*

Ripae fraxino multa, multa populo vestiuntur, quas
perspicuus amnis velut mersas viridi imagine adnumerat.
5 rigor aquae certaverit nivibus, nec color cedit. adiacet
templum priscum et religiosum. stat Clitumnus ipse
amictus ornatusque praetexta; praesens numen atque etiam
fatidicum indicant sortes. sparsa sunt circa sacella com-
plura, totidemque di. sua cuique veneratio, suum nomen,
quibusdam vero etiam fontes. nam praeter illum quasi
parentem ceterorum sunt minores capite discreti; sed
6 flumini miscentur, quod ponte transmittitur. is terminus
sacri profanique: in superiore parte navigare tantum, infra
etiam natare concessum. balineum Hispellates, quibus

illum locum divus Augustus dono dedit, publice praebent,
praebent et hospitium. nec desunt villae, quae secutae
7 fluminis amoenitatem margini insistunt. in summa nihil
erit ex quo non capias voluptatem. nam studebis quoque:
leges multa multorum omnibus columnis, omnibus parietibus inscripta, quibus fons ille deusque celebratur. plura
laudabis, nonnulla ridebis; quamquam tu vero, quae tua
humanitas, nulla ridebis. vale.

TACITUS

An aura of mystery surrounds the figure of Cornelius
Tacitus. We do not know whether his first name (*praenomen*) was Publius or Gaius; the dates of his birth (A.D.
56 or 57) and death (probably at or near the end of Trajan's
reign in 117) are uncertain; his birthplace could have been
in northern Italy or Gaul (perhaps Forum Julii (Fréjus),
see page 228). Even his literary survival 'hangs on a slender
thread': we depend on a single manuscript for *Annals* I–VI,
and another single manuscript for *Annals* XI–XVI and the
whole of the *Histories*. There was even, towards the end of
the last century, a 'Bacon wrote Shakespeare' type theory,
easily and speedily refuted, that the *Annals* were a Renaissance forgery.

Tacitus began his official career under Vespasian, whose
revival of the art of oratory encouraged him to train and
practise in this field. In 77 he married the daughter of
Julius Agricola, a distinguished soldier and governor of
Britain (78–84, but these dates are disputed). He became
a quaestor in 81 or 82, under the emperor Titus, and praetor
under Domitian in 88. He was then posted abroad, perhaps
to govern a minor province, and returned in 93 to find his
father-in-law dead, rumoured poisoned by Domitian. Four

years of obscurity (93 96) during the worst of Domitian's tyranny, when, as Tacitus himself admits, it was safer to be obscure, were followed by a consulship in 97, in an atmosphere of hope that the new emperor, Nerva, would restore real power to the republican offices. It was then that he delivered a funeral oration on Verginius Rufus, a distinguished general and guardian of the Younger Pliny (see page 59); and in 100, in company with Pliny (his friend and admirer who addressed to him, among others, his two famous letters on the eruption of Vesuvius) secured the exile of Marius Priscus, ex-governor of the province of Asia, for extortion. Happier under the more enlightened principate of Trajan (89–117), he became proconsul in Asia 112–113, but thereafter we know nothing. He probably devoted his last years to the composition of his major work, the *Annals*.

Though most of Tacitus' writings are historical, one, the *Dialogue on Orators*, once thought to be his earliest work but now dated by some scholars as late as 107, reveals his interest in oratory and is Ciceronian in style and manner. He wrote two historical monographs, the *Life of Agricola* (published in 98) describing his father-in-law's governorship of Britain and the background to it, and *On the Origin and Geographical Position of the Germans*, a work which from time to time makes barbed contrasts between the corruption of his fellow-countrymen and the robust simplicity of the Germans, who 'have learned bribery from us' and 'have provided us with more triumphs than victories'. His major works are: the *Histories* (published 104–109) covering the period from Galba to Domitian, of which only the first four books and part of the fifth survive, dealing with 69, the year of civil war and 'the Four Emperors' (Galba, Otho, Vitellius and Vespasian) and the beginning of the principate of Vespasian in 70; and the *Annals*, composed later but embracing the earlier period from the death of Augustus (A.D. 14) to the

death of Nero in 68, in 16 books, but there are yawning gaps:
we lack over two years of Tiberius, the whole of Caligula
and two years of Claudius (Books VII–X); and the last
two years of Nero (most of XVI).

As a historian Tacitus claims to be impartial, to write *sine
ira ac studio* ('without passion and without bias'). He has
been accused of reading into Tiberius what he knew of
Domitian, and of concentrating on the crimes of the court
to the exclusion of the solid achievement in the provinces.
But the sources he used were mainly hostile to the imperial
system; little survives to refute them, and we cannot be
sure there was a more favourable tradition even in his time.
His purpose is a moral one (*Annals* III, 65): to glorify
virtue and denigrate vice. That he did more of the latter
than the former is largely in the nature of his subject-matter,
and Napoleon, who called him a 'traducer of humanity'
deserves the retort (*Oxford Classical Dictionary* on Tacitus)
'from one who spent his powers annihilating humanity this
verdict is interesting, but simply untrue'.

Our concern is with Tacitus as a *writer*. Here it is all too
easy to be sidetracked by that overworked and misleading
word 'style'.[1] Scholars tell us we find in Tacitus a stylistic
trinity — brevity, variety and poetic colour — and so indeed
we do (a few examples are mentioned in the Notes). But to
compile a list of examples, out of context, is merely to stock
a museum while the genius of Tacitus slips out through the
window. Better to watch Tacitus at work in a self-contained
episode, and this we shall endeavour to do. The passages
we have chosen are contrasted. In the first (No. 8 below)
the interest is in the matter rather than the manner. We all
like to hear about our distant ancestors and Tacitus himself,

---

[1] We owe much in our approach to Tacitus to a stimulating essay on
Tacitus' Narrative Technique by Professor Quinn in *Latin Explorations*
(Routledge), though some of his ideas are perhaps too advanced for our
readers and a few, even, for the editors!

writing for less involved Romans, says geographical and
ethnographical description (*situs gentium*) interests and
stimulates the reader (*Annals* IV, 33). Moreover his
declared aim is to counter with fact (*rerum fide*) the 'ignorance
dressed up as eloquence' (*nondum comperta eloquentia percoluere*) of his predecessors. Yet even here, in a superficially
'dead-pan' passage, the instinct for epigram at times bursts
through: a couple of well-aimed lunges at the British
climate — *crebris imbribus ac nubibus foedum* (3, 3), *multus
umor terrarum caelique* (3, 6); and a final sideswipe at his
fellow-countrymen: British pearls must be second-rate if
Roman greed can leave them alone (3, 6).

With the second passage, in Part II, it is different. Tacitus
himself apologises to his Roman readers for the grim catalogue of vice he is recording (*Annals* IV, 33); our own revul-
sion should be even stronger. So Nero murdered his mother
— he also fiddled (or rather, played the lyre), did he not?,
while Rome burned, and came to a sticky end. Who cares?
It was all such a long time ago and a long way away. Tacitus
absorbs himself so deeply in his episodes and characters[1]
and radiates that personal involvement so powerfully in his
writing that he somehow takes his reader by the scruff of the
neck, as it were, and makes him or her care too. How he
does it we shall endeavour to analyse in the Introduction
and Notes to the passage from Tacitus (No. 16) in Part II.

Consider, at the end, whether a case could not be made for
learning Latin *just* to read Tacitus. For here a translation
is of little use. With Tacitus to translate is to emasculate,
for he does with Latin what English cannot do. Read his

---

[1] The faculty of deep personal involvement in episode and character
has also been observed and studied in Virgil by Brooks Otis (*Virgil, A
Study in Civilised Poetry*, Oxford University Press) who calls it 'empathy'.
Scholars have spent much time illustrating Tacitus' 'poetic colour' from
Virgilian borrowings; this deeper debt of Tacitus to Virgil, so far
relatively unexplored, could well be investigated further.

Latin and any English translation side by side and then ask yourself which is the 'dead' and which the 'living' language. You may well be surprised at the answer; and the translator, whoever he was, would be the last person to disagree with you.

8. Britain and the British (*Agricola* 10–12)

Britain has been invaded many times in the pre-historic periods by migrants from the mainland of Europe who brought their own civilisation with them and made this island their permanent home until they were dispossessed by the next wave of invaders. The Celtic Iron Age in Europe is divided into two main periods of about four centuries each, 'Hallstatt' from about 850 B.C. and 'La Tène' from about 450 B.C., so called from the places in Europe where the remains of their cultures have been most closely studied. Pressure from central Europe caused Celtic communities to move slowly westwards and led to invasions by Hallstatt settlers in south-west England from about 550 to 300 B.C. (Iron Age A) and by La Tène immigrants on the east coast of Scotland and England and in the south-west of England from about 300 to 150 B.C. (Iron Age B). These were followed in the third and most highly civilised La Tène period, from about 125 to 50 B.C. (Iron Age C) by a Germano-Celtic people called the Belgae from north-west France and Belgium which overran Kent, Essex, and Hertfordshire. The earlier invaders brought with them the Celtic language, the use of iron for tools and weapons (instead of bronze), the practice of light ploughing, the establishment of hill forts, and the art of making pottery on the wheel; the Belgic invaders also introduced deep ploughing, gold coinage, and a comparatively well-advanced standard of civilisation.

Western Scotland, Wales, and other remote districts were

less fully advanced in culture than the Belgic invaders, and some tribes were still almost in the Bronze Age (which began in Britain in about 1650 B.C.), hardly yet using the iron tools introduced by the Iron Age A settlers. The Druidic religion, which Caesar tells us (*B.G.* VI, 13–18) included belief in the transmigration of souls and the practice of offering human sacrifices, was probably brought to Britain by the earliest Celtic invaders. The Celts, both Gauls and British, worshipped the spirits of nature (lakes, mountains, forests, trees) and their own gods, some of whose names are known to us, for which Caesar gave approximate Roman equivalents, but on the whole we know little about the Celtic religion. Very little knowledge of the Celtic language survives, but it is almost certain that it was spoken in one form or another all over Britain (see page 174).

The first writer to describe Britain was the Greek traveller, Pytheas of Marseilles, who sailed round the island in about 325 B.C., landed more than once, and spoke to the inhabitants, presumably through an interpreter; only fragments of his account survives. Other Greek geographers were Posidonius (*c.* 80 B.C.), Diodorus Siculus (*c.* 40 B.C.), and Strabo (*c.* 25 B.C.). Roman writers were Julius Caesar, who gives in his *Gallic War* V, 12–14, a description of the island based on earlier information and on his two invasions of 55 and 54 B.C., Pomponius Mela (*c.* A.D. 45) and the Elder Pliny (d. A.D. 79), besides Livy and Fabius Rusticus (a friend of Seneca), whom Tacitus mentions in 2, 3, but whose accounts have been lost. Pytheas and the other Greek authors call these islands the 'Pretanic Isles', and Julius Caesar seems to have been the first to use the name *Britannia* and *Britanni.*

Caesar followed the Greek geographers in thinking that Britain was triangular in shape with a perimeter of 2000 Roman (1840 English) miles; this is a good result, for the distance in a straight line along the coasts is 1500 English miles and for a ship sailing round and avoiding the smaller estuaries and bays it is about 3000 English miles (this distance would be almost doubled if every yard of the heavily indented coast-line of Scotland were included). But all the early writers, including Tacitus, thought that the coast of Gaul ran in an almost straight line south-west from the mouth of the Rhine to the north coast of Spain and that the south coast of Britain was parallel to it; our east coast was therefore to them the north coast (Scotland lying almost west of England), and our west coast ran from north to south-east, with Ireland (Hibernia) lying between the north-west coast of Britain and Spain, as shown on the sketch map given below.

MAP OF ANCIENT BRITAIN, ACCORDING TO
JULIUS CAESAR AND TACITUS

Julius Caesar made two expeditions to Britain in 55 and 54 B.C. In the late summer of 54 he landed with a force of two legions near Deal, repelled two British attacks, and returned to Gaul after spending less than a month in the island, during which he advanced only a few miles from the coast; the expedition was hardly more than a reconnaissance. In July 54 he made a second invasion with a much larger force, five legions and 2000 cavalry. After landing, this time unopposed, probably a little south of Sandwich, he marched inland, crossed the Thames, expelled Cassivellaunus, the leader of the united British forces, from his stronghold at Wheathampstead (near St Albans), and forced him to accept terms. But the lateness of the season (mid-September) and the threat of risings in Gaul compelled Caesar to return to the continent after demanding hostages and an annual tribute, which was probably never paid. Britain was then left undisturbed by the Romans for nearly a hundred years.

Commius, king of the Atrebates in northern Gaul, who had aided Caesar in both expeditions to Britain, turned against the Romans and in 50 B.C., after the final defeat of the Gauls, crossed to Britain and settled among another branch of the Atrebates in Hampshire. Here he soon became ruler of most of the central part of southern Britain and was succeeded as king by his three sons in turn. Meanwhile Cassivellaunus of the Catuvellauni in Hertfordshire, who had opposed Caesar in 54, was extending his power over the neighbouring tribes. One of his successors at about the beginning of the Christian era was Cunobelinus (Shakespear's Cymbeline), whose authority extended over Kent and most of the 'Home Counties' as far as Oxfordshire, with Camulodunum (Colchester) as his capital. His brothers or sons seem to have seized the kingdom of the last of the successors of Commius south of the Thames. Besides these two powerful kingdoms there were the Iceni in East Anglia, the Dobuni in the Cotswolds, and the Brigantes in Yorkshire, all of whom were prosperous communities, and there was considerable trade between Britain and the continent.

During this period exiled British princes more than once appealed to Rome for help, but Augustus and Tiberius decided to take no action and to leave Britain to its own devices. Caligula (Gaius) planned but did not carry out an expedition, and it was left to Claudius to make a full-scale invasion in A.D. 43 and begin the eventual conquest of this island, which is summarised on page 78.

1, (10). *Geography. Britain lies west of Germany, east of Spain, and north of Gaul, and (excluding Caledonia) is shaped like an axe-head. The Orkneys and Thule lie farther north, in a sluggish sea, and the northern part of the island is intersected by many rivers and firths.*

1 Britanniae situm populosque, multis scriptoribus memoratos, non in comparationem curae ingeniive referam, sed quia tum primum perdomita est. ita quae priores nondum comperta eloquentia percoluere rerum fide tradentur.
2 Britannia, insularum quas Romana notitia complectitur maxima, spatio ac caelo in orientem Germaniae, in occidentem Hispaniae obtenditur, Gallis in meridiem etiam conspicitur; septentrionalia eius, nullis contra terris, vasto
3 atque aperto mari pulsantur. formam totius Britanniae Livius veterum, Fabius Rusticus recentium eloquentissimi auctores oblongae scapulae vel bipenni adsimulavere. et est ea facies citra Caledoniam, unde et in universum fama: sed transgressis immensum et enorme spatium procurrentium extremo iam litore terrarum velut in cuneum tenuatur.
4 hanc oram novissimi maris tunc primum Romana classis circumvecta insulam esse Britanniam adfirmavit, ac simul incognitas ad id tempus insulas, quas Orcadas vocant,

invenit domuitque. dispecta est et Thule, quia hactenus
5 iussum et hiems adpetebat. sed mare pigrum et grave
remigantibus perhibent ne ventis quidem perinde attolli,
credo quod rariores terrae montesque, causa ac materia
tempestatum, et profunda moles continui maris tardius
6 impellitur. naturam Oceani atque aestus neque quaerere
huius operis est, ac multi rettulere; unum addiderim,
nusquam latius dominari mare, multum fluminum huc
atque illuc ferre, nec litore tenus adcrescere aut resorberi,
sed influere penitus atque ambire, et iugis etiam ac montibus
inseri velut in suo.

2 (11). *Ethnography. The Caledonians (in northern Scotland) are similar in appearance to the Germans, the Silures (in
South Wales) to the Spaniards, and the people of south-east
Britain to the Gauls, who probably invaded and occupied most
of the island, for the language and customs of both countries are
similar. The British are more high-spirited than the Gauls,
being not yet accustomed to Roman rule.*

1 Ceterum Britanniam qui mortales initio coluerint, indigenae an advecti, ut inter barbaros, parum compertum.
2 habitus corporum varii atque ex eo argumenta. namque
rutilae Caledoniam habitantium comae, magni artus Ger-
manicam originem adseverant; Silurum colorati vultus,
torti plerumque crines et posita contra Hispania Hiberos
veteres traiecisse easque sedes occupasse fidem faciunt;
proximi Gallis et similes sunt, seu durante originis vi, seu
procurrentibus in diversa terris positio caeli corporibus
3 habitum dedit. in universum tamen aestimanti Gallos
vicinam insulam occupasse credibile est. eorum sacra
deprendas ac superstitionum persuasionem; sermo haud
multum diversus, in deposcendis periculis eadem audacia
4 et, ubi advenere, in detrectandis eadem formido. plus

tamen ferociae Britanni praeferunt, ut quos nondum longa pax emollierit. nam Gallos quoque in bellis floruisse accepimus; mox segnitia cum otio intravit, amissa virtute pariter ac libertate. quod Britannorum olim victis evenit: ceteri manent quales Galli fuerunt.

3 (12). *The strength of the British in war lies in their infantry, sometimes in their chariots. They are brave fighters, but cannot combine against a common foe. The climate is foggy but not very cold, and in the far north the nights are short. The soil is fertile owing to the prevailing dampness. Gold, silver, and other metals are found in Britain, and pearls of inferior quality.*

1 In pedite robur; quaedam nationes et curru proeliantur. honestior auriga, clientes propugnant. olim regibus parebant, nunc per principes factionibus et studiis distra-
2 huntur. nec aliud adversus validissimas gentes pro nobis utilius quam quod in commune non consulunt. rarus duabus tribusve civitatibus ad propulsandum commune periculum conventus: ita singuli pugnant, universi vin-
3 cuntur. caelum crebris imbribus ac nebulis foedum; asperitas frigorum abest. dierum spatia ultra nostri orbis mensuram; nox clara et extrema Britanniae parte brevis, ut finem atque initium lucis exiguo discrimine internoscas.
4 quod si nubes non officiant, aspici per noctem solis fulgorem, nec occidere et exsurgere, sed transire adfirmant. scilicet extrema et plana terrarum humili umbra non erigunt
5 tenebras, infraque caelum et sidera nox cadit. solum praeter oleam vitemque et cetera calidioribus terris oriri sueta patiens frugum pecudumque fecundum: tarde mitescunt, cito proveniunt; eademque utriusque rei causa,
6 multus umor terrarum caelique. fert Britannia aurum et argentum et alia metalla, pretium victoriae. gignit et Oceanus margarita, sed subfusca ac liventia. quidam artem

abesse legentibus arbitrantur; nam in rubro mari viva ac spirantia saxis avelli, in Britannia, prout expulsa sint, colligi: ego facilius crediderim naturam margaritis deesse quam nobis avaritiam.

This account of the geography of Britain comes from Tacitus' biography of his father-in-law Julius Agricola (40–93), who served in this island as a junior officer against Boudicca in 61 and again as commander of the XXth Legion in Scotland in 70. Between 43 and 51 Aulus Plautius and his successor Ostorius Scapula subdued most of southern Britain and extended Roman power to the line of the Fosse Way, from Lincoln to south Devon; in one of the campaigns of 43 Maiden Castle in Dorset (see Plate 8) was taken by storm. Caratacus led a rising of the Silures of South Wales against Scapula in 51 and Boudicca a more serious rebellion of the Iceni against Suetonius Paulinus in 61. Successive governors pacified the south and began to overcome Yorkshire and Wales.

In 78 Agricola became governor and during his six years' office advanced as far as the Forth-Clyde line and even won a victory at Mons Graupius (not yet identified) in the Highlands of Scotland. His governorship was successful both in the peaceful south and the warlike north, until he was recalled, possibly out of jealousy, by Domitian. Hadrian built his famous stone Wall (122–127) from Newcastle to Carlisle, 73 miles long, ten feet thick, and twenty feet high, which remained the frontier (except for some 40 years from 140 when the turf Antonine Wall from Forth to Clyde was the northern boundary) until the withdrawal of Roman troops from all the frontiers to defend Rome against the barbarians at the beginning of the fifth century left this island at the mercy of the invading Saxons.

PART II

9 (*a*). An Orator Defies Death (*Philippic* II, 118 to end)

In some ways Cicero's *Second Philippic* is his finest speech in his finest hour, and this is the peroration. After the murder of Julius Caesar in March 44 B.C. it soon became clear that Antony intended to assume the mantle of dictator himself. He exploited Caesar's will, recruited armed supporters and illegally made himself governor of all Gaul, Caesar's own province, for five years. Brutus and Cassius fled to the East in August; the republican cause appeared hopeless. At the end of August Cicero returned from Greece, only to be criticised by Antony for his absence from a meeting of the Senate. On 2 September he replied with the *First Philippic*, a moderate speech which provoked a fierce reply from Antony. In October Cicero withdrew to the country and composed the *Second Philippic*, never delivered as a speech but published as a pamphlet: it is a scathing attack on Antony's whole career, but ends with a desperate appeal to him to change his ways at the eleventh hour. This, and the further twelve Philippics that followed, despite Cicero's hopes of playing off 'the boy' Octavian against Antony, brought him little real success and in the end led to his death (see p. 14). It is the measure of Cicero's versatility that while he was composing this speech, with all its bitter invective, he was also putting the finishing touches to his treatise *On Friendship* (see p. 15).

1–3 (118). *Think of your country, Antony, and your ancestors, not your associates, whatever your relationship with*

me. Your behaviour is for you to decide; mine I shall declare.
In my youth I defended the State against Catiline; as an old
man I shall not fear you. I would gladly offer my life for my
country's freedom. Twenty years ago I said death could not
come too soon for a man who had been consul. I say it with more
reason now I am old. Death for me, after a life of action and
honours, is even to be desired. My prayer is that I may leave
Rome free and that men's fortunes may match their service to
their country.

1   Respice, quaeso, aliquando rem publicam, M. Antoni,
quibus ortus sis, non quibuscum vivas considera: mecum,
ut voles: redi cum re publica in gratiam. sed de te tu
2 videris; ego de me ipse profitebor. defendi rem publicam
adulescens, non deseram senex: contempsi Catilinae gladios,
non pertimescam tuos. quin etiam corpus libenter obtulerim, si repraesentari morte mea libertas civitatis potest, ut
aliquando dolor populi Romani pariat quod iam diu parturit!
3 etenim si abhinc annos prope viginti hoc ipso in templo
negavi posse mortem immaturam esse consulari, quanto
verius nunc negabo seni? mihi vero, patres conscripti, iam
etiam optanda mors est, perfuncto rebus eis quas adeptus
sum quasque gessi. duo modo haec opto, unum ut moriens
populum Romanum liberum relinquam — hoc mihi maius
ab dis immortalibus dari nihil potest — alterum ut ita cuique
eveniat ut de re publica quisque mereatur.

9 (*b*). Ethics of a Salesman (*De Officiis* III, 54–55)

We all know that when we buy something it is marvellous
and, though expensive, 'cheap at the price'; when we sell
something it is worthless, and the person who relieves us of
it 'for a song' is really doing us a favour. Between the value
of a commodity to vendor and purchaser is an area of

1. *Spartan warrior at Thermopylae*

A modern memorial to the Three Hundred Spartans who died fighting to defend the pass against the invading Persians in 480. See Piece No. 1.

2. *Inscription commemorating the Spartans killed at Thermopylae*

Near the statue of the warrior is a stone slab bearing the epitaph written by Simonides, which is translated into Latin by Cicero in No. 1.

3. *The Wall of Servius at Rome*

Servius Tullius (No. 4) probably built a defensive earthwork (*agger*) to include most of the ancient city of Rome. In 378 B.C. a complete circuit was built of stones two foot square, of which about 100 yards still stands outside the Termini Railway Station, wrongly called the 'Servian Wall'.

4. *A Roman Dinner*

This relief from the third century A.D. shows four men reclining at a table, two of them eating roast chicken and bread rolls while the other two exchange toasts with a fifth, perhaps the host, who is standing. On the left two slaves are pouring wine into a mixing-bowl. See page 48, 'Trimalchio's Feast.'

5. *View of Naples and Vesuvius from Posilipo*

The promontory directly in front is the Castello dell' Ovo, now a barracks, and beyond it is the main part of the Bay and town of Naples. The coast road to Puteoli and Baiæ is immediately behind the spectator, and about half a mile further inland is the Naples Tunnel (No. 6).

6. *Pliny's mysterious spring near Torno on Lake Como*

A sketch to illustrate No. 7(*a*), since photographs are not allowed. The hidden spring feeds the pool, attractively backed by a grotto cut in the sheer rock face, which is overhung with rich greenery. The pool periodically overflows into a waterfall that cascades noisily into the lake below.

7. *The Source of the Clitumnus*

This delightful pool is well described by Pliny in No. 7(*b*).

8. *Aerial view of Maiden Castle,*
   near Dorchester in Dorset

This is the largest (45 acres) and most impressive of the Iron Age British hill-forts. It was begun in neolithic times (*c.* 2000 B.C.) and was enlarged by successive settlers until it was taken from the Durotriges in A.D. 43 by the Second Augusta Legion under Vespasian (future emperor) during the invasion of Britain under Aulus Plautius. The east gate is at the top of the photograph.

9. *Backbone of a Briton killed at*
   Maiden Castle by a Roman ballista bolt

The skeletons of 38 British defenders of Maiden Castle were found in a war-cemetery near the east gate of the fort, where the Romans made their main attack with heavily-armed legionaries supported by ballista missiles. This man died facing the enemy.

ONE FOOT

10. *A Roman water pipe*

The inscription is IMP(ERATORE) VESP(ASIANO) VIIII T(ITO) VII CO(N)S(ULIBUS) CN(AEO) IULIO AGRICOLA LEG(ATO) AUG(USTI) PR(O) PR(AETORE), which means 'when the Emperor Vespasian was consul for the ninth time and the Emperor Titus consul for the seventh time, Gnaeus Julius Agricola being legate of Augustus with the rank of praetor', i.e. Governor of Britain, in A.D. 79. The pipe was found in Eastgate Street, Chester, in 1899 and is now in the Grosvenor Museum.

Britanie descriptio:

At in & iniuersis fama:

H. dmari:

11. *A manuscript of Tacitus, Agricola,*
showing the beginning of his
description of Britain

No. 8 begins at the second line on this page. This manuscript
dates from the fifteenth century and is in the Vatican Library
at Rome.

bargaining open to persuasion or deception which the recent Description of Goods Act (1967) attempts to regularise. Cicero here explores this problem in an extract from *On Duties* (see p. 15) which might be called 'applied ethics'. This little debate puts the cases for scrupulous honesty and sharp practice equally cogently. Cicero gives his own opinion later in no uncertain terms: a string of seven adjectives dismiss the smart salesman as a 'shifty, deep, artful, treacherous, underhand, sly, habitual rogue' (*De. Off.* III, 57). Today the flattering advertisements of house-agents and the legal axiom *caveat emptor* ('let the buyer beware') keep the solicitors and surveyors in business; and in a fiercely competitive world Diogenes has more disciples than Antipater.

1 (54 to 55, line 6). *Suppose a man wants to sell a house which is insanitary and defective. Is he acting dishonestly or illegally if he suppresses these faults to get a high price? Yes, says Antipater; it is worse than not showing a lost traveller the way, which at Athens is treated as an offence, for the purchaser is being deliberately misled.*

1   Vendat aedes vir bonus propter aliqua vitia, quae ipse norit, ceteri ignorent; pestilentes sint et habeantur salubres, ignoretur in omnibus cubiculis apparere serpentes, sint male materiatae, ruinosae, sed hoc praeter dominum nemo sciat:
2 quaero, si haec emptoribus venditor non dixerit aedesque vendiderit pluris multo quam se venditurum putarit, num
3 id iniuste aut improbe fecerit? 'ille vero', inquit Antipater. 'quid est enim aliud erranti viam non monstrare, quod Athenis exsecrationibus publicis sanctum est, si hoc non est, emptorem pati ruere et per errorem in maximam fraudem incurrere? plus etiam est quam viam non monstrare; nam est scientem in errorem alterum inducere.'

2 (55, line 6 to end). *No, says Diogenes; he did not even ask* *you to buy it. People are not blamed for misleading advertise-* *ments; still less should those be who merely refrain from praise.* *The purchaser can exercise his own judgement; the vendor does* *not have to justify everything he says, so how can he be asked* *to justify what he does not say? It would be absurd for a seller* *and auctioneer to advertise the faults of what is for sale.*

1   Diogenes contra: 'num te emere coegit qui ne hortatus quidem est? ille quod non placebat proscripsit, tu quod placebat emisti. quod si qui proscribunt villam bonam beneque aedificatam non existimantur fefellisse, etiam si illa nec bona est nec aedificata ratione, multo minus qui 2 domum non laudarunt. ubi enim iudicium emptoris est, ibi fraus venditoris quae potest esse? sin autem dictum non omne praestandum est, quod dictum non est id praestandum putas? quid vero est stultius quam venditorem eius rei quam vendat vitia narrare? quid autem tam absurdum quam si domini iussu ita praeco praedicet: "domum pesti-lentem vendo"?'

9 (*c*). Domestic Design (*Epistulae ad Quintum Fratrem* III, 1, 1–2, 4–5)

Cicero wrote this letter from Arpinum in September 54 B.C. to his brother Quintus, who was away serving as a commanding officer in Caesar's army in Gaul and Britain (further details of Quintus' career appear later, on p. 88). At Arpinum Quintus, like his brother Marcus whose birth-place it was, owned several estates and seems, here, to be reflecting rising fortunes in domestic expansion. Marcus Cicero, in this letter, reveals yet another of his many talents, a flair for estate management. We note three special merits: first, though he offers opinions, he leaves the major decisions to his brother, quite properly, for it is his house and he is footing the bill; then, as it is all too obvious that the men on the site needed supervision, he is quite prepared to act firmly, not least with the feckless and dilatory Diphilus; and finally, in dealing with the private roads, he shows tact and consideration with neighbours. This should be remembered to his credit when his shortcomings as a politician are so seldom forgiven.

1 (1–2). *At your Manilian place Diphilus, though slow, had nearly finished. I liked the paved colonnade, but must see that the stucco suits. The pavement was getting well laid, but I ordered some changes in the ceilings. As for the small hall you wanted in the colonnade, I prefer it as it is. The house is not large enough for it, nor for rooms opening off it. In the baths I moved the hot chamber to prevent the chimney being under the bedrooms. I liked the siting of the bedroom and other winter room. Diphilus had the columns badly placed and will have to change them. He should finish in a few months, and Caesius keeps an eye on him.*

MARCVS QVINTO FRATRI SALVTEM

1 In Maniliano offendi Diphilum Diphilo tardiorem; sed tamen nihil ci restabat praeter balnearia et ambulationem et aviarium. villa mihi valde placuit propterea quod summam dignitatem pavimentata porticus habebat, quod mihi nunc denique apparuit postea quam et ipsa tota patct ct columnae 2 politae sunt. totum in eo est, quod mihi erit curae, tectorium ut concinnum sit. pavimenta recte fieri videbantur; 3 cameras quasdam non probavi mutarique iussi. quo loco in porticu te scribere aiunt ut atriolum fiat, mihi ut est magis placebat. neque enim satis loci videbatur esse atriolo neque fere solet nisi in iis aedificiis fieri in quibus est atrium

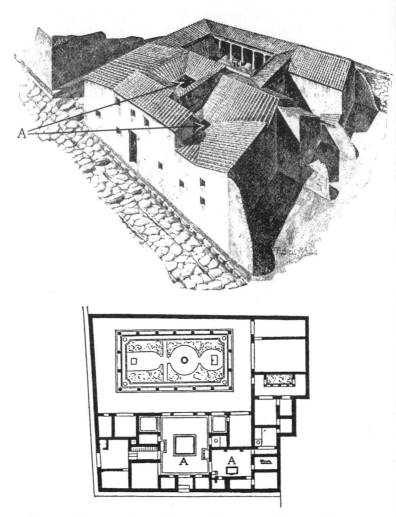

PLAN AND EXTERIOR (restored) OF THE HOUSE OF THE VETTII AT POMPEII
Note the two atria (marked A), one by the entrance, the other to the right,
distinguishable by the rectangular water tank (*impluvium*) in each

maius nec habere poterat adiuncta cubicula et eiusmodi
4 membra. tu tamen si aliter sentis, rescribe quam primum.
in balneariis assa in alterum apodyteri angulum promovi
propterea quod ita erant posita ut eorum vaporarium esset
5 subiectum cubiculis. subgrande cubiculum autem et
hibernum alterum valde probavi quod et ampla erant et loco
posita ambulationis uno latere, eo quod est proximum
6 balneariis. columnas neque rectas neque e regione Diphilus
collocarat. eas scilicet demolietur. aliquando perpendiculo
7 et linea discet uti. omnino spero paucis mensibus opus
Diphili perfectum fore; curat enim diligentissime Caesius,
qui tum mecum fuit.

2 (4–5). *At Laterium I found the private road in good con-*
dition, though part will have to be gravelled. Varro has made
up his part but Lucusta has not touched his. I shall see him in
Rome about it, also Taurus about channelling water through
his farm. I understand from your bailiff, Nicephorus, that
you gave him a contract for the villa but then added to the work
without increasing the price, so he has done nothing. I approve
the additions and have congratulated the gardener on his
tasteful use of ivy. The chänging-room is as cool and mossy
as could be.

1 Idibus Septembribus in Laterio fui. viam perspexi;
quae mihi ita placuit ut opus publicum videretur esse,
praeter CL passus (sum enim ipse mensus) ab eo ponticulo,
2 qui est ad Furinae, Satricum versus. eo loco pulvis non
glarea iniecta est (et mutabitur), et ea viae pars valde
acclivis est; sed intellexi aliter duci non potuisse, praesertim
cum tu neque per Lucustae neque per Varronis velles
ducere. Varro viam ante suum fundum probe munierat;
3 Lucusta non attigerat. quem ego Romae aggrediar et, ut
arbitror, commovebo et simul M. Taurum, quem tibi audio

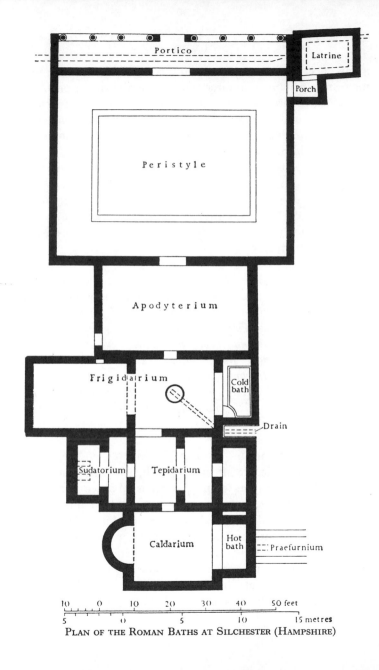

PLAN OF THE ROMAN BATHS AT SILCHESTER (HAMPSHIRE)

promisisse, qui nunc Romae erat, de aqua per fundum eius
4 ducenda rogabo. Nicephorum, vilicum tuum, sane probavi
quaesivique ex eo ecquid ei de illa aedificatiuncula Lateri de
5 qua mecum locutus es mandavisses. tum is mihi respondit
se ipsum eius operis HS $\overline{XVI}$ conductorem fuisse sed te
postea multa addidisse ad opus, nihil ad pretium; itaque
6 se omisisse. mihi me hercule valde placet te illa ut consti-
tueras addere; quamquam ea villa, quae nunc est, tamquam
philosopha videtur esse quae obiurget ceterarum villarum
7 insaniam. verum tamen illud additum delectabit. topiarium
laudavi; ita omnia convestivit hedera, qua basim villae, qua
intercolumnia ambulationis, ut denique illi palliati topiariam
facere videantur et hederam vendere. iam apodyterio nihil
alsius, nihil muscosius.

9 (d). Domestic Discord (*Ad Atticum* V, 1, 3–4)

This letter was written by Cicero in May 51 B.C. at
Minturnae (in central Italy) to Atticus, the wealthy banker
with whom, from student days, he maintained a lifelong
friendship and candid correspondence. Atticus' writings,
which have not survived, included a one-volume history of
Rome and a genealogical treatise on certain Roman families,
and he also helped to establish the date of the foundation of
Rome for the Calendar. The most striking thing about him
was his unfailing kindness (this emerges in the Life of
Atticus written by Cornelius Nepos; see page 25): he looked
after Cicero's wife Terentia while he was in exile, and
Antony's wife Fulvia during the siege of Mutina (see pages
13–14). He also acted as Cicero's publisher, and to him and
Tiro (see page 90) we owe the preservation of Cicero's
letters to Atticus himself and his friends.

Atticus' sister, Pomponia, was married to Cicero's
younger brother Quintus, who had been praetor in 62,

governor of Asia from 61 to 58, and then served with Pompey in Sardinia in 56 and Caesar in Gaul in 54. Here his camp was attacked on two occasions (by the Nervii in 54 and the Sugambri in 53), in situations where his gallantry redeemed what greater caution might have avoided. In 51–50 he served with his brother in Cilicia (see page 12). Joining Pompey in the Civil War he was afterwards pardoned by Caesar, but was executed with his brother by Antony in 43. While in Gaul he was said to have composed four tragedies in 16 days.

Whatever the rights and wrongs of the domestic quarrel described below — and perhaps the hint of impetuousness in politics and in the field suggests that Quintus was not blameless — Marcus Cicero does not come out of it very well. He served Quintus better on his estates than in his marital affairs. For what did he expect Atticus to do in response to this family-biased tittle-tattle? Even assuming he could be persuaded that his sister was to blame, he would hardly have done Quintus a favour by taking her to task about it, as Marcus implies he should. It is this sort of thing that makes 'in-laws' a stock music-hall joke. The best advice to those, like Cicero, who take sides in relatives' marriage squabbles is the time-honoured advice in *Punch* about getting involved in marriage itself — 'Don't'.

1 (3–4). *At Arpinum I talked with my brother about you, and then about our discussion of your sister at Tusculum. Quintus' attitude was kindly, and if there had been a quarrel over expenditure, did not resent it. Next day we lunched at Arcanum. Though Quintus was polite in discussing arrangements for invitations, Pomponia took offence because Statius had seen to the meal. Quintus said this sort of thing was a daily occurrence.*

1 Vt veni in Arpinas, cum ad me frater venisset, in primis
nobis sermo isque multus de te fuit. ex quo ego veni ad ea
quae fueramus ego et tu inter nos de sorore in Tusculano
2 locuti. nihil tam vidi mite, nihil tam placatum quam tum
meus frater erat in sororem tuam, ut, etiam si qua fuerat ex
ratione sumptus offensio, non appareret. ille sic dies.
3 postridie ex Arpinati profecti sumus. ut in Arcano Quintus
maneret dies fecit, ego Aquini, sed prandimus in Arcano.
nosti hunc fundum. quo ut venimus, humanissime Quintus
'Pomponia' inquit, 'tu invita mulieres, ego viros accivero.'
nihil potuit, mihi quidem ut visum est, dulcius idque cum
4 verbis tum etiam animo ac vultu. at illa audientibus nobis
'ego ipsa sum' inquit 'hic hospita,' id autem ex eo, ut opinor,
quod antecesserat Statius ut prandium nobis videret. tum
Quintus 'en' inquit mihi, 'haec ego patior cotidie.'

2 (4). *I was upset, too, but hid my feelings. She would not
take her place at table, and refused the food that Quintus sent
up to her. Next day, at Aquinum, Quintus told me her attitude
had not changed. You can tell her yourself I consider her
behaviour unkind.*

1 Dices 'quid quaeso istuc erat?' magnum; itaque me
ipsum commoverat; sic absurde et aspere verbis vultuque
responderat. dissimulavi dolens. discubuimus omnes
2 praeter illam, cui tamen Quintus de mensa misit. illa reiecit.
quid multa? nihil meo fratre lenius, nihil asperius tua sorore
mihi visum est; et multa praetereo quae tum mihi maiori
3 stomacho quam ipsi Quinto fuerunt. ego inde Aquinum.
Quintus in Arcano remansit et Aquinum ad me postridie
mane venit mihique narravit nec secum illam dormire
voluisse et cum discessura esset fuisse eiusmodi qualem
ego vidissem. quid quaeris? vel ipsi hoc dicas licet, humanitatem ei meo iudicio illo die defuisse.

9 (*e*). Concern for the Health of a Former Slave
(*Ad Fam.* XVI, 4, 1–3)

This letter was written by Cicero at Leucas, in western Greece, on 7 November 50 B.C., to Marcus Tullius Tiro. Tiro had been Cicero's slave but was later manumitted by him and, as usual with a freedman (*libertus*), assumed the first name (*praenomen*) and second name (*nomen*) of his former master, Marcus Tullius. Though a slave he was a well-educated man (for the slave-market, being supplied from captives of pirates and prisoners of war, included men of all backgrounds) who acted as Cicero's secretary, edited some of his speeches and the *Letters to Friends*, including a number to himself, and wrote a biography of his master. He used a kind of shorthand which he invented himself (abbreviations derived from it in later times were called after him *notae Tironianae*) and was said to be better than others at correcting errors and deciphering his master's handwriting. On this occasion Cicero, on his way back from Cilicia (see page 12) had been obliged to leave Tiro at Patrae, at the west end of the Corinthian Gulf, because of ill-health. His care and concern for Tiro — note the greetings from all the male members of the family with its touching suggestion that Tiro was something of an 'institution' — emerges in every sentence of this letter.

The existence of slavery was an unpleasant feature of Roman civilisation, and the treatment of slaves working in chain-gangs on the large estates (*latifundia*) or trained to butcher each other in the amphitheatre 'to make a Roman holiday' is nauseating. But the family slave lucky enough to have a considerate master fared much better. Cicero seizes the opportunity to practise the Stoic doctrine of the brotherhood of man (see page 54) and this enlightened attitude to a bad institution grew in later times, notably with

Seneca and Pliny (see page 122), foreshadowing St Paul's 'neither Greek nor barbarian, slave nor free' and the liberation movement of Wilberforce, still to be completed in some parts of the world today.

1–4 (1–2). *Your letter upset me, though it reassured me at the end. You must not travel until you are completely recovered. I am not quite satisfied with your doctor, despite good reports of him, and have given him and Lyso detailed instructions about you. I have also asked Curius to look after you, for Lyso, like many Greeks, is rather casual. Spare yourself no pains or expense to get better. I have asked him to give you whatever you need, and the doctor should be given something to increase his concern for you.*

TVLLIVS TIRONI SVO S. P. D. ET CICERO ET
Q. FRATER ET Q. F.

1   Varie sum adfectus tuis litteris, valde priore pagina perturbatus, paulum altera recreatus. qua re nunc quidem non dubito quin, quoad plane valeas, te neque navigationi neque viae committas. satis te mature videro, si plane confirmatum

2   videro. de medico et tu bene existimari scribis et ego sic audio; sed plane curationes eius non probo; ius enim dandum tibi non fuit, cum κακοστόμαχος esses. sed tamen

3   et ad illum scripsi accurate et ad Lysonem. ad Curium vero, suavissimum hominem et summi offici summaeque humanitatis, multa scripsi, in his etiam ut, si tibi videretur, te ad se traferret; Lyso enim noster vereor ne neglegentior sit, primum quia omnes Graeci, deinde quod, cum a me litteras accepisset, mihi nullas remisit. sed eum tu laudas;

4   tu igitur quid faciendum sit iudicabis. illud, mi Tiro, te rogo sumptu ne parcas ulla in re, quod ad valetudinem opus sit. scripsi ad Curium quod dixisses daret. medico ipsi puto aliquid dandum esse, quo sit studiosior.

5–6 (3). *Your services to me are boundless, but the greatest of all will be to let me see you in good health. You should have a good voyage with the quaestor Mescinius, an agreeable person. But after thinking of your health, think of the voyage. You must not hurry and risk your health, which is my sole concern.*

5   Innumerabilia tua sunt in me officia domestica, forensia, urbana, provincialia, in re privata, in publica, in studiis, in litteris nostris; omnia viceris, si, ut spero, te validum
6   videro. ego puto te bellissime, si recte erit, cum quaestore Mescinio decursurum. non inhumanus est teque, ut mihi visus est, diligit. et cum valetudini tuae diligentissime consulueris, tum, mi Tiro, consulito navigationi. nulla in re iam te festinare volo; nihil laboro, nisi ut salvus sis.

9 (*f*). An Author's Lapse (*Ad Atticum* XVI, 6, 4)

This little 'tailpiece' from a letter to Atticus was written at Vibo, in south-west Italy, in July 44, when Cicero, now despairing of a republican revival after Caesar's murder, was thinking of sailing to Greece. It illustrates his honesty in the smallest matters, where nobody could accuse him of trying to make an impression. He finds he has used the same preface in two different books he had sent to Atticus. How many authors would bother about such a trifle? People do not read prefaces anyway, and if they do they would not notice. Not so Cicero; he must put it right even, or perhaps especially, with a life-long friend who would generously forgive a trivial oversight. All this while he is preoccupied about the future of his country and the role in it, if any, he has to play. A good note, this, on which to take our leave of Cicero, the man who, we should now realise, was so much more than the luckless author of *o fortunatam natam me consule Romam.*

1–3 (4). *A confession: I inserted the same preface in 'On Glory', which I sent you, as I did in Academica III, forgetting I had used it already when I put it in at Tusculum. Reading the Academica on the boat I noticed my mistake and so have dashed off a new preface. Cut out the old one and stick in the new. Greetings to your wife and my darling Attica.*

1 Nunc neglegentiam meam cognosce. 'De Gloria' librum ad te misi. at in eo prohoemium idem est quod in Academico tertio. id evenit ob eam rem quod habeo volumen prohoemiorum. ex eo eligere soleo cum aliquod
2 σύγγραμμα institui. itaque iam in Tusculano, qui non meminissem me abusum isto prohoemio, conieci id in eum librum quem tibi misi. cum autem in navi legerem Aca-
3 demicos, agnovi erratum meum. itaque statim novum prohoemium exaravi et tibi misi. tu illud desecabis, hoc agglutinabis. Piliae salutem dices et Atticae, deliciis atque amoribus meis.

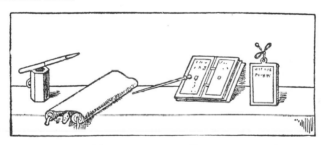

ROMAN WRITING MATERIALS, FROM A POMPEIAN WALL PAINTING
Left to right: ink-pot and pen; papyrus roll book (see note on *volumen*); stilus, double and single writing tablets (see note on *exaravi*)

NEPOS

10. Hannibal's Adventures after the Defeat of Carthage
(*Hannibal* 9–11)

Six pages in this part of the book recount episodes in the life of Hannibal, the great Carthaginian general who, in the Second Punic War (218–202 B.C.), brought the rising power of Rome to the brink of defeat. His is a fascinating story, well told and attractively illustrated in Sir Gavin De Beer's book, *Hannibal* (Thames and Hudson). The passage from Livy (No. 12) describes Hannibal's crossing of the Alps, and the earlier part of his life up to that point is briefly sketched in the Introduction there. The extract below comes from the brief biography of Hannibal by Cornelius Nepos (see page 25), which lacks the grandeur and detail of Livy's story but fills in some gaps in Hannibal's life after the surrender of Carthage in 202. A brief outline of his career from the crossing of the Alps to his death follows, excluding those episodes where Nepos tells the story for you.

Though the ordeal of the Alps had reduced Hannibal's army from something under 50,000 men to about 26,000 and he had lost most of his elephants, he managed to defeat the Romans in four decisive battles: at the Ticinus and the Trebia, in northern Italy (218); at Lake Trasimene, in Etruria (217); and, after a short but successful period of 'delaying tactics' by Quintus Fabius Maximus Cunctator ('the delayer'), who avoided pitched battles, at Cannae, in southern Italy (216), where the rash action of Varro, one of the consuls, in crossing the river Aufidus led to the annihilation of the Roman army. Though some of the cities of southern Italy joined Hannibal after Cannae, he could not keep a firm hold on them. Their loyalty to Rome prevailed in the end, and even a sudden swoop on Rome by Hannibal, which brought his army within three miles of the city (his cavalry actually rode up to the Colline Gate to the south of the city), could not shatter the Romans' nerve nor save Capua and Syracuse from recapture by them. Hannibal was soon in difficulties with supplies, and the attempt of his brother, Hasdrubal, to reach him with reinforcements by crossing the Alps from Spain was thwarted by the Roman victory, and Hasdrubal's death, at the battle of the Metaurus in 207. Soon after the young general Scipio Africanus, who had already distinguished himself in Spain, crossed to Africa, and his successes there forced the recall of Hannibal to Africa. There Scipio defeated him at the battle of Zama in 202.

Hannibal now urged Carthage to sue for peace, and remained there until 195, when, harassed by his political enemies and fearing that the Romans would demand his surrender, he fled to king Antiochus of Syria, who was himself soon involved in war with Rome. After the defeat of Antiochus at Magnesia in 190 the Romans demanded Hannibal's surrender, and at this point our extract from Nepos takes up the story. At length the Romans, infuriated at the discomfiture of their ally, Eumenes of Pergamum, by Prusias of Bithynia, in which the ingenuity of Hannibal described below played no small part, sent Flaminius to Prusias to ensure Hannibal's surrender. He was cornered in a fort in 183 but, helped by a faithful slave, took poison which he kept in a ring (the *anulus* with which Juvenal made great play — see *Two Centuries of Roman Poetry*, page 224) and died true to the oath he had sworn (see pages 107–8) always to be the enemy of Rome and never to surrender to her.

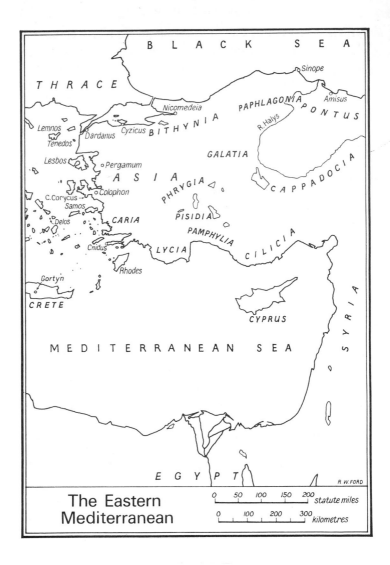

BLACK SEA

THRACE

Sinope

Nicomedeia

PAPHLAGONIA

Amisus

PONTUS

Lemnos

Cyzicus

BITHYNIA

R.Halys

Dardanus

Tenedos

GALATIA

Lesbos

Pergamum

ASIA

CAPPADOCIA

C.Corycus

Colophon

PHRYGIA

Samos

PISIDIA

Delos

CARIA

PAMPHYLIA

CILICIA

Cnidus

LYCIA

Rhodes

SYRIA

Gortyn

CRETE

CYPRUS

MEDITERRANEAN SEA

EGYPT

R.W.FORD

The Eastern Mediterranean

| 0 | 50 | 100 | 150 | 200 | statute miles |

| 0 | 100 | 200 | 300 | kilometres |

1 (9). *After the defeat of Antiochus Hannibal fled to the Gortynians, in Crete. To safeguard his possessions against their greed he filled some jars with lead, covering their tops with gold and silver, and deposited them in a temple. His valuables he placed in some bronze statues and left them casually in the courtyard. The Gortynians, falling for the trick, carefully guarded the 'treasures' in the temple (but allowed Hannibal to take away his bronze statues when he departed.)*

1 Antiocho fugato verens ne dederetur, quod sine dubio accidisset si sui fecisset potestatem, Cretam ad Gortynios
2 venit, ut ibi, quo se conferret, consideraret. vidit autem vir omnium callidissimus magno se fore periculo, nisi quid providisset, propter avaritiam Cretensium; magnam enim secum pecuniam portabat, de qua sciebat exisse famam.
3 itaque capit tale consilium. amphoras complures complet plumbo, summas operit auro et argento. has praesentibus principibus deponit in templo Dianae, simulans se suas fortunas illorum fidei credere. his in errorem inductis statuas aeneas, quas secum portabat, omnes sua pecunia
4 complet easque in propatulo domi abicit. Gortynii templum magna cura custodiunt, non tam a ceteris quam ab Hannibale, ne ille inscientibus iis tolleret secumque duceret.

2 (10). *Escaping with his property Hannibal went to help Prusias of Bithynia with his war against Eumenes, an ally of Rome. He won the support of other kings and compensated for naval inferiority by a ruse. Numerous poisonous snakes in earthenware jars were loaded onto his ships. He told the marines to concentrate on Eumenes' ship. The snakes would protect them from the rest. He promised to indicate Eumenes' ship and offered a reward for his capture or death.*

1   Sic conservatis suis rebus Poenus illusis Cretensibus omnibus ad Prusiam in Pontum pervenit. apud quem eodem animo fuit erga Italiam neque aliud quicquam egit quam
2 regem armavit et exercuit adversus Romanos. quem cum videret domesticis opibus minus esse robustum, conciliabat ceteros reges, adiungebat bellicosas nationes. dissidebat ab eo Pergamenus rex Eumenes, Romanis amicissimus,
3 bellumque inter eos gerebatur et mari et terra: quo magis cupiebat eum Hannibal opprimi. sed utrobique Eumenes plus valebat propter Romanorum societatem: quem si removisset, faciliora sibi cetera fore arbitrabatur. ad hunc
4 interficiundum talem iniit rationem. classe paucis diebus erant decreturi. superabatur navium multitudine: dolo erat pugnandum, cum par non esset armis. imperavit quam plurimas venenatas serpentes vivas colligi easque in vasa
5 fictilia conici. harum cum effecisset magnam multitudinem, die ipso, quo facturus erat navale proelium, classiarios convocat iisque praecipit, omnes ut in unam Eumenis regis concurrant navem, a ceteris tantum satis habeant se defendere. id illos facile serpentium multitudine consecuturos.
6 rex autem in qua nave veheretur, ut scirent, se facturum: quem si aut cepissent aut interfecissent, magno iis pollicetur praemio fore.

3 (11). *Just before the battle Hannibal sent a herald in a skiff with a message for Eumenes. He was shown which was the king's ship, pointed it out to his own men, and returned. Eumenes, finding that the message merely insulted him, was puzzled but joined battle. The Bithynians concentrated on Eumenes' ship and forced him to flee to his defences. The other Pergamene ships were pelted with the jars and, finding their ships full of snakes, fled in terror. Thus, and by other such devices at other times, Hannibal discomfited his enemies.*

(b)

(a)

(a) SIGN OVER BOOTMAKER'S SHOP AT POMPEII
(b) BADGE OF ROYAL CORPS OF SIGNALS
Both show the figure of Mercury with caduceus
(see note) winged hat and sandals

1 Tali cohortatione militum facta classis ab utrisque in
proelium deducitur. quarum acie constituta, priusquam
signum pugnae daretur, Hannibal, ut palam faceret suis
quo loco Eumenes esset, tabellarium in scapha cum caduceo
2 mittit. qui ubi ad naves adversariorum pervenit epistu-
lamque ostendens se regem professus est quaerere, statim
ad Eumenem deductus est, quod nemo dubitabat quin
aliquid de pace esset scriptum. tabellarius ducis nave
3 declarata suis eodem, unde erat egressus, se recepit. at
Eumenes soluta epistula nihil in ea repperit nisi quae ad
irridendum eum pertinerent. cuius etsi causam mirabatur
neque reperiebat, tamen proelium statim committere non

4 dubitavit.   horum in concursu Bithynii Hannibalis praecepto universi navem Eumenis adoriuntur.   quorum vim
rex cum sustinere non posset, fuga salutem petit, quam
consecutus non esset, nisi intra sua praesidia se recepisset,
5 quae in proximo litore erant collocata.   reliquae Pergamenae
naves cum adversarios premerent acrius, repente in eas
vasa fictilia, de quibus supra mentionem fecimus, conici
coepta sunt.   quae iacta initio risum pugnantibus concita-
6 runt, neque quare id fieret poterat intellegi.   postquam
autem naves suas oppletas conspexerunt serpentibus, nova
re perterriti, cum, quid potissimum vitarent, non viderent,
puppes verterunt seque ad sua castra nautica rettulerunt.
7 sic Hannibal consilio arma Pergamenorum superavit, neque
tum solum, sed saepe alias pedestribus copiis pari prudentia
pepulit adversarios.

SALLUST

11. Caesar and Cato Compared (*Catiline* 53, 6 and 54)

This passage from Sallust's *Catiline* follows his versions
of speeches by Caesar and Cato urging respectively life
imprisonment and the death penalty for the conspirators.
Lucius Sergius Catilina, a spendthrift aristocrat who formed
a revolutionary movement to cancel debts and set up a
radical government in Rome, had already been involved in
an abortive plot to kill the consuls of 65 B.C., but managed
to escape prosecution.   In 63 he plotted to seize the city,
having collected an army of malcontents in Etruria, but was
defeated in his bid for the consulship by Cicero.   The latter
forestalled a plot to kill him, denounced Catiline to the
Senate and forced his withdrawal to Etruria.   Meanwhile
Lentulus, Catiline's second-in-command, had approached
some ambassadors from Gaul, who were visiting Rome, for

support. But Cicero had persuaded the Gauls to trap Lentulus into giving written evidence of his intentions; he then had Lentulus and his confederates arrested, faced them with their signatures on the incriminating documents, and persuaded the Senate, despite Caesar's plea for mercy, to order their summary execution. Cicero had the sentence carried out forthwith, and announced it to the people in the Forum in one word — *vixerunt* ('they have lived', i.e. are dead).

The two men who form the subject of Sallust's contrasting profiles were indeed very different. Gaius Julius Caesar (100–44) was an aristocrat and talented orator who, like Sallust himself, joined the popular party. He became quaestor in 68, aedile in 65 and *Pontifex Maximus* (chief priest at Rome) in 63, the year of Catiline's conspiracy. Praetor in 62 and afterwards governor of Spain, but disappointed in his hope of a 'triumph' on his return, he formed the First Triumvirate with Pompey and Crassus in 60 and secured his election as consul for 59. Appointed governor of Cisalpine Gaul and Illyricum, he spent the years from 59–50 in the conquest of Gaul. But in the later part of this term his links with the other triumvirs were broken (his daughter Julia, married to Pompey, died in 54 and Crassus was killed in battle against the Parthians in 53) and he returned to find himself facing the opposition of the Senate, led by Pompey. The Civil War (49–45) followed, and Caesar's victories at Pharsalus, in Greece (48), followed by the death of Pompey, at Thapsus, in Africa (46), and at Munda, in Spain (45) left him master of the Roman world. Back at Rome he set about various reforms, but, whether because he planned or because he seemed to plan an imperial dynasty, he was assassinated by Brutus and Cassius and the other conspirators on the Ides of March, in 44.

Marcus Porcius Cato 'Uticensis' (95–46) was the great-grandson of Cato the Censor (see page 17). He lost both parents in childhood and was brought up by his uncle, M. Livius Drusus. In 67 he served as a military tribune in Macedonia, and in 63 supported Cicero in his demand for the execution of the Catilinarian conspirators but later in the year opposed him in his defence of Lucius Murena on a charge of bribery. As tribune in 61 he conciliated the populace by increasing cheap doles of corn, but his general attitude in politics was one of diehard obstructionism and had the effect of cementing together the members of the First Triumvirate, all of whom had been thwarted by him in various ways. Not content with helping to secure for Caesar, as consul in 59, an obstructive colleague in Bibulus, Cato lost no chance to impede Caesar on his own account. But in 58 Clodius, obliging here too as he had been in dealing with Cicero (see page 12) forced him to undertake the annexation of Cyprus. On his return Cato became praetor in 54, and in the Civil War joined Pompey, holding Utica, in Africa, against Caesar's troops and committing suicide after the battle of Thapsus in 46. An unamiable champion of lost causes, whose epitaph by the poet Lucan (A.D. 39–65) few can forbear to quote — *victrix causa deis placuit, sed victa Catoni* ('the conquering cause pleased the gods, the conquered, Cato', *Pharsalia* I, 128) — he nevertheless stood firmly for a mixture of Stoic and old Roman principles. It was said that after his accounts were lost on the voyage back from Cyprus nobody doubted his word. There is no such story about Caesar.

To attempt, as Sallust did, to evaluate these two men side by side is a hazardous exercise, and a warning to those who seek to assess by too facile contrast the great men of history, literature and art. Greek legend told of a brigand named Procrustes, who laid his victims on a bed, and if they were too long for it, cut short their limbs; but if they were too

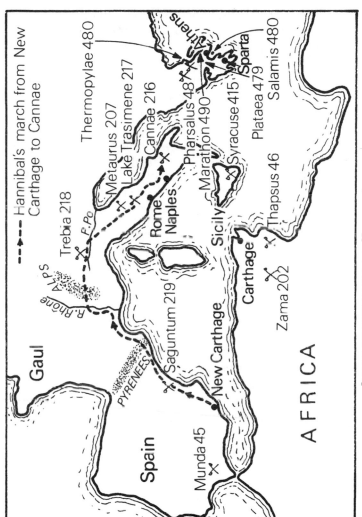

IMPORTANT BATTLE SITES AND HANNIBAL'S MARCH

short he stretched them to fit. Sallust's subjects suffer more than a little from this Procrustean formula of contrast. For instance it was not Caesar's 'generosity' or 'mercy' that made him famous and great, but the conquest of Gaul and his victories in the Civil War. Again, much that would upset the balance is perforce omitted. We hear nothing of the arrogant ruthlessness that caused Caesar, when captured by pirates in his early life, to put up the price of his ransom and, after his eventual release, to track them down and execute them (other examples are mentioned in the Notes). There is nothing of his cynical manipulation of the creaking Roman constitution, as in his disregard of Bibulus' veto during his consulship which earned it the name of the 'consulship of Julius and Caesar'; or his election of a friend, Caninius Rebilus, to the consulship for half a day (from 1 p.m. (after lunch) till midnight) for services rendered, caus- ing Cicero to observe ruefully (*Ad Fam.* VII, 30) that in the consulship of Caninius nobody had lunch, but that the consul showed exceptional vigilance in never sleeping during his consulship. Nor is justice done to his personal mag- netism that could make a man like Curio, a Pompeian tribune whose transfer fee cost Caesar a fortune, ready, because he could never face his general after losing his army (*Bell. Civ.* II, 42), to lay down his life in battle for Caesar near where Cato later laid down his for his conscience. Nor is the picture of Cato complete: *nihil largiundo*, § 4, 'by never stooping to bribery' is qualified by his alleged connivance at bribery to secure the election of Bibulus (Suet. *Jul.* 19, 1) and a certain amount of political intrigue (*factione cum factioso*, § 7) on his own account; and 'integrity of life' could be a mixed asset, and good for a laugh, when it reached the extremes of Stoicism (riotously exploited by Cicero in his speech *For Murena*, especially § 61) that made all crimes equal, and killing one's father no worse than killing a chicken. Sallust's device of contrasting profiles, attractive reading as it is for its neat antithesis and epigrams, can mislead us and mask a good deal of the truth. For Sallust's bed of Procrustes Cato was more than a shade too small and Caesar several sizes too big.

1-3 (53,6-54,2). *I shall give an account of the characters of Cato and Caesar, two outstanding men of my time. In birth, age, eloquence and nobility of soul they were equal, but their renown was different. Caesar owed his to his favours and generosity, Cato to uprightness of life and austerity.*

1 Sed memoria mea ingenti virtute, divorsis moribus fuere viri duo, M. Cato et C. Caesar, quos quoniam res obtulerat, silentio praeterire non fuit consilium, quin utriusque naturam et mores, quantum ingenio possum, aperirem
2 igitur eis genus, aetas, eloquentia prope aequalia fuere,
3 magnitudo animi par, item gloria, sed alia alii. Caesar beneficiis ac munificentia magnus habebatur, integritate vitae Cato. ille mansuetudine et misericordia clarus factus, huic severitas dignitatem addiderat.

4-7 (54, 3-6). *Caesar was renowned for giving and forgiving, Cato for never offering presents; one was good-natured, a refuge for the unfortunate, the other steadfast, a scourge for the wicked. Caesar would work hard, neglect himself for his friends, give anything worth giving. He sought an army and a campaign to win glory. Cato preferred restraint, propriety and austerity. He did not compete in wealth or party strife, but in merit, self-control and righteousness. Being good was more his concern than seeming good; so the less he sought fame the more it pursued him.*

4 Caesar dando, sublevando, ignoscundo, Cato nihil largiundo gloriam adeptus est. in altero miseris perfugium

5 erat, in altero malis pernicies. illius facilitas, huius con-
stantia laudabatur. postremo Caesar in animum induxerat
laborare, vigilare; negotiis amicorum intentus sua neglegere,
nihil denegare quod dono dignum esset; sibi magnum
imperium, exercitum, bellum novom expetebat, ubi virtus
6 enitescere posset. at Catoni studium modestiae, decoris,
7 sed maxume severitatis erat. non divitiis cum divite neque
factione cum factioso, sed cum strenuo virtute, cum modesto
pudore, cum innocente abstinentia certabat; esse quam
videri bonus malebat; ita quo minus petebat gloriam, eo
magis illum sequebatur.

AFRICAN ELEPHANT
(Carthaginian silver coin
minted in Spain about 220 B.C.)

INDIAN ELEPHANT
(Etruscan bronze coin,
enlarged, of 217 B.C.)

HANNIBAL
(Carthaginian silver coin,
minted in Spain about 220 B.C.)

LIVY

12. Hannibal at the Summit of the Alps (XXI, 35, 4 to 37)

We have already (No. 10) seen something of Hannibal's resourcefulness and tenacity in his declining years after his country's defeat. This extract from Livy shows him at the summit of achievement. For the crossing of the Alps was his major goal; that accomplished, he saw the victorious sequel assured. His reasons for this were sound enough. Surprise is the essence of military success. Though to us the invasion of Italy from the north may seem no great surprise, it surprised the Romans as much as, if not more than, a seaborne invasion would have done, even had that been feasible. They had been invaded from the north only once, by the Gauls at the beginning of the fourth century B.C., but that, at the outbreak of the Second Punic War in 218 B.C., was over a century and a half ago, and memories were short. Moreover they regarded the Gauls as universal enemies, Hannibal's no less than their own, and in crossing the Alps he had them to reckon with. If the Alps could not overcome him, the Gauls would, or so it seemed. When Hannibal said to his men *cetera plana, proclivia fore* (1,6) he meant more than that the rest of the journey would be level or downhill; the Alps conquered, victory in the crucial battles to come (see page 94) seemed a foregone conclusion.

Hannibal had earned his success the hard way in early life. After their defeat in the First Punic War (264–241 B.C.), fought largely in Sicily and Africa, the Carthaginians turned their attention to Spain. In 237 they sent their general Hamilcar, accompanied by his young son Hannibal, to extend their foothold there and strengthen their army with the sturdy and courageous Spanish tribesmen. Hamilcar made his son swear a solemn oath before the altar that he would never be a friend of the Roman people; he then set about the conquest of southern and eastern Spain, and on his death in 229 was succeeded by his son-in-law Hasdrubal, who pushed his forces northwards nearly to the Ebro and established a base at New Carthage on the south-east coast. On the murder of Hasdrubal in 221 Hannibal, now aged 25 and already an experienced leader and the darling of the troops, succeeded him. He at once extended his power by subduing native tribes and became a threat to Saguntum, a town to the east of New Carthage with whom Rome had a treaty of friendship although they had no army stationed in Spain. Hannibal exploited a local dispute to attack this town in 219, and captured it after an eight-month siege. Already Hannibal had plans for the invasion of Italy from Spain, and though his capture of Saguntum led to a declaration of war by Rome it also removed a threat to his rear in the future march eastwards. Before the Romans could move he collected an army of some 50,000 men, crossed the Pyrenees and reached the Rhone. The Romans sent an army under P. Cornelius Scipio to challenge him, but it reached the river only to find that Hannibal had already crossed it, ferrying over his elephants on specially constructed rafts, and was on his way to Italy. The ascent of the Alps, with the hostility of local tribes and treacherous guides adding to the rigours of nature, was a superhuman feat, but though, at the outset of this passage, Hannibal had reached the summit his troubles were not over.

1 (35, 4–12). *Reaching the summit of the Alps the Cartha-*
ginians camped there for two days and were caught up by
straggling baggage-animals. A snow storm increased the troops'
despondency, but the march was continued. Then Hannibal
went ahead to a vantage-point, showed them the plains of the
Po valley below, and promised an easy journey in the future

and the conquest of Italy in one or two battles. The descent begah with little hindrance from the enemy, but proved steep and treacherous, causing men and beasts to fall over each other.

1 Nono die in iugum Alpium perventum est per invia pleraque et errores, quos aut ducentium fraus aut, ubi fides iis non esset, temere initae valles a coniectantibus iter 2 faciebant. biduum in iugo stativa habita, fessisque labore ac pugnando quies data militibus; iumentaque aliquot, quae prolapsa in rupibus erant, sequendo vestigia agminis in 3 castra pervenere. fessis taedio tot malorum nivis etiam casus, occidente iam sidere Vergiliarum, ingentem terrorem 4 adiecit. per omnia nive oppleta cum signis prima luce motis segniter agmen incederet, pigritiaque et desperatio in 5 omnium vultu emineret, praegressus signa Hannibal in promonturio quodam, unde longe ac late prospectus erat, consistere iussis militibus Italiam ostentat subiectosque 6 Alpinis montibus Circumpadanos campos moeniaque eos tum transcendere non Italiae modo, sed etiam urbis Romanae: cetera plana, proclivia fore; uno aut summum altero proelio arcem et caput Italiae in manu ac potestate habituros. 7 procedere inde agmen coepit, iam nihil ne hostibus quidem 8 praeter parva furta per occasionem temptantibus. ceterum iter multo, quam in ascensu fuerat — ut pleraque Alpium ab Italia sicut breviora ita arrectiora sunt — difficilius fuit. 9 omnis enim ferme via praeceps, angusta, lubrica erat, ut neque sustinere se a lapsu possent, nec, qui paulum titubassent, haerere adflicti vestigio suo, aliique super alios et iumenta in homines occiderent.

2 (36). *The ledge became narrower still, and a landslip halted them. Going forward to reconnoitre, Hannibal decided to attempt a detour. But though the vanguard made progress over a layer of freshly fallen snow, their trampling on it flattened*

it to the bare ice, so that those following slipped, with no vege-
tation to check their fall, while the animals' hooves penetrated
the ice and they were stuck fast.

1   Ventum deinde ad multo angustiorem rupem, atque ita
rectis saxis, ut aegre expeditus miles temptabundus mani-
busque retinens virgulta ac stirpes circa eminentes de-
2 mittere sese posset.   natura locus iam ante praeceps recenti
lapsu terrae in pedum mille admodum altitudinem abruptus
3 erat.   ibi cum velut ad finem viae equites constitissent,
miranti Hannibali, quae res moraretur agmen, nuntiatur
4 rupem inviam esse.   digressus deinde ipse ad locum visendum.   haud dubia res visa, quin per invia circa nec trita
5 antea quamvis longo ambitu circumduceret agmen.   ea vero
via insuperabilis fuit: nam cum super veterem nivem intactam nova modicae altitudinis esset, molli nec praealtae
6 facile pedes ingredientium insistebant;   ut vero tot hominum
iumentorumque incessu dilapsa est, per nudam infra glaciem
7 fluentemque tabem liquescentis nivis ingrediebantur.   taetra
ibi luctatio erat, glacie non recipiente vestigium, et in prono
citius pedes fallente, ut, seu manibus in adsurgendo seu
genu se adiuvissent, ipsis adminiculis prolapsis iterum
corruerent;   nec stirpes circa radicesve, ad quas pede aut
manu quisquam eniti posset, erant: ita in levi tantum
8 glacie tabidaque nive volutabantur.   iumenta secabant
interdum etiam infimam ingredientia nivem, et prolapsa
iactandis gravius in conitendo ungulis penitus perfringebant,
ut pleraque velut pedica capta haererent in dura et alte
concreta glacie.

3 (37). *Thus checked they encamped on the ridge and set about*
constructing a road.   A bonfire was made from the branches of
huge trees to heat the rock and then they melted it by pouring
on vinegar.   A zigzag path of easy gradient was engineered

which baggage-animals and even elephants could use. Four days were taken for this, while the animals nearly starved on the pastureless wastes. Lower down, in terrain wooded and watered by streams, the animals were grazed and the men rested. Three days later they reached the plains, with less forbidding country and inhabitants.

1 Tandem nequiquam iumentis atque hominibus fatigatis, castra in iugo posita, aegerrime ad id ipsum loco purgato: 2 tantum nivis fodiendum atque egerendum fuit. inde ad rupem muniendam, per quam unam via esse poterat, milites ducti, cum caedendum esset saxum, arboribus circa immanibus deiectis detruncatisque struem ingentem lignorum faciunt, eamque, cum et vis venti apta faciendo igni coorta esset, succendunt, ardentiaque saxa infuso aceto putrefaciunt. 3 ita torridam incendio rupem ferro pandunt, molliuntque anfractibus modicis clivos, ut non iumenta solum, sed 4 elephanti etiam deduci possent. quadriduum circa rupem consumptum iumentis prope fame absumptis: nuda enim fere cacumina sunt, et, si quid est pabuli, obruunt nives. 5 inferiora vallis apricos quosdam colles habent, rivosque 6 prope silvas et iam humano cultu digniora loca. ibi iumenta in pabulum missa, et quies muniendo fessis hominibus data. triduo inde ad planum descensum iam et locis mollioribus et accolarum ingeniis.

PETRONIUS

13. A Proud Father (*Satyricon* 46)

In Part I we heard a story told by one of the ebullient guests at Trimalchio's banquet (see page 48). In this passage another guest talks about his son. There are two things to notice before we leave you to enjoy this delightful glimpse of the family life of Echion the rag-collector (or whatever precisely he was). First, the vividness with which the character of this successful tradesman comes through — one could almost imagine his thumbs in the arm-holes of his waistcoat if he had one. Respectful to the learning of Agamemnon but a shade suspicious that his silence conceals arrogance, generous in his hospitality, with a hint that his 'place in the country' is really quite something, he is inordinately proud, as self-made men often are, of his son and heir, but not above a little sharp practice over the goldfinches ('it's for the lad's good, really, y'see'). Then, to round it off, some decided ideas about the boy's career — the Echions of this world tend to have very firm ideas about what 'the lad' will do and are equally determined that he shall not follow in father's footsteps — and a sententious remark about the value of a good education: *omne ignotum pro magnifico est* ('everything unknown is impressive'), as Tacitus observes (*Agricola* 30).

The second thing to notice here is how limited were the facilities for education in Rome at this time (see also *Two Centuries of Roman Poetry*, page 107). State schools were virtually non-existent, and private schools were alarmingly varied in quality and few and far between outside the towns. Echion was forced to rely on two tutors for his son, and was lucky to find one of them good. It was this situation which the Younger Pliny imaginatively sought to remedy by founding his school at Comum (see No. 15). And there is another thing. A question in a recent general paper asked: 'By whom were you chiefly educated at school, your teachers or your friends?' It was the second possibility here envisaged that Echion's son missed, and for which Pliny sought to provide.

12. *The Atrium of the 'House of the Silver Wedding' at Pompeii*

View from the main entrance, looking towards the Peristyle (see below). Note the *compluvium* in the roof, the *impluvium* in the floor, and the doors on each side leading to the *cubicula* (bedrooms). Quintus Cicero's villa at Arpinum (No. 9 (*c*)) was probably too small for two such *atria*, though large establishments like the 'House of the Vettii' (see p. 84) had them.

15. Money-changer in his 'Bank'

Second century A.D. relief from the Palazzo Salviati, Rome. Note how his right hand rests on his coins as he deals with a customer. No doubt Cicero's banker friends Atticus and Curius (No. 9(e)) exercised similar caution.

13. The Peristylium of the 'House of the Silver Wedding' at Pompeii

This is an open garden surrounded by a colonnade. Between the two pillars in the left background is the entrance to the *atrium*. Cicero does not use the word *peristylium* for the garden of his brother's house (No. 9(c)), preferring *ambulatio*, which implies something more expansive, for which there would be room in the country. This too had a colonnade, which caused the architect Diphilus so much trouble.

14. Apodyterium (changing-room) of the Stabian Baths at Pompeii

The Stabian Baths are the oldest surviving public baths of the Roman period and date from the second century B.C. The walls of this changing room are entirely decorated with stucco and have what appear to be open lockers on the right. Presumably the *apodyterium* of Quintus Cicero's villa (No. 9(c)) was smaller and less elaborate.

16 and 17.
Busts of
Julius Caesar and
Marcus Cato

The portrait bust of Julius
Caesar, found at Tusculum and
now in the Castello dei Aglie at
Turin, was probably carved in his
lifetime. That of Cato was found
at Volubilis in Africa. The
cynical half-smile of the former,
the intent, earnest expression of
the latter, perhaps reflect the
qualities of character attributed
to them by Sallust (No. 11).

18. *Mosaics of a cat killing a partridge,*
    and ducks, from Pompeii

These mosaics are in the National Museum at Naples. The first helps to
bring to life the Echion's somewhat shabby confession about his son's
goldfinches (No. 13) and both show the painstaking observation of Roman
mosaic artists in the portrayal of animal life.

19. *Scene in a draper's shop*

From a first century A.D. relief in the Uffizi Gallery, Florence.   Assistants are displaying a piece of cloth to customers as Echion (No. 13) would have displayed his blankets.

21. *The Roman amphitheatre at Forum Iulii (Fréjus)*

This town of Provence, probably founded as a colony by Julius Caesar and later made a naval base by Augustus, was chosen by Pliny for the convalescence of his slave, Zosimus (No. 15(b)) and was the birthplace of Tacitus' father-in-law, Agricola and possibly Tacitus himself.

20. *Etruscan player of twin flutes*

From the 'Tomb of the Leopards' at Tarquinia, first half of fifth century
B.C. This fresco helps to bring to life the instrument tuner by the
Trickling Fountain in Rome, who contributed to the city cacophony that
disturbed Seneca's peace (No. 14).

22. *A Roman trireme*

Relief from the Vatican Museum. The figures and superstructure, though strangely proportioned, convey something of the atmosphere in which the 'accident' staged for Agrippina occurred (No. 16).

23. *The Bay of Baiae*

Here Nero entertained his mother to dinner, and from here the fateful vessel sailed (No. 16).

1–4 (46, 1–4). *I suppose, Agamemnon, you despise our chatter, good talker and learned as you are. Still, come and see my place in the country. We'll find something to eat despite the ravages of the weather. My youngster is doing well and, if he is spared, will do anything for you. He is clever and always at his books, but too keen on keeping pet birds. I got rid of his goldfinches and blamed a weasel, but now he has other hobbies and likes to paint.*

1   Videris mihi, Agamemnon, dicere: 'quid iste argutat molestus?' quia tu, qui potes loquere, non loquis. non es nostrae fasciae, et ideo pauperorum verba derides. scimus
2 te prae litteras fatuum esse. quid ergo est? aliqua die te persuadeam, ut ad villam venias et videas casulas nostras? inveniemus quod manducemus, pullum, ova. belle erit, etiam si omnia hoc anno tempestas disparpaliavit: inveniemus ergo unde saturi fiamus. et iam tibi discipulus crescit
3 cicaro meus. iam quattuor partes dicit; si vixerit, habebis ad latus servulum. nam quicquid illi vacat, caput de tabula non tollit. ingeniosus est et bono filo, etiam si in aves
4 morbosus est. ego illi iam tres cardeles occidi, et dixi quia mustella comedit. invenit tamen alias nenias, et liben-
5 tissime pingit.

5–8 (46, 5–8). *He's well ahead with Greek and is taking to Latin literature. One tutor knows his stuff but is self-satisfied and unreliable. The other knows less but teaches the boy more than he knows himself. He even comes round on holidays and is happy with whatever you give him. I've bought the boy some law books. There's money in that, and he has had enough dabbling with poetry. If he objects I'll make him learn a trade. I told him studying is for his good. Phileros succeeded as a lawyer but was a porter not long ago. Education is an investment, and a trade never dies on you.*

Ceterum iam Graeculis calcem impingit et Latinas coepit non male appetere, etiam si magister eius sibi placens sit, nec uno loco consistit, sed venit, abit. scit quidem litteras, 6 sed non vult laborare. est et alter non quidem doctus, sed curiosus, qui plus docet quam scit. itaque feriatis diebus solet domum venire, et quicquid dederis, contentus 7 est. emi ergo nunc puero aliquot libra rubricata, quia volo illum ad domusionem aliquid de iure gustare. habet haec res panem. nam litteris satis inquinatus est. quod si resilierit, destinavi illum artificii docere, aut tonstreinum aut praeconem aut certe causidicum, quod illi auferre non 8 possit nisi Orcus. ideo illi cotidie clamo: 'Primigeni, crede mihi, quicquid discis, tibi discis. vides Phileronem causidicum: si non didicisset, hodie famem a labris non abigeret. modo, modo collo suo circumferebat onera venalia, nunc etiam adversus Norbanum se extendit. litterae thesaurum est, et artificium numquam moritur.'

Seneca

14. The Psychology of Noise (*Epistulae Morales* 56, 1–6, 14 to end)

This letter is one of the 124 written by Seneca to Lucilius Iunior (see page 54), and as in many of them he approaches his subject from a personal experience — in this case the fact that he lived above noisy public baths. The subject of noise is perennially topical. A Noise Abatement Society has been founded in England, and we are constantly exercised about which part of the country shall be lumbered with London's third airport, or whether a third airport is needed at all. The very name of the current favourite, Foulness, seems an added recommendation. Nor is it certain, at the time of writing, whether the giant supersonic Concorde will be permitted to land in America at all. Noise in Seneca's time lacked this scale, but it had the persistence to be a serious nuisance, and Seneca had picked the right place for it. The Roman baths, from being simple wash-houses where men could clean up, had grown in Seneca's time into huge recreation centres for both sexes, with gymnasia, gardens, libraries, lecture halls and reading rooms as well as the cold (*frigidarium*), warm (*tepidarium*) and hot (*calidarium*) chambers and changing rooms of the baths proper. The fee was trifling (a *quadrans*, or quarter of a Roman penny (*as*), as Cicero, in his speech *pro Caelio*, indicates in a joke while giving an amusing account of an alleged rendezvous of some poisoners at the Senian Baths in Rome) and the public baths were therefore patronised by all classes, even those who, like Quintus Cicero (see page 83) had their own private baths but enjoyed the social contacts of public establishments. In later times these public baths became places of phenomenal size and splendour. The Baths of Caracalla (emperor A.D. 211–217), for instance, remains of which can still be seen at Rome, were as high as the nave of St Paul's and covered an area as large as the entire Houses of Parliament or the British Museum. The baths that provoked Seneca's train of thought would have been a much smaller establishment, but he gives a lively word- and, in places, sound-picture of its multifarious noisy activities. The letter suggests that he would be in sympathy with the youth of today in preferring the inarticulate *crepitus* of a transistor radio to the over-articulate *vox* of a chatterbox, but few would accept his truly Stoic conclusion that noise can and should be conquered.

1–2 (56, 1–2). *I cannot see why quiet is so essential to the student. I have lodgings above a bath-house, noisy with the grunts of people taking exercise, the slap of massage, the din of a ball-game, brawling, a thief being caught, the splash of bathers diving in, the cries of hawkers.*

SENECA LVCILIO SVO SALVTEM

1   Peream si est tam necessarium quam videtur silentium in studia seposito. ecce undique me varius clamor circumsonat: supra ipsum balneum habito. propone nunc tibi omnia genera vocum quae in odium possunt aures adducere: cum fortiores exercentur et manus plumbo graves iactant, cum aut laborant aut laborantem imitantur, gemitus audio, quotiens retentum spiritum remiserunt, sibilos et acerbissimas respirationes; cum in aliquem inertem et hac plebeia unctione contentum incidi, audio crepitum illisae manus umeris, quae prout plana pervenit aut concava, ita sonum mutat. si vero pilicrepus supervenit et numerare coepit
2   pilas, actum est. adice nunc scordalum et furem deprensum et illum cui vox sua in balineo placet, adice nunc eos qui in piscinam cum ingenti impulsae aquae sono saliunt. iam biberari varias exclamationes et botularium et crustularium et omnes popinarum institores mercem sua quadam et insignita modulatione vendentes.

3–5 (56, 2–5). '*You must be made of iron, or deaf, to endure this', you say. It troubles me no more than the sound of waves or falling water. Voices, which catch the attention, distract me more than mere noise, which just fills the ears: like passing carriages, a carpenter or man sawing in a nearby block, a horn or flute player by the Trickling Fountain. Intermittent noise is worse than a continuous din, but I have steeled myself to endure the shouts of a coxswain giving the time to his crew. One can endure bedlam without provided one's emotions are not in turmoil and there is inner peace.*

3 'O te' inquis 'ferreum aut surdum, cui mens inter tot
clamores tam varios, tam dissonos constat, cum Chrysippum
nostrum adsidua salutatio perducat ad mortem.' at mehercules ego istum fremitum non magis curo quam fluctum aut
deiectum aquae, quamvis audiam cuidam genti hanc unam
fuisse causam urbem suam transferendi, quod fragorem Nili
4 cadentis ferre non potuit. magis mihi videtur vox avocare
quam crepitus; illa enim animum adducit, hic tantum aures
implet ac verberat. in his quae me sine avocatione circumstrepunt essedas transcurrentes pono et fabrum inquilinum
et serrarium vicinum, aut hunc qui ad Metam Sudantem
5 tubulas experitur et tibias, nec cantat sed exclamat: etiamnunc molestior est mihi sonus qui intermittitur subinde quam
qui continuatur. sed iam me sic ad omnia ista duravi ut
audire vel pausarium possim voce acerbissima remigibus
modos dantem. animum enim cogo sibi intentum esse nec
avocari ad externa; omnia licet foris resonent, dum intus
nihil tumultus sit, dum inter se non rixantur cupiditas et
timor, dum avaritia luxuriaque non dissideant nec altera
alteram vexet. nam quid prodest totius regionis silentium,
si adfectus fremunt?

(*Seneca, in a passage omitted here, argues that even night and
sleep cannot bring peace to a troubled spirit. We must remain
active, like a general exercising his troops to avoid boredom,
and achieve true detachment so that ambition, greed, concern
for possessions do not make us anxious.*)

6–7 (56, 14–15). *Be sure you are truly at peace when noise
does not reach you nor voices distract you. 'Is it not simpler
to move?', you say. Of course, and I intend to. But I wanted
to test myself. Now I shall adopt the easy remedy of Ulysses
against the Sirens.*

6   Tunc ergo te scito esse compositum cum ad te nullus clamor
pertinebit, cum te nulla vox tibi excutiet, non si blandietur,
non si minabitur, non si inani sono vana circumstrepet.

7   'quid ergo? non aliquando commodius est et carere convicio?' fateor; itaque ego ex hoc loco migrabo. experiri
et exercere me volui: quid necesse est diutius torqueri, cum
tam facile remedium Ulixes sociis etiam adversus Sirenas
invenerit? vale.

ULYSSES AND THE SIRENS
from an entrance ticket to the Museum at Delphi

PLINY

15 (a). The First Grammar School at Comum (4, 13)

Pliny wrote this letter to Cornelius Tacitus, the great
historian (see page 67), who at the time was known chiefly
as an orator and advocate. As consul in A.D. 37 he delivered

the funeral oration on Pliny's guardian, the general Verginius Rufus (see page 39). But he was also working on his first major historical work, the *Histories*, for which Pliny later supplied eye-witness accounts of the eruption of Vesuvius (*Letters* 6, 16 and 20) and details of the events of the year 93 (7, 33). In another letter Pliny is proud to be equated with Tacitus as an orator (9, 23).

This letter is a landmark in the history of education, though its importance is seldom recognised.[1] We have noted Echion's problem (see page 112) over his son's education when living in the country; but the situation in the towns was not much better. Horace's father moved from Venusia to ensure a good education for him (see *Two Centuries of Roman Poetry*, page 51), just as the father from Comum in this letter was obliged to send his son to school at Milan. There were very few state schools; private schools varied alarmingly in quality, and boarding schools were unheard of. Pliny's great contribution here is twofold: first, he devoted some of his considerable wealth to providing a secondary school for his home town (he also endowed a public library at Comum and a fund for the maintenance of a number of free-born children (1, 8)); secondly he involves the parents in their sons' education not only through the payment of fees but also in the choice of teachers. Thereby he became the first school governor, self-appointed, and pioneer in a long line of benefactors, individual and corporate, who have dedicated their resources and energies to create Trusts for providing education as something other than merely an activity for private profit or just another state service, all too often starved of resources or a plaything of party politics, or both.

---

[1] For the importance of Pliny's school in the development of grammar schools in England see *The Grammar School*, Robin Davis (Penguin Books), Chapter 1.

Pliny begins (in a paragraph omitted here) with an apology, through pressure of work, for anticipating with a begging letter a request he later intends to make in person.

1–5 (4, 13, 3–5). *I heard from a fellow-townsman of Como and his son that the boy is at school at Milan because there are no teachers at Como. Pointing out that children are happier and better controlled when educated in their home town, and the expense is less, I suggested that parents should club together to engage teachers, adding to their salaries what is saved on away-from-home expenses. Having no children of my own, I offered to add, as a present to my home town, a third of whatever sum the parents themselves contribute.*

1 Proxime cum in patria mea fui, venit ad me salutandum municipis mei filius praetextatus. huic ego 'studes?' inquam.
2 respondit: 'etiam.' 'ubi?' 'Mediolani.' 'cur non hic?' et pater eius (erat enim una atque etiam ipse adduxerat puerum): 'quia nullos hic praeceptores habemus.' 'quare
3 nullos? nam vehementer intererat vestra, qui patres estis' (et opportune complures patres audiebant) 'liberos vestros hic potissimum discere. ubi enim aut iucundius morarentur quam in patria aut pudicius continerentur quam sub oculis
4 parentum aut minore sumptu quam domi? quantulum est ergo collata pecunia conducere praeceptores, quodque nunc in habitationes, in viatica, in ea quae peregre emuntur (omnia autem peregre emuntur) impenditis, adicere merce-
5 dibus? atque adeo ego, qui nondum liberos habeo, paratus sum pro re publica nostra, quasi pro filia vel parente, tertiam partem eius quod conferre vobis placebit dare.

6–9 (4, 13, 6–9). *I should have promised the whole amount, but feared my gift might be abused, as often happens when*

teachers are hired at public expense. If the appointment of
teachers were left to parents, they would be conscientious as
their own money was involved as well as mine. So meet and
decide, I said; I want my contribution to be as large as possible.
Children should be brought up in their home-town and learn to
love it and stay there. I hope you will choose such good teachers
that children from other towns will be attracted here.

6 'Totum etiam pollicerer, nisi timerem ne hoc munus meum
quandoque ambitu corrumperetur, ut accidere multis in
locis video, in quibus praeceptores publice conducuntur.
7 huic vitio occurri uno remedio potest, si parentibus solis ius
conducendi relinquatur, isdemque religio recte iudicandi
8 necessitate collationis addatur. nam qui fortasse de alieno
neglegentes, certe de suo diligentes erunt dabuntque operam,
ne a me pecuniam non nisi dignus accipiat, si accepturus et
9 ab ipsis erit. proinde consentite conspirate maioremque
animum ex meo sumite, qui cupio esse quam plurimum,
quod debeam conferre. nihil honestius praestare liberis
vestris, nihil gratius patriae potestis. educentur hic qui hic
nascuntur, statimque ab infantia natale solum amare frequentare consuescant. atque utinam tam claros prae
ceptores inducatis, ut in finitimis oppidis studia hinc
petantur, utque nunc liberi vestri aliena in loca ita mox
alieni in hunc locum confluant!'

Pliny then asks Tacitus (in a paragraph here omitted) to
look for possible teachers among his following of students.
But he will not commit himself to anyone recommended.
The choice must be the parents'. Tacitus may send anyone
who has confidence in his own abilities, but must realise that
that confidence will be the only certainty he brings.

15 (b). Convalescence of a sick Slave (5, 19)

Valerius Paulinus, to whom Pliny wrote this letter, was consul in A.D. 97. He came from Gallia Narbonensis (Provence), and had estates at Forum Julii (Fréjus).

We have already seen (page 90) Cicero's concern for his former slave, Tiro. This civilised attitude is also shown by Seneca, who reminds Lucilius (*Letter* 47) that chance could turn today's master into tomorrow's slave (this could have happened to Julius Caesar in his youth (see page 104) had he been delivered by his pirate captors to the slave market before he made his escape), so one should treat one's slaves well. Other letters of Pliny (2, 6 and 8, 16) reveal a similar concern for members of his household, both slaves and freedmen, and he shows little sympathy for the brutal Larcius Macedo (3, 14), whose cruelty to his slaves drove them to murder him in the public baths. The Stoic doctrine of the brotherhood of man (see page 54) and the spread of Christian ideals, helped by the civilised attitude of men like Cicero and Pliny, did much to make slavery more tolerable in practice than its inhuman name implies.

1–5 (5, 19, 1–5). *I am glad that you, as I do, treat your household well. My freedman Zosimus has a special claim on my sympathy. He has many fine qualities and is talented at acting, reciting and playing the lyre. I owe him much for his services to me and feel an affection for him which, as happens by nature, my fear of losing him has increased.*

C. PLINIVS VALERIO PAVLINO SVO S.

Video quam molliter tuos habeas; quo simplicius tibi confitebor, qua indulgentia meos tractem. est mihi semper in animo hoc nostrum 'pater familiae'. quod si essem natura

asperior et durior, frangeret me tamen infirmitas liberti mei
Zosimi, cui tanto maior humanitas exhibenda est, quanto
3 nunc illa magis eget. homo probus officiosus litteratus; et
ars quidem eius et quasi inscriptio comoedus, in qua plurimum facit. nam pronuntiat acriter sapienter apte decenter
etiam; utitur et cithara perite, ultra quam comoedo necesse
est. idem tam commode orationes et historias et carmina
4 legit, ut hoc solum didicisse videatur. haec tibi sedulo
exposui, quo magis scires, quam multa unus mihi et quam
iucunda ministeria praestaret. accedit longa iam caritas
5 hominis, quam ipsa pericula auxerunt. est enim ita natura
comparatum, ut nihil aeque amorem incitet et accendat
6 quam carendi metus; quem ego pro hoc non semel patior.

6–9 (5, 19, 6–9). *Some years ago, when an impassioned
recitation by him caused a haemorrhage, I sent him to Egypt.
He returned with health restored, but once again voice strain
has produced a warning cough, and blood. I would like to send
him to your place at Forum Julii, where the climate and milk
is beneficial to his complaint. Please arrange with your people
to offer him hospitality and meet his expenses. These will be
few, as he denies himself not only delicacies, but even the
essentials for his health. I will see he has sufficient journey-
money.*

6 Nam ante aliquot annos, dum intente instanterque pronuntiat, sanguinem reiecit atque ob hoc in Aegyptum missus
a me post longam peregrinationem confirmatus redît nuper;
deinde dum per continuos dies nimis imperat voci, veteris
infirmitatis tussicula admonitus rursus sanguinem reddidit.
7 qua ex causa destinavi eum mittere in praedia tua, quae
Foro Iulii possides. audivi enim te saepe referentem esse
ibi et aera salubrem et lac eiusmodi curationibus accom-
8 modatissimum. rogo ergo scribas tuis, ut illi villa, ut

domus pateat, offerant etiam sumptibus eius, si quid opus
9 erit. erit autem opus modico; est enim tam parcus et
continens, ut non solum delicias verum etiam necessitates
valetudinis frugalitate restringat. ego proficiscenti tantum
viatici dabo, quantum sufficiat eunti in tua. vale.

TACITUS

16. A Murder Ship Miscarries (*Annals* XIV, 3–5)

Agrippina the Younger, mother of the emperor Nero,
came of blood that had freely spilled blood and itself been
freely spilled. She was the great-granddaughter of the
emperor Augustus. Her father, Germanicus, had won
renown quelling mutinies and campaigning in Germany, but
was recalled by Tiberius and sent to the East, where he died
in suspicious circumstances in A.D. 19; her mother, Agrippina the Elder, had herself spent much of her life in the
camp with Germanicus, even controlling panic-stricken
troops on the Rhine when there was a risk of a German
breakthrough (*Annals* I, 69), but was banished soon after
her husband's death and starved herself to death in 30; her
two older sons, Nero and Drusus, were probably murdered
by Sejanus and Tiberius respectively.

With this background Agrippina the Younger conceived
a twofold ambition: to see her son, Nero, as emperor, and
through him to rule herself as the petticoat power behind
the throne. She set to work with military precision. Twice
married already (Nero was the son of her first husband,
L. Domitius Ahenobarbus), in 48 she secured as her third
husband the emperor Claudius, helped, it was said, by a
freedman named Pallas. Though Claudius already had a
son, Britannicus, by his previous wife Messalina, she
persuaded him, in 50, to adopt her own son Nero, five years

Britannicus' senior, as his heir. By the twin weapons of poison and secret trial she removed several possible rivals, and recalled Seneca from exile (see page 52) to be Nero's tutor. He 'came of age' (assumed the *toga virilis*, see page 222) at thirteen, two years prematurely; received other honours, made his first speech in the Senate and married Claudius' daughter Octavia (his step-sister) at the age of fifteen.

In 54 Claudius, having outlived his usefulness, died from a dish of poisoned mushrooms. Tacitus, describing Agrippina's thoughts before Claudius died (*Annals* XII, 65) in terms that bear a strong family likeness to Nero's own matricidal meditations in 1, 1–4 below, has no doubts where few doubts can remain. Agrippina's first ambition was secured, and there was fair promise (for Nero was still only sixteen) of the second. A few minor obstacles, an aunt of Nero's here, a proconsular great-grandson of Augustus and a freedman there, she quickly disposed of by murder or palace-inspired suicide. Coins bearing confronting busts of herself and Nero with her own titles on the obverse (see page 131) and Nero's relegated to the reverse advertised what she was about (indeed the story below was in a sense 'A Tale of Two Coins', for Nero thought an emperor should have a coin, like the second one on page 131, to himself, not in junior partnership with his mother); and the Senate was obliged to meet on the Palatine when it took her fancy to hear a debate. But when she attempted to sit beside Nero at a reception of some Armenian ambassadors, he publicly rebuffed her. In retaliation she started to show affection for Britannicus. Born too early to have learned the lesson of Frankenstein, she was shocked to witness her new favourite's prompt death by poison, and seemed momentarily to grasp that the murderer of a step-brother might in time graduate to matricide (*parricidii exemplum intellegebat, Annals* XIII, 16). The pupil of Seneca was learning faster, it seemed, from his mother. But her shock was short-lived. She next devoted her vindictive affections to Nero's wife, Octavia.[1] This was the last straw, and Nero clutched it eagerly. Agrippina was promptly banished from the palace.

Nero was already 'eager to kill his mother' (*interficiendae matris avidus, Annals* XIII, 20), but somehow Seneca and Burrus (see page 52) restrained him for a time. They had reckoned without Nero's new mistress, Poppaea Sabina, whose husband, Otho, was a friend of Nero's and a future emperor. Poppaea preferred a present one, so Otho was conveniently dispatched to govern the remote province of Lusitania. But there was still Nero's wife, Octavia. Poppaea was shrewd enough to see that there was little hope of clinching the matter by a divorce for Nero while Agrippina remained. So she taunted him with being his mother's puppet and Nero, thus provoked, 'put off no longer the crime he had long contemplated' (*diu meditatum scelus non ultra Nero distulit, Annals* XIV, 1). So opens Book XIV of the *Annals*, and the grim drama of how Nero went about it, of which the first act appears below, soon follows.

We have already observed (page 70) how Tacitus so identifies himself with his characters that he involves the reader, too, in a temporarily assumed personality. Notice, as you read this story, how he does it. First a few circumstantial details, and then Nero's dilemma. Murder it must be, but how? From then on Tacitus *becomes* Nero, and he and the reader together plan the matricide. The macabre

[1] The eventual fate of this unhappy girl 'who virtually died on her wedding day' (*nuptiarum dies loco funeris fuit, Annals* XIV, 63) showed the grim price of involvement with Nero. She was put to death in 62 at the whim of Nero's second wife Poppaea: the crime, adultery with (of all people!) Anicetus; the method, suffocation in a vapour-bath, in the manner adopted later by Seneca (see page 53).

shopping list of possible means, each rationally rejected —
then Anicetus, a sinister figure with a sinister plan. Nero
conveniently at Baiae on religious business — the sham
welcome and the special ship — the suspense when an informer puts Agrippina on guard — the starlit night and
calm sea, menacing as celestial detectives — the vagueness
about the mechanics of the collapsible ship and what
actually happened — the violent end of Agrippina's friends
and her own unobtrusive escape. We have tried in the
Notes to help you not only to understand the Latin but also
to enjoy to the full the subtle skill with which Tacitus tells
his story. His task, he says, recalling the glorious exploits
related by Livy and other predecessors, is cramped and
inglorious (*nobis in arto et inglorius labor, Annals* IV, 32).
But he could spread his wings for all that and, as great
writers do (in their different ways Dickens and Dostoevsky
in particular come to mind), achieved glory through the
inglorious.

1 (XIV, 3). *Nero, though avoiding Agrippina, found her
intolerable and decided to kill her. But poison would look
suspicious after Britannicus' death, and she was alert to plots
and had taken antidotes. Stabbing risked detection and an
assassin could not be trusted to obey his orders. Anicetus,
freedman admiral, once Nero's tutor and Agrippina's enemy,
proposed a collapsible ship which would throw her overboard.
Human agency could not be blamed for the accidents of the sea.
When she was dead, Nero could honour her memory.*

1 Igitur Nero vitare secretos eius congressus, abscedentem
in hortos aut Tusculanum vel Antiatem in agrum laudare,
2 quod otium capesseret. postremo, ubicumque haberetur,
praegravem ratus interficere constituit, hactenus consultans,
3 veneno an ferro vel qua alia vi. placuitque primo venenum.

sed inter epulas principis si daretur, referri ad casum non poterat tali iam Britannici exitio; et ministros temptare arduum videbatur mulieris usu scelerum adversus insidias intentae; atque ipsa praesumendo remedia munierat corpus.

4 ferrum et caedes quonam modo occultaretur, nemo reperiebat; et ne quis illi tanto facinori delectus iussa sperneret

5 metuebat. obtulit ingenium Anicetus libertus, classi apud Misenum praefectus et pueritiae Neronis educator ac mutuis

6 odiis Agrippinae invisus. ergo navem posse componi docet, cuius pars ipso in mari per artem soluta effunderet ignaram:

7 nihil tam capax fortuitorum quam mare; et si naufragio intercepta sit, quem adeo iniquum, ut sceleri adsignet quod venti et fluctus deliquerint? additurum principem defunctae templum et aras et cetera ostendandae pietati.

2 (XIV, 4). *The plan was approved. Nero was conveniently at Baiae for a festival. He feigned a reconciliation and, as women do, Agrippina readily believed the good news. On her arrival from Antium Nero welcomed her warmly, took her to Baiae, showed her the splendid ship, apparently a compliment to her, and invited her to dinner (at Baiae). Uneasy because of a warning brought by an informer, she travelled to Baiae by sedan-chair. Nero's attentions relieved her anxiety; he was boyish and serious by turns, kept her late and clung to her at the farewell, whether from pretence or genuine emotion.*

1   Placuit sollertia, tempore etiam iuta, quando Quin-

2 quatruum festos dies apud Baias frequentabat. illuc matrem elicit, ferendas parentium iracundias et placandum animum dictitans, quo rumorem reconciliationis efficeret acciperetque

3 Agrippina, facili feminarum credulitate ad gaudia. venientem dehinc obvius in litora (nam Antio adventabat) excepit

4 manu et complexu ducitque Baulos. id villae nomen est quae promunturium Misenum inter et Baianum lacum flexo mari

5 adluitur. stabat inter alias navis ornatior, tamquam id
quoque honori matris daretur: quippe sueverat triremi et
6 classiariorum remigio vehi. ac tum invitata ad epulas erat,
ut occultando facinori nox adhiberetur. satis constitit
exstitisse proditorem, et Agrippinam auditis insidiis, an
7 crederet ambiguam, gestamine sellae Baias pervectam. ibi
blandimentum sublevavit metum: comiter excepta superque
8 ipsum collocata. iam pluribus sermonibus, modo familiaritate iuvenili Nero et rursus adductus, quasi seria consociaret,
tracto in longum convictu, prosequitur abeuntem, artius
oculis et pectori haerens, sive explenda simulatione, seu
periturae matris supremus aspectus quamvis ferum animum
retinebat.

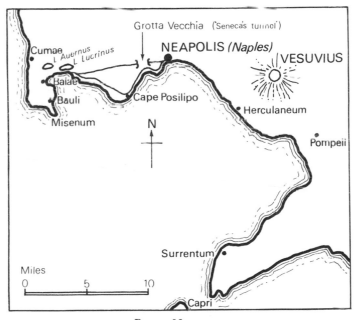

BAY OF NAPLES

3 (XIV, 5). *Heaven sent a starlit night and calm sea. The
ship sailed. Two friends were near Agrippina, Crepereius by
the tiller, Acerronia leaning over her feet happily discussing
Nero's changed attitude. The canopy-roof collapsed under
pressure of lead weights. Crepereius was crushed to death, but
Agrippina and Acerronia were saved by the projecting sides of
the couch. The ship failed to collapse. The accomplices were
impeded by the numbers on board, and the crew's attempt to
capsize the ship was frustrated by others throwing their weight to
the opposite side to provide a gentler slide into the water.
Acerronia, pretending to be Agrippina and calling for help, was
battered to death; Agrippina kept quiet. Though slightly
wounded she swam till picked up by fishing vessels, and so
reached the shore and home.*

1 Noctem sideribus illustrem et placido mari quietam
2 quasi convincendum ad scelus di praebuere. nec multum
erat progressa navis, duobus e numero familiarium Agrippinam comitantibus, ex quis Crepereius Gallus haud procul
gubernaculis adstabat, Acerronia super pedes cubitantis
reclinis paenitentiam filii et reciperatam matris gratiam
per gaudium memorabat, cum dato signo ruere tectum
loci multo plumbo grave, pressusque Crepereius et statim
3 exanimatus est. Agrippina et Acerronia eminentibus lecti
parietibus ac forte validioribus, quam ut oneri cederent,
4 protectae sunt. nec dissolutio navigii sequebatur, turbatis
omnibus et quod plerique ignari etiam conscios impediebant.
5 visum dehinc remigibus unum in latus inclinare atque ita
navem submergere: sed neque ipsis promptus in rem
subitam consensus, et alii contra nitentes dedere facultatem
6 lenioris in mare iactus. verum Acerronia, imprudentia dum
se Agrippinam esse utque subveniretur matri principis
clamitat, contis et remis et quae fors obtulerat navalibus
7 telis conficitur: Agrippina silens eoque minus agnita

(unum tamen vulnus umero excepit) nando, deinde occursu lenunculorum Lucrinum in lacum vecta villae suae infertur.

Whatever happened to the collapsible ship Nero had burned his boats, and could not turn back. Perhaps at Seneca's suggestion he convinced himself that the messenger who brought news of his mother's escape was an assassin threatening his own life. Anicetus was instructed to ensure (this time without gimmickry) that she met the fate she had escaped before through mistaken identity — like Acerronia she was battered to death, but in her own home and by two of Anicetus' officers armed with club and sword. Tacitus records that astrologers had foretold to Agrippina that her son would be emperor but that he would murder his mother. 'Let him kill', she replied, 'provided that he reigns' (*occidat dum imperet, Annals* XIV, 9, 5). She had her way, and paid the price.

     1.   2.

COINS OF NERO AND AGRIPPINA

From the British Museum. On the first coin Agrippina has pride of place; the more important obverse or 'head', with confronting busts of herself and Nero, contains all her imperial titles: *Agripp(ina) Aug(usta) divi Claud(ii uxor) Neronis Caes(aris) mater*. Nero achieves no more than a genitive case as being her son, and his own name and titles are relegated to the less important reverse or 'tail'. Matricide seemed the only way to the splendid isolation of the second coin.

NOTES

PART I

Cicero

1. 'Brave Men Despise Death' (*Tusculan Disputations* I, 96–102)

1.

1. The first *quam* is 'how much' (=*quantum*) and the second is 'how', with *elato*; 'how much pleasure (the thought of) Theramenes gives me!, what a lofty spirit he had!', lit. with how lofty a spirit he is, ablative of quality. A brief account of Theramenes is given in the Introduction to this piece. **cum legimus,** 'when we read (the story)', told by Xenophon in his *Hellenica* II, 3, 56. **non miserabiliter,** 'in a way that does not arouse our pity', because we admire his courage. **qui cum,** 'when he . . .'; see the note on *quo sonitu* below. The 'Thirty Tyrants' (Theramenes had been one of them) were oligarchs who drew up a new constitution for Athens after its surrender to the Spartans in 404. **ut sitiens,** 'as though (he were) thirsty'; the poison was hemlock, which was supposed to chill the extremities of a man's body until the cold reached his heart and caused his death; it was the usual method of executing criminals at Athens. Theramenes showed his contempt for death by drinking the poison willingly and pretending to play the game called 'cottabus' with its dregs. At banquets a feaster would throw out the last drops (*reliquum*) of his wine into a saucer floating in a bowl of water and containing a little image of Hermes (Mercury) 'in such a way that it made a ringing sound'; at the same time he uttered the name of the person whom he loved. Cicero represents Theramenes as combining this with drinking the health of Critias, with the words 'to (the health of) the handsome Critias', who had procured his death. **quo sonitu reddito,** 'and when it had made this noise', a 'connecting' relative pronoun, like *qui* above, referring to a noun in (or in this case understood from) the previous sentence; it is translated by the same case of *hic, haec, hoc*. **nominare . . . sint,** 'to name (the person) to whom they are going to hand the cup', an indirect question, more easily taken as a relative clause in English. Feasters used to pass the cup counter-

clockwise (not clockwise, as we pass the port or a loving cup), each man toasting the neighbour on his right at table.

2. **praecordiis . . . contineret,** 'he had within him the death which he had absorbed in(to) his vitals'. *vere* goes with *est auguratus.* **cui . . . praebiberat,** 'whose health he had drunk in the poison'. **brevi,** 'in a short time'; Critias was killed in the following year, 403, in a battle between the Thirty and the exiled democrats.

3. **laudaret, si . . . iudicaret,** an unfulfilled present conditional, 'who would praise this calmness of a great spirit if he considered death to be an evil?'. **in eundem . . . scyphum,** an example of the figure of speech called 'zeugma' or 'syllepsis', in which a verb is taken with two nouns but in a slightly different sense with each; 'he went (historic present) to the same prison and (drank) the same cup (of poison)'; in English it is often used with a slightly comic sense, e.g. 'he took his hat and his leave'; see also No. 4 (Livy), 3, 6. **paucis post annis,** in 399; see page 21. **eodem . . . Theramenes,** 'by a verdict of his judges as wicked as that by which Theramenes (was condemned) by the Tyrants', lit. by the same crime of his judges as Theramenes of the Tyrants. **eius oratio . . . multatum,** 'the speech of Socrates which Plato represents (*facit*) him as having made (*usum*) when already sentenced to death'. Cicero now translates or paraphrases part of Plato's *Apology* (40 C to the end), in which Socrates addressed his judges after the verdict and death penalty had been pronounced.

2.

1. **magna . . . spes,** 'I am very hopeful', followed by a present infinitive, *evenire,* instead of the usual future infinitive; 'that the fact that (*quod* with the subjunctive in *oratio obliqua*) I am being sent . . . is for my own good', lit. is turning out well for me. **necesse est** is followed either by a subjunctive, with or without *ut,* or by an infinitive; the *ut* is here omitted perhaps because another *ut*-clause follows; 'it must be that one of two things should happen, either that . . .'. **migretur,** impersonal passive, 'that in death we change our abode', lit. that a change of abode is made.

2. **quam ob rem,** 'wherefore'. **sive** is here followed not by another *sive* (or *seu*) but by *sin,* 'but if'; *sive* should therefore be translated as 'if', not 'whether'. **ei somno qui,** we omit the demonstrative adjective and say 'like the sleep which'. **di boni,**

vocative used in an exclamation, like our 'good heavens!'. **quid lucri,** partitive genitive, 'what a gain it is to die'. **quam multi,** 'how many', usually *quot*. **qui . . . anteponantur,** a generic or consecutive subjunctive, lit. of such a kind that they would be preferred, but we say simply 'that would be preferred'. **cui si . . . temporis,** 'and if the coming (*futura*) eternity of all ensuing time is like this sleep'. **me,** ablative of comparison, with *est* understood as the verb for *quis*.

3. The antecedents of *dicuntur* and *excesserunt* are *ea* and *ei* (understood) respectively; 'if the stories that are told are true', followed by the indirect statement 'that death is a change of abode to those regions which the dead (lit. those who have departed) inhabit'; the two relative clauses are in the indicative although in *oratio obliqua* because they are 'defining' relative clauses, not part of what is actually being said. **multo,** ablative of measure of difference, 'surely (*iam*) much happier'. **tene . . . venire . . . haec . . . potest ?,** *ne* is the interrogative particle, and *te . . . venire* is an accusative and infinitive noun-clause which is summed up by *haec . . . potest, haec* being 'attracted' from the neuter of the noun-clause to agree in gender with *peregrinatio*; 'the fact that . . . you should come . . . and meet . . . , can this seem to you (judges) to be an ordinary journey?'. *evaseris* is future perfect, 'when you have (lit. shall have) escaped', and *appellentur* and *vixerint* are generic subjunctive again, lit. the kind of people who are called, but we use the indicative in English and do not distinguish it from the ordinary relative clause *qui . . . volunt*. Socrates is addressing his judges (hence *vobis*), but *te* is the indefinite second person singular, like our 'you' or 'one'. In the *qui . . . volunt* clause we should omit the object, *se*, in translation, and say 'who wish to be reckoned as (lit. in the number of) judges'. Minos, king of Crete, his brother Rhadamanthus, king of Lycia, and Aeacus, another son of Zeus (Jupiter), became judges in the Underworld after their death because of their justice and piety on earth; to these Plato added Triptolemus, king of Eleusis, the originator of ploughing and sowing. **cum fide,** 'honourably'.

4. **quanti,** genitive of value; 'how much, I wonder (*tandem*, used in emphatic questions), would you think it worth (potential subjunctive; see the note on Pliny 7 (b), 4) that you should be allowed . . .'. Orpheus and Musaeus were mythical Greek poets and musicians, Homer the author of the *Iliad* and *Odyssey*, and Hesiod the seventh-century author of a poem on country life

Allen, Greenough 452, 1

called 'Works and Days'. **si . . . , vellem,** an unfulfilled present conditional clause, 'if it were possible (lit. if it could happen), I should be willing . . .'. **ut . . . invenire,** 'that I might be permitted to discover (the truth of) what I am saying'. **adficerer** is another unfulfilled conditional sentence, but *cum convenirem* takes the place of the *si*-clause; 'with what delight I should be filled when (almost equivalent to '*if*') I met . . .'. Palamedes and Ajax were Greek heroes at the siege of Troy; Palamedes incurred the enmity of Ulysses (Odysseus in Greek, Ulixes in Latin) and was killed on a false charge of treachery trumped up by him, and Ajax committed suicide after being defeated in the contest for the weapons of Achilles. **circumventos,** 'ruined', or 'overthrown'.

5. **temptarem . . . damnarer,** 'I should also test the wisdom . . . and I should not be condemned to death (lit. by the head, i.e. on a capital charge) for that reason when I asked these questions as I used to do here.' Socrates says that he would follow his usual practice of cross-questioning people, even in the Underworld, about the truth of their beliefs, as he used to do in Athens, a practice that indirectly and partly led to his accusation and condemnation. 'The supreme king' was Agamemnon, leader of the Greeks in the expedition against (*ad*) Troy, Sisyphus was a king of Corinth famous for his cunning, and Ulysses was the wiliest of the Greeks at Troy; all would be suitable objects of Socrates' methods of interrogation.

6. **ne . . . timueritis,** the formal negative command, less common than *nolite timere*; 'do not you judges either, you (*ii*) who voted for my acquittal, fear death'. Socrates was condemned by a majority of the 501 judges (281 to 220). **ne . . . quidem** is 'not even', normally with an indicative verb. **nec . . . mortuo,** 'for indeed no evil (partitive genitive) can befall anyone who is good either in life or in death', lit. alive or dead. **eius res,** 'his fortunes', or 'his interests'. **nec habeo quod succenseam,** 'and I have no reason to be angry with . . .'; *quod* is adverbial accusative, lit. nor have I with regard to which, and *succenseam* is generic or consecutive subjunctive, lit. of such a kind that I should. . . . **nisi quod,** 'except that'.

7. **haec** refers to his previous statements; supply *dixit* as the verb. **hoc modo,** 'in this manner'. **melius extremo,** '(is) better than the end (of his speech)', ablative of comparison. **abire . . . vos,** accusative and infinitive after *tempus est*; 'it is time that we should depart from here, myself to die, you . . .'. **ut vitam agatis,** 'to go on living'. **utrum,** 'which of the two courses'. The position

of *neminem* at the end of the sentence is emphatic; it is here used as an adjective agreeing with *hominem*, 'no human being at all'. About ten lines of Cicero's comments on this speech of Socrates are omitted here.

3.

1. **quid**= *cur*. **praestantes . . . gloria,** 'men who were outstanding because of the fame of their virtue . . .'; in philosophy *virtus* means the abstract quality of 'virtue', in other contexts usually 'courage'. *cum* with the perfect subjunctive is 'since', but here we should say 'for'. **cuius . . . proditum est,** 'of whom not even the name has been handed down to us'. **tanto opere,** often in one word, *tantopere*, 'so much'. **ad eam,** referring to *mortem*, i.e. 'to execution'. The 'ephors' were the five officials at Sparta, appointed annually and with authority even over the two hereditary kings; two ephors accompanied one of the kings in war and supervised his actions. **vultu . . . hilari,** ablative of description, 'and had a cheerful and happy face', lit. was with a cheerful . . . . *inimicus* was a private enemy, not an enemy of the state.

2. Lycurgus was the legendary lawgiver of the Spartan constitution, which dated from about the seventh century B.C. and consisted of the two kings and the five ephors, a Council of thirty elders, and an assembly of all citizens aged 30 and over; it was thus nominally a monarchy but actually an oligarchy. By the fifth century the ruling class was the full citizens, called *Spartiatae*, brought up, boys and girls alike, under the strictest discipline but with little intellectual education, to serve their country, the men as soldiers and the women as the mothers of soldiers. This produced the finest and bravest army in Greece, whose warriors were famed for the simplicity and discipline of their lives, but they lacked all breadth of outlook and feeling for art or literature; they were the exact opposite of the quick-witted and artistic Athenians, and were inept and therefore disliked in their relationships with foreign states. Trade and business was in the hands of the non-Spartan inhabitants of the surrounding towns, though coined money was not used in the state. The original inhabitants, now reduced to serfdom, were called 'helots'. The name of the country was Laconia, of it capital Lacedaemon or Sparta, and of the inhabitants in general Lacedaemonians, among whom the Spartiatae (about 8000 in 480) were greatly outnumbered by the other two classes. **qui . . . multaverit,** a causal relative clause, 'because he has punished me with a (lit. that) penalty which I could pay . . .';

possem is generic subjunctive (the kind of penalty that I could pay) and potential, hence the change from primary to historic sequence, with a conditional clause ('if I wanted to do so') implied. **o virum . . . dignum,** exclamatory accusative, 'how worthy of Sparta was this man!'. **ut . . . videatur,** this consecutive clause depends on *adeo* ('to such an extent') understood, *qui . . . fuerit* is another causal relative clause, and *tam magno* (usually *tanto*) *animo* is ablative of quality; 'so much so that since he was a man of such high spirit he seems to me indeed to have been undeservedly condemned'. But Cicero forgets that sometimes the most guilty criminals meet death with the greatest courage.

3. **tales innumerabiles,** 'such men in countless numbers'. **nostra,** i.e. *Romana.* **quid** (=*cur*) **nominem,** deliberative question, 'why need I name . . . ?'. **cum,** 'since'. Marcus Porcius Cato (234–149), 'the Censor', a man of stern and upright character, was one of the earliest Roman 'annalistic' historians (see page 40) in a book called *Origines*, which has not survived and which Cicero is presumably quoting here. **alacres . . . profectas (esse), unde,** 'marched willingly to a position from which . . .'. *arbitrarentur* is subjunctive in *oratio obliqua* and is also generic, 'the sort of place from which . . .', supply *esse* with *redituras*, as with *profectas*.

4. **pari animo,** 'with equal courage'. The gallant defence of the pass of Thermopylae by Leonidas for three days against the enormous Persian army of Xerxes in 480 is mentioned on page 27. Besides his Three Hundred Spartans, Leonidas had about 6000 men from different Greek cities, of whom the Thebans and Thespians held the eastern end of the pass against the enemy who were led over the mountains by treachery, while the Spartans defended the western end alone. Four thousand Greeks were killed, including all the Spartans. Herodotus (Greek historian, d. *c.* 425) records in VII, 228 the famous epitaph written by Simonides of Ceos (d. *c.* 468), which Cicero here translates into a Latin elegiac couplet of which a verse paraphrase (omitting *sanctis* and *patriae*, neither of which appears in the original Greek, and making *legibus* singular) is

> 'O stranger, tell at Sparta that you saw
> Us lying her, obedient to her law'.   (Plate 1)

Spartae is locative, and for the sake of the metre *nos* and *te* have been transposed, but the sense shows that *te* is the subject of *vidisse*. **e quibus unus,** 'one of them', i.e. one of the Spartans.

Herodotus says that the conversation was between Dieneces, a Spartan, and another Greek, not between a Spartan and a Persian, as Cicero says; if it was a Persian, he must have shouted in Greek across the interval between the two armies, or perhaps made the remark at a parley during a truce.

5. **tandem,** used in an emphatic question, as in 2, 4; 'of what character, indeed, were the Spartan women?', the singular being used for the women generally. *quae* here is not 'she' but 'one of them'. **interfectum,** supply *eum* and *esse*. *audisset* = *audivisset*. *genueram* is from *gigno*; 'for this reason I had borne him, that he should be one who would not hesitate to . . .'; *qui non dubitaret* is a generic or consecutive subjunctive (the sort of person who would not hesitate). **esto,** third person singular imperative of *esse*; 'so be it', or 'very well'. *fortes . . . Spartiatae* is vocative, 'you brave and hardy Spartans'. **vim,** 'power', i.e. over its citizens.

CORNELIUS NEPOS

2. The Life of Aristides

I.

1. **Themistocli,** probably genitive (not dative), according to Nepos' usual practice with Greek names whose nominative ends in -*cles*, though he uses the -*is* ending for other Greek names with nominative in -*es*, like *Aristides, -is* in § 3. The Life of Themistocles (*c.* 514–459 B.C.) comes just before that of Aristides in Nepos. Themistocles was a man of outstanding ability and eloquence, with which he persuaded the Athenians to carry out his plans (generally for the great benefit of the city) and the judges to acquit him when he was accused of accepting bribes from the Persians, but he was unprincipled and venal, quite unlike Aristides, whose honour could not be purchased. **obtrectarunt** is a contracted form of *obtrectaverunt*, and with *inter se* means 'they were rivals', lit. they were opposed between themselves, or 'they were at variance with one another'.

2. **in his,** 'in the case of these men'. **quanto . . . innocentiae,** 'how superior eloquence was to integrity', lit. by how much it was superior; Nepos of course means in the opinion of men, judging from the way in which Aristides was treated by the Athenians. **ut unus . . . appellatus,** 'that he is the only one in the history of mankind, at least of whom we have heard, who was called by the

name (of) "the Just" '. **audierimus** is a (contracted) perfect subjunctive in a consecutive clause with a 'limiting' force; *de quo* would be more common with *audire* in this sense. **testula illa,** 'by the well-known vote of the potsherd'. In 610 the Athenian statesman Cleisthenes brought in a law whereby if one or more of the leading men were thought to be aiming at supreme power a vote should be taken of the whole people and if more than 6000 citizens wrote on a fragment of pottery (a convenient form of writing material for this purpose) the name of the same person, he should go into exile for ten years without loss of civil rights. Aristides was thus 'ostracized' (the word is derived from *ostrakon*, the Greek for a potsherd) in 482, and Themistocles himself suffered the same fate in 471 but never returned to Athens.

3. **qui,** another example of the 'connecting' relative pronoun at the beginning of a new sentence, referring to a noun in the preceding sentence, here Aristides; it is translated by the same case of *hic, haec, hoc,* 'this man' or 'he'; so also *cui* in the next sentence, **concitatam,** 'which had been stirred up (against him)'. **cedens.** 'when he was withdrawing from the struggle (with Themistocles)'. **ut . . . pelleretur,** indirect command depending on **scribentem,** 'writing (on a potsherd) that he should be banished from . . .'. *patria* is ablative of separation. **dicitur,** 'he is said'; we often use an impersonal verb ('it is said') but Latin never does so. **quare** = *cur.* **quid . . . duceretur,** 'what Aristides had done to be considered worthy of . . .', lit. why he should be considered, deliberative subjunctive. The Greek author Plutarch (*c.* A.D. 100) in his Life of Aristides says that the man referred to in this story could not write and asked Aristides to do so for him, whereupon Aristides found that he had to write his own name on the potsherd for the reason given by Nepos. In 1932, during archaeological excavations in the *Agora* (market place) at Athens, a number of *ostraka* or potsherds were found in a disused well, including four bearing the name of Aristides and two the name of Themistocles. See page 29.

4. The subject of *placere* is *eum*, i.e. Aristides, but we should say 'but that he (the stranger) did not like him', instead of 'that he (Aristides) was not pleasing to him'. **elaborasset** = *elaboravisset,* subjunctive in a causal clause in *oratio obliqua,* 'because he had taken such particular pains to be called . . .'; no doubt an entirely unjust accusation, but typical of one kind of human nature.

5. **legitimam poenam,** 'the full legal penalty' of ten years' exile. **descendit,** 'came down upon', or 'invaded'. *quam* here

=*postquam*; this use is found also in Livy, and may be due here partly to the fact that *postquam* appears earlier in the sentence. *sexto* is an error for *tertio*, for Aristides was ostracized in 482 and recalled in 480. **erat expulsus,** the pluperfect is used instead of the perfect indicative with *postquam* when the exact interval of time is mentioned. **scito,** 'by the decree'; the usual Latin form is *plebiscitum* (hence our 'plebiscite'), which at Rome was a resolution passed by the plebeians alone.

2.

1. **pugnae apud Salamina** (Greek accusative singular), it is unusual for a prepositional phrase to depend on a noun without a verb; this would normally be *pugnae apud Salamina commissae*. **prius quam liberaretur,** since there is no idea of purpose in this clause Cicero and other classical authors would have written *liberatus est*, but Nepos and later writers often use the imperfect subjunctive in a purely temporal clause. *poena* (another ablative of separation) refers to Aristides' ostracism, but Nepos is probably mistaken in thinking that he was not officially recalled until after the battle. **idem,** 'he again'. *praetor* was the title of a high Roman magistrate, inferior only to the two consuls, which Nepos uses for one of the ten 'generals' appointed each year at Athens. At Plataea Mardonius was killed and his army routed, so probably *fusus* and *interfectus* have been accidentally transposed; lower down (in 2, 2) Mardonius is again said to have been *fugatus*, which is the same as *fusus*, a repetition of the error.

2. **neque ... memoria,** 'there is no other famous exploit of this man in war except the record of this command'. **multa,** in agreement with *facta* understood, or perhaps with some word like *exempla*, 'many instances'. **in primis ... ut summa,** 'in particular that (*quod*) it was due to his uprightness . . . that the chief command . . .', lit. it was brought about by his uprightness . . . . *Graeciae* = *Graecorum*, which other writers would normally say. *quo duce,* ablative absolute without a verb, 'under whose leadership', lit. who (being) leader.

3. **et intemperantia ... ut,** 'it was due both (*et*) to the arrogance . . . that . . . '. *Aristidis* depends on *iustitia*, though separated from by *factum est*. Pausanias behaved very badly while in command of the Greek naval forces, even assuming the dress and manner of a Persian despot, and was suspected of intriguing with the Persians, so that he was recalled to Sparta in 477. **omnes fere,** an exaggera-

tion, for only some of the Aegean islands and maritime cities of northern Greece and Ionia (the west coast of Asia Minor) joined Athens in the Confederacy when Sparta seemed to be slack in pursuing the war against Persia. **hos duces,** 'them (the Athenians) as leaders'.

3.

1. **quos,** referring to *barbaros*, i.e. the Persians, in the previous sentence. *quo* is used in a purpose clause when there is a comparative adjective or adverb; 'in order (lit. by which) to repulse them more easily'. **si conarentur,** the subjunctive is used because it expresses the thoughts of the members of the Confederacy, 'if (as they thought) they should try'; this is called 'virtual *oratio obliqua*'. **ad classes . . . constitueret,** the order of clauses must be reversed in English; 'Aristides was chosen to decide how much money each state should contribute for the purpose of building . . .'. *pecuniae* is partitive genitive, *daret* indirect deliberative question (the direct question was 'how much is each to contribute?'), and *qui constitueret* a relative clause of purpose. The distributive adjectives *quad-ringena et sexagena* are used because 460 talents were to be con-tributed each year. A talent was a sum of money consisting of 60 *minae*, a *mina* was a sum consisting of 100 *drachmae*, and a *drachma* was a silver coin weighing a little less than a 5p. piece but with a far higher purchasing power at that time; a talent was equivalent to about 250 gold sovereigns, again with a very much higher value. A few of the larger cities at first supplied ships and crews instead of money, but later nearly all paid 'tribute' to a total value of 460 talents (sometimes less), with which Athens built ships and in time made herself head of a maritime empire. **Delon** (Greek accusative), accusative of motion towards, Delos being a small island. **id,** 'that place', neuter because it is 'attracted' into the gender of *aerarium*.

2. **quae,** a connecting relative pronoun; 'all this money'. **postero tempore,** 'at a later date', about 454. **hic qua . . . indicium,** 'there is no surer proof of Aristides' disinterested conduct', lit. with what self-restraint this man was, ablative of quality. **quam quod, cum,** 'than the fact that, although . . .'. *qui* is an old form of the ablative in a relative clause of purpose, 'he scarcely left (the means) whereby he could be carried out to burial'.

3. **quo factum est ut,** 'the result of this was that . . .', lit. by which it was brought about that. . . . **de communi aerario,** 'out of the Public Treasury', probably of Athens rather than of the

Confederacy, now kept at Athens. **dotibus datis,** 'with the present of a dowry (each)', ablative absolute. *autem* is 'now', or it can be omitted. **post quartum annum quam** = *quarto anno postquam*; in this phrase *post* governs *quartum annum* as well as combining with *quam* to form the conjunction *postquam*, as in No. 4 (Livy), 2, 3; Nepos is using the Roman 'inclusive' method of reckoning, for Aristides' death in 468 was by our calculation only three years after Themistocles' ostracism from Athens in 471.

SALLUST

3. The Early History of Rome (*Catiline* 6, 7, 9)

I.

1. **sicut ego accepi,** 'according to the tradition that I have heard', lit. as I have heard; there were several versions of the story, the main form of which is given on page 35. There was a gap of over 400 years between the traditional dates of the fall of Troy (1184) and the foundation of Rome (753), so that no Trojan could have played any part in founding the new city, even if there is any truth in the Greek story of their coming to Italy, of which there is no archaeological evidence. Sallust ignores the well-established Roman legend of Romulus and ascribes the foundation to the Trojans. **condidere** = *condiderunt*, an alternative form often used by Sallust. **Aenea duce profugi,** 'as exiles under the leadership of Aeneas', ablative absolute without a verb, lit. Aeneas (being) leader. **incertis sedibus,** 'with no fixed abode', referring to the wanderings of Aeneas from Troy to Thrace, Delos, Crete, Epirus, Carthage, Sicily, and finally to Latium in Italy, as told in Virgil's *Aeneid*. The *Aborigines* were the original inhabitants of the district of Latium, probably the people known as *Latini*. **sine legibus,** perhaps a reference to the so-called 'Golden Age' of man's innocence, when it was said that there was no need of laws or government (*imperio*).

2. **in una moenia,** 'into one city'; *unus* is thus used with plural nouns that have a singular meaning. **dispari genere,** ablative of description, '(being people) of different origin . . .'. The absence of a conjunction between the two pairs of words is called 'asyndeton' and is common in Sallust. **alio . . . viventes,** 'one race living in one way, the other in another', or 'each with its own mode of life'; *alio* here = *altero*. **memoratu,** supine in -*u*, used with certain adjectives with the meaning of an English in-

finitive, lit. it is incredible to say, followed here by an indirect question, 'it is unbelievable (or "an incredible story") how easily they . . .'; the same phrase occurs in 2, 3. **coaluerint,** from *coalesco.* **brevi,** 'in a short (time)'. *concordia* is ablative; 'became a state by (living in) harmony'. *dispersa* refers to the Aborigines, *vaga* to the migrating Trojans.

3. **postquam** is here followed by an imperfect instead of the usual perfect indicative; the imperfect *videbatur* means 'began to . . .'; 'after their state (*res = respublica*), increased in population (*civibus*), civilisation, and territory, began to seem fairly (*satis*) prosperous . . .'. **sicut . . . habentur,** 'as generally happens in human affairs', lit. as most of mortal (things) are held.

4. **finitumi,** in agreement with *reges* as well as with *populi*. Sallust spells with *u* instead of the normal *i* such words as *finitumus, accipiundus, legitumus, minumus, lubido, maxumus,* all of which are noted in the Vocabulary. **temptare, esse,** historic infinitive, used by all writers to express a vivid series of events, instead of an imperfect indicative; there are several examples in this chapter; tr. 'began to assail them'. **pauci,** 'only a few'. *auxilio* is predicative dative, lit. were as a help, i.e. 'came to their help'. **aberant,** 'kept themselves clear of . . .'. The enemies of Rome were the kings of Etruria (the country north of Latium) and the federations of tribes like the Aequi and. Volsci; her allies were towns in the Latin League.

5. **domi militiaeque,** locative, with *intenti*, 'actively engaged at Rome and in the field'. **alius alium hortari,** 'encouraged one another'. **post,** an adverb. *ubi* generally has a perfect, not a pluperfect, indicative, as in § 7, *ubi . . . convortit.* **magis . . . beneficiis,** 'more by giving than by receiving services'. **parabant,** 'won', or 'made for themselves'.

6. **imperium . . . habebant,** 'they had a government based on law, the name of the government (being) a "monarchy" ', lit. (and) the name of the government, royal. **delecti . . . erat,** 'chosen (men), whose bodies were enfeebled . . . (but) whose minds were strong . . .'. *consulebant* would generally be used instead of *consultabant*; 'took counsel for the good of the state', or 'formed the council of the state'. **curae similitudine,** 'because of the similarity of their duties', i.e. they were like fathers to the people; but the *senatores* (derived from *senex*, an old man) were more probably called *patres* because they were *patres familiae*, heads of families.

7. **post**, an adverb again. **conservandae . . . fuerat,** 'had tended to preserve liberty . . .'; the genitive of the gerundive is here used predicatively to express purpose, for which the dative is more common. **superbiam,** the last of the kings, the second Tarquin, was called *Superbus* because of his arrogant tyranny. **se convortit** (=*convertit*), 'became', or 'turned into'. **more,** 'their form of government', or 'their constitution'. **binos . . . fecere,** 'appointed yearly magistracies and pairs of magistrates'; the highest officials were originally called 'praetors', and later 'consuls', when the praetors took second place with judicial powers. **minume . . . hominum,** 'that men's spirits would be least able to become arrogant . . .'.

2.

1. **sed,** not 'but', but 'now', like *autem*. **ea tempestate** = *eo tempore*, i.e. in 509, after the expulsion of the Tarquins. *quisque* here has a plural verb, *coepere* (= *coeperunt*); 'each man began to distinguish himself more and to display his abilities with greater readiness', lit. to keep . . . more in readiness.

2. **nam,** '(this was not so before,) for . . .'. **regibus,** dative of the agent with a past participle passive, *suspectiores*, here used as a comparative adjective, 'more suspected by . . .'. **boni . . . mali,** masculine plural, 'the good . . . the evil'. **aliena virtus,** 'another person's merit'.

3. **incredibile memoratu est,** supine in -*u*, as in 1, 2, to be taken first in this sentence; 'it is unbelievable how strong the state became . . .' lit. it is incredible to relate how much it grew (from *cresco*), indirect question. **adepta,** passive instead of the usual deponent participle (from *adipiscor*) in an ablative absolute. **cupido gloriae,** objective genitive, 'desire for glory had come upon them'; so also *belli patiens, gloriae certamen* ('rivalry for glory'), *laudis avidi,* and *pecuniae liberales* in § 6.

4. **iuventus,** collective singular, = *iuvenes*. **belli,** another objective genitive; 'as soon as (*simul ac*, often printed as one word) they could endure (the hardships of) war'. **per . . . militiae,** 'a soldier's duties (or "the practice of warfare") by hard toil'. **militaribus equis,** 'war-horses' or 'horses trained for war'. **lubidinem** (=*libidinem*) **habebant,** 'took pleasure in . . .'; notice the plural, though preceded by *erat* and *discebat*; the subject is *iuventus*.

5. **ullus,** with *labor* and *hostis* as well as with *locus*; 'no hardship was unfamiliar'. **asper aut arduus,** 'too difficult or too steep'.

6. **inter ipsos,** 'with one another'. **se quisque . . . properabat,** the *se* is unnecessary because *properare* normally takes a prolative infinitive, 'each man was eager to . . .', but Sallust has inserted *se* as the subject of *ferire*, lit. 'each man hurried on that he himself should strike . . .', perhaps because *se* is so often used in phrases with *quisque*. **dum . . . faceret,** subjunctive in *oratio obliqua* depending on the thought implied in *properabat*; 'to be seen while doing such a deed'. **eas . . . eam,** referring to the exploits just mentioned, which would normally be *id* or *ea* but are 'attracted' to agree with the nouns that follow; 'this they regarded as wealth, this as high fame . . .'. **divitias honestas,** 'wealth honourably won'.

7. **memorare . . . possem . . . ni . . . traheret,** an unfulfilled condition in present time; 'I could relate on what battlefields . . . , what cities . . . , were it not that this project would be drawing me too far away from my subject'; *parva manu* is 'with a small body of troops', *pugnando* = *oppugnando*, and the indirect questions have their verbs in primary sequence (perfect subjunctive) although the conditional clause on which it depends is historic. **natura munitas,** 'naturally fortified'. *nos* is like our 'editorial we', but *nos* and *noster* are frequently used, especially by poets, for *ego* and *meus*. Chapter 8 of *Catiline* is here omitted because it is mainly a digression on Greek and Roman historians.

3.

1. **boni mores colebantur,** 'virtue (or "good moral conduct") was practised'. By *concordia* Sallust means 'harmony' between the two classes (patricians and plebeians) in the state, as mentioned on page 36, but to say that it was *maxuma* or that the rich nobles were free from *avaritia* is entirely untrue. The order of words in *concordia maxuma, minuma avaritia* (instead of *concordia maxuma, avaritia minuma*), where the words or phrases are arranged ABBA instead of the usual ABAB (as in 'I cannot dig, to beg I am ashamed'), is called a 'chiasmus', from the shape of Greek letter *chi* (χ); there is another example in § 3, and others in No. 7 (Pliny) (b), 4 and 6 and No. 8 (Tacitus), 1, 6 and 3, 5. **bonum,** neuter adjective used as a noun, 'the good', or 'goodness'.

2. **cum hostibus,** 'only with the enemy'. **de virtute,** 'to win the prize for merit'. There are several examples of 'asyndeton', the absence of co-ordinating conjunctions, in this sentence and the next. The usual meaning of *supplicium* is 'punishment', but here it has its original meaning of 'an offering to the gods'; this was

accompanied by a sin-offering, often the execution of a criminal, from which the later meaning of the word was derived. **domi,** locative, meaning 'in their own homes', or 'in their domestic expenses'. **in amicos,** 'towards their friends'.

3. **artibus,** 'principles'. The order of words in *audacia . . . aequitate* is a 'chiasmus', as explained in the note on § 1. **seque remque publicam,** 'both . . . and', like *et . . . et.*

4. **maxuma documenta haec,** 'the following striking proofs of this', which are given in the two *quod*-clauses in apposition, 'that in war . . .; but (*vero*) in peace . . .'. **vindicatum est,** impersonal passive, 'punishment was inflicted on those who contrary to orders . . .'. T. Manlius Torquatus was killed on his father's orders for doing this in the Latin War of 340, and Q. Fabius Maximus was barely saved by the people from suffering the same fate on the orders of the Dictator in the Second Samnite War of 325. *quique = in eos qui,* and *quam qui = quam in eos qui.* **tardius,** 'too slowly', with *excesserunt. signa* in the plural generally means the military standards, of which every maniple (double century) had its own, in addition to the 'eagle' of the legion and the standards of the (later) cohorts; in battle they were the rallying-points for the soldiers, who followed them wherever they were carried and defended them to the death. **loco,** with *cedere,* 'to give ground when hard pressed' (*pulsi*). **ausi erant** is perhaps used ironically.

5. **imperium agitabant,** 'they governed', when they had defeated the enemy. **et accepta iniuria,** 'even when they had received an injury'. We must emphasise again that in his desire to extol the 'good old days' of the early Republic Sallust has given an exaggerated and highly idealised picture of the history of those times, which he has intentionally distorted to suit his theme.

LIVY

4. How Servius Tullius became King at Rome (I, 39–41)

1.

1. **visu . . . mirabile,** 'marvellous in its appearance and its outcome'; *visu* is not the supine of *video* (as is usual in the phrase *mirabile visu,* 'marvellous to behold'), but the ablative of *visus,* a noun like *eventu.* **puero dormienti,** dative of advantage, often used in close relationship with a noun, with more emphasis than, but equivalent to, a possessive genitive; 'the head of a boy . . . while

he was asleep'. **cui . . . nomen,** 'whose name was Servius . . .';
grammatically *Servio Tullio* should be in the nominative case, but
in such sentences the name is often 'attracted' into the dative to
agree with the antecedent; so too 'my name is Tullius' is either
nomen mihi Tullius est or *nomen mihi Tullio est.* **ferunt,** 'men say',
or 'the story is'. *arsisse* is from *ardeo.*

2. **ad tantae rei miraculum orto,** 'which arose at the miraculous
appearance of such an event'. **excitos (esse) reges,** 'the king and
queen were aroused'; the indirect statement depends on *ferunt* in
the previous sentence and goes down to *abisse* (=*abiisse*), but the
subject of *retentum* (*esse*) is *eum* understood, referring to *quidam
familiarium,* and of *vetuisse* it is *eam,* i.e. the queen. There is no
object for *restinguendum,* but the context shows that it means 'to
put out the fire'. *donec experrectus esset,* 'until he should awake';
the pluperfect subjunctive represents in *oratio obliqua* the future
perfect of Tanaquil's own words, *donec experrectus erit,* lit. until
he shall have awoken, for which we say 'until he awakes'. **et
flammam,** 'the flame also'.

3. **viro,** 'her husband'. **viden,** a colloquial form of *videsne.*
tam humili cultu, 'in so humble a style', as a slave, which according to one story his mother was, either by birth or by capture in
war. *educamus* is from *educare,* not *educere.* **scire licet,** 'you may
be sure (lit. it is permitted to know) that he will one day (*quondam*)
be a glory (*lumen*) to our doubtful fortunes . . .'. For *praesidium*
the predicative dative *praesidio* might have been used ('a defence
to the royal house when it is in trouble'), but it is put in the same
case as *lumen.* Tanaquil was skilled in the Etruscan lore of
prophecy, according to the legend. **materiam . . . nutriamus,**
'let us bring up . . . (one who is destined to be) the cause of great
renown to our country and our family', lit. publicly and privately;
the adverbs qualify the adjective and noun between which they are
placed.

4. **liberum** (=**liberorum) loco coeptum (esse) haberi,** 'began
to be regarded as their own child', lit. in the place of children; the
indirect statement depends on *ferunt* in § 1 again, although *inquit*
and Tanaquil's own words intervene. *coeptum* is passive because
the infinitive depending on it, *haberi,* is passive; the active of
coepi is used when the dependent infinitive is active. **artibus . . .
excitantur,** 'in the accomplishments whereby men of ability
(*ingenia*) are encouraged to the pursuit of . . .'; *excitantur* is
indicative because it is not really part of the indirect statement but

a 'defining' relative clause, or a statement made by Livy. **evenit . . . esset,** 'this easily came to pass, because it was (lit. which was) the will of the gods'; *quod . . . esset* is a causal relative clause, and *cordi* is locative, 'close to the heart of the gods', i.e. pleasing to the gods, with *dis* (possessive) dative of advantage, like *puero dormienti* in § 1. **vere indolis regiae,** 'of a truly royal nature', genitive of description, with *esse* understood. **nec . . . quisquam Romanae iuventutis,** 'and . . . no one among the Roman youth'. **ulla . . . potuit,** 'could be compared (with him) in any accomplishment'.

5. **hic tantus honor,** 'this great honour', or 'so great an honour as this', **quacumque . . . habitus,** '(which was) conferred upon him for whatever reason'. The object of *prohibet* is *nos* understood; 'prevents us from believing that he was the son of a slave-woman (ablative of origin) and had himself when young . . .'. **eorum . . . qui,** 'I am more of the opinion of those writers who say (*ferunt*) . . .'; Livy refers probably only to Valerius Antias, one of the 'annalists' mentioned on page 40; up to now he has been following the account given by Licinius Macer. *Ser.* (= *Servii*) *Tulli* depends on *uxorem,* and *viro occiso* refers to the same man, the supposed husband of Ocrisia and father of the younger Servius Tullius; 'that the pregnant wife of . . . , after her husband had been killed, . . . had been rescued (*prohibitam*) from slavery . . . and had given birth to a child . . .'. *qui . . . fuerat* is indicative, although inside an indirect statement, for the same reason as *quibus . . . excitantur* in 1, 4. **cognita,** 'recognised', or 'known for what she was', because of her noble appearance. *in domo* is used instead of *domi* because it means 'in the house' (or 'palace'), not 'at home'.

6. **tanto beneficio,** 'because of so great a kindness', *et . . . et,* 'both . . . and'. The infinitives in this section are all in indirect statement still depending on *ferunt* in § 5. **inter mulieres** 'between the two women', *auctam = auctam esse.* **ut . . . eductum,** 'as one brought up from childhood . . .'. **fuisse,** 'was held'. **fortunam . . . fecisse,** 'his mother's misfortune . . . had brought it about (*fecisse*) that he was believed to have been born from a slave-woman'. *venerit* is subjunctive in a causal clause in *oratio obliqua* and perfect (instead of the normal pluperfect required by strict sequence depending on the historic tense of *fecisse*) because it represents the primary tense used in *oratio recta*, *venit*, 'she has come' (as in 2, 3), whereas *crederetur* is the usual historic tense; but in English we must translate *venerit* as 'she had come', i.e. 'had fallen into the hands'.

2.

1. **ex quo** =*ex quo tempore*, 'from the time when'; the traditional
dates of the reign of Tarquinius Priscus are 616–578 and of Servius
Tullius 578–534. **non apud . . . erat,** 'was (held) in the very
highest (lit. by far the greatest) honour not only by (*apud*) the
king . . .'; *honore* is ablative of description, lit. was (a man) with
honour; in 1, 6 we have the ablative with *in*, to give the same
meaning.

2. The long sentence in §§ 2 and 3 contains what is called an
'anacoluthon', i.e. a change of construction half-way through it,
which is common in everyday speech but unusual in a formal
history like this. *filii duo* has no verb, for after the *etsi* clause,
which ends at *ne Italicae quidem stirpis*, the construction changes to
the historic infinitive *tum impensius iis indignitas crescere*, in which
iis refers to *Anci duo filii* and *tum* is repeated; it is perhaps best to
translate the first *tum* as *autem*, 'now', omit *etsi*, put a full-stop at
stirpis, and begin a new sentence by translating the second *tum* as
'but'. **pro indignissimo habuerant,** 'had considered it the
greatest outrage', lit. had held (it) as a most disgraceful thing,
followed by the indirect statement *se . . . pulsos* (*esse*) and *regnare . . .
advenam . . . stirpis*. **patrio regno,** ablative of separation, 'from . . .'.
tutoris fraude, the half-Greek, half-Etruscan Tarquinius Priscus
contrived to become the chief adviser of Ancus Martius (640–616),
who named him as his young sons' guardian in his will, but on the
death of Ancus Tarquin sent the two boys off on a hunting expedition and in their absence got himself appointed king. *et* or
sed should be inserted before *regnare*. *non modo* when followed by
ne . . . quidem is regularly used instead of *non modo non*, 'not only
not . . . but not even . . .'. Tarquin's father was Demaratus, who
was exiled from Corinth and settled at Tarquinii, a town of Etruria
about 60 miles north-west of Rome, where he married an Etruscan
wife; his elder son Lucumo married another Etruscan woman,
Tanaquil, but being of mixed blood he was despised by the Etruscans
and decided to migrate to Rome, where he took the name of Tarquinius from the town of Tarquinii and eventually became king in
the way just described. **impensius . . . crescere,** 'their indignation
began to increase (even) more greatly'; *iis* is the (possessive) dative,
here of disadvantage, like *puero dormienti* in 1, 1, and *crescere* is
historic infinitive as explained in the note on *temptare*, *esse* in No. 3
(Sallust), 1, 4. **si . . . rediret,** this does not quite mean 'if', but 'at

the thought that . . .', and is sometimes used after verbs expressing emotion, in imitation of the ordinary Greek usage; 'at the thought that even after (the death of) Tarquin the royal power would not revert to them'.

3. **sed praeceps . . . caderet,** still in the *si*-clause; 'but would fall headlong even further than that (*porro inde*, lit. onwards from there) into (the hands of) a slave'; *servitia* is plural used for singular and refers only to Servius Tullius, though Livy did not believe the story about his servile origin. *ut* is 'with the result that . . .'. **post . . . quam . . . tenuerit,** *post* governs *centesimum annum* and also combines with *quam* to form the conjunction *postquam*; lit. after about the hundredth year that Romulus . . . , i.e. 'about a hundred years after Romulus held . . .', equivalent to *centesimo anno postquam*, as in No. 2 (Nepos), 3, 3, where the clause was *post annum quartum . . . quam erat expulsus*; the pluperfect is more common than the perfect when the exact interval of time is mentioned. It was 100 years from the death (or apotheosis) of Romulus to the accession of Tarquin, and 138 years to his death. *deo* and *serva* are both ablative of origin, as in 1, 5 and 6, and the verbs *tenuerit*, *fuerit*, *possideat* are in primary sequence in *oratio obliqua* in the same tenses as were used in *oratio recta*, like *venerit* in 1, 6. *donec* meaning 'as long as' takes the same tense as the main verb, like *dum. id* refers to *regnum*. **cum . . . tum,** 'not only . . . but also'. *fore* is infinitive in indirect statement depending on a verb of saying understood from the previous sentence; '(they said that) it (*id*, looking forward to the *si*-clause) would be a general disgrace . . . to (lit. of) the Roman name . . .'. **virili stirpe salva,** ablative absolute without a verb; 'while the male stock . . . was still alive'. **Romae,** objective genitive, 'sovereignty over Rome', or perhaps locative.

4. **statuunt,** historic present, like most of the verbs in the rest of this chapter, used in a vivid narrative, to be translated either as present or past in English. *stimulabat*, though singular, has two subjects, *et iniuriae dolor*, 'both their indignation at the wrong (done to them)' (objective genitive), and the *et quia . . . privatus* clause, 'and the fact that (lit. because) the king was likely to be a more severe . . . than a private individual (would be)'. **si superesset,** subjunctive in 'virtual' *oratio obliqua* without an introductory verb, expressing the thoughts of the sons of Ancus; 'if he should survive'; so also *delegisset*, which represents the future perfect of direct speech. *Servio occiso* is equivalent to a conditional clause; 'further-

more (*tum*), if Servius was killed'. **quemcumque . . . videbatur,** 'he seemed likely to appoint as heir . . . the same person,
whoever else it was, whom he chose as his son-in-law', lit. the
same, whomever other he should have chosen. *insidiae* here of
course does not mean 'an ambush' but 'a plot', or 'a secret attack'.

5. **delecti ad facinus,** 'being chosen to do the deed'. **ferramentis** is put inside the relative clause but must be taken as the
antecedent of *quibus*; 'with the rustic tools to which each was
accustomed'; *uterque* here has a plural verb. **quam potuere**
(=*potuerunt*) **tumultuosissime,** 'causing as much uproar as they
could'; the verb *posse* is often omitted in this phrase, e.g. *quam
celerrime.* **specie rixae,** 'under the pretence of quarrelling'.
penitus . . . pervenisset, 'had penetrated far into . . .'.

6. **vociferari, obstrepere,** historic infinites, as in 2, 2. **alter
alteri,** 'each one tried to shout the other down'. **rem . . . orditur,**
'began to state his case, according to their previous arrangement'.

7. **cum . . . averteret** 'when the king, intent upon him (i.e. upon
the speaker), was turning completely away'; *totus* is used ad-
verbially. **elatam . . . deiecit** =*extulit . . . et deiecit.* **se foras
eiciunt,** 'rushed out of the palace', lit. out of doors.

3.

1. **qui** = *ei qui*, lit. those who were around, i.e. 'his attendants',
or 'the bystanders'. **illos fugientes,** not 'those fleeing' nor 'the
fugitives', which would be *fugientes* alone, but 'the two shepherds
as they were fleeing'. The verb for *clamor concursusque* is *est*
(=*fuit*) or *fit* (=*factus est*), understood, and *mirantium* is plural
agreeing with *civium* which is understood from the sense of *populi*;
we might bring out the change from singular to plural by translating *mirantium* as 'while men were wondering . . .'. **rei,** partitive
genitive; *quid rei* is a little more vague than *quae res*, and the whole
phrase could be translated 'what was going on'. **(ea) quae . . .
sunt,** '(the remedies) which are (or "were") necessary for healing
a wound'; *curando vulneri* is dative of purpose, and *opus* is often
also used with *est* and a noun in the ablative case to mean 'there is
need of . . .'. **si spes destituat,** this is subjunctive in 'virtual *oratio
obliqua*', as in 2, 4, showing what Tanaquil thought; 'she devised
other means of safety (to protect herself) if hope proved false'.
The tenses subordinate to a historic present can be in primary
sequence but are usually in historic sequence, as most of the verbs
are in this chapter; but *destituat* and *sinat* (in § 3) are perhaps

primary because they represent the tenses of what Tanaquil thought
or said (see the last note on 1, 6). The change of tense in the main
verbs *iubet* and *eiecit* in the same sentence is probably only for the
sake of variety. The other main verbs in this chapter of short, vivid
sentences are historic present, as far as *simulat* in § 6.

2. **paene exsanguem virum,** 'her almost lifeless husband'.
Supply *eum* as the object of *orat*, and *esse* with *inultam*, 'not to allow
the death . . . to be unavenged'. **ludibrio,** predicative dative, 'to
be a laughing-stock to her enemies'.

3. **Servi,** vocative of *Servius*. **vir,** 'a man', i.e. a brave man.
tuum, . . . non eorum, 'belongs to you, . . . not to those who . . .'.
sequere, imperative; 'follow the guidance of the gods', lit. the
gods (as) leaders. **hoc caput,** 'this head of yours', which she was
then perhaps touching. **igni** =*igne*, in the ablative absolute clause;
'when they poured divine fire around it', as described in 1, 2.
excitet, jussive subjunctive, 'let it spur you on'. **expergiscere,**
Livy makes Tanaquil use the same word (here imperative) as she
had used in 1, 2, implying that whereas before he had merely
awakened from sleep as a child he must now wake up in earnest and
seize the opportunity to become king. **et nos, peregrini,** 'we too
(i.e. Tarquin and Tanaquil), though foreigners, . . .', referring to
Tarquin's half-Greek, half-Etruscan origin and her own entirely
Etruscan birth. **non unde sis,** 'not whence you were born',
another indirect question, like *qui sis*; Tanaquil evidently regarded
him as the son of a slave, not the son of a nobleman of Corniculum,
which was the later story believed by Livy (1, 5–6). *tua* agrees
with *consilia*, from which it is separated, for the sake of emphasis,
by *re subita*, 'because of this sudden crisis'. **at . . . sequere,** 'at
any rate follow my counsels', or 'follow mine'.

4. **impetus,** 'pushing'. **ex superiore parte,** 'from the upper
storey', an anachronism, because houses in early Roman times
consisted of only a large hall (*atrium*) with small rooms round it.
in Novam Viam versas, 'that faced the *Nova Via*', a street that
ran along the northern foot of the Palatine Hill; the kings usually
lived in the Regia, a palace built by King Numa near the eastern
end of the Forum, which in the Republic was the official residence
of the Chief Priest. **ad Iovis Statoris,** 'near the (temple) of Jupiter
the Stayer', which was vowed to Jupiter by Romulus if he 'stayed'
the flight of the Romans from the Sabines in the very early days
of Rome, but it was apparently not built until 294 B.C., at the foot of
the Palatine Hill in the angle formed by the *Nova Via*, the *Sacra*

Via (almost parallel with it), and the *Clivus Palatinus* (which ran at right angles southwards up the Palatine Hill); *templum* is often omitted in Latin before a name in the genitive case, just as we say 'St Paul's' instead of 'St Paul's Church' or 'Cathedral'.

5. **iubet,** supply *eos* as the object. **bono animo esse,** 'to be of good cheer', ablative of quality. The rest of the section is all in indirect statement introduced by 'she said', understood from *iubet*. **fuisse,** used with *sopitum* instead of the normal *esse* to mean that the king had been, and still was, stunned. **haud alte descendisse,** 'had not sunk deeply'. Livy says *corpus* here, but *caput* in 2, 7. **ad se redisse,** 'had recovered consciousness', like our phrase 'to return to oneself'. **inspectum (esse),** i.e. by doctors. **omnia salubria esse,** 'all (the indications) were favourable'. The subject of *confidere* and *iubere* is *se*, i.e. Tanaquil. *eos* refers to *cives*, understood from *populum* in § 4 (see also *populi, mirantium* in 2, 1). **dicto audientem esse** =*parere*; 'she was ordering the people to obey . . .'. **eum iura redditurum (esse),** 'he would administer justice'. *alia* =*cetera*.

6. **trabea,** a short purple cloak worn by a king, Etruscan in origin. **cum trabea et lictoribus prodit,** an example of 'zeugma' or 'syllepsis', in which a verb is taken with two nouns but in a slightly different sense with each, as in No. 1 (Cicero), 1, 3; here we must say 'came forward clad in a royal robe and accompanied by the lictors'. *prodit* is from *prodeo*, and *sede regia* is a local ablative without *in*, common in poetry and sometimes used in prose, generally with an adjective like *totus* or *medius*. **alia . . . simulat,** 'passed judgement on some (cases) and pretended that he would consult the king about others'. **per speciem . . . vicis,** 'on the pretext of discharging the duties of another'; deponent verbs that govern the ablative, like *fungor*, are used in the 'gerundive attraction' construction because in old Latin such verbs governed the accusative. **suas opes,** 'his own position'; *opem* (no nominative) in the singular means 'help', in the plural 'wealth' or 'resources'; in § 7 it means 'strength', or 'position' again. **palam factum est,** 'the truth was revealed', lit. it was made openly. **praesidio . . . munitus,** 'defended by a strong bodyguard'. *primus regnavit* would normally mean 'was the first to rule', but here *primus* seems to mean 'at first', *primo*. We should insert *sed* before *voluntate*, 'but with the consent of the Senate'.

7. **iam tum,** i.e. immediately after the attack on Tarquin. **ut,** 'when'. The position of Suessa Pometia in the land of the Volsci,

south of Latium, is unknown. **exsulatum,** the supine in -*um* is used to express purpose after a verb of motion; 'had gone into exile at (lit. to) . . .'.

PETRONIUS

5. The Werewolf (*Satyricon* 61, 6–62)

1.

1. **servirem,** nearly all those present at the banquet, including the host, Trimalchio, and his wife, were ex-slaves, *liberti*, freedmen who had been given their freedom by their former masters or had purchased it out of their savings (*peculium*). **in Augusto Vico,** 'in Narrow Street', the name of a street at Cumae, like *Vicus Longus, Alta Semita* ('High Street'), and *Via Nova* (No. 4 (Livy), 3, 4), which were streets at Rome. Niceros was at this time the slave of Gaius, who owned an inn in Narrow Street and an estate in the country, where there was another inn for the use of estate-workers and travellers. Terentius and Melissa were also his slaves and managed the inn at Cumae, where Niceros met and fell in love with Melissa; they had probably been sent temporarily to manage the inn on the estate, until Terentius died there. **quomodo dii** (=*dei*) **volunt,** 'as the gods willed it', historic present. **noveratis,** 'you used to know' or 'you remember', lit. you knew; the pluperfect of *nosco*, whose perfect, *novi*, means 'I know'. **bacciballum,** a word of uncertain origin and meaning, found only here, possibly derived from *bacca*, 'a berry'; it might be translated 'a pretty little peach of a girl'; its gender is neuter, though here referring to a girl.

2. **si quid . . . negatum (est),** 'if I asked for anything, it was never refused me'. **fecit,** equivalent to *si fecit*; 'if she made tuppence'; an *as* was a copper coin worth one-tenth of a *denarius*, which was a silver coin a little smaller than a 5p. piece but with a very much higher purchasing power. A *sinus* was a fold in a garment which could serve as a pocket, 'I put it into her pocket'. **fefellitus sum,** a colloquial form of *falsus sum*, from *fallo*.

3. **contubernalis,** i.e. Terentius; slaves could not contract a legal marriage, but an owner would allow a male and female slave to live together; their children were called *vernae*, 'home-bred slaves'. Here we should call Terentius Melissa's husband, as she is called his *uxor* in § 1. **ad villam,** 'on the estate', i.e. at the inn

on their master's country-estate which they had probably been sent to manage for a time. *villa* normally means 'a country house', but here it means the estate generally, and in 2, 11 it is the courtyard of the inn there. **supremum diem obiit,** 'died', lit. met his last day, perhaps conveniently for Melissa and Niceros. **per scutum per ocream,** a proverbial expression, 'by hook or by crook', lit. by shield and greave (leg armour worn by Roman soldiers). Notice the 'asyndeton', absence of a coordinating conjunction, in this phrase, as also in *egi aginavi*, 'I plotted and planned'; *agino* is another colloquial word used by Petronius. **pervenirem,** deliberative indirect question, 'how I could reach her'; he could not leave the inn without his master's permission or in his absence, which fortunately occurred just at that time. **scitis,** used parenthetically, like our 'you know', without affecting the syntax of the main clause, which is no doubt a proverbial saying, the kind of remark that simple folk in all countries like to make — an apt touch of characterisation by Petronius.

2.

1. **ad scruta scita expedienda,** 'to look after some bits and pieces', lit. elegant trifles. Apparently all Niceros' schemes for meeting Melissa depended on his master's leaving home, which he could not influence in any way, however much 'he plotted and planned'. Capua was about 20 miles from Cumae to the north-east.

2. **persuadeo,** historic present, here governing an accusative instead of the normal dative. **hospitem nostrum,** 'one of our guests', at the inn in Narrow Street where Niceros was employed. **fortis tamquam Orcus,** 'as brave as the devil', or 'as brave as hell'; Orcus was a name for the Underworld, also applied to Pluto, the god of the Underworld, and to death. The soldier was presumably on leave from his legion.

3. **apoculamus nos,** another colloquial word; 'we got ourselves off'. **gallicinia,** 'cock-crow', plural for singular, the beginning of the last of the four 'watches' of the night, about 3 a.m. in summer. *meridie* is ablative of 'time when', lit. as though at midday.

4. **monimenta,** the tombstones that lined the roads outside towns. **homo meus,** 'my friend', or like our own colloquial use of 'my man'. **ad . . . facere,** 'to make for'; the soldier seems to have given Niceros no reason for turning aside to the tombstones. **cantabundus,** either because he was looking forward to seeing Melissa or perhaps to keep up his spirits in case the graves were

haunted.   Some verbs have the ending *-bundus* as an alternative
to a present participle, e.g. *temptabundus* in Part II, No. 12 (Livy),
2, 1. *numero* is a verb; he counted the tombstones to pass the time.

5. **ut**, 'when'.   **secundum**, a preposition.   **esse**, historic infinitive; 'my heart was in my mouth' is our expression (lit. my soul
was in my nose); *mihi* is dative of advantage, almost equivalent to a
possessive genitive, as in No. 4 (Livy), 1, 1.

6. **ut mentiar . . . facio**, lit. I value nobody's fortune so highly
(genitive of value) that I should tell lies, i.e. 'I wouldn't tell a lie
about this for any money'.   Some remarks on 'lycanthropy', the
belief that human beings could turn into wolves, are printed after
the Latin text of Petronius.

7. **quod coeperam dicere**, 'as I was saying', lit. which I had
begun to say.

9. **qui** (=**quis**) **. . . ego**, 'who could be nearer dying of terror
than I was?', lit. who was dying . . . unless I (was); *mori* is historic
infinitive.   **umbras cecidi**, 'I was killing shadows all the way',
i.e. he thought that the shadows were men (or ghosts) and cut at
them with his sword.   **donec pervenirem**, we should say 'until I
reached', but the subjunctive implies 'until I could reach' and
suggests his hurry to get to his girl-friend's house.

10. **ut larva**, 'like a ghost', or 'as pale as a ghost'.   **animam
ebullivi**, 'I was at my last gasp', lit. I made my breath boil over.
mihi per bifurcium, 'down my legs'; the dative is used as in
§ 5.   **mortui erant**, 'were lifeless', or 'dull'.   **vix umquam**,
'hardly . . . at all'.   Here again there is 'asyndeton', absence of co-
ordinating conjunctions, with short, vivid sentences.

11. **mirari, quod . . . ambularem**, 'to express surprise that
(lit. because) I was out walking so late', or we might say 'so early'
because it was now nearly dawn — he had set out *circa gallicinia*,
2, 3. *ante* is an adverb.   **adiutasses** = **adiutavisses**, 'you could
have helped us'; it usually governs an accusative case.   **villam**,
here the courtyard or enclosure round the inn, where the sheep
were folded for the night.   **pecora . . . misit**, 'worried the sheep and
spilt (or "let") their blood like a butcher'; *illis* is the (possessive)
dative of advantage (here disadvantage), like *mihi* in § 10.   **nec
tamen derisit**, 'but yet he did not make fools of us'.   **servus
noster**, 'one of our slaves'; Melissa was herself a slave, but
probably she and her late husband were allowed to employ slaves
to do the domestic and farm work while they managed the inn.

12. **ut**, 'when'.   **operire oculos amplius**, 'keep my eyes closed

any longer', which suggests that he had tried to get some sleep before hearing about the wolf's attack. **luce clara,** 'when it was full day', a little later than *prima luce*. **Gai . . . fugi,** 'I hurried back to the house of my master Gaius'. **tamquam caupo compilatus,** 'like a defrauded innkeeper', a proverbial saying found in one of Aesop's *Fables* (423). **illum,** we generally omit this when it is used adjectivally as the antecedent of a relative pronoun, 'the place where . . .'. **nisi,** 'except'.

13. **miles meus,** 'my soldier', as in 2, 4 — but *Melissa mea* in § 11 is 'my dear Melissa'. *bovis* is an ante- and post-classical form of *bos*. **panem gustare,** 'eat a bite of food'. **non si me occidisses,** the sentence in full would be 'I could not . . . (and I should not have been able to do so) not even if you had killed me', i.e. threatened to kill me, but the words as they stand are probably intentionally comic, for a dead man cannot eat.

14. **viderint,** jussive perfect subjunctive; 'let others see what they think', **genios . . . habeam,** 'may I incur the anger of your guardian spirits'; every man and every house had a *genius* that looked after him and it; it was often painted on the wall of the house in the form of a serpent. *vestros* shows that Niceros was addressing all the guests, as does *noveratis* in 1, *scitis* in 13, and *nolite* in 2,6, but *occidisses* in § 13 is singular, like our indefinite second person singular, 'you' or 'one'.

SENECA

6. Thoughts in a Tunnel (*Epistulae Morales* 57)

With *salutem* supply *dicit* or *dat*, 'sends greetings to his (friend) . . .'. Pliny has *S* alone, for *salutem*. Cicero usually has *S.D.* In Latin capital *V* is used both for *V* and (as here) for *U* (see page 2).

1. **a Bais** (=*Baiis*), Baiae was a sea-side resort on what is now the Bay of Pozzuoli, about twelve miles west of Naples by sea, very popular with well-to-do Romans but with a somewhat dubious moral reputation. A preposition is usually omitted with names of towns unless the meaning is 'from (or "to", with *ad*) the neighbourhood of . . .', but Roman writers (especially Livy) often use the preposition when this meaning seems unnecessary, as in this sentence. **deberem,** we might say, 'when it was time for me to return to . . .'. **esse,** 'was raging'. **ne . . . experirer,** 'that I should

not have to endure a sea-voyage (lit. a ship) again'. **et,** 'and yet'.
luti is partitive genitive depending on *tantum*, 'so much mud',
and *tota via* is local ablative without *in*, often found with *totus* and
similar adjectives.   **navigasse** =*navigavisse*; Seneca means that
travelling on the muddy roads was as uncomfortable as going by
sea; 'that I can seem to have ...'. **totum ... fuit,** 'I had to endure
the full fate of athletes ...'; wrestlers were first massaged with oil
to make their muscles supple and then sprinkled with sand to
prevent an opponent's hand from slipping; Seneca says that after
the anointing with wet mud on the open road the dust-sprinkle in
the Neopolitan Tunnel received them. *nos* often =*me* (or *ego*), but
probably here refers to Seneca and his companions.

2. **carcere, facibus,** ablative of comparison, with *esse possit*
('could be') understood as the verb; the comparison is an example
of the figure of speech called 'oxymoron' (the combination of
opposite ideas to give emphasis), because prisons are usually small
and torches bright, not 'dim'. The torches were placed at intervals
along the walls of the tunnel to give some light to travellers. **quae
... ipsas,** 'which made it possible for us, not to see (anything else)
amid the darkness, but (to see the darkness) itself'; the light was
so dim that it merely intensified the darkness. **ceterum,** adverbial
accusative, lit. for the rest, i.e. 'but'. Two imperfect subjunctives
in a conditional clause are used for an unfulfilled present condition;
'if the place provided any light, the dust, a thing which is oppressive
... even in the open, would hide it', lit. would remove it. **quid
illic,** 'what (is it like) there ... ?', i.e. how much worse is it there.
cum, 'since'. Evelyn's account of his visit to the tunnel in 1645
(quoted in the Introduction to this Letter) shows that by his time a
spiramentum, passage for ventilation, had been made through the
roof of the tunnel into the open air. **inter se contraria,** 'quite
incompatible with one another', lit. in conflict with each other.
eadem via is another local ablative without *in*. **laboravimus,** 'we
struggled with both ...', or 'we suffered from ...'.

3. **aliquid quod cogitarem,** 'something to think about', a
relative purpose clause. **ictum animi,** 'excitement', or 'thrill'.
sine metu mutationem, 'a (mental) change unaccompanied by
fear'; Seneca evidently did not feel the terror of enclosed places
that we call claustrophobia. *simul ac* here =*et simul* (not *simulac*,
'as soon as'). **qui ... absum,** 'who am far removed from being an
average man, to say nothing of not being a perfect man'; *nedum*
in Ciceronian Latin means 'still less', in Silver Latin sometimes

(as here) 'still more'. Like most Stoic philosophers, Seneca thought that the entirely perfect and wise man could practically never be found. **de illo . . . perdidit,** 'about a person over whom fortune has lost her power'; the 'perfect man' of Stoic philosophy was thought to be liberated from the vicissitudes of fortune. **huius . . . ferietur,** 'even such a man's mind will be struck (by a thrill of excitement)'.

4. **quaedam,** neuter accusative plural; 'certain emotions'. **mi Lucili,** vocative. *virtus* here is not philosophic 'virtue' but ordinary 'courage', to which *illam* refers; 'nature reminds it of its own mortality', i.e. that even courage, and brave men, must one day pass away. The subject of *adducet* and the verbs that follow is 'the perfect man'. **ad tristia . . . ad subita,** 'at sad news . . . at sudden apparitions'. **in . . . constitutus,** 'when standing on the edge of it'. **despexerit,** future perfect in a conditional clause, for which we say simply 'if he looks down at', not 'if he shall have . . .'. **hoc,** neuter nominative 'this reaction'. **rationi,** 'by reason', dative of the agent used after an adjective with a passive meaning, though as *ratio* is not a living agent the ablative of the instrument might have been used.

5. **et paratissimi,** we should omit *et* and say 'who are . . .', or put a comma instead. **videre non possunt,** 'cannot bear to see'. *alienum,* as well as *suum,* agrees with *sanguinem.* **ad . . . inspectionemque,** 'at having to touch and look at a newly-inflicted wound . . .'. **et purulenti,** *et* is omitted again in English; 'at an old wound that is festering'. **linquuntur animo,** lit. are left by their senses, i.e. 'they faint'. **gladium . . . vident,** 'receive a sword-stroke more willingly than they see (it inflicted)'.

6. **ut dicebam,** 'as I was saying'; Seneca now returns to his feelings in the tunnel. **non quidem perturbationem,** 'not indeed a disturbance of mind'. **ad,** 'at'. **redditae lucis,** 'of restored daylight', at the end of the tunnel. **illud mecum loqui,** 'to discuss in my own mind the following thought', followed by an indirect question *quam inepte. . . timeremus,* 'how foolishly we fear (lit. feared) certain things to a greater or less degree, since the outcome of them all is the same'; the dependent verbs are in historic sequence after *coepi,* though we should use present tenses in English. **quid interest utrum,** 'what difference does it make whether . . .'. **nihil (interesse) invenies,** 'you will find that there is no difference'. **erunt qui . . . timeant,** 'there will be some who fear the latter catastrophe more', i.e. being crushed by a landslide

from a mountain; *erunt qui* introduces a consecutive or generic subjunctive, lit. there will be people of such a kind that they fear. **utraque,** 'each calamity'. **adeo,** 'indeed'. **effectus** is accusative plural with a singular meaning; 'not the result, but what causes (*efficientia*) the result'.

7. The teaching of the Stoic philosophers is outlined in the Introduction to Cicero (page 54). It was not part of their regular beliefs that 'the soul of a man who has been crushed (from *extero*) by a great weight cannot remain in existence and is at once destroyed (lit. scattered)'; this passage is the only authority for such a doctrine. **non ... liber,** 'it has not had a free means of departing (from the body)'. *fuerit* is subjunctive in *oratio obliqua* depending on *existimant.* **non facio,** this seems to mean 'I am not doing so', i.e. I am not referring to the Stoics; but the argument is not easy to follow, for if Seneca is not referring to them why should he mention them at all, and to whom is he really referring? Perhaps *non facio* refers to *existimant,* the verb in the relative clause and means 'I do not do that', i.e. I do not think that this particular Stoic belief is true, a statement which he elaborates in the words that follow. Two sentences that deal with the arguments about this doctrine are omitted here. **de illo ... esse,** 'we must examine (or "inquire into") the following point, whether (*an = num*) it (the soul) can be ...'. **hoc certum habe,** 'be sure of this', followed by the indirect statement *illam ... posse.* The conditional clause and the causal clause in this sentence of *oratio obliqua* remain in the indicative instead of being put in the subjunctive (like *quia fuerit* earlier in this section), which would be the normal usage in Ciceronian Latin. **nulla ... aeterno est,** 'there is no (rule of) immortality that has an exception to it and nothing can injure that which is everlasting'. **vale,** the usual ending of a Roman letter, equivalent both to our formal 'yours faithfully', our less formal 'yours sincerely', and our familiar 'yours ever'.

PLINY

7 (a). A Mysterious Spring (4, 30)

S. stands for *salutem,* with *dicit* or *dat* understood, 'sends greetings to his (friend) ...', as in the heading to Seneca's letter (No. 6). *C.* is for *Gaius* (in the early Latin alphabet *C* and *G* were both written *C*), and capital *V* is used both for *V* and (as here) for *U*.

1. **ex patria mea,** i.e. from the neighbourhood of Novum
Comum (Como) in Cisalpine Gaul, which was incorporated into
Italy proper in 42 B.C. **pro,** 'as'. **altissima,** 'most profound'.

2. **per saxa,** 'through the rock', but the visible stream, that
becomes a cascade, flows into the lake over the rocks. **excipitur . . .
facta,** 'is caught in a little artificial grotto', in a little dining-room
made by hand; it was probably hewn out of the rock by one of the
previous owners of the estate as a picnic place, though the roar of
the water today makes conversation beside the grotto difficult.
The absence of a conjunction between the last two verbs is called
'asyndeton'. *Larium lacum* is Lake Como. **paulum retentus,**
'after being checked there for a short time', lit. a little.

3. **huius mira natura (est),** 'the nature of this spring is remarkable'. **in die,** the preposition would be omitted in Ciceronian
Latin. What Pliny means by 'three times a day' (probably 'every
six hours') is discussed on page 61. **statis auctibus,** 'with a
regular increase'; the singular makes better sense in English.
deprenditur, 'can be observed', implying greater detail than
cernitur. The neuter *id*, 'it', refers to the whole action of the spring.
recumbis, either addressed to Licinius Sura or perhaps the
indefinite second person singular, like our 'you' or 'one'. No doubt
couches were provided for visitors on which to recline beside the
grotto, supported on the left elbow in the usual Roman fashion at
meals. **vel subtrahitur vel adsurgit,** 'it ebbs and flows', lit. 'it
either ebbs or flows'.

4. Supply *seu* before *anulum*; if you put a ring or anything else
on the dry (edge)'. **si . . . videas,** 'if you were to watch . . . you
would see both (actions happening) a second and a third time',
after six and then another six hours' interval. The change of
mood from indicative to subjunctive in the two conditional clauses
suggests that only guests staying at the villa would be likely to
return to the grotto to see the spring working again.

5. **aliquis,** here used as an adjective instead of *aliqui*; 'does
some hidden (lit. more hidden) current of air . . .'. **modo . . .
modo,** 'at one time . . . at another time'. **prout . . . expulsus,**
'as it blocks (the way) when forced in and leaves it free (lit. departs)
when forced out'. Pliny is here applying to a particular case his
uncle's theory, based on a Stoic idea that the world has its own
breath that causes natural phenomena, in this case entering 'the
mouth and outlet of the spring' and alternately blocking and
releasing the flow of water.

6. **quod . . . videmus,** 'we see this happen in . . . other (vessels) of the same kind', i.e. with long and narrow bottle-necks, as described in *quibus . . . exitus,* 'which have no wide and continually (lit. immediately) open outlet'. *ceteris,* 'the other', is here used for *aliis,* 'other'; it is neuter plural, as is shown by *illa,* 'those (vessels)'. *quamquam* is used here, as sometimes in English, without a finite verb, 'although tilted upsidedown', lit. face downwards and leaning. **per quasdam . . . quod effundunt,** 'hold back what they are pouring out with as it were repeated gurgling sounds on account of certain stoppages caused by the opposing (inrush of) air', a good description of the 'glug-glugging' noise made by liquids running out of an upturned bottle.

7. **oceano . . . fonti,** supply *est* with both words; 'has the spring also the same natural property as the sea', lit. is there to the spring the nature which there is to the ocean. **quaque ratione . . . hac** = *et hac ratione . . . qua,* the antecedent, *ratione,* being put inside the relative clause; 'and is this small amount of water alternately made to ebb and (lit. or) flow in the same (*hac*) way as (*qua*) the sea (*ille*) is driven forward or sucked back'. The Elder Pliny knew about the lunar attraction that causes tides (*Natural History,* 2, 232), but it seems from this passage that his nephew did not.

8. **ut . . . ita,** 'as . . . so'. **obvio aestu,** 'by the opposing tide', a force which is hardly perceptible in the almost tideless Mediterranean. **quod . . . repercutiat,** a consecutive or generic subjunctive, lit. such as drives back, but we can hardly say more than 'which drives back'. Pliny does not say what he imagines this 'something' to be, but the mention of contrary winds and tides seem merely to repeat the two previous theories put forward in §§ 5–6 and 7. All three of these theories, and the fifth in § 10, are equally impossible.

9. Here too *est* must be supplied with *certa mensura* and with *rivus;* 'is there a fixed amount (of water) in a hidden reservoir (lit. in hidden channels), and while it (*quae dum*) is accumulating what (i.e. the same quantity as) it had discharged the flow is smaller and slower, (but) when it has accumulated it, it gushes out faster and in greater volume'. This appears to be the nearest attempt at the correct explanation, that there is a natural siphon (see page 62), except that the flow ceases altogether for every alternate three hours instead of becoming 'smaller and slower'. Greek scientists and engineers, and their Roman successors or contemporaries, had been acquainted with the theory and use of siphons for several centuries

B.C., but generally on a small scale, e.g. for mixing liquids in containers, though King Eumenes II of Pergamum (*c.* 170 B.C.) supplied water to Pergamum by a siphon; but on account of leakages caused by faulty construction and high water-pressure the Romans preferred to convey water in aqueducts raised on arches or in underground pipes. In his very brief reference to the spring at Torno (see page 61) the Elder Pliny does not suggest a reason for the ebb and flow, though with his wide knowledge of science and nature he must have been familiar with the theory of siphons. But his non-scientific nephew, the Younger Pliny, evidently did not know about siphons (or about the cause of the tides); the *sipo* mentioned by him in X, 33 (not included in this book) refers to some kind of device used in fire-engines, perhaps something like our 'stirrup-pump'.

10. **nescio quod,** an adjective, from *nescio qui* (the substantive is *nescio quis*), in which the *nescio* does not change or effect the mood of the verb, lit. I do not know what . . . , i.e. 'some . . . or other'; here *nescio quod* agrees with *libramentum*, with *est* understood; 'is there some hidden and unseen force of water which when it has drained away starts the spring and sets it in motion and when it has filled up again checks and blocks it'. *libramentum* also means a 'counterpoise', which Pliny perhaps thinks of as sinking when full to block the passage of water and rising when empty to release it; but it is difficult to see how water in a counterpoise, or the counterpoise itself, could have a natural rise and fall.

11. **scrutare,** imperative. **potes,** 'you have the ability to do so'. **si satis . . . efficitur,** 'if I have described clearly what happens'. It would be interesting to know what reply Licinius gave to this letter, but Pliny did not preserve his correspondents' answers or refer to them in later letters.

7 (*b*). The Source of the Clitumnus (8, 8)

S. as usual stands for *salutem dicit*, 'sends greetings to . . .'.

1. **Clitumnum fontem,** we should say 'the source of the Clitumnus'. **si nondum,** *vidisti* must be understood here, and *te . . . vidisse* with *puto*, but we can omit these verbs in English and say 'if not yet, and I think not yet'. *narrasses* = *narravisses*, 'you would have told me', with *alioqui*, 'otherwise', taking the place of *si vidisses*. **vide, quem . . . vidi,** 'do go and see it, as I did . . .'. Supply *me* as the object of *paenitet*, 'I regret having put it off so

long', lit. it makes me repent me of my lateness, an impersonal verb.

2. **cupressu,** collective singular with plural meaning. The trees that used to grow on the lime-stone hillside have now all disappeared. *subter* here follows the noun that it governs. **exprimitur . . . imparibus,** 'gushes out of several channels of unequal size'; there are now eight main springs and countless smaller ones, from which the neighbouring village once took its name of Le Vene, Italian for 'The Channels'; the springs are now called I Fonti on maps. **eluctatus . . . gurgitem,** 'forcing its way out of the eddies that it makes'. **lato . . . vitreus,** 'it broadens out into (lit. with) a wide expanse, (so) clear and glassy'. **iactas,** 'that have been thrown into it', by priests or visitors who offered them as votive gifts to the river-god; the custom of visitors' throwing coins into the Fountain of Trevi at Rome (no connection with the small town of Trevi near the Clitunno) as an offering to obtain a return visit to the city, or into a wishing well in England to obtain a thing wished for, is kept up even today. *possis* is the indefinite second person singular again, 'you' or 'one', as in No. 7 (*a*), 3–4.

3. **ipsa sui copia,** 'by its own volume'; *sui* is the genitive of *se*, lit. by the very volume of itself. The slope of the ground, though almost imperceptible to the eye, must contribute more to the rapid flow of the stream than Pliny realised. **fons adhuc et iam,** '(one moment it is) still a spring and then (*iam*) . . .'. *amplissimum* is 'deep' rather than 'wide', for the Clitunno is not really a large river and *navium* are merely 'boats'; the genitive is objective, governed by *patiens*, 'able to bear boats'. **quas . . . perfert,** 'which it allows to pass one another (*transmittit*) and sends them on their way (*perfert*) even (*quoque*) when they are meeting and moving in opposite directions on a contrary course', lit. with contrary effort. *ipse, validus, idem,* and *adversus* are masculine to agree with *Clitumnus* understood. **illa, qua,** both adverbs, 'in the direction in which it is itself hurrying', i.e. downstream. **quamquam** is used again without a verb; 'although over level ground', a statement already discussed in a note at the beginning of this section. **remis non adiuvetur,** 'it does not need the assistance of oars', to send boats downstream. *idem* is lit. the same (stream), but we should say 'but at the same time it is with the greatest difficulty overcome in the opposite direction by means of oars . . .'.

4. **iucundum utrumque (est),** lit. each thing is pleasant, i.e. 'it is equally enjoyable for those who are boating (*fluitantibus*) for

amusement and pleasure to alternate toil . . . , whenever they change direction'. *flexerint* is perfect subjunctive in an indefinite clause, which in Ciceronian Latin would be indicative. The order of words in *laborem otio, otium labore* (ABBA instead of the usual ABAB) is called 'chiasmus', from the shape of the Greek letter *chi* (χ); there is another example in the next sentence, *fraxino multa, multa populo*, and in § 6; see also No. 3 (Sallust), 3, 1 and 3, and No. 8 (Tacitus), 1, 6 and 3, 5. **fraxino . . . populo,** another collective singular, which with *multa* can be singular in English too; 'with many an ash-tree, many a poplar'. **velut . . . adnumerat,** 'allows us to count (lit. counts) with their green reflection as though they were sunk (in the water)'. **certaverit,** a potential subjunctive, almost equivalent to a conditional sentence with the *si*-clause omitted; 'would rival snow', i.e. 'the water is as cold as snow, and as sparkling', lit. the colour does not give way to it; *color* must refer to the brightness, not the whiteness, of snow. For some general remarks on Pliny's love of the natural beauty and scenery, see the final paragraph of the Notes on this extract.

5. **templum,** not the little early Christian church of S. Salvatore, on the river bank, which was probably built with stones taken from the Roman shrine and is called 'the temple' on the map. **Clitumnus,** i.e. a statue of the river-god. **amictus . . . praetexta,** 'dressed and adorned with a magistrate's embroidered toga', either carved and painted on the statue or perhaps a real toga; ordinary citizens used to wear the plain white *toga virilis*, and only higher magistrates (and boys) the toga with a purple embroidered edge. **sortes,** these 'oracular lots' were tablets inscribed with prophecies more or less relevant to the enquiries likely to be made by worshippers at the temple; they were drawn at random by the priest and therefore 'testified to the presence and prophetic power of the deity', lit. that the deity was present and prophetic. **circa,** an adverb. **totidemque di,** lit. and as many gods, i.e. 'each one having its own god'. **sua cuique,** the nominative of the reflexive possessive adjective is often used with the dative of *quisque* (here with *est* understood); 'each one has his own cult', i.e. his own sanctity and worshippers. **quibusdam . . . fontes,** 'some of them indeed also have their own springs'. **praeter . . . ceterorum,** 'besides the one (which is) as it were the parent stream of the others'. **capite discreti,** 'with separate sources', lit. separated at the source; for these springs, see the second note on § 2. **flumini,** 'with the main stream', dative after *miscentur*. **transmittitur,** 'is spanned'.

6. **is (pons est)** . . . **profanique,** 'that bridge is the boundary between the sacred and the ordinary part of the stream'. **navigare . . . concessum (est),** 'it is permitted only (*tantum*) to sail, below (the bridge) to bathe as well'; to bathe in the sacred water would pollute it. **Hispellates,** the people of Hispellum, now Spello, 12 miles north of the springs. **divus,** the 'good' emperors (and Julius Caesar, not an emperor but the first to receive this honour) were deified after their death and worshipped as gods; *divus* can be translated as 'the late emperor' or 'the deified'; the emperor Augustus died in 14 A.D. **dono,** dative of purpose, 'as a gift'. Notice the 'chiastic' arrangement (explained in the note on § 4) of *balineum . . . praebent, praebent et* (= 'also') *hospitium.* The *balineum* was no doubt the usual Roman bathing establishment with hot air circulating in a 'hypocaust' under the floor to provide a 'Turkish' bath for visitors to the shrines. *nec desunt* . . . , 'there are also several . . .', lit. nor are there lacking. . . . **secutae . . . amoenitatem,** 'placed wherever the river is most beautiful', lit. following the beautiful scenery of the river.

7. **ex quo non capias,** 'from which you will not derive', a generic subjunctive, lit. of such a kind that. . . . **studebis,** 'you will be able to do some research'. **multa multorum inscripta,** 'many inscriptions written by many people', not formal *tituli* but the informal scribblings now called *graffiti*, here made by the hands of worshippers. Many such *graffiti* have been found in Pompeii and Herculaneum, towns which were buried by volcanic ashes or lava in the eruption of Vesuvius in A.D. 79. They include initials or names of lovers with the date of their meeting, election slogans, names of successful charioteers, 'tips' for chariot races long since run, humorous verses, in fact the usual material that is to be found scribbled on walls in all countries. An example is given overleaf. But we may hope that the writing on the temple-walls at the source of the Clitumnus were more reverent than this. *plura* here = *plurima,* 'most of them', and *nonnulla* is 'some of them'. **quamquam,** 'and yet'. **quae tua humanitas (est),** 'such is your good nature', i.e. you are of course (*vero*) too good-natured to laugh at any of them, however simply or badly they express the gratitude of the worshippers towards the god of the river; Pliny at once corrects his previous statement that Romanus will laugh at them.

This letter of Pliny is almost unique in Latin prose for its sensitive appreciation of the natural beauty of the source of the Clitumnus. Cicero in his *De Natura Deorum* (II, 98 *ff.*) writes in general

A ĎẎMIROR Jïⁱ·PARⱥE Ş·NŮⁿ CⓘCIDISŚE‾
QⱯ/I Ṭ.OṬ⁻ S C R I P TORⱯⱯ TAⱯDIAˑ SⱯSTINⱯAŞ

'I Wonder, O Wall'

This elegiac couplet was scratched on the wall of the amphitheatre at Pompeii (C.I.L. iv, 2487), and should run

> *admiror, paries, te non cecidisse ruinis*
> *qui tot scriptorum taedia sustineas,*

but the writer was so eager to get in the *te* that he started it after the *ad* of *admiror* and finally put it before instead of after *paries*; he could not remember the last word of the hexameter and put a dash instead. A rough rhyming translation is

> 'I wonder, O wall, that your stones do not fall,
> So scribbled upon by the nonsense of all.'

terms of the wonders of nature and of animal and human life, but not in praise of any particular landscape and mainly as evidence for the existence of the gods. Roman poets, especially Virgil in his *Georgics* and Horace in some of his *Odes*, e.g. III, 13, *Fons Bandusiae* (included in *Two Centuries of Roman Poetry*), provide us with many fine descriptions of Italian scenery, some of them inspired by this very river, as is mentioned in the Introduction to the piece. But Pliny is one of the very few prose authors who have written a poetic description of a place of natural beauty. The first four sections of this letter are worth re-reading with the object of seeing what a fine picture he paints of a place which retains today much, if not all, of its former charm, as may be seen to a certain extent from the photograph on Plate 7. Only a truly poetic imagination could have produced such a vivid description.

Tacitus

8. Britain and the British (*Agricola*, 10–12)

1.

1. **situm,** 'geographical position'. The plural *populos* refers to the different tribes living in Britain. **multis scriptoribus,** dative of the agent, often used with past passive participles, nearly always

with gerundives, and sometimes with other parts of passive verbs (*Gallis* in § 2 is an example of its use with a present indicative passive); for the earlier writers on Britain, see the Introduction to this piece (page 72). **non . . . ingenii,** 'not to make (*in*) a comparison of my diligence and ability (with theirs)'. **referam,** 'I shall describe'. **tum primum,** 'at this period for the first time'; Agricola's recent campaigns provided more accurate information about Britain, though in fact Tacitus mentions only eleven geographical names of places or peoples in this island, of which four are names of tribes. Agricola's conquest of Scotland lasted for 30 years, until it was abandoned in the time of Trajan. The antecedent of *quae* is *ea* understood, which is the subject of *tradentur*; 'matters which my predecessors adorned with an eloquent style because they were not yet (fully) discovered will be described with the truth of (established) facts.' *percoluere* = *percoluerunt.*

2. **quas . . . complectitur,** 'which Roman knowledge (of geography) includes'. **spatio ac caelo,** 'in extent and geographical position'; *caelum* here refers to the portion of the sky under which a country lay, as marked out by astronomers. **in . . . obtenditur,** 'faces Germany to the east . . .'; *Germania* began at the Rhine and (to the Romans) included Scandinavia. The map of Ancient Britain on page 73 and the description given above it shows clearly what Tacitus and his predecessors thought was the position and shape of Britain and the neighbouring coasts of Europe; the truth was not generally established until the time of Ptolemy (A.D. 150). **Gallis . . . inspicitur,** 'is actually in sight of Gaul . . .', lit. is seen by the Gauls, dative of the agent, as in § 1; Tacitus thought that the English Channel was equally narrow all along its length. **septentrionalia eius,** 'its northern shores'. **nullis contra terris,** 'there being no land opposite them', ablative absolute, with *positis* understood, or with *contra* used as an adjective.

3. **Livius,** the historian Livy, whose account of Caesar's invasions of Britain has been lost. **Fabius Rusticus,** a friend of Seneca, wrote a history of Nero's reign, also lost, which may have included a description of Britain. **eloquentissimi,** referring to literary style rather than to historical accuracy; 'Livy, the most eloquent (or simply "the best") of the old, Fabius Rusticus of the recent authors'. In *Germania* 28, 1 Tacitus calls Julius Caesar *summus auctorum*, 'greatest of historians', so it is strange that he does not here mention his description of Britain; perhaps he

thought that Caesar's account had been superseded by those of the later writers mentioned here. **oblongae . . . adsimulavere** (=-*erunt*), 'have compared the shape . . . to an elongated shoulder-blade or axe-head'. The reading *scapulae* instead of the MS *scutulae*, is suggested by R. M. Ogilvie, who thinks that *bipennis* here means a single-headed axe (*securis*) instead of the double-headed axe which it generally means in poetry. Figure 1 shows an axe (blade to the right),

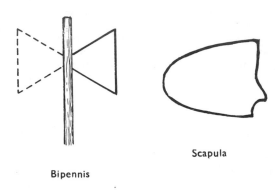

Scapula

Bipennis

with a dotted line showing the second blade of a double-axe, and figure 2 is a human shoulder-blade, of roughly similar shape. From the map on page 73 we see that Caesar and his predecessors thought that the whole island was approximately triangular or axe-shaped (with the cutting edge formed by the south coast). After hearing about Agricola's exploration of Scotland, Tacitus agreed that Britain was roughly triangular south of the Forth–Clyde isthmus, but said that north of that line a huge tract of land tapered northwards like a wedge. (*scutula* was thought by previous editors to mean a dish of elongated rhomboidal form, like a rectangle tilted to one side, but this has no resemblance at all either to a double- or a single-headed axe. **et est ea,** 'and indeed that is . . .'. **unde . . . fama,** 'from which also (comes) the report (that it has that shape) as a whole'; the 'triangular' shape of Britain of course does not take into account the indentations of the Bristol Channel and the Thames estuary. **transgressis,** dative of 'the person judging', like *aestimanti* in 2, 3; 'when one has crossed (into Caledonia)', lit. to those who have crossed. **spatium . . . tenuatur,** 'a . . . tract of land jutting out from the very extremity of the coast tapers as it were into a wedge'; *extremo iam litore* seems to refer to the Forth–Clyde isthmus, which a stranger might expect to be the most northerly extremity of Britain. *litore . . . tenuatur* is an accidental hexameter.

4. **novissimi maris,** 'of the remotest sea'. **tunc primum . . . adfirmavit,** 'then for the first time (i.e. during the governorship of Agricola, Tacitus' father-in-law, for which see page 78) definitely proved', what had been accepted as true by all writers since the time of Pytheas in *c.* 325 B.C. Tacitus describes in *Agricola* 38, 4 this voyage by a Roman fleet, which in fact only partly circumnavigated Britain, for it sailed round Cape Wrath and a little way down the west coast before returning to its starting place somewhere on the east coast of Scotland. In the previous summer (A.D. 83) a cohort of the German tribe of the Usipi serving as auxiliary troops in Britain mutinied and murdered their Roman officers. They then seized three galleys, sailed without pilots round the coast of Britain, almost certainly northwards from west to east, suffering great hardships on the voyage, during which they had to resort to cannibalism, and finally were captured as pirates by other German tribes and sold into slavery. A few of them were sold from one owner to another and eventually reached the Roman province of Gaul, where their remarkable adventure became known. Tacitus describes this first historical circumnavigation of Britain, in *Agricola* 28. The Orkneys were 'unexplored' (*incognitas*) but not 'unknown', for Pytheas may have put in there, and Mela and the Elder Pliny knew of them. The subject of *vocant* is 'the inhabitants', or the vague 'people' generally. **domuit,** surely in no more than a nominal conquest, though Agricola's men may have landed and explored the islands. **dispecta,** 'seen from a distance'. Thule is first mentioned by Pytheas as being a six days' voyage north of Britain; he may have meant Iceland. Thule here is perhaps Mainland, the largest of the Shetlands, or Foula, the highest. With *hactenus iussum* supply *est* and *progredi*, 'they were ordered to proceed (only) so far'.

5. The subject of *perhibent* is probably not 'people' generally but the Romans who were on this expedition; 'they say that the sea, which is sluggish and heavy to oarsmen (lit. to those rowing),

is not disturbed even by winds (i.e. still less by oars) as much (as other seas)'. Pytheas described the outer ocean as being a mixture of sea, land, and air, like jelly-fish (perhaps referring to half-melted ice), which could neither be walked on or sailed through; beyond this there was solid ice. But there is probably a reference here to the North Atlantic Drift, currents off the western shores of the Shetlands that together with the fog and absence of winds make it difficult for sailing ships to make headway; contrary winds and tides south of the islands sometimes cause sailing ships to remain motionless for several days. **credo,** 'I suppose'. **rariores (sunt),** 'are scarcer there'. *causa ac materia* is in apposition to *terrae montesque*; the Romans believed that such obstacles were the cause of strong winds. **tardius impellitur,** 'is set in motion more slowly'.

6. **neque . . . ac,** an unusual combination of conjunctions; 'it is both no part of this work ("characteristic" genitive) to enquire into . . . and moreover (*ac*) many writers have described them', such as the Greek authors Aristotle, Pytheas, and Posidonius, who all wrote about the tides. *aestus* is accusative plural. **unum addiderim,** a potential subjunctive, almost equivalent to a conditional sentence with the 'if'-clause omitted; 'one thing I would add'. **latius dominari,** 'hold wider sway'. **multum . . . ferre,** 'many tidal currents (partitive genitive) flow in various directions'; this translation takes *ferre* as an intransitive verb, but it may be transitive, with *mare* as the subject and *multum fluminum* the object, 'the sea carries many currents to and fro'. The order of words in *dominari mare, multum fluminum . . . ferre* is a 'chiasmus', for which see 3, 5, and the notes on No. 3 (Sallust), 3, 1 and No. 7 (Pliny), (*b*), 4. **litore tenus,** '(only) on (lit. as far as) the shore'; *tenus* is placed after the noun that it governs. **iugis . . . in suo,** 'it forces its way among highlands . . . , as though it were in its own domain', an apt description of the firths and sea-lochs of western Scotland, no doubt obtained from Agricola himself.

2.

1. **ceterum,** 'but', an adverb, really an adverbial accusative, lit. with regard to the rest, used by Tacitus to show that he is returning to his main subject after a digression on the geography of Britain. **qui . . . coluerint,** an indirect question depending on *parum compertum (est)*, with *et utrum fuerint* to be supplied before *indigenae*; 'it has not been fully discovered what people originally inhabited . . .

(and whether they were) natives or immigrants'. **ut inter barbaros,** 'as (might be expected) in the case of barbarians', who would not know their own origins. **habitus corporum,** 'their physical characteristics'. *sunt* must be supplied with this phrase, and something like *trahi possunt*; 'from that (variation several) arguments can be drawn'.

2. **Caledoniam habitantium,** 'of the inhabitants of Caledonia', lit. of those inhabiting . . . , an imitation of the Greek construction of the article with a participle. The absence of a conjunction (*et*) between *rutilae comae* and *magni artus* is called 'asyndeton'. The Germans and Celts both had reddish hair and large limbs, the Germans slightly more so, and were believed by the Romans to be of the same stock; the Caledonians were probably a mixture of the old native neolithic stock and of immigrant Celts. The Silures lived in south Wales, and their 'swarthy faces (and) generally curly hair' were probably due to their being immigrant Celts who intermarried with an earlier dark-skinned non-Aryan stock of the later Stone Age. Ethnologists give the name 'Iberian' to this race, which lived in various parts of the Mediterranean coastal area, including Spain, but it is unlikely that they came to Britain from the Iberian peninsula during the Iron Age; Tacitus' error in thinking that they did so arose from the false belief in '(the fact that) Spain lies (lit. is placed) opposite', *posita contra Hispania*, a phrase that is part of the subject of *fidem faciunt*, 'makes one believe that the pre-historic Spaniards . . .'. *contra* is an adverb, and the supposed position of Spain in relation to Britain is shown in the map on page 73. *eas sedes* is 'those districts', i.e. South Wales, where the Silures lived. **proximi . . . sunt,** '(those who are) nearest to the Gauls are also like (them)'; this refers to the similarity of the customs of the Kentish tribes to those of their kinsfolk on the opposite coastal-regions of Gaul, the Belgae, who crossed over to south-east Britain between about 125 and 50 B.C. (see page 71). **seu . . . seu,** the double conditional clause is unusual because the first *seu* has an ablative absolute and the second a finite verb; there is another (not quite similar) example in Part II, No. 16 (Tacitus), 2, 8; 'whether because the force of their (common) origin persists or (because) when (two) countries project (and approach each other) in different directions (i.e. north and south respectively) their geographical position has given (similar) characteristics to their physical appearance (lit. to their bodies)'; for *caeli*, see the note on *spatio ac caelo* in 1, 2.

3. **in universum aestimanti,** 'when one considers (the question) generally', lit. to one judging, like *transgressis* in 1, 3 (see the note there). **credibile est,** 'we can believe'. Tacitus was correct in this belief; see pages 71–74. **eorum . . . persuasiones,** 'you would find (in Britain) the sacred rites and religious beliefs (of the Gauls)', which the Gallic invaders had brought with them. This is no doubt a reference to Druidism (see page 72), of which Caesar gives an account in *B.G.* VI, 13–14, though he is probably wrong in saying that the cult originated in Britain; *deprendas* is a potential subjunctive, explained in the note on *addiderim* in 1, 7, but here it seems to differ little from 'you will find'; the second person singular is here indefinite, like our 'you' or 'one'. Supply *est* with *diversus* (and with *audacia* and *formido*), 'does not differ much (from that of the Gauls)'. At the time of Caesar's invasions in 55 and 54 B.C. the Celtic language seems to have been spoken in one form or another both in Gaul and in southern Britain and (probably) in the north of Scotland, and each dialect was understood by speakers of the other forms, so this statement of Tacitus is correct. No traces of a pre-Celtic language survive in any place-names in Britain. But practically nothing is known about the once widely-spread Celtic language, which had no alphabet of its own, and though the Druids, and probably others, could write in Greek and Roman characters, it produced no literature except some poetry transmitted orally by the Druids, and only names of people and places and a few inscriptions in Greek or Latin survive. **audacia . . . formido,** Caesar (*B.G.* III, 19, 6) and Livy (X, 28) say the same thing about the boldness of the Gauls at the beginning of a battle and their subsequent cowardice in defeat. **ubi . . . advenere** (= *-erunt*), 'when they have reached (the point of danger)'.

4. **plus ferociae,** 'more spirit', partitive genitive. **ut quos . . . emollierit,** a generic or consecutive subjunctive; 'as (they are people) whom . . .', lit. of such a kind that. . . . *nam* implies 'as is the case with the Gauls, for . . .'. **accepimus,** 'we have learned', e.g. in Caesar, *B.G.* VI, 24, 1, where Caesar says that at one time the Gauls surpassed the Germans in courage. *pariter = simul.* **Britannorum,** partitive genitive, 'this experience (*quod*) befell those of the British who were conquered some time ago', i.e. in the Claudian invasion of A.D. 43, when much of southern and central England was subdued (see pages 75, 78). **ceteri,** those tribes living in the north and west of the island. **fuerant,** i.e. before the Roman conquest under Julius Caesar, 59–51 B.C.

3.

1. **in pedite robur,** 'their main strength (lies) in their infantry', a collective noun; but Caesar says that the British had cavalry as well. **et curru,** 'with the chariot also'; Caesar calls these charioteers *essedarii* (*B.G.* IV, 33), Tacitus *covinnarii* (*Agricola* 35, 3). Later Roman writers say that the chariots were armed with scythes, but Caesar and Tacitus say nothing of this and there is no archaeological evidence to support it. **honestior (est),** 'is of nobler birth', i.e. the noble drove the chariot, while his clients of lower rank (probably one to each chariot) fought for him. So also in Caesar's time the British *auriga* drove the fighting man into battle and withdrew until it was time to pick him up again; but in Gaul (and in Homeric times) the charioteer was of lower, the fighter of higher rank. **olim,** Caesar mentions four kings in Kent (*B.G.* V, 22) who apparently accepted the orders of Cassivellaunus of the Catuvellauni as commander-in-chief of the British forces opposing the Romans. **nunc,** in the time of Tacitus no kings held power, because the people 'were drawn apart by factions and rivalry among the (various) chieftains'.

2. **nec aliud (est) . . . consulant,** 'nothing is more advantageous for us (in war) against . . . than the fact that they do not consult together for the common good'. **rarus . . . conventus,** 'a combination of two or three states for . . . (is) rare'. **singuli . . . universi,** 'as individual (tribes) . . . as a whole'.

3. **foedum (est),** 'is gloomy'. **asperitas frigorum,** 'excessive cold'; in *B.G.* V, 12, 7 Caesar says that the climate in Britain is more temperate than in Gaul, with less severe cold, a statement with which English people today would not agree. **ultra . . . mensuram (sunt),** 'exceeds the (usual) length in our (part of the) world', i.e. in Italy. Tacitus refers only to summer time; Caesar (*B.G.* V, 13, 3) verified the greater length of a summer's day in Britain by means of a water-clock, and the Elder Pliny (*N.H.* II, 186) was nearly correct in saying that the length of the longest day in Italy is 15 hours and in Britain 17 hours, which is true for a point midway between the north of Scotland and London. **extrema parte,** 'in the extreme north', a local ablative without *in*. **ut . . . internoscas,** 'so that you can distinguish between . . . by (only) a brief interval', five hours in the shortest summer night. *internoscas* is both consecutive and potential subjunctive (see the note on *addiderim* in 1, 5).

4. **quod si,** 'and if'; *quod* is an adverbial accusative, lit. with regard to which. *officiant* is subjunctive in a *si*-clause in *oratio obliqua* depending on *adfirmant*; 'if clouds do not block the view'. *fulgorem* is the 'glow' of the sun, which can be seen even in the Midlands long after sunset on a clear summer night. The subject of the infinitives is *solem* understood, and *transire* means 'passes along the horizon'; in fact it is just below the horizon, but the glow does not last all night even in the north of Scotland. For *adfirmant*; see the note on *vocant* in 1. 4. **scilicet . . . cadit,** 'in fact the flat extremities (lit. most distant and flat parts) of the earth, with (only) a low shadow, do not throw the darkness up high, and night falls below the (level of the) sky and stars'. Tacitus seems to have regarded the earth as a disc, flat at the edges but with mountains elsewhere, surrounded by the ocean and with the sky as an inverted bowl, set with stars, above it; night was the shadow of the earth cast by the sun below it, but at the edges, where the sun was only just below the earth, the shadow was so low that it did not darken the sky. It is strange that Tacitus apparently did not know that the earth is a sphere, a fact that was known to the Greeks (Pythagoras in the sixth century B.C. and Aristotle in the fourth century) and to educated Romans like Cicero and the Elder Pliny.

5. **solum (est) . . . patiens frugum,** 'the soil can bear (all) produce except . . .'; *frugum* and *pecudum* are objective genitives, and the order of words in *patiens frugum pecudumque facundum* is another 'chiasmus' (ABBA instead of ABAB), as in 1, 6; see the references to Sallust and Pliny in the note on that passage. **cetera . . . sueta,** 'the other crops which usually grow in . . .'; *calidioribus terris* is a local ablative without *in*. **tarde . . . proveniunt,** the subject is of course *fruges*, though *pecudum* was mentioned last; the natural order of events is reversed, for emphasis, and the absence of a co-ordinating conjunction ('asyndeton') suggests 'though . . . yet'. **eademque . . . causa,** 'and the reason for both facts (is) the same'.

6. Some gold was mined in Carmarthenshire, and silver (only in combination with lead) in the Mendips, Shropshire, Flintshire, and Yorkshire; tin in Cornwall, and iron ore in the Weald of Sussex, Norfolk, and the Forest of Dean. **pretium** =*praemium*, 'the reward for victory' (objective genitive), but it is unlikely that the hope of mining precious metals influenced Claudius in his decision to invade Britain in A.D. 43. **gignit et,** 'also produces'. The Elder Pliny (*N.H.* IX, 116) calls British pearls *parvos et*

decolores, 'small and discoloured'. **quidam,** 'some writers'.
artem abesse legentibus, 'that those who gather them lack the skill
(to dive for them)'. **in rubro mari,** the Indian Ocean, or perhaps
only the Persian Gulf, or the Red Sea. **saxis avelli,** 'are torn from
the rocks', either dative after a verb of taking away or ablative of
separation depending on the preposition compounded in the verb;
the infinitive and the subjunctive *expulsa sint* ('thrown up on the
shore'), depend on *arbitrantur*. **crediderim,** 'I should believe',
potential subjunctive, like *addiderim* in 1, 7. **naturam,** 'quality';
if the pearls were really good, the greed of the Romans (*nobis*)
would surely have found a way of gathering them.

PART II

CICERO

9 (*a*). An Orator Defies Death (*Philippic* II, 118 to end)

1. **respice . . . M. Antoni,** 'Antony, think, I beg you, at long
last, of your country . . .'. Everything in this sentence is calculated
to suggest a last desperate appeal. *respicere* is often used of the
concern the gods show for men, and men, by implication, should
show for their country. *quaeso*, the older alternative form to
quaero, is used of direct personal pleading. *aliquando* indicates
something overdue, almost too late: 'at the eleventh hour' as we
say. *rem publicam* and *M. Antoni* are juxtaposed, hinting at the
bond between self and country which Cicero suggests Antony
ought to have and never has had. And Antony is addressed
directly by name. *Antoni*, the usual vocative form of nouns in
-ius. **quibus . . . considera,** 'think of your forbears, not your
associates', lit. those from whom (ablative of origin) you have
sprung, not (those) with whom you live. *vivas*, subjunctive in a
dependent question. Cicero's mention of 'forbears' refers in
particular to M. Antonius, Antony's grandfather (143–87), consul
in 99, who lost his life in opposing the revolutionary supporters of
Marius; he was a distinguished orator and one of the chief spokes-
men in Cicero's dialogue *De Oratore*. (Perhaps also to Antony's
father, M. Antonius Creticus (died 72) for his part in the campaigns
against Sertorius and the pirates (74–72), though he was none too
successful here and shared his son's extravagant habits.) **mecum,
ut voles,** 'let your future relationship with me be as you please',

G

lit. deal (some such imperative as *age* or *redi in gratiam* being understood) with me as you will wish.   Note the precise tense usage in *voles* — Cicero is thinking of the future, not the present. **redi . . . in gratiam,** 'reconcile yourself with your country', lit. return into favour with. . . . **sed . . . videris,** 'but your behaviour is for you to decide', lit. you will have seen about yourself.   The future perfect is used as a polite imperative.   **ego . . . profitebor,** 'as for me, I shall make a personal declaration', lit. speak out myself about myself.

    2. **defendi . . . senex,** 'when I was a young man, I defended the state; in my old age I shall not forsake it'.   This splendid sentence, set beside an English translation, well illustrates the twofold strength of Latin: (*a*) its economy — English needs 19 words, 14 of them trivial sounding monosyllables, to say what Cicero says in 6; (*b*) the flexibility of order which an inflected language enjoys: verb — object — subject balanced against verb — object (understood) — subject.   Note the idiom *adulescens,* 'as a young man', *senex,* 'as an old man' (so also *puer,* 'as a boy' =in my boyhood) which furthers the economy of words.   In *adulescens* Cicero is referring with justifiable pride to his early career as a barrister when, in 80, aged 26, by defending Roscius Amerinus, he defied Sulla's powerful former slave Chrysogonus; and in 70, still only in his thirties, when he challenged Verres (praetor in Sicily in 75 when Cicero was his quaestor) and all the abuses of provincial government by championing the Sicilians against their governor.   He probably also included his suppression of the Catilinarian conspiracy in 63 (see page 100), for the Romans regarded their *adulescentia* as extending to age 45, when they ceased to be liable for military service.   Those who dismiss Cicero in his later life as weak and vacillating too easily forget his earlier courage.   **contempsi Catilinae gladios,** a direct reference to the armed conspiracy of Catiline.   Juvenal sarcastically quotes these words, after deriding Cicero's poetry, when he says:

> Antoni gladios potuit contemnere, si sic
> omnia dixisset.

(See *Two Centuries of Roman Poetry,* page 114, and note on page 219).   Note the careful balance of this sentence, responding to the balance of the one before.   **quin etiam,** 'on the contrary', lit. how not even — of something more striking than what has just been said. **obtulerim,** 'I should offer', potential subjunctive, with some such condition as 'if I were asked' understood. The perfect subjunctive is often used, where the present might be expected, of a cautious statement. So *dixerim, crediderim*, 'I should be inclined to say, believe'. **si repraesentari . . . potest,** 'if by my death the freedom of the state can be redeemed here and now'. *repraesentare* is a specialist word of the Roman business world meaning 'to secure by cash payment'. Cicero's metaphor says in effect that he would pay 'in cash' by his death for the restoration of liberty in Rome. Note that this conditional clause does not depend on *obtulerim* but is a separate assumption which for the moment Cicero regards as real (hence the indicative *potest*). He says in effect: granted that by my death etc., then I would offer my life if I were asked. **ut . . . parturit,** 'so that at long last the birth pangs of the Roman people can deliver the child (liberty) with which it has now so long been in labour'. It may seem that on close scrutiny Cicero's elevated language, like some of Shelley's poetry, has got out of hand. Rome has long been pregnant with a child — liberty — of which she is at last to be delivered by a cash payment in the currency of Cicero's death. But great oratory gains its effect from emotion and atmosphere, which can dazzle the critic's microscope.

    3. **abhinc . . . viginti,** in 63, in the Fourth Speech against Catiline. **hoc ipso in templo,** the temple of Concord, where that speech was delivered and where the present speech, though in fact never delivered but circulated as a pamphlet, was delivered in Cicero's imagination. **negavi . . . consulari,** 'I declared that death could not come prematurely to a man who had been consul'. Cicero echoes his own words (*Cat.* 4, 3): *nam neque turpis mors forti viro potest accidere neque immatura consulari,* 'for to a brave man death cannot come as a disgrace, nor prematurely to one who has been consul'. **quanto . . . seni,** 'now much more truthfully can I say this of myself now that I am old'. *posse mortem immaturam esse* is understood from the previous sentence, and *mihi* with *seni*, lit. by how much more truly shall I deny that death can be premature to (me) an old man. **patres conscripti,** 'Senators', lit. enrolled fathers, the formal term of address to members of the Senate who were officially enrolled by the *censor* either as sons of Senators or after holding the office of quaestor or above. **optanda,** 'something to be desired'. **perfuncto,** 'after I have discharged', agreeing with *mihi* and governing the ablative *rebus*. **rebus . . . gessi,** 'the office I have attained and the deeds I have performed'. The meaning of *rebus* is determined by its context, and here differs from the two

verbs that govern the relatives which refer to it: first it means 'office' (Cicero was quaestor and consul) with *adeptus sum* (the regular phrase for attaining office is *magistratum adipisci*); then the 'deeds', with *gessi*, which he carried out while in office. **duo modo haec,** 'these two things only'. **hoc . . . maius . . . nihil,** 'nothing greater than this'. *maius* agrees with *nihil* and *hoc* is ablative of comparison. **ut . . . mereatur,** 'that each man's fortunes may match his service to the state', lit. that it may so turn out to each as each deserves of the state.

9 (*b*). Ethics of a Salesman (*De Officiis* III, 54–55)

1.

vendat, 'suppose he sells', lit. let him sell, jussive subjunctive used here of a hypothesis or imaginary case. **aedes,** 'house', plural in this sense; in the singular it means 'temple'. **vitia,** 'flaws', 'defects'. **norit,** contracted form of *noverit*, perfect subjunctive with present meaning, for *noscere* means to 'get to know'. *norit* and *ignorent* are either generic subjunctives, 'of a kind which he knows about', or they may be jussives again, taking *quae* as a connecting relative (= *et ea*): 'and suppose he knows of them, others do not'. Note the 'asyndeton' (omission of a conjunction) in *norit, ignorent*, emphasising the contrast. **habeantur salubres,** 'suppose it has the reputation of being healthy', lit. is held (to be). Note the subjunctive, again jussive, as Cicero fills in the details of his imaginary case. **ignoretur,** 'suppose it is not realised that', impersonal passive. **apparere serpentes,** 'that vermin are to be found', lit. appear. **male materiatae,** 'badly timbered', from *materia*, 'timber', the commonest 'material' of ancient construction, hence its modern extended use.

2. **quaero, si . . . num . . . fecerit,** 'I ask whether he acted . . . if . . .'. *dixerit, vendiderit, putarit* (contracted form of *putaverit*) and *fecerit* are all perfect subjunctives: the last in a dependent question, the others in subordinate clauses in a dependent question. Note that *num* means 'whether' and *si* (which never means 'whether' or 'if' in a question) introduces the conditions. **pluris multo,** 'for a much higher price'. *pluris* is genitive of price (the genitive being used instead of the usual ablative for the words *pluris, minoris, tanti* and *quanti*) and *multo* is an ablative of measure of difference, lit. by much. **quam . . . putarit,** 'than he thought he would (sell it)'. **iniuste aut improbe,** 'unjustly or dishonourably', i.e. against the

law or against the moral code. These *may* coincide, but not necessarily, and Cicero is very precise in his language.

3. **ille vero,** 'certainly he has', supply *fecit*. **Antipater,** a Stoic philosopher who died shortly before 44 B.C. He introduced the Younger Cato (see No. 10 (Sallust), page 101) to the Stoic philosophy and wrote a number of books whose titles include *On Duty*, *On the Soul* and *On Marriage*. **quid est . . . monstrare . . . si hoc non est,** 'for what else is not showing the way to a man who is lost . . . if it is not (the same as) this', i.e. this (*emptorem pati ruere . . .*) is exactly the same as not showing the way to. . . . **quod . . . sanctum est,** 'which at Athens is forbidden under penalty of public cursing'. **ruere,** 'make a hasty deal', lit. rush, or perhaps 'fall into ruin'. **in maximam fraudem incurrere,** 'incur a heavy loss'. *fraus* here is a legal term meaning 'loss of property' not 'deception'. It is thus used, for instance, in the Twelve Tables of the (Roman) Law. **plus etiam est,** 'it is even worse', lit. more. **scientem . . . inducere,** 'deliberately (lit. knowing) to lead another astray (lit. into error)' *scientem* is accusative case in agreement with *aliquem* understood, subject of the infinitive, lit. it is (someone) knowing to. . . . Note that *alterum*, here used for *alium*, does not agree with *errorem* but is the object of *inducere*, while *errorem* is governed by *in*.

2.

1. **Diogenes,** of Sinope on the Black Sea, a leading representative of the Cynic school of philosophy, lived in the fourth century B.C. and was renowned for his simple mode of life and rejection of the comforts of civilisation — a creed glamourised by the story of his living in an earthenware tub in Athens. The Cynics derived their name either from the gymnasium of Cynosarges in Athens, where they had their school, founded by Antisthenes, a pupil and friend of Socrates, or from the Greek κύων, *kyon* (a dog), because of their canine contempt for knowledge and current morality. Their concern was the practical side of morality — well illustrated in the earthy realism of Diogenes in this passage — and they regarded 'virtue', secured by freedom from wants and desires, as the sole basis for happiness. In this way they have something in common with Buddhism and the 'non-attachment' of Aldous Huxley's *Ends and Means*. Their model was the Greek hero Heracles. **num . . . coegit,** 'he did not force you to buy it, did he?', suggesting a negative answer. **ne hortatus quidem est,** 'did not even encourage you to'. *ne . . . quidem* wraps itself round the word to which

it applies, rather like *ne . . . pas* in French. Here the sense is 'did not even encourage you, let alone force you to buy'. **quod non placebat,** 'something he did not like', lit. what was not pleasing, object of *proscripsit*. **quod si qui,** 'but if those who. . . .' **proscribunt,** 'advertise . . . as being . . .'. **aedificata ratione,** 'well built', lit. built by plan. **multo minus, qui . . .** 'much less guilty of deception are those who . . .', lit. much less are thought to have deceived, *existimantur fefellisse* being understood from earlier in the sentence. *multo* is ablative of measure of difference. **laudarunt,** contracted form of *laudaverunt*.

2. **iudicium emptoris est,** 'the choice (lit. judgement) is the buyer's', reflecting a basic principle of Roman law, *caveat emptor*, 'let the buyer beware'. **fraus,** 'deception' here, not 'loss' as in 1, 3 above. **quae** is interrogative, 'what . . . ?'. **sin autem,** 'but if again . . .' introducing a second counter to Antipater's argument. **praestandum est,** 'is to be made good', of which *dictum omne* ('everything that has been said') is the subject. **quod . . . putas,** 'do you think what has not been said must be made good', lit. what . . . said, that must be. . . . The demonstrative *id* emphasises the relative clause which anticipates and defines it. **quam venditorem,** 'than for the seller to . . .', accusative case for the subject of an infinitive as in 1, 3 above: *scientem . . . inducere*. **eius rei quam vendat vitia,** 'the defects of what(ever) he is selling'. *vendat* is generic subjunctive, of a generalised statement. **domini iussu,** 'on the owner's instruction'. **praeco,** the auctioneer, who announced the sale by a trumpet blast. **quam si praedicet,** subjunctive of *praedicare*, 'as if he were to say . . .', in an unreal comparison following *tam absurdum*.

9 (*c*). Domestic Design (*Epistulae ad Quintum Fratrem*
III, 1, 1–2, 4–5)

In the title, with SALUTEM, supply DAT, lit. gives greetings. This is the Roman equivalent of our 'Dear Quintus'.

1.

1. **in Maniliano,** 'at your Manilian estate' somewhere near Cicero's villa at Arpinum. Its exact location is unknown, or indeed whether the prefix of the word refers to a place or a person named Manilius who formerly owned it. The suffix *-anum* is often applied to villas or estates, as in Cicero's own villas at Tusculum

(*Tusculanum*) and Formiae (*Formianum*) or the 'estate' reserved for prisoners in Rome, the *Tullianum*, an underground prison named after the Roman king Servius Tullius (see Part I, No. 4) who by tradition had it built. **Diphilum,** the architect responsible for the development of Quintus Cicero's villa. **Diphilo tardiorem,** 'going slow even for Diphilus', lit. slower than Diphilus (himself), an idiom borrowed from Greek, Cicero being more or less bilingual in Latin and Greek. *Diphilo* is ablative of comparison. **nihil ei restabat,** 'nothing was left for him (to do)', i.e. he had finished everything except. . . . **ambulationem,** 'cloister' or 'promenade', which might be covered or open. Cicero was particularly fond of these as suitable places to sit or pace about in while discussing philosophy. He called his own at Tusculum a 'gymnasium' and asked Atticus (*Ad Att.* I, 6 and 10) to look out for suitable statues to adorn it. **aviarium,** 'aviary'. The Romans frequently had birds as pets. Catullus' lady-love, Lesbia, had a favourite sparrow (*Two Centuries of Roman Poetry*, page 37 and Plate 3a) and Ovid wrote a mock lament on the death of a pet parrot (*Amores* II, 6), while in Petronius Echion's son was a fancier of goldfinches (No. 13, 4, *A Proud Father*). **pavimentata porticus,** 'paved cloister', clearly different from the *ambulatio* mentioned above as unfinished. This would be a square or rectangular colonnade of the type that surrounded the garden of well-to-do Romans' houses (see Plate 13), called the 'peristyle' from the pillars which enclosed it (*style* is the Greek for 'pillar'). **quod . . . postea quam,** 'which I did not fully appreciate until', lit. which appeared to me now at last after. *nunc* (or *tum*) *denique* is a common phrase meaning 'then and not till then'. **tota patet,** 'it was fully opened'. *patet* is present tense because the verb expresses the state of being open rather than the act of opening. **politae sunt,** columns of houses and temples were regularly polished and often painted to catch the full glory of the Mediterranean sun.

  2. **totum . . . concinnum sit,** 'everything depends on the stucco harmonising, which will be my concern', lit. everything is in that, which will be a care to me, so that. . . . *curae* is predicative dative and *sit* is subjunctive in a result clause. Cicero may be thinking of the choice of colour for the stucco on the walls, or he may have in mind decorations or pictures of the type found on the walls of houses in Pompeii and Herculaneum: in a letter to Atticus (I, 10, 3) he is concerned about the choice of figures to include on the stucco of the *atrium* walls (*typos . . . quos in tectorio atrioli possim*

includere).   **recte fieri,** 'to be being properly laid'.   **cameras,**
'ceilings'.   *camera* properly means an 'arch' or 'vaulted roof' (from
the Greek word meaning 'to bend') but its use was extended to
include first the whole roof or ceiling, then, internationally, to
embrace the whole room: Italian *camera*, German *Kammer*,
Russian *komnata*, French *chambre*, English *chamber*.   Finally it
was applied to any box-shaped object or confined space: so we
speak of a 'meeting *in camera*' i.e. in secret and also apply it to any
photographic apparatus, from the original box cameras of earlier days.

3. **quo loco . . . fiat,** 'as for the place in the cloister where
they tell me you write that a small entrance-hall is to be built', lit. in
which place in the cloister they say you write that. . . .   *scribere* is
followed by a dependent command here as it is used of a written
order.   The subject of *aiunt* is presumably Diphilus and the
builders who showed Cicero round the villa.   **mihi . . . magis
placebat,** 'I liked it better as it is', lit. it pleased me more; it is not
clear from this whether Cicero means that he prefers (*a*) a small
secondary *atrium* sited elsewhere than in the cloister (some of the
larger Roman houses like the House of the Vettii and the House of
the Fauns at Pompeii had one) or (*b*) no second smaller *atrium* at
all.   **satis loci . . . atriolo,** 'enough room for a smaller hall', i.e. in
the cloister if Cicero means there is an *atriolum* sited elsewhere.
But the rest of the sentence implies that there should be no smaller
atrium at all and that (*b*) above is the correct interpretation.
neque fere . . . fieri, 'nor is it generally usual' (to have a second
atrium or *atriolum*).   **atrium maius,** 'a larger hall', i.e. than the
present one, which seems to suggest that the main hall is too small
to justify the existence of an *atriolum*.   **adiuncta . . . membra,**
'bedrooms and apartments of that kind opening off it'.   *membra*
is here used of rooms which are attached to ('open off') the hall as
limbs are to the body.

4. **quam primum,** 'as soon as possible', lit. how very soon,
with some form of *posse* understood, a common idiom formed by
quam and a superlative adjective or adverb.   **assa,** 'Turkish baths'
or 'hot room'; access to these would be from the central changing
room (*apodyterium*), as in the larger Stabian Baths at Pompeii, and
seem to have been either at basement level or on the ground
floor with bedrooms on the first floor above them.   **ut eorum
vaporarium . . . cubiculis,** 'that their chimney was (or "would
have been") sited under the bedrooms'.   This arrangement of
Diphilus, in a house designed for a hot climate, defies comment.

5. **subgrande cubiculum,** 'the fair-sized bedroom'. The prefix *sub-* usually adds the meaning 'somewhat' or 'rather', and appears in our word 'subfusc', of the darkish suits worn by men on formal occasions. **hibernum alterum,** 'the other winter one' (bedroom). **ampla . . . posita,** neuter plural, agreeing with both bedrooms. **loco posita,** 'in the right position', lit. placed in their (proper) place. **ambulationis uno latere,** 'on one side of the promenade'. **eo . . . balneariis,** 'the one nearest the baths'. Though it is not possible from the information in this letter to visualise clearly the plan of the Manilian villa, the siting of these two winter bedrooms both near the *ambulatio,* whose aspect would doubtless have been towards the sun, and the baths would ensure the maximum warmth in winter.

6. **columnas . . . collocarat,** 'Diphilus had got the columns neither perpendicular nor opposite one another'. *collocarat,* contracted form of *collocaverat.* Once again Diphilus had blotted his copybook. Without seeing his handiwork we cannot be sure whether *e regione* means 'in a straight line' i.e. with the two rows of pillars exactly parallel, or 'equidistant'; whether, diagrammatically, the pillars were at fault by being placed

thus: 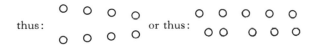 or thus:

Perhaps Cicero meant both faults. **scilicet . . .** 'of course he'll have to . . .'. *demolietur* is a 'military future', equivalent to an imperative, like the drill sergeant's 'squad will advance'.

7. **aliquando,** 'one of these days', sarcastic. **perpendiculo et linea,** ablatives governed by *uti.* The *perpendiculum* is a builder's plumb-line, consisting of a plank with a hole towards the bottom and a ball of lead suspended from the top by string of a length to enable the lead ball to fit into the hole. If the pillar is truly perpendicular, the string will be flush with the plank and the lead ball half inside the hole as shown overleaf. *linea,* though sometimes also used of a plumb-line, here appears to be a measuring tape for checking that the pillars are equidistant in each direction. **omnino,** 'all things considered'. In view of the practice of builders and of Cicero's own earlier remarks about Diphilus — *Diphilo tardiorem* — perhaps 'a few months' for completion was

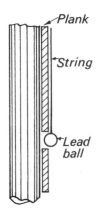

optimistic. But the key may lie in *Caesius*, of whom we know nothing, except that he appears from a reference to him in a later sentence in the letter (not included here) to have been a kind of clerk of the works. If his name was some sort of *cognomen* or nickname (from *caedere*, 'to beat'), equivalent to 'Basher', this would explain the assurance of Cicero's words *curat enim diligentissime*, 'keeps a close eye on him'.

2.

1. **Idibus Septembribus,** 'on 13 September', the Ides of the month being on the 13th except in March, July, October and May, when they were on the 15th. **Laterio,** another property of Quintus Cicero in Arpinum. **opus publicum,** 'a public highway'. Main roads were the responsibility of the state and were maintained by the aediles, though their original building was often undertaken by higher magistrates, some of whom gave their names to the roads like the Via Appia, the Via Aurelia and the Via Flaminia, which retain their original names to this day. Minor roads to farms or estates were the responsibility of those through whose properties they passed, though not by 'road charges' such as are levied today on residents in new housing estates, but personally or by using their own labourers or slaves. The Elder Cato, in his handbook on farming (*De Re Rustica*) reminds his readers of this obligation.

CL passus, '150 (Roman) paces'. The Roman pace was a double one, equivalent to five Roman feet. But as the latter was somewhat shorter than ours (·97 British feet), for the Romans, like the modern Italians, were of somewhat smaller average build than ours, the 150 paces (=750 Roman feet) of this stretch of road would have been about 725 feet or just over 240 yards. **sum enim ipse mensus,** 'for I paced it out myself'. **ponticulo,** note Cicero's fondness for diminutives in his *Letters,* seen in this and *atriolum* earlier. These were common in spoken Latin and are an important element derived from it in modern Italian. Compare Catullus' use of them and the note in *Two Centuries of Roman Poetry,* page 173 (on *Veraniolum*). **ad Furinae,** 'by the temple of Furina', *templum,* governed by *ad,* being understood as in 'St. Paul's', where church or cathedral is understood. *Furina* is an old Italian goddess about whom little was known even in Cicero's time. Cicero connects her tentatively (*ut ego interpretor, De Natura Deorum* III, 18, 46) with the Greek Furies or Eumenides; and Varro says she had a priest assigned and a festival on 23 July, the *Furinalia* (too late in the year to appear in the surviving books of Ovid's *Fasti,* which terminate in June). **Satricum versus,** 'in the direction of Satricum', a small town on the Appian Way, now Casale di Conca, near Anzio. Note the position of *versus,* after the name of the place.

2. **pulvis . . . iniecta est,** 'the road has been surfaced with earth, not gravel', lit. earth, not gravel has been thrown on. **mutabitur,** 'will be changed', i.e. properly surfaced with gravel. **aliter duci non posse,** (the road) 'could not have gone any other way'. **per Lucustae . . . Varronis,** 'through Lucusta's or Varro's land', *agrum* being understood. Compare *ad Furinae* (*templum*) above. Lucusta and Varro were owners of the neighbouring estates to Quintus'. **probe munierat,** 'had made up properly'. *munire* refers to the elaborate foundations and various layers of a properly built Roman road.

3. **aggrediar et . . . commovebo,** 'I will get onto him and, as I think, stir him up'. **M. Taurum . . . promisisse,** 'M. Taurus — I hear he gave you a promise'. **qui nunc Romae erat,** 'who *is* now at Rome'. *erat* is an 'epistolatory imperfect'. It was a convention of Roman letter-writing that the writer composed his letter from the point of view of the recipient, and thus often used the imperfect tense of events which were present to him but would be past when the letter came to be read. Taurus *is* at Rome when Cicero is writing; by the time Quintus received the letter he could

have left — hence *erat*.   **de aqua . . . ducenda,** 'about channelling water through his farm'.   The passage of a watercourse through private property was an important matter in ancient times because of the intense flooding that occurred in the rainy season.   The speech of Demosthenes *Against Callicles* is an amusing example of the kind of litigation that could arise over watercourses — worthy of a place among A. P. Herbert's *Misleading Cases*.

4. **sane probavi,** 'I thought very highly of'.   *sane* intensifies the word to which it applies and is particularly common in conversational Latin, as in Cicero's letters and Catullus' short poems.   **ecquid** (=*numquid*) **ei . . . mandavisses,** 'whether you had given him any instructions . . .'.   **aedificatiuncula,** 'little place', another splendid example of the use of diminutives in conversational Latin.   Clearly the villa at Laterium was far less pretentious than the 'Manilian place'.   **Lateri,** is locative case.

5. **eius operis HS X̄V̄Ī conductorem fuisse,** 'had contracted for the work there for a figure of 16,000 sesterces'.   The bar over X̄V̄Ī indicates that the sum is expressed in units of 1000 sesterces (of which HS is an abbreviation).   The rough modern equivalent value of the sesterce, the main unit of Roman coinage, still appears in some books as 2½d, but this takes no account of recent inflation.   The Italian Professor Bagnani put it more realistically at 1s 9d in 1956, and the figure today should be at least 2s (10 new pence), making the sum here mentioned something like £1600.   **multa addidisse . . . ad pretium,** 'you had added many items to the work, (but) nothing to the price'.   Quintus evidently drove a hard bargain and paid the penalty.   **omisisse,** 'had let it drop'.

6. **me hercule,** a common oath.   *hercule* is vocative of Hercules, and some imperative like *audi* or *defende* is understood, governing *me*; or the phrase may be an abbreviation of *me Hercules iuvet*, 'may Hercules help me'.   Swearing by the strong man of Greece is a fit way of emphasising a statement, rather like our 'by George', no doubt St. George of England.   **te illa . . . addere,** 'your carrying out the proposed addition', lit. that you should add those things as you had decided.   The accusative and infinitive clause *te illa addere* is the subject of *placet*.   **quae nunc est,** 'in its present form', lit. which it now is.   **tamquam philosopha . . . quae obiurget . . . insaniam,** 'seems to be like a moralist with a mission to reprove the frivolity of the other villas (in the area)'.   *obiurget* is subjunctive in a relative clause of purpose: Cicero is playfully suggesting that the villa in its present austere form has the purpose of reproaching

other villas. The practice of investing their villas with a personality was a not uncommon conceit of the Romans. Cicero, quoting Homer, describes his villa at Arpinum as a 'rugged but kindly nurse' (*Ad Att.* I. 11), no doubt thinking of its rugged site in the Apennines, while the Younger Pliny (*Ep.* IX, 7) had two villas on Lake Como, one of which he called Tragedy because it was raised above the lake on rocks or piles like the buskins (high boots) worn by actors in tragedy, the other Comedy because it lay at the water's edge, as if wearing the low slippers worn by actors in comedy. Cicero, while giving his blessing to Quintus' proposed improvements, seems to regret the loss of austerity to the place caused by his brother's attempt to keep up with the local villa-owning Joneses.

7. **verum tamen,** 'all the same'. Quintus is probably to be understood as the object of *delectabit*: 'the extension (*illud additum*, lit. that (being) added) will please you at any rate'. **topiarium,** 'the landscape gardener'. **qua . . . qua,** 'both . . . and'. **basim,** 'the foundation wall'. **intercolumnia ambulationis,** 'the spaces between columns in the promenade'. **denique illi palliati,** 'in fact those Greek figures'. The *pallium* was the Greek cloak, and the Romans made a distinction, in their early comedies, between those performed in Greek dress — *fabulae palliatae*, and in Roman dress — *fabulae togatae*. The placing of statues between columns was common practice: Cicero (*In Verrem* II, 1, 19) refers to *signa omnibus intercolumniis disposita* ('statues erected in all the spaces between columns'). **topiariam facere,** 'to behave like topiary artists'. *artem* is understood with *topiariam*. **hederam vendere,** 'to show off the ivy'. *vendere* often has the sense of 'showing off' or 'displaying for approval' as a salesman displays his wares. **iam . . . muscosius,** 'now nothing is cooler or more mossy than the changing-room'. *apodyterio* is ablative of comparison. Though small this modest villa still seems to have been well-appointed, with *ambulatio* and baths, implicit in the word *apodyterio*.

9 (d). Domestic Discord (*Epistulae ad Atticum* V, 1, 3–4)

1.

1. **ut,** 'when'. **Arpinas,** 'my estate at Arpinum', a neuter adjective agreeing with *praedium* understood. Arpinum, some 60 miles south-east of Rome, was Cicero's birthplace, and this villa was a favourite haunt of his (see previous passage No. 9 (c), 2, 6). **nobis**

... **fuit,** 'we had a talk, and a long one too, about you'. *isque multus,* lit. and that much, with *sermo.* **ex quo,** 'after that', lit. from which (talk). **veni ad,** 'I went on to discuss'. **ea quae fueramus . . . locuti,** 'what we had (already) discussed', a sort of plu-pluperfect, as if *locuti* were an adjective rather than a participle. The difference in meaning from an ordinary pluperfect, if any, is not always clear: perhaps here it adds a note of finality, and Cicero is apologising for raising again a matter apparently already settled. **ego et tu inter nos,** 'privately', *inter nos* making clear that no one else was present. **in Tusculano,** 'at my estate at Tusculum', some 15 miles south-east of Rome, near Frascati. **sorore,** Pomponia, Atticus' sister, married to Cicero's brother Quintus.

2. **nihil . . . placatum,** 'I have not seen anyone so kind or so conciliatory as . . .', lit. nothing so . . . , neuter because the person's behaviour is being described. **in,** 'towards'. **ut,** 'with the result that'. **si qua . . . offensio,** 'if there had been any offence on the score of expenditure'. It is extraordinary how some editors, apparently from male prejudice, leap to take Quintus' side in this domestic quarrel of nearly 2000 years ago. Pomponia, we are told, besides being a shrew, was extravagant. How do we really know she was either? Or that 'Marcus did Quintus a bad turn by bringing about his marriage to the masterful Pomponia'? We have only Cicero's side of the story, and the fact that Pilia, Atticus' wife, apparently took Quintus' part (*Ad Att.* V, 11, 7) — a fact which Cicero admits having discovered by opening somebody else's correspondence! — decides nothing. We can tell from the account of Quintus Cicero's exploits in Gaul that though courageous he could be impetuous (*B.G.*V, 39 and VI, 36); and not a few regular soldiers, by being domineering husbands, create for themselves domineering wives. He could well have been at fault in this domestic squabble, or there may have been faults on both sides. The present editors, therefore, out of chivalry to their schoolgirl readers if for no other reason, propose to remain firmly neutral.

3. **ille sic dies,** 'so much for that day', *erat* understood. **ut . . . dies fecit,** 'the date required Quintus to stop at Arcae', where Quintus had an estate. It seems to have been some sort of festival, and Quintus would be expected there among his tenants as a kind of local squire. **ego Aquini,** 'I was at Aquinum', *eram* understood. *Aquini* is locative case. Aquinum was a few miles south-east of Arcae. **nosti,** contracted form of *novisti* with present meaning 'you know', lit. have got to know. **quo,** 'there', lit. whither.

humanissime, 'very pleasantly'. **ego viros accivero,** 'I will take care of (lit. summon) the men'. The future perfect here is more polite than the future simple. **potuit,** supply *esse*; 'nothing could have been more considerate (lit. sweeter)'. **ut,** 'as'. **idque,** 'and that'. **cum ... tum,** 'not only ... but also'. **animo,** 'feeling' or 'intention'.

4. **audientibus nobis,** 'in our hearing', ablative absolute. **ego ipsa,** 'I, the mistress ...'. **hic hospita,** 'a stranger in my own house', lit. here. **id autem ex eo,** supply *ortum est.* 'but the real cause of the trouble was', lit. that arose from the fact that. . . . **Statius,** a favourite servant of Quintus, of whom Pomponia seems to have been jealous, apparently with good reason. Cicero himself wrote a letter to Quintus (*Ad Q.F.* II, 1, 1) reproaching him for the excessive favour and influence he allowed to this slave, and he disapproved (*Ad Att.* II, 18, 4) when Quintus gave Statius his freedom. **ut ... videret,** 'to see to our meal'. **en,** 'you see?', lit. behold.

2.

1. **quid, quaeso, istuc erat?** 'what, I ask, was there in that?', lit. what . . . was that (point of yours). *istuc* = *istudce*, the suffix *-ce* adding emphasis. **me ipsum commoverat,** 'she had upset me as well' (as Quintus). **sic absurde et aspere ... responderat,** 'her reply and expression had been so uncalled-for (lit. out of tune, irrational) and sharp'. **dissimulavi dolens,** 'I did not show my feelings', lit. being distressed, I concealed (the fact). **discubuimus,** 'we took our places at table', reclining, as the Romans did, on their left elbows on the couches of the *triclinium* (dining-room). **de mensa misit,** 'sent her (some food) from the table', presumably to her room, where she was sulking.

2. **quid multa?,** 'in short', lit. why should I say much, *dicam,* deliberative subjunctive, understood. **nihil ... visum est,** 'I never saw anything so polite (lit. nothing seemed more polite than . . .) as my brother or so rude as your sister'. Note the order of words, where like is contrasted with like by juxtaposition in the middle and separation at the extremes. This is called 'chiasmus', from the Greek letter χ (*chi*) because the words are 'crossed over' from their normal position (ABBA instead of ABAB). Thus to emphasise his point — my brother was an angel, your sister was the other thing — by word order was hardly the height of tact on Cicero's part. But Atticus was a long-suffering person, and we are not surprised to hear (Nepos, *Atticus* 22) that he starved himself to

death when afflicted by an incurable illness. **mihi maiori stomacho . . . fuerunt,** 'caused me greater anger', *stomacho* being a predicative dative, here qualified by the comparative *maiori*.

3. **ego inde Aquinum,** supply *abii*. *Aquinum* is accusative of motion towards without a preposition, as is usual with names of towns. **Aquinum ad me . . . venit,** 'came to me at Aquinum', lit. came to Aquinum to me, the usual idiom in Latin, and logical: for one first goes to the town and then finds the person. **fuisse eiusmodi . . . vidissem,** 'behaved just as I had seen her', lit. was of such a kind as I had seen. *vidissem* is subjunctive in a dependent clause in reported speech. **quid quaeris,** 'well?', lit. what do you ask? **vel . . . dicas . . . licet,** 'you can tell her this to her face'. *licet* here takes subjunctive instead of the usual dative and infinitive. *vel* intensifies *ipsi*, lit. even to herself. **humanitatem ... defuisse,** 'she had been lacking in kindness', lit. kindness had been lacking to her, reported statement after *dicas*. *meo iudicio,* 'in my opinion'.

9 (*e*). Concern for the Health of a Former Slave
(*Ad Fam.* XVI, 4, 1–3)

S.P.D. = *salutem plurimam dat*, 'send warmest greetings'. CICERO is Cicero's son, Marcus, and Q.F. (Quintus Filius) is Quintus' son. This letter is from the whole family though the elder Cicero (TULLIVS) wrote it and used the first person singular all through.

1. **varie . . . litteris,** 'your letter caused me mixed feelings', lit. I was variously affected by. . . . **perturbatus,** 'upset', *not* 'perturbed', a condition better reserved for characters in Victorian novels. **altera** = *secunda*. **qua re,** 'therefore'. **non dubito quin . . . committas,** 'I do not doubt that you should not . . .'. *quin* with the subjunctive is the normal construction after *dubitare* when negative, introducing a fact of which there is no doubt, but *committas* has the added force of a command, of what Tiro *should* not do, not merely what he is not doing. **quoad plane valeas,** 'until you are absolutely fit'. *valeas* is subjunctive, as regularly with conjunctions meaning 'before' or 'until', where there is an idea of purpose (compare No. 10 (Nepos), 3, 1). **te neque . . . viae committas,** 'risk travelling by sea or land', lit. entrust yourself to sailing or the road. **satis ... videro, si ... videro,** 'I shall see you soon enough if (when I do) I see you fully recovered'. Note the future perfects, expressively used to show that the two actions are to be coincident and interdependent; and there is a touch of finality

about it, as if Cicero were saying, with affectionate firmness, 'and I don't want any argument about it'.

2. **de medico**, his name was Asclapo, probably derived from Asclepius, or, in the Latin form of the name, Aesculapius, the Greek patron god of doctors. The medical profession was not highly regarded in Rome and was often left to Greeks or slaves. For Martial's view of doctors see *Two Centuries of Roman Poetry*, pages 108–9; and Plates 15(*a*) and (*b*) in that book are instructive. No wonder Cicero needed reassurance on the credentials of Tiro's doctor. **bene existimari scribis**, 'you write that he is well thought of'. *existimari*, lit. a good opinion is held, is impersonal passive infinitive. **ius . . . fuit**, 'you should not have been given soup'. **cum κακοστόμαχος** (*kakostomachos*) **esses**, 'when your stomach was upset'. Cicero, being bilingual in Latin and Greek, often uses a Greek word, here an adjective meaning 'having a bad (κακός) stomach (στόμαχος), when there is no neat equivalent in Latin, much as we sometimes draw the *mot juste* from French. Here we might say 'when you were *indisposé*'. **accurate**, 'with detailed instructions'. **Lysonem**, Lyso was Cicero's host at Patrae, and he had left Tiro in his care, though not without justifiable misgivings. In a later letter (*Ad Fam.* XVI, 9), written after Cicero reached Brundisium, he regrets that Lyso had pressed Tiro to go to a concert before he was fit and Tiro had been too polite to refuse.

3. **Curium**, Curius was a money-lender at Patrae and a friend of Cicero and Atticus, with whom he no doubt shared business interests in banking. Cicero felt Tiro would be safer with a fellow Roman. **suavissimum . . . humanitatis**, 'a most charming, obliging and kindly fellow'. *offici* and *humanitatis* are genitives of description. **multa scripsi, in his etiam ut**, 'I have written at length (lit. much) asking him, among other things, also to. . . . **si tibi videretur**, 'if that is what you would like'. **traferret**, contracted form of *transferret*, subjunctive in an indirect command after *scripsi*, of written instructions, and *videretur* is subjunctive in a clause depending on an indirect command. **Lyso . . . noster**, 'our friend Lyso', spoken of in affectionate terms despite the criticism that follows. **neglegentior**, 'a little casual', lit. more careless (than he should be). The comparative often has this sense of 'rather' or 'somewhat', without any specific object of comparison. **quia omnes Graeci**, 'because all Greeks are', supply *neglegentes sunt*. Cicero, though a great admirer of Greek culture, is less enthusiastic about the Greeks themselves (compare also *Ad Q.F.* I,

1, 5, 16 and *Pro Flacco* 9–12, the latter passage, it is true, aiming
to undermine witnesses who happen to be Greek), though he does
not show Juvenal's fierce hatred of the *Graeculus esuriens* (*Satire*
III, 75 *ff.*), the Greek who will do anything (even become a doctor!)
for a square meal:

> He has a whole bundle
> Of personalities with him — schoolmaster, rhetorician,
> Surveyor, artist, masseur, diviner, tight-rope walker,
> Magician or quack, your versatile hungry Greekling
> Is all by turns. Tell him to fly — he's airborne.
>
> (translated by Peter Green — Penguin Classics)

cum . . . nullas remisit, 'he did not acknowledge my letter', lit.
when (or although) he had received a letter from me, he did not
send me one back.

4. **laudas,** 'you speak well of him'. **sumptu,** 'expense', dative
governed by *parcas*, an alternative ending for *-ui* usually found
only in poetry, but sometimes also in prose. Note how *sumptu* is
placed outside the *ne*-clause for emphasis. **quod ad valetudinem
opus sit,** 'that is necessary for your health'. *quod* is nominative
with *opus sit* (though the ablative is equally common), and attracted
into the gender of its complement, as regularly happens in relative
clauses. *sit* is subjunctive in a subordinate clause inside a dependent request (*rogo ne . . . parcas*), and is probably also generic:
'any sort of thing which may be necessary'. **quod dixisses daret,**
'to advance you any (money) you ask for'. *ut* is understood, introducing the dependent command. *dixisses* is a subordinate clause
inside it, pluperfect subjunctive for a future perfect of the original
words. Cicero said to Curius: *dabis* (or less politely *da*) *quod
(Tiro) dixerit*. **aliquid . . . studiosior,** 'the doctor should be given
something (i.e. a fee on account) to make him take greater interest'.
quo is regularly used instead of *ut* in a purpose clause containing a
comparative adjective (*studiosior*) or adverb.

5. **tua . . . in me officia,** 'your services to me'. Note the order,
with *tua* displaced to emphasise it: yours in particular, the services
you have done me. **forensia,** 'in the courts'. Legal business was
conducted in the Forum, and Tiro acted as secretary in Cicero's
cases. **provincialia,** 'in the provinces'. Tiro accompanied
Cicero when he was governor of the province of Cilicia (southern
Asia Minor) in 52, and may have helped him prepare the case
against Verres after his experiences there as quaestor in 75. **litteris,**

'my writings', probably wider in application than just 'correspondence'. **omnia viceris . . . ,** 'you will surpass all those
services . . .'. Note how once again, as in 1 above, Cicero uses a
double future perfect for a similar effect. Getting well is the finest
service of all Tiro can render him.

6. **bellissime . . . decursurum,** 'will have a first-rate journey
home with Mescinius if all goes well'. *bellus* and its adverb *belle*
are common in conversational Latin, as in Catullus (see *Two
Centuries of Roman Poetry*, page 80, and note on page 171) and
Petronius (No. 13, *A Proud Father*, § 2). Mescinius Rufus, who
was Cicero's quaestor in Cilicia, could not be trusted (Cicero tells
us *Ad Att.* VI, 3, 1) with the province because he was 'unreliable,
wanton and light-fingered' (*levis, libidinosus, tagax*); but Cicero,
as a governor, like the Memmius to whom Catullus objected (see
Two Centuries of Roman Poetry, page 82 and note on pages 175–6),
had exceptionally high standards, and Mescinius, for all his faults,
could have made an excellent travelling companion. **decursurum,**
lit. run down from. The Romans spoke of 'coming down from'
(also *decedere*) a province as business men today 'come down' from
London, or students from a university. **non inhumanus,** 'quite
agreeable', lit. not unkind. **ut mihi visus est,** 'my impression
was', lit. as he seemed to me. **cum consulueris,** 'when you have
taken every possible care of your health'. *consulere* with a dative
means 'to do one's best for' a person or thing. **consulito navigationi,** 'take care over your voyage'. *consulito* is a more formal
alternative to the usual imperative *consule*. **nihil laboro nisi ut,**
'my only concern is that . . .', lit. I trouble about nothing except
that. . . .

9 (*f*). An Author's Lapse (*Ad Att.* XVI, 6, 4)

1. **cognosce,** 'learn all about', lit. get to know. **'De Gloria'**
this work of Cicero has been lost, but it could well have resembled
in its treatment of the theme his works On Friendship (*De Amicitia*)
and On Old Age (*De Senectute*), which are extant. **prohoemium,**
'preface' to a book. The word also means a 'prelude' in music.
quod, 'as'. **in Academico tertio,** 'in the third book of the
Academica'. This work of Cicero on philosophical theories of
knowledge was published in two editions, the first in two books,
the second revised and expanded to four. The first book of the
second edition and the second book of the first survive, but not the

third book referred to here nor the other books.   **id evenit ob eam rem quod . . . ,** 'this happened because . . .', lit. this happened on account of the following fact because.   **volumen,** Roman books were written in vertical columns on a roll of papyrus, which was rolled open (*volvere*) when read.   Hence our word 'volume'.   **eligere soleo,** 'my habit is to make a selection'.   σύγγραμμα (syngramma) 'composition', from the Greek word 'to write'. Here again, as in 9(*e*) 2, Cicero finds the exact word he wants for 'literary composition' more readily in Greek; we might likewise borrow from French 'when I have begun writing some *oeuvre*'.

2. **in Tusculano,** Cicero's villa at Tusculum (see note on 9(*d*), 1) where he wrote several of his books on philosophy and oratory, including the *Tusculan Disputations*, from Book I of which the first passage in Part I of this book is taken.   **qui non meminissem,** 'since I did not remember', causal relative with subjunctive. **me abusum isto prohoemio,** 'that I had used up that preface'. The prefix *ab-* conveys the sense of completeness — once used it could not be used again.   *uti* and its compounds govern the ablative — hence *prohoemio*.   **conieci . . . librum,** 'I slipped it into that book'.   *conicere*, the normal word for hurling a missile, suggests Cicero's careless haste — as we might say 'I flung it into the book'.   **in navi,** Cicero had written this letter at Vibo, on the west coast of Bruttium, in southern Italy, with a vague plan to cross to Greece to escape the aftermath of the murder of Caesar. **Academicos,** 'the books of the *Academica*', *libros* understood.

3. **statim . . . exaravi,** 'I at once hacked out a new preface'. *exarare*, meaning 'to plough', is applied by Cicero to the impression made by writing with a metal stilus on wax tablets as a ploughshare cuts into the soil.   **tu . . . agglutinabis,** 'please cut out the other preface (lit. that one) and stick this one in'.   The future is here used as a polite imperative.   **Piliae . . . Atticae,** 'give my regards to Pilia and Attica'.   Pilia was Atticus' wife and Attica his daughter, also affectionately called *Atticula* by Cicero in *Ad Att.* VI, 5, 4. **deliciis atque amoribus,** 'my pet and darling', lit. my delight and loves, conversational endearments also used by Catullus, e.g. of Lesbia's sparrow (*deliciae*) and his friend Varus' girl-friend (*amores*) — *Two Centuries of Roman Poetry*, pages 37 and 82.

CORNELIUS NEPOS

10. Hannibal's Adventures after the Defeat of Carthage
(*Hannibal* 9–11)

1.

1. **Antiocho fugato,** ablative absolute. **verens ne dederetur,** 'fearing that he would be surrendered (to the Romans)'. The imperfect subjunctive, not the present, is used here, referring to the future, because the verb on which *verens* depends is historic. The so-called 'present participle' is really a 'contemporary participle', and the tense of the main verb with which it is contemporary determines the tense sequence that follows. **quod . . . accidisset,** 'as . . . would have happened', lit. which (thing). *accidisset* is pluperfect subjunctive in a past unfulfilled condition. **si sui fecisset potestatem,** 'if he had allowed himself to be taken' (in Syria), lit. caused power over himself. **Cretam ad Gortynios venit,** 'came to the Gortynians in Crete', lit. came to Crete to the Gortynians. This is the usual Latin idiom, and typically precise. He came to Crete first, and then to the Gortynians. Compare No. 9 (Cicero) (*d*), 2, 3. Crete is regarded as a 'small island' and therefore has no preposition. **quo se conferret,** 'where to go', lit. betake himself, an indirect deliberative question whose verb is therefore subjunctive for two reasons. Hannibal's thoughts were 'where am I to go . . .', *quo me conferam?*

2. **vir omnium callidissimus,** 'being the cleverest of men', a descriptive phrase in apposition to the subject (understood), Hannibal. **in magno se fore periculo,** note the word order: the separation of adjective and noun by the accusative and infinitive *se fore* gives extra emphasis to the former. **nisi quid providisset,** 'unless he took some precautions'. *providisset* is subjunctive in a dependent clause in reported speech, and the pluperfect tense represents a future perfect in direct speech. Hannibal said to himself *in magno ero periculo nisi quid providero*. **magnam . . . pecuniam,** again the separation of *magnam* and *pecuniam* gives greater emphasis to *magnam*. Also the 'sandwiching' of *secum* makes a composite picture. He had a great deal of money and it was 'with him' — hence the seriousness of the danger. **exisse famam,** 'news had leaked out', lit. rumour has gone out. **capit,** historic present, used to make the narrative more vivid. **tale,** 'the following', lit. such a.

3. **summas (amphoras),** 'the tops (of the jars)'. Note that in expressions like 'top of', 'middle of', and 'bottom of' Latin uses an adjective in agreement with the noun where English has a noun phrase. Note also the 'asyndeton' (omission of a conjunction joining the two verbs) in this sentence, which stresses here the contrast between the apparent value and real worthlessness of the contents of the jars. We should insert 'but . . .'. **praesentibus principibus,** 'in the presence of the leaders', ablative absolute. **fortunas,** generally plural meaning 'possessions' or 'property', whereas we say 'his fortune'. **fidei,** 'protection', lit. trust. So, in law, a 'trust' is a document designed to 'protect' a person or property against abuse. **in errorem inductis,** 'deceived', lit. led into error, **abicit,** 'put down', lit. threw down.

4. **non tam a ceteris quam ab . . . ,** 'not so much from the others as from . . .'. **inscientibus iis,** 'without their knowledge', ablative absolute.

2.

1. **Poenus,** 'the Carthaginian', i.e. Hannibal. **Pontum,** the neighbouring kingdom, to the east. It is not known why Prusias was here at the time. Note the accusative, after *in*, because motion is implied. **apud quem** (=*apud eum*), 'at his court', connecting relative. **eodem animo fuit erga Italiam,** 'maintained the same attitude towards Italy', lit. was with the same mind. *animo* is ablative of description. **neque aliud quicquam egit quam regem armavit,** 'he gave his whole attention to arming the king', lit. did nothing else than arm. . . .

2. **domesticis opibus . . . robustum,** 'none too strong in personal resources'. *minus* goes with *robustum*, and the comparative has the more general sense of 'rather' or 'somewhat', without any specific object of comparison. **Pergamenus,** 'of Pergamum', the state to the west of Bithynia. Its king, Eumenes, was the ally of Rome in the war against Philip of Macedon (200–196) and Antiochus of Syria (195–190) and in 133 his successor, Attalus III, bequeathed his kingdom, enlarged by territory conquered from Antiochus, to the Romans, who made it the Province of Asia. **Eumenes,** as the friend and ally of Rome, would be the natural enemy of Hannibal who, even after the defeat of Carthage, 'never ceased to war with the Romans in spirit' (*numquam destiterit animo bellare cum Romanis*, Nepos, *Hannibal* 1).

3. **quo,** 'for that reason'. Note the displacement of the subject

Hannibal towards the end of the sentence, thereby giving it emphasis: 'Hannibal of all people . . .', i.e. because Eumenes was an ally of Rome (to whom Hannibal as a boy had sworn eternal enmity) and dependent on Roman support. **utrobique,** 'in both spheres', i.e. on land and sea. **quem si removisset,** 'if he got rid of him' (Eumenes). *quem* is a connecting relative, and the plu-perfect subjunctive is used in a dependent clause in reported speech representing a future perfect in direct speech. Hannibal's thought was *si eum removero, cetera mihi faciliora erunt.* **cetera,** 'everything else', lit. the rest. **ad hunc interficiundum,** 'to kill him', gerundive of purpose. *interficiundum* (=*interficiendum*) is an archaic form of the gerundive, common in Sallust (see note on page 203), Lucretius and earlier Latin writers.

4. **classe . . . erant decreturi,** 'they intended to fight a decisive naval battle', lit. were going to decide by fleet. **superabatur,** 'he was inferior . . .'. **erat pugnandum,** 'it was necessary to fight', impersonal gerundive of obligation. **vivas colligi,** 'to be collected alive'. Note the use of the infinitive here for a dependent command after *imperare*, a regular usage when the dependent verb is *passive*; when it is active *ut* with the subjunctive is the rule.

5. **classiarios,** 'the marines', supply *milites*, lit. the soldiers of the fleet. **ut in unam . . . navem,** 'to concentrate their attack on King Eumenes' ship', lit. charge against the ship of King Eumenes alone. Note the separation in word order of *unam* and *navem*, which gives special emphasis. They were to charge Eumenes' ship and no other. So too the extraction of *omnes* from the relative clause in which it belongs adds emphasis: 'all without exception', 'one and all'. **satis habeant,** 'be satisfied', lit. regard as enough. **tantum** with *se defendere*, 'merely to defend themselves'. **id . . . consecuturos.** Note the change of construction from dependent command to dependent statement, made clear in Latin by the shift to accusative and infinitive. In English it is often necessary, though not essential here, to make this shift of construction clear by an insertion such as 'he added that . . .', whereas such an insertion in Latin would be quite unnecessary and incorrect. The whole of the rest of the chapter continues the reported speech; hence *se facturum* and *magno praemio fore.*

6. **rex . . . facturum,** great care is needed here with the order of words, which is almost the reverse of the English order, and note that *rex* is the subject of *veheretur*. 'He (Hannibal) would let them know in which ship the king (Eumenes) was sailing.' Though the

order seems strange to us, it is natural to Latin, where inflexions make it possible. Hannibal anticipates the natural question from the sailors 'How shall we know which is the king's ship?' and supplies the answer: 'I will see to it that you do'. **autem,** 'furthermore', as often, not 'however' (here). **cepissent aut interfecissent,** subjunctives in dependent clauses in reported speech, representing original future perfects in direct speech: *si ceperitis aut interfeceritis*. **magno iis pollicetur praemio fore,** 'he promised it would earn them a great reward', lit. it would be for a great reward to them. **praemio** is predicative dative, somewhat strangely used for the expected *se magnum praemium daturum esse*, but *praemium* sometimes means 'advantage' as well as 'reward', and Hannibal's suggestion here is the less specific 'it would be to their great advantage' or 'he would make it well worth their while'.

3.

1. **tali . . . facta,** 'after he had encouraged the troops in this way', ablative absolute. Beware of confusing *cohortatione*, 'encouragement', with *cohors*, a 'cohort' or division of the Roman army. **ab utrisque,** 'on both sides', lit. by both parties. **quarum acie constituta,** 'when the fleets had been drawn up in line', lit. when a battle-line had been established of them. *quarum* is a connecting relative referring to *classis* (each side's fleet) in the previous sentence, and *acie constituta* is ablative absolute. **priusquam . . . daretur,** 'before the battle signal could be given'. *priusquam* is followed by the subjunctive when it conveys an idea of purpose (Hannibal's purpose was to anticipate the battle signal in sending his message) and this is best brought out in English by the insertion of 'could'. **ut palam faceret suis,** 'to reveal to his men', lit. to make (it) publicly. **cum caduceo,** 'with the herald's staff'. The *caduceus* was an olive stick, 'the symbol of peace' (*pacis signum* in the words of the antiquarian Varro) carried by heralds and especially associated with Mercury, the messenger of the gods. The figure of Mercury with *caduceus* is still the centrepiece of the badge of the Royal Corps of Signals, because that Corps transmits the messages of the army (see illustration on page 99).

2. **nemo dubitavit quin,** 'nobody doubted that'; *quin* with the subjunctive is the regular construction with *dubitare* meaning 'to doubt' when it is negative. Contrast its use in § 3 below with infinitive meaning 'to hesitate'. **aliquid de pace esset scriptum,** 'it was some communication about peace', lit. something about

peace had been written. **nave declarata suis,** 'having pointed out
the ship to his own side'. **eodem unde,** 'to the same place from
which'.

3. **soluta epistula,** 'after opening the letter', i.e. after breaking
or untying the tape with which the scroll or tablets would have
been bound. **nisi . . . pertineret,** 'except what has been designed
to make fun of him', lit. pertained to mocking him. The subjunctive is generic or perhaps consecutive. **ad irridendum eum**
is gerundive of purpose. What the message contained is left to the
reader's imagination — perhaps something unprintable! **cuius . . .
causam,** 'the reason for it' (the letter); *cuius* is a connecting
relative. It is worth noting that five of the twelve sentences in this
chapter begin with a connecting relative, which should never be
translated literally. **neque reperiebat,** 'and could not find it'.
dubitavit, see note on § 2 above.

4. **Hannibalis praecepto,** 'on Hannibal's order'. **quam** refers
to *salutem*, not *fuga*, and care is needed with the order of words to
make this clear: 'sought by flight the safety which he would not
have secured without retreating', lit. unless he had retreated.
praesidia, 'defences'.

5. **reliquae Pergamenae naves.** Note that this is the subject
of the *cum*-clause, not of the main sentence, placed outside it for
emphasis. Translate: 'when the rest of the Pergamene ships . . .'.
conici coepta sunt, 'began to be thrown'. *coepi,* when used with a
passive infinitive, is regularly 'attracted' into the passive. **quae
iacta,** 'when these were thrown, they . . .', *quae* is a connecting
relative referring to *vasa fictilia* in the previous sentence. **pugnantibus,** 'among the fighting men' (of the enemy). *concitarunt,*
contracted form of *concitaverunt.* **poterat intellegi,** 'it was not
possible to understand', lit. it could not be understood. *posse* with
a passive infinitive is the simplest way in Latin to express 'it is
possible to . . .'. **fieret,** 'was being done'.

6. **serpentibus.** Note how, for emphasis, the word has usurped
the normal position of the verb *conspexerunt*: 'after they realised
that it was with snakes (of all things, not just earthenware jars)
that their ships were filled'. **nova re,** 'by the strange event'.
quid vitarent, 'what they were to avoid', indirect deliberative
subjunctive. **puppes,** 'ships' not 'sterns'. An example of
metonomy, the figure whereby a person or thing is designated more
colourfully by something associated with them. So we often use
'the Crown' to refer to the monarch who wears it.

7. **consilio,** 'by ingenuity', lit. plan, but often used of a clever plan or stratagem. **neque tum solum,** 'and not only then'. **alias,** 'on other occasions', an adverb.

SALLUST

11. Caesar and Cato Compared (*Catiline* 53,6 and 54)

1. **memoria mea,** 'within my lifetime', lit. memory, ablative of 'time within which'. **ingenti virtute divorsis moribus,** 'of immense worth though of different character'. *virtus* is much wider in meaning than 'virtue' and includes all the qualities that make a true man (*vir*). *divorsis* is an archaic form of *diversis*. Archaisms of language are favoured by Sallust. Note the 'asyndeton' (see Note on No. 10 (Nepos), 1,3), particularly common in Sallust, a writer who strives for antithesis after his Greek model, Thucydides (see p. 33). We naturally insert 'though' or 'but'. **fuere** (=*fuerunt*), 'there were' or 'there lived'. **quoniam res obtulerat . . . non fuit consilium,** 'since the occasion has brought them to our notice, I do not intend . . .'. Sallust here uses the *epistolatory* past, common in letter-writing (see Note on 9 (Cicero) (*c*), 2, 3); tenses which for him would be perfect and present (*obtulit, est*) are cast, from the reader's point of view, into the pluperfect and perfect. **quin,** 'without', 'and not', followed by a subjunctive of result, lit. so as not to. This use of *quin =ut non* should be distinguished from its use with negative verbs of 'doubting'. **naturam et mores,** 'disposition and character', the former referring to what is born in a person, the latter to the character which results from his habits (*mos* in the singular means 'habit' or 'custom'). **quantum ingenio possum,** 'to the best of my ability', lit. how much I can by my inborn talent.

2. **eis,** 'in them'. **genus,** 'birth'. Caesar was a member of the patrician Julian family, traced back by Virgil to Iulus, son of Aeneas, grandson of Anchises and the goddess Venus; Cato's family (*gens Porcia*) was in origin plebeian, but ennobled by office and public honours. **aetas,** Cato (born 95), was in fact about five years younger than Caesar (born about 100). **eloquentia,** perhaps somewhat flattering to Cato, for Caesar, as an orator, ranked second only to Cicero. **prope aequalia fuere,** 'were almost equally matched'. *fuere =fuerunt. aequalia* is neuter plural as the complement of several abstract nouns following the rule, though

only one of them (*genus*) is neuter. **magnitudo animi par, item gloria,** 'in nobility of soul and renown alike they were equal', lit. their greatness of soul (was) equal, likewise their glory. **sed alia alii,** 'but the renown of each was different'. The full Latin is *sed alia gloria alii* (dative) *erat*. We might expect *alteri* where only two people are involved, but Sallust, in his striving for antithesis, prefers *alii* to balance *alia*, here meaning 'different', a sense which *altera alteri* would not give.

3. **beneficiis ac munificentia,** 'favours and generosity', most of which were calculated to further his own career, but this would not be immediately apparent to contemporaries, and Sallust, who himself had cause to be grateful to Caesar (see page 31) would not stress it. **magnus habebatur,** 'was held to be great', with both Caesar and Cato as subject in this carefully balanced sentence. **ille,** 'Caesar', lit. the former. **mansuetudine et misericordia,** 'gentleness and mercy'. Of these qualities Caesar's plea for mercy in the trial of the Catilinarian conspirators in 63 is an example, but he could be ruthless when it suited him, as in his massacre of the Usipetes and Tencteri in Gaul in 55 *pour encourager les autres*, and his unchivalrous treatment of the captive Vercingetorix when celebrating his triumph for the Gallic War in 51. His mercy was the calculating kind, and he admits as much in a revealing letter preserved among Cicero's letters to Atticus (*Ad Att.* IX, 7c): *haec nova sit ratio vincendi, ut misericordia et liberalitate nos muniamus,* 'Let this be a new technique of conquest, to build one's defences by mercy and generosity'. **severitas,** 'sternness', of which his support of Cicero's plea for execution of the Catilinarian conspirators was an example, contrasting with Caesar's advocacy of leniency.

4. **dando, sublevando, ignoscundo . . . nihil largiundo.** Although this sentence says much the same as the previous one, the cascade of ablative gerunds ('by giving' etc.) give it more power, stressing activities rather than qualities. Note the archaic forms *ignoscundo, largiundo* (=*ignoscendo, largiendo*), common in Sallust, like other archaisms of language (e.g. the superlative in -*umus* and accusative singular in -*om*, see *novom* in § 5 below), but occasionally found in other writers as well (e.g. *interficiundum* in No. 10 (Nepos), 2, 3). **in altero . . . pernicies.** Again note the careful balance of this sentence. Variations on the theme of contrast in the two men appear throughout the passage: *ille . . . huic, Caesar . . . Cato, in altero . . . in altero, illius . . . huius.* But

the balanced contrast of qualities is here enhanced by distributed alliteration in Miseris perfugium, Malis pernicies. Something of the effect can be obtained, though not precisely in the same way, by translating: 'in the one was a refuge for the wretched, in the other a scourge for scoundrels'. **facilitas,** 'good nature', lit. easiness to deal with.

5. **in animum induxerat,** 'had schooled himself to . . .', lit. brought into his mind, followed by the infinitives *laborare, vigilare.* Note again the effect of the 'asyndeton' (omission of *et*). **negotiis amicorum intentus,** 'absorbed in the affairs of his friends'. **sua neglegere,** 'to neglect his own', *negotia* understood. *neglegere* and *denegare* are also infinitives depending on *induxerat*; or they may be historic infinitives (see note on page 144), very common in Sallust, in a separate sentence, though this seems less likely. **quod dono dignum esset,** 'which was worth the giving'. *dono* here is almost the equivalent of an abstract noun or supine in -*u*. It could also mean 'worthy of a gift' (in return), but perhaps this would be too subtle, though Sallust gets nearer the truth with the implication 'worth his while in the giving'. It was worth Caesar's while, for instance, to give bribes and influence to Clodius to safeguard his political interests at Rome while he was away campaigning in Gaul. *esset* is generic subjunctive, lit. of such a kind as to be. . . . **magnum imperium,** 'a great command', such as his propraetorship in Spain after being praetor in 62 and even more his proconsular command in Gaul and Illyricum from 58 to 50 after being consul in 59. **bellum novom,** 'an entirely new war', not merely a campaign to finish off, as Sulla's and Pompey's had been in the East. Caesar's campaigns in Gaul, Germany and Britain were on largely new ground. *novom* is an archaic form of *novum.* **ubi virtus enitescere posset,** 'where his brilliance could shine forth'. *posset* is subjunctive in a purpose clause with an adverbial relative, *ubi* being equivalent to *ut ibi*, i.e. *ut in eo bello.*

6. **at Catoni studium . . . erat,** 'but Cato's taste was for . . .', lit. of. **modestiae,** 'self-control' (from *moderari*, 'to restrain'), *not* 'modesty'. **maxume severitatis,** 'most of all for austerity'. *maxume* is an archaic form of *maxime.*

7. **non divitiis . . . certabat,** 'he did not vie in riches with the rich, nor in intrigue with the intriguer, but with the energetic in good deeds, with the man of restraint in self-control, with the blameless in avoiding wrong'. Again note the careful balance of this sentence, and the use of 'chiasmus' (see Note on No. **9** (Cicero)

(*d*), 2,2): in the first two aims rejected by Cato the aim comes before the person — *divitiis cum divite, factione cum factioso*; in the three aims pursued by him the person precedes the aim — *cum strenuo virtute*, etc. **esse quam videri bonus malebat,** 'he preferred to be rather than appear to be a good man'. The implication here that Caesar's ambition was the opposite, though not entirely fair, contains some truth. Certainly his record of the Gallic and Civil Wars is a brilliant public relations exercise designed to show his exploits in their most favourable light. **ita . . . sequebatur,** 'so the less he courted fame the more it pursued him'. *quo . . . eo,* lit. by how much . . . by that (much). In this near-epigram at the conclusion of a chapter Sallust foreshadows the practice of Tacitus, who in many ways modelled his style on him. Like so many epigrams this presents only part of the story, for Cato's fame was overshadowed by that of men like Pompey, Caesar and Cicero. Nearer the truth, as we recall Cato's heroic suicide at Utica described in the *Bellum Africum* (88), is this epitaph:

> nothing in his life
> Became him like the leaving it; he died
> As one that had been studied in his death
> To throw away the dearest thing he ow'd
> As 'twere a careless trifle. (*Macbeth* I, iv, 7)

LIVY

12. Hannibal at the Summit of the Alps (XXI, 35,4 to 37)

1.

1. **nono die,** presumably from leaving the foot of the mountain. Polybius, the Greek historian who describes Hannibal's crossing of the Alps, also assigns nine days from the foot to the summit. **in iugum perventum est,** 'they arrived at the summit' or 'the summit was reached', impersonal passive. **per invia pleraque,** 'over ground mostly trackless', supply *loca.* **et errores . . . faciebant,** 'and over roundabout ways which were caused either by the treachery of the guides or, when(ever) they did not trust them, because they blindly entered valleys, guessing at the way', lit. over (*per* understood) roundabout routes which either the deceit of the guides or . . . valleys blindly entered by them guessing the way caused. *esset* is subjunctive of repeated action, commonly

found in Livy and later writers in imitation of a Greek construction. In Cicero and Caesar it would have been indicative, even after *cum*, which normally takes subjunctive in past time meaning 'when', but indicative if it means 'whenever'.

2. **biduum,** 'for two days', accusative of duration of time. **stativa habita,** 'a permanent camp was established', supply *castra* with *stativa* and *sunt* with *habita*. **fessisque labore ac pugnando . . . militibus,** 'and to the soldiers, exhausted with effort and fighting . . .'. Note the word order, with *fessis* and *militibus* given pride of place at the beginning and end of the sentence to dominate the picture. To Hannibal his men were paramount, and so, in his battle scenes and descriptive passages, they were to Livy, thus causing confusion to scientific historians who look in vain in him for precision over topography, times and tactics. **quae prolapsa in rupibus erant,** 'which had stumbled among the rocks', again the separation of *prolapsa* from its auxiliary verb *erant* sharpens this picture of the suffering animals. **sequendo,** 'by following', gerund. **pervenere** = *pervenerunt*.

3. **fessis . . . adiecit,** 'wearied as they were by the strain of so many misfortunes, a snow-storm, as the last straw (*etiam*) . . . threw them into great fear'. *fessis* is dative of indirect object with *adiecit*, lit. a fall of snow added great fear to men tired by. . . . **occidente iam sidere Vergiliarum,** 'for the constellation of the Pleiades was now setting'. This refers to the first *visible* setting of the Pleiades (a constellation of seven stars, in mythology the seven daughters of Atlas, pursued by Orion and turned with him into a constellation — also called *Vergiliae* from *vergere*, 'to set' because at certain times their setting was visible) in the morning, just as the sun begins to rise, so that the setting of the constellation in the west can be seen before the brightness of the sun, rising in the east, outshines it. This fixes the date at 26 October, and the occurrence of a fall of snow so early in the year is one piece of evidence that Hannibal used a high pass, taking him above the snow-line.

4. **per omnia nive oppleta cum . . . motis,** 'when the advance was made (lit. the standards were moved) and the army began to go forward slowly at dawn over ground everywhere covered with snow', supply *loca* with *oppleta*, lit. all places covered with snow. The *signum*, or battle-standard, was the focus of troop movements and appears in many phrases: *signa inferre*, 'to attack', *signa referre*, 'to withdraw', *signa conferre*, 'to engage' (of opposing armies). So, in the motion-picture that Livy is here presenting,

the movement of the standards catches the eye first as the sign of advance, then the movement of the column itself — *agmen incederet*. **pigritiaque et desperatio . . . emineret**, 'and listlessness and despair showed clearly in the countenance of everyone'. Again note Livy's approach to history: he specifies the expression on men's faces and leaves later scholars to speculate and argue about the name and location of the pass.

5. **praegressus signa**, 'going ahead of the vanguard', where the *signa* would be. **in promunturio quodam . . . prospectus erat**, 'on some vantage point, from which there was an extensive view', lit. a view far and wide. So Livy follows precision in physiognomy with vagueness in topography. **consistere iussis militibus**, 'made the soldiers halt and . . .', ablative absolute, better rendered here, as often, by a separate clause. **subiectosque . . . campos**, 'and the plains around the Po, lying below the Alps'.

6. **moeniaque eos transcendere**, 'and told them that they were at that moment scaling the walls . . .'. The transition from Hannibal's pointing out (*ostentat*) the plains and starting to speak is immediately clear in Latin from the shift to an accusative and infinitive clause *eos . . . conscendere*. In English we must make this clear by inserting a verb of saying — 'he told them that . . .' — which Latin does not need. **cetera plana, proclivia fore**, 'the rest would be level or downhill', but both words in Latin have the added suggestion of something straightforward and easy. **summum**, 'at most', adverbial accusative. **habituros**, 'they would hold', supply *eos* before and *esse* after, but both pronoun and auxiliary verb are commonly omitted by Livy in reported speech.

7. **iam nihil . . . temptantibus**, 'and now not even the enemy interfered with them at all (lit. tried nothing) except by stealthy raids as chance offered'. **hostibus . . . temptantibus**, ablative absolute.

8. **ceterum iter multo quam in ascensu fuerat . . . difficilius fuit**, take in the order *ceterum iter multo difficilius fuit quam. . . .* 'The rest of the journey (or "but the journey" — *ceterum* can be an adjective with *iter* or an adverb) was much more difficult than it had been on the ascent'. *multo* is ablative of measure of difference with *difficilius*, lit. more difficult by much. **ut pleraque . . . sunt**, 'just as the slope of the Alps on the Italian side is generally steeper in proportion as it is shorter'. *pleraque Alpium*, lit. most areas or routes of the Alps, supplying *loca* or *itinera* or perhaps no specific word, for a neuter adjective or pronoun is often used vaguely in

this way with a partitive genitive. *ab Italia*, 'on the Italian side'. *ab* sometimes has this sense, as also in the phrase *a te sto*, 'I am on your side'. *sicut . . . ita*, lit. just as . . . so, of things exactly proportional. Those who have toiled up the long haul of, say, the St. Gothard Pass from Andermatt on the Swiss side and then paused to gaze down at the breathtaking hairpin bends and 'Tremezzo loops' of the road down on the Italian side, with Airolo nestling like a toy town below, will confirm the truth of Livy's observation.

9. **omnis ferme via,** 'practically every road' or 'almost the whole of the road'. **praeceps, angusta, lubrica,** note how 'asyndeton' (omission of *et*) makes the hazards of the descent appear even more formidable. **neque sustinere se ab lapsu possent,** 'they could not keep themselves from falling'. **qui paulum titubassent,** 'those who had become a little unsteady on their feet'. *titubassent* (= *titubavissent*) is subjunctive either because it is generic ('any who . . .') or by attraction to the subjunctive *possent* in the result clause on which this relative clause depends. **nec . . . haerere adflicti vestigio suo,** 'were thrown down and could not retain their footing', lit. stick in their footprint (*vestigio*), i.e. the place where they were standing when they fell. *haerere*, like *sustinere* in the previous line, is governed by *possent*. **aliique super alios . . . occiderent,** 'and fell one on top of the other', lit. some over others.

2.

1. **ventum,** supply *est*, 'they reached', impersonal passive. **ad multo angustiorem rupem,** 'to a much narrower cliff', lit. narrower by much. *multo* is ablative of measure of difference. **ita rectis saxis,** 'with rocks so perpendicular', ablative of description. **ut . . . possent,** 'that (only) with difficulty could an unencumbered soldier, feeling his way and clinging with his hands to bushes and roots projecting around, lower himself'. *expeditus*, 'unencumbered', i.e. by arms and equipment. *temptabundus*, verb adjectives in *-bundus* with similar meaning to a present participle are not uncommon in Livy; other examples are *contionabundus* and *moribundus*, from which 'moribund' is derived, and *cantabundus* in Part I, No. 5 (Petronius), 2, 4.

2. **natura iam ante praeceps,** 'by its nature already steep before'. **in . . . altitudinem abruptus erat,** 'was broken off sheer to a depth of . . .'. **admodum,** 'fully', with *mille*. Livy here

seems to have misunderstood the Greek historian Polybius, or a Roman source derived from him, in two important respects: (*a*) Polybius (III, 54) speaks of a road made too narrow to pass along owing to a landslip along its side, in the direction of the route. Livy sees it as a landslip *across* the line of march, and so in § 3 uses the expression *velut in finem viae*, 'as though they had come to the road's end'. (*b*) Polybius clearly means the landslip had narrowed the road for a distance of 1000 feet along its length. Livy has converted this to a *depth* of 1000 feet, and so presents the picture of the road suddenly terminating in a 1000 foot drop. Diagrams make this clear:

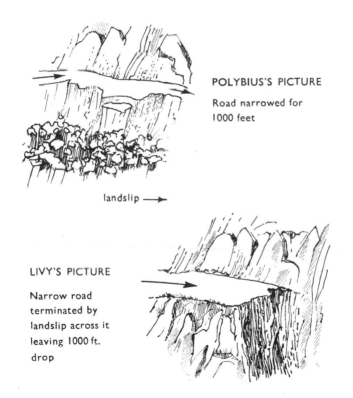

POLYBIUS'S PICTURE

Road narrowed for
1000 feet

landslip ⟶

LIVY'S PICTURE

Narrow road
terminated by
landslip across it
leaving 1000 ft.
drop

3. **ad finem viae,** 'at the end of the road'. **miranti Hannibali . . . nuntiatur.** 'while Hannibal wondered . . . he was told', lit. to Hannibal wondering it is reported.

4. **digressus,** supply *est.* **ad locum visendum,** 'to inspect the place', gerundive of purpose. **haud dubia res visa quin circumduceret,** 'it seemed there was nothing for it but to lead the army round . . .', lit. it seemed no doubtful matter that he would have to lead round. . . . *circumduceret* is subjunctive after *quin* used with a negative expression of doubt, but here (compare note on No. 9 (Cicero) (*e*), 1) it is a necessity rather than a fact of which there is no doubt, so *circumduceret* is jussive subjunctive as well as being subjunctive after *quin.* **per invia . . . antea,** 'over a trackless and hitherto untrodden neighbourhood', lit. over trackless places round about and . . . ; supply *loca* with *invia* and *trita.* **quamvis longo ambitu,** 'however long the detour', lit. by a detour as long as you like.

5. **intactam,** i.e. unmelted since the previous spring, another indication that Hannibal was on a high pass above the snow-line. **nova . . . esset,** 'there was a new layer (of snow)', supply *nix* with *nova.* **modicae altitudinis,** genitive of description. **molli . . . insistebant,** 'the men, as they trod on it, kept their foothold easily, for it was soft and not very deep', lit. the feet of the men treading stood firm on it, being soft. . . . Supply *nivi* with *molli nec praealtae*, dative after *insistebant*: such compound verbs commonly have a dative of the word their prepositional prefix would have governed = *in nive . . . sistebant.*

6. **incessu dilapsa est,** 'it was crushed (lit. it disappeared) by the trampling of . . .'. **per nudam . . . nivis,** 'over the bare ice beneath and the running slush of melting snow'. It is not clear whether, in their detour, they had stumbled on a buried glacier or a frozen stream-bed, but in any case we all know the difficulties even of walking on ice-packed pavements made more treacherous when covered by a fresh fall of snow.

7. **glacie . . . fallente,** 'as the ice did not afford a foothold and made their feet slide more quickly downhill from under them'. *in prono* suggests a forward and downward motion. Their feet slipped down the slope and they fell on their backs. **pedes fallente,** lit. deceiving their feet, i.e. making them insecure. **ut** =*ita ut,* 'with the result that'. **seu . . . se adiuvissent,** 'whether they helped themselves up with their hands or their knees', lit. helped themselves in rising. *adsurgendo* is a gerund. *adiuvissent,*

subjunctive of repeated action (see note on 1.1.) or attracted into the subjunctive *corruerent* in the result clause. **ipsis adminiculis prolapsis**, 'when these supports themselves slipped', ablative absolute. **ad quas . . . eniti posset**, 'by which (lit. against which) anyone could pull himself up with foot or hand'. *posset* is subjunctive in a relative clause of purpose. **in levi . . . volutabantur**, 'they slid about on nothing but (lit. only) smooth ice and thawing snow'. *levi*, the sense requires that this is from *lēvis*, 'smooth', not *lĕvis*, 'light'.

8. **etiam secabant . . . nivem**, 'would sometimes even cut into the lowest (layer of) snow as they went along'. *ingredientia* goes with the subject, *iumenta*. **et prolapsa . . . perfringebant**, 'and stumbling, as they struck out too violently (*gravius*) with their hooves in an effort to rise (lit. by throwing their hooves more violently in struggling (to rise)) would break clean through it'. **ut pleraque velut pedica capta**, 'with the result that a large number of them, as if caught in a trap', *pleraque* and *capta* with *iumenta*, *pedica* being ablative of instrument or place where. **alte concreta**, 'deeply frozen'.

3.

1. **nequiquam . . . fatigatos**, 'worn out to no purpose', ablative absolute. **posita**, supply *sunt*. **loco purgato**, 'after the place had been cleared of snow', ablative absolute again. **ad id ipsum**, 'for that very purpose'. **tantum nivis**, 'so much snow', lit. of snow, partitive genitive. **fodiendum atque egerendum fuit**, 'had to be dug and carted off'. *fodiendum* and *egerendum* are gerundives of obligation agreeing with *tantum*.

2. **ad rupem muniendam**, 'to make a road along the cliff', gerundive of purpose after *ad*, dependent on *milites ducti*. *viam munire*, the normal expression for 'to build a road', is here extended, by substituting *rupem* for *viam*, to mean 'to make a cliff road'. **per quam unam via esse poterat**, 'their only possible route', lit. through which alone there could be a way. **milites ducti**, 'soldiers were brought up to . . .'. *milites* is also the subject of the main verbs *faciunt*, *succendunt* and *putrefaciunt*, but it is better to treat *ducti* as a finite verb, follow it by 'and', and start a new sentence after *faciunt*. Otherwise in English this sentence, an example of Livy's periodic structure at its best (or perhaps 'worst' for the struggling translator!) becomes somewhat un-

wieldy. It may help to analyse its structure thus: *milites, ducti ad . . . muniendam* (participle with gerundive of purpose)/*per quam . . . poterat* (relative clause with *rupem*)/*cum . . . saxum* (causal clause)/*arboribus . . . detruncatisque* (ablative absolute)/*struem . . . faciunt* (main clause)/*eamque* (*cum . . . coorta esset*) *succendunt* (second main clause with temporal clause inserted)/*ardentiaque . . . (infuso aceto) putrefaciunt* (third main clause with ablative absolute inserted). **caedendum esset,** 'had to be cut through', gerundive of obligation. **circa,** 'round about', an adverb. **deiectis detruncatisque,** 'had been cut down and cleared of branches'. **et vis venti apta faciendo igni,** 'a wind also of sufficient strength to make it burn', lit. a force of wind suitable for making a fire. *faciendo igni,* a dative gerundive of purpose after *apta* for the somewhat commoner *ad* with accusative. The object of *succendunt* is *eam* (*que*), referring to *struem.* This chapter well illustrates the two commonest uses of Latin gerundive: (*a*) with the verb *esse* to express obligation: 3, 1, *fodiendum atque egerendum fuit*; 3, 2, *cum caedendum esset saxum.* (*b*) in phrases of purpose: 3, 2, *ad rupem muniendam* and *igni faciendo.* For good measure there is an instrumental or causal gerund to follow in § 6: *muniendo fessis.* **ardentiaque saxa infuso aceto putrefaciunt,** 'and cause the glowing rocks to crumble by pouring vinegar over them'. The later historians Appian (Greek) and Ammianus Marcellinus (Latin) also record this incident, and the Elder Pliny refers to the practice. It is also mentioned by Juvenal (X, 153) — see *Two Centuries of Roman Poetry*, page 114, and note on page 222 (line 26). There is no reason to disbelieve the story: heated rock will split if liquid is poured over it, and the acid in vinegar (which, when mixed with water, was the ordinary drink of Roman soldiers and readily available to Hannibal) will melt limestone rock even without heating. There is even a mention of *acetum* when a tunnel was pierced, in 1480, under the summit of the *Col de la Traversette*, believed by some to have been the pass Hannibal used (see Gavin de Beer, *Alps and Elephants* and *Hannibal*, and Leonard Cottrell, *Enemy of Rome*). Their theory has been contested by Wallbank in *Journal of Roman Studies*, 1956, page 37 *ff.* — perhaps 'demolished' (Walsh, *Livy*, footnote on page 156) is putting it too strongly — but the accounts of de Beer and Cottrell, who made the journey themselves and tell an exciting story, are well worth reading and, to the editors, remain convincing). Polybius does not mention the story, but for him the problem is a different one, of widening a ledge made too narrow by the landslip, and he speaks of 'building out' from it, making a sort of terrace.

3. **torridam incendio rupem ferro pandunt,** 'after thus heating the crag with fire they opened a way through it with iron tools', lit. iron, presumably axes, crowbars and metal wedges. **molliuntque anfractibus modicis clivos,** 'and lessened the steepness of the slopes with zigzags of an easy gradient', lit. softened the slopes by moderate winding paths. The practice is mentioned by Caesar in *B.G.* VII, 46, *circuitus ad molliendum clivum,* 'deviation to ease the slope', and it is a fundamental principle of mountain pass engineering, though nowadays somewhat superseded by tunnel and viaduct as, for instance, in the splendid stretch of the *Autostrada del Sole* between Bologna and Florence, which dispenses, by this means, with anything that can be called a 'pass' at all.

4. **consumptum,** 'was spent', supply *est.* **iumentis . . . absumptis,** 'and the animals nearly perished . . .', ablative absolute, but better rendered here by a second main clause. **si quid est pabuli,** 'such fodder as there was', lit. if there was anything of fodder, object of *obruunt.*

5. **inferiora vallis,** 'the lower slopes of the valley', supply *loca.* **rivosque prope silvas,** *prope* can both precede and follow the word it governs, so 'streams beside woods' and 'woods beside streams' are both possible, though perhaps the former is preferable. **iam humano cultu digniora loca,** 'places that began to be more fit for human habitation'. *iam* with a comparative often suggests a gradual process. *·cultu* is ablative after *dignus,* 'worthy of', 'fit for'.

6. **missa . . . data,** supply *est* and *sunt* to make the participles finite verbs. **muniendo fessis,** 'exhausted with road building'. *muniendo* is an ablative gerund of cause or instrument. **triduo . . . descensum,** 'in three days they made the descent'. *triduo* is ablative of time within which and *descensum* (supply *est*) impersonal passive. **et iam . . . ingeniis,** 'where the natural conditions and character of the people alike grew less forbidding', lit. with both places and characters of the inhabitants (being) more gentle, ablative of attendant circumstances. *iam* with a comparative of a gradual process as in § 5 above.

PETRONIUS

13. A Proud Father (*Satyricon* 46)

1. **mihi,** the speaker is Echion, by trade a rag-collector (*centonarius*) or maker of patchwork cloth and blankets (*centones*) which, when soaked in water, were used to extinguish fires (Caesar, *B.C.* 2, 9; 3, 44). **Agamemnon,** a teacher of rhetoric, the art of public speaking, which was the chief element in Roman higher education (see *Two Centuries of Roman Poetry*, note on page 224). **quid iste argutat molestus,** 'What's that bore going on about?' *argutare*, in classical Latin a deponent verb, means to chatter in a shrill (*argutus*) voice. *molestus*, lit. troublesome. Echion is of course referring to himself as Agamemnon sees him. **qui potes loquere, non loquis,** 'a good talker like you don't talk', lit. you who can speak do not speak. Note how *loqui*, a deponent verb in classical Latin, has become active like *argutare* above. This example of the simplification of the written language in spoken Latin is a stage in the transition to later Romance languages derived from it. **non es nostrae fasciae,** 'you're a cut above us', lit. not of our bundle, a proverbial expression of the class or 'bundle' of people to whom one belongs; genitive of description. **pauperorum,** vernacular for the classical Latin *pauperum*. **prae litteras fatuum esse,** 'are off your head with all that learning', lit. silly because of. . . . *prae* governing the accusative is another feature of Petronius' conversational Latin.

2. **quid ergo est,** 'never mind!', an idiomatic phrase dismissing what has gone before, like the French *que voulez-vous* or the modern slang 'so what?' **aliqua die,** in Petronius, as in Latin verse, *dies* is sometimes feminine even when it does not refer to a special day. **te persuadeam,** in classical Latin *persuadere* governs the dative. The subjunctive is either of a wish or a cautious future, 'can I hope to persuade you' (a use often found in Vulgar Latin). **casulas nostras,** 'our little bit of a cottage', diminutive of *casa*. Such diminutives are common in conversational Latin (see note on No. 9 (Cicero) (*c*), 2, 1) and perhaps plural through false analogy with *aedes* (plural = house). **inveniemus quod manducemus,** 'we'll find a bite to eat'. *manducemus* is subjunctive in a relative clause of purpose, and is the slang word for *edere*; from it are derived words meaning 'to eat' in Romance languages: Italian *mangiare*, French *manger*. **belle erit,** 'it'll be nice', a conversa-

tional expression also found in Catullus and Cicero's letters (see note on No. 9 (Cicero) (*e*), 6). **omnia hoc anno tempestas disparpaliavit**, 'this year the foul weather has made havoc of everything'. The text is corrupt here, though the general meaning is clear. Sedgwick (*Addenda* in 1949 edition) suggests this word, a vulgar coinage from *palea*, 'chaff', and perhaps *dispar*, 'uneven', conveying the havoc of a hurricane. Compare the French *éparpiller*, 'to scatter'. **ergo**, 'anyway', resuming his train of thought after the remark about the weather. **unde saturi fiamus**, 'enough to fill our bellies', lit. whence we may be full, a relative adverb clause of purpose where *unde = ut inde*, that from there. **tibi discipulus crescit**, 'is growing up to be a pupil of yours', i.e. in rhetoric. **cicaro meus**, 'my lad'. *cicaro* is either a vulgar form of Cicero, 'my budding orator', or, like the name Cicero itself, derived from *cicer*, 'a chick-pea', much as we say 'my chickabiddy' of a child.

3. **iam quattuor partes dicit**, 'he can already divide by four', lit. says his four parts, perhaps referring to the four-times table or to the ability to deal in fractions of four, i.e. division by four. **si vixerit**, 'if God spares him', lit. if he shall have lived. **habebis . . . servulum**, 'you'll have him ready to do anything for you', lit. a little slave at your side. **quidquid illi vacat**, 'in his spare time', lit. whatever is free for him. **caput de tabula non tollit**, 'he doesn't take his head out of his exercise book', lit. does not lift his head from his writing-tablets. The *tabula* was a pair of hinged wooden tablets, coated on the inside with wax and shutting up like a book, on which pupils wrote with an iron pen, *stilus*. **bono filo**, 'there's good stuff in him', lit. with good thread (ablative of description), an apt metaphor for Echion, the blanket-maker. **in aves morbosus est**, 'he's crazy about birds', another example of the fondness of the Romans for birds as pets. Compare Quintus Cicero's aviary in No. 9 (Cicero) (*c*), 1, 1, and notes there.

4. **illi**, dative of disadvantage, virtually possessive here, 'his three goldfinches'. **cardeles**, common as pets. Some scholars believe Lesbia's pet 'sparrow' may have been a goldfinch. **dixi quia mustella comedit**, 'I told him a weasel ate them'. *quia*, in time the Romans, like many a modern Latin student, found the accusative and infinitive too much for them and gradually replaced it by *quod* or *quia* with the indicative, which found its way into Romance languages as the Italian *che* and French *que*. But not consistently so, for in § 1 we have the classical construction *scimus te . . . esse*. **mustella**, weasels were kept by the Romans as pets

and to kill mice.   They were the equivalent for them of the domestic cat; for the cat in ancient times, though known to the Egyptians as a sacred animal, was not common.   The cat appearing on a mosaic at Pompeii (see Plate 18) and also the cat in Phaedrus' fable were probably wild cats; though there is what appears to be a domestic cat behind the master's chair in the picture of a music lesson represented on a Greek vase and also, on a Roman lamp, a cat climbing a ladder — both in the British Museum.   And the Elder Pliny refers to the domestic cat more than once as a well-known animal.   **nenias,** 'hobbies', lit. songs or trifles.   **libentissime pingit,** 'thoroughly enjoys painting', lit. paints very willingly.

5.   **ceterum Graeculis calcem impingit,** 'but he is getting his Greek behind him', lit. is giving a kick to his Greek.   Supply *litteris* with *Graeculis*, and note the diminutive, perhaps suggesting elementary studies.   The teaching of Greek before Latin is also recommended by Quintilian, writing on Roman education (*Inst. Or.* I, 1, 12), both because Latin, being in general use, will be picked up anyway and because Latin learning is derived from Greek, so that the latter should be studied first.   **et . . . non male appetere,** 'and has begun to take to his Latin quite well'; with *Latinas* supply *litteras* again.   **sibi placens,** 'self-satisfied', lit. pleasing to himself.   **nec uno loco . . . non vult laborare,** 'he's unreliable (lit. does not stop in the same place) — he just comes and goes.   He knows his stuff (lit. knows letters indeed) but does not want to work.'   The text is uncertain here.   The translation of J. P. Sullivan (*Penguin Classics*) has been adopted with his emendation *venit* (*abit. scit qui*) *dem litteras*, applying all these remarks to the unreliable teacher and not, as some have done, partly or wholly to the boy, for whom, apart from those venial goldfinches, Echion has nothing but praise.

6.   **alter,** 'another (teacher)', though it has been taken to mean another son of Echion, surely wrongly, for the whole tone of the passage suggests an only son, the apple of his father's eye; and *plus docet quam scit* seems an odd thing to say of a pupil.   **curiosus,** 'conscientious'.   **feriatis diebus . . . venire,** 'makes a habit of coming round (to our) home on holidays', i.e. to give extra lessons.   **quicquid dederis,** 'whatever you give him (in cash or kind)', lit. will have given, future perfect with typical Latin precision, though we might have expected *erit* rather than *est* with *contentus*.

7.   **libra rubricata,** 'law books with headings in red'.   The rubrics, or instructions in a prayer book, were so called because originally they were printed in red (*ruber*).   *libra* (from *librum*,

neuter) is an alternative vernacular form of *liber*. **ad domusionem,** 'for home use', a composite coinage from *domus* and *utor*. **aliquid de iure gustare,** 'get a taste of law', lit. taste something about. **habet panem,** 'has a living in it', lit. bread.   So we speak of a man's 'bread and butter', and compare the slang expression (when asking about someone's career) 'What do you do for a crust?' **satis inquinatus est,** 'has dabbled enough in', lit. is sufficiently stained with.   **quod si resilierit,** 'but if he objects', lit. jumps back from it.   *quod si,* 'but if', lit. with regard to which if; *quod* is adverbial accusative and a connecting relative.   Note the mixed conditional sentence, lit. if he will have objected (referring to the future), I have decided.   **artificii,** 'a trade'.   We should expect *artificium*, a double accusative being normal with *docere*.   Perhaps *aliquid* is understood or has dropped out of the text, making a partitive genitive phrase, 'some trade', lit. something of trade; or it may be like the use of *doctus* with the genitive: *eum artificii docere = eum artificii doctum facere*.   Note that the Romans made no distinction between trade and profession: barber, auctioneer and lawyer all pursue a trade *(artificium)*.   **quod ... Orcus,** 'something he can't lose till he dies', lit. which nothing but (his departure to) the Underworld (or the god of the Underworld, Orcus being sometimes used for Pluto) could take from him.   *possit* is subjunctive in a relative clause of purpose, or more probably generic.

8. **Primigeni,** vocative of *Primigenius*, the boy's name.   **tibi discis,** 'you learn for your own good', lit. for yourself, dative of advantage.   **Phileronem,** a self-made and successful barrister in Cumae.   **hodie ... abigeret,** 'he'd be starving today', lit. would not be driving hunger away from his lips.   Note the mixed conditional sentence: the *si*-clause has a pluperfect subjunctive of a supposition in the past — if he had not studied (but he did): the main clause an imperfect subjunctive of what would now be happening — he would be starving — (but he is not).   **modo, modo,** 'it's no time at all since', lit. recently, repeated for emphasis. **collo,** 'on his back', lit. neck.   Philero appears to have been some sort of hawker or travelling salesman.   **nunc autem adversus Norbanum se extendit,** 'now he can even measure up to Norbanus', lit. extends himself face to face with Norbanus, i.e. in wealth and success.   Norbanus was a popular magistrate at Cumae, mentioned in an earlier chapter of the *Cena Trimalchionis* (45, 11) for the gladiatorial shows he put on to win votes.   **litterae thesaurum est et artificium nunquam moritur,** 'an education is an

investment (lit. letters are a treasure) and a proper profession (lit. trade) never dies'. *thesaurum*, a neuter variant of the classical Latin form *thesaurus*. Echion's summing-up seems tailor-made for a school or polytechnic in search of a motto.

SENECA

14. The Psychology of Noise (*Epistulae Morales* 56, 1–6, 14 to end)

1. **pereand si,** 'I can't for the life of me see that . . .', lit. may I perish if . . . seems. **in studia seposito,** 'for a man who has shut himself away to study', lit. placed aside for studies, dative after *necessarium*. **ecce . . . circumsonat,** 'here I am with a babel of noise echoing all round me', lit. look, from all sides varied shouting sounds round me. **supra ipsum balneum,** 'right over a public bath', lit. above the bath itself, a very different proposition from the peace and seclusion of the private baths of Quintus Cicero's villa (see No. 9 (Cicero) (*b*), 1, 4). **propone nunc tibi,** 'just picture to yourself'. **in odium possunt aures adducere,** 'can disgust the ears', lit. can bring the ears to hatred. **fortiores exercentur,** 'the tougher types take exercise'. In poetry and later Latin *fortis* can mean 'strong' as well as 'brave'. *exercentur* is equivalent to a reflexive or intransitive verb; as *exercere* is transitive the active requires an object. Seneca could have written *se exercent* instead. **manus plumbo graves iactant,** 'swing their lead dumb bells', lit. throw about hands heavy with lead. **aut laborantem imitantur,** 'or pretend to strain', lit. imitate a straining man. **gemitus,** 'grunts'. **retentum spiritum remiserunt,** 'release their pent-up breath'. **sibilos et acerbissimas respirationes,** 'I hear hissing and strident (lit. very sharp) gasps', supply *audio*. **cum . . . incidi,** 'when my attention has chanced upon (lit. I have fallen upon) some idle fellow, satisfied with just a cheap massage'. *plebeia*, something which the *plebs*, or ordinary folk, can afford. **crepitum illisae manus umeris,** 'the smack of a hand cracking down on his shoulders', *umeris* dative after *illisae*. **prout plana pervenit aut concava,** 'according to whether it lands on him flat or hollowed'. Ancient masseurs apparently lacked the gentle touch. **pilicrepus,** it is not clear whether this is some sort of umpire whose job it is to count the balls (*pilas numerare*), perhaps some form of keeping the score; or whether it is the ball-player himself, who makes a noise

(*crepare*) with the ball (*pila*) either by bouncing it or by shouting the score. **actum est,** 'that's the last straw', lit. it is done, impersonal passive.

2. **scordalum et furem deprehensum,** 'the rowdy and thief caught in the act'. **cui . . . placet,** the bath baritone who 'liked the sound of his own voice', lit. whom his own voice pleases, can be traced back even earlier than Seneca; Horace mentions him in *Sat.* I, 4, 76. **cum ingenti impulsae aquae sono,** 'with an almighty splash', lit. huge sound of water struck against. **biberari,** 'drink seller'. The word is not found elsewhere but has good manuscript authority and seems a natural derivative from *bibere* ('to drink'); one would expect to find the ancient equivalent of Coca-Cola on sale at the baths. **exclamationes** and other accusatives which follow are objects of *adice* supplied from the previous sentence. **mercem sua quadam et insignita modulatione vendentes,** 'hawking their wares each with some distinctive intonation of his own',

3. **o te . . . surdum,** 'o man of iron or stone-deaf', accusative of exclamation. **cui mens . . . constat,** 'to keep your reason . . .', lit. for whom the mind stands firm among. . . . **cum . . . mortem,** 'though endless "good-days" were the death of (lit. brought to death) our (fellow-Stoic) Chrysippus'. *nostrum* because, like Seneca, he was a Stoic. Living in the third century B.C. he was a pupil of Zeno and Cleanthes, and is often quoted by Cicero as an authority on Stoicism. *perducat,* historic present. **mehercules,** 'by George', see note on 9 (Cicero) (*c*), 2, 6. **deiectum aquae,** 'falling water'. **cuidam genti . . . transferendi,** 'this reason alone caused a certain tribe to move their city . . .', lit. this was the one cause of transferring. . . . The gerund governing a direct object becomes commoner in later Latin than the gerundive alternative: Cicero might have written *urbis suae transferendae*. **fragorem Nili cadentis,** 'the roar of a Nile cataract'. This story is mentioned in Cicero (*Rep.* 6, 19) and again in Seneca (*Nat. Quaest.* 4, 2, 5).

4. **magis . . . crepitus,** 'it seems to me that the (human) voice is more distracting than mere noise'. Seneca makes a valid distinction here between words (*vox*), which one is tempted to try to follow and understand, and inarticulate noise (*crepitus*) which hinders concentration less. Many students find that a background of music does not impede and can actually help study — but a radio talk is a different matter. **illa** refers to *vox*. **animum adducit,** 'demands attention', lit. draws the mind (to it). **hic** refers to

crepitus. **aures implet et verberat,** 'fills the ears and batters away at them'. **quae me sine avocatione circumstrepunt,** 'which make a din all round me without (causing) distraction'. **pono,** 'I include'. **inquilinum,** 'living in the same block'. The blocks of flats (*insulae*) in which the less well-to-do residents of Rome lived would often have a shop or workshop on the ground floor, and these wooden structures, often cheaply and badly built (see *Two Centuries of Roman Poetry*, page 74), were far from sound-proof. **ad Metam Sudantem,** 'near the Trickling Fountain', lit. sweating turning-post. A *meta* was a conical column placed at the turning points in the Roman Circus. This *Meta Sudans* seems to have been a fountain of similar shape with multiple jets which, when playing, resembled perspiring pores (*sudare* means 'to sweat') of the skin. The remains of such a structure have been found near the Colosseum in Rome, and there could well have been a similar one near these baths. **tubulas experitur et tibias,** 'tunes (lit. tests) his horns and flutes', presumably a street musician or vendor of musical instruments whose 'pitch' was by the Trickling Fountain. **nec cantat sed exclamat,** 'does not play a tune but just blasts away'.

5. **etiamnunc,** 'furthermore', introducing a fresh distinction between noises. Just as articulate sounds are more distracting than mere noise, so an intermittent noise disturbs Seneca more than a steady one. **qui intermittitur subinde,** 'an intermittent but repeated noise', i.e. a frequent alternation of noise and pause, of which the road-mender's pneumatic drill is an excruciating modern example. **omnia ista,** 'all those noises'. **vel pausarium,** 'even a boatswain'. The *pausarius* would give the timing of the strokes (*modos*) to the rowers much as the cox of a boat-race crew calls 'in-out, in-out', and also tell them when to ease oars — hence his name *pausarius* (from *pausa*, 'a pause'). Ovid (*Met.* 3, 618) also describes the process: *qui requiemque modumque/voce dabat remis.* **sibi intentum esse** 'to concentrate', lit. be intent on itself. *sibi* refers to *animum.* Strictly the reflexive pronoun refers back to the subject of the sentence, in this case *ego* contained in *cogo*, but is sometimes applied to another important word which is the logical though not the grammatical subject. *animum* is here emphasised by its position as first word, and Seneca is thinking of his mind rather than himself. **omnia . . . resonent,** 'though all is bedlam outside'. *licet* with subjunctive commonly has the meaning 'although', lit. it is allowed that. **dum,** 'provided that', with the

subjunctive. The normal negative in this sense is *ne*, but Seneca's use of *non* may be conversational, or perhaps because the negative belongs closely with the verbs *rixentur* and *dissideant*, emphasising that the passions should 'be at peace'. **nihil timultus,** 'no commotion', lit. nothing of . . ., partitive genitive. Note that Seneca is here thinking of study for its own sake, not work to earn a living. He is not saying, therefore, that *cupiditas* and *avaritia*, which might be motives for hard work, are not in conflict with distracting emotions like *timor* and *luxuria* (the self-indulgence which can stop a man from working); rather that all these passions are under control, and the mind left free for disinterested study, an important element in the Stoic way of life. **nec altera alteram vexet,** 'and do not harass each other', lit. the one does not harass the other. **totius regionis silentium,** 'silence throughout the neighbourhood'. **si adfectus fremunt,** 'if the emotions are in uproar'.

6 **tunc ergo,** 'then and only then', emphatic. **scito,** the more formal imperative; compare No. 9 (Cicero) (*e*), 6, *consulito*. **cum . . . pertinebit,** when no clamour affects you', lit. concerns (or reaches) you. **te . . . tibi excutiet,** 'shakes you out of yourself'. *tibi* is dative after a compound verb of the word its prepositional prefix would have governed = *te ex te quatiet*. **non si . . . circumstrepet,** 'not if it booms round you emptily with meaningless din'. *vana*, with *vox* understood, has the force of an adverb.

7. **quid ergo,** 'that's all very well', lit. so what?, dismissing the previous sentence as impossibly idealistic. **commodius,** 'simpler', 'better', lit. more convenient. **et carere convicio,** 'just to be free from the din'. *et* here intensifies, meaning 'even', not 'and'. **experiri et exercere me volui,** 'I wanted to test and train myself', like a true Stoic in an act of self-discipline. **cum,** 'since', for after a primary main verb (*est*) *cum* meaning 'when' would take the indicative. **adversus Sirenas,** the reference is to Homer, *Odyssey* 12, 277 *ff.*, where Odysseus, to steel himself and his crew against these fabulous creatures whose irresistible singing lured men onto the rocks around the island where they dwelt, filled his men's ears with beeswax and had himself lashed to the mast of his ship. But he also told his men to row past the island as quickly as possible. This is Seneca's point. Having proved to oneself that the distraction of noise can be overcome by self-discipline it is foolish to tempt providence by staying with it when there is no need.

PLINY

15 (*a*). The First Grammar School at Comum (4, 13)

1. **in patria mea,** 'in my native town', Novum Comum (the modern Como) where Pliny spent most of his life, and where the name Pliny is still something of a legend. Statues of himself and his uncle (the Elder Pliny) flank the entrance to the cathedral, and there is a *Via Plinia* named in his honour. **ad me salutandum,** 'to pay his respects to me', lit. to greet me, gerundive of purpose. Such formal calls by dependents on their patrons were usually made at dawn, and were sometimes a source of annoyance to either or both. See *Two Centuries of Roman Poetry*, page 160. **praetextatus,** '(still) wearing the purple-bordered toga (of boyhood)'. This, also worn by magistrates, was discarded for the plain white toga of manhood at about the age of fifteen with a sort of 'coming of age' ceremony. The boy was then registered in his family 'tribe' and assumed the rights and duties of a citizen. **studes?** 'are you at (secondary) school?' *studia* and *studere* commonly refer in Pliny's letters to the second stage of Roman education, a course in rhetoric given by a *rhetor* following the course in Greek and Latin language and literature given by *grammaticus*. Pliny himself learned his 'grammar' at a primary school in Comum (*Ep.* 1, 19, 1).

2. **etiam,** 'yes', the usual Latin for affirmation, though an alternative would be to repeat the verb in the question — *studeo*. (See *Two Centuries of Roman Poetry*, page 170, note on line 5). **Mediolani,** 'at Milan', locative case. This was the chief city of Cisalpine Gaul in north Italy and today has become a huge Chicago-like skyscraper industrial city with one of the most bewildering one-way-traffic systems in Europe. **erat enim una,** 'for he was with him'; *una* is an adverb here. **quare nullos?** 'why have you none?', supply *habetis*, inferred from *habemus*.

3. **vehementer intererat vestra,** 'it is vitally important to you'. *vestra* is ablative feminine singular of the possessive adjective agreeing with *re* understood. This is the normal construction with *interest* and *refert*, and the genitive is used of nouns: *vestra* or *Caesaris interest*, 'it concerns you' or 'Caesar', lit. it is involved with your affair or Caesar's affair. Note the tense of *intererat*: Latin uses the imperfect tense of something which was true and continues to be true. But in this situation English uses the present; for if we said 'it was vitally important' we should imply that it was so

at the time but now no longer is, and give quite the wrong sense here. **qui . . . estis,** the antecedent is *vos* contained in *vestra*. **liberos . . . discere,** 'that your children should learn', accusative and infinitive after *intererat*. **hic potissimum,** 'here of all places', lit. especially. **iucundius morarentur,** 'could they stay more happily', potential subjunctive, equivalent to a present impossible conditional sentence with 'if they had the choice' understood. They would like to stay at home but they cannot. **aut pudicius continerentur,** 'or be kept under stricter control'. Pliny stresses here, as elsewhere, the moral content of education. **aut minore sumptu,** 'or (kept) with less expense', supply *continerentur*.

4. **quantulum est ergo . . . pecunia,** 'how little it would cost you, then, if you put your money together, to . . .', lit. how little it is, then, when the money has been put together. The ablative absolute *collata pecunia* is here equivalent to a conditional clause, and Pliny uses the indicative *est* for greater vividness, as if the project were already in hand. **conducere praeceptores,** 'to engage teachers'. For the most part schools in Pliny's day were private enterprise affairs. A teacher would establish himself in a room, open-fronted shop, or even a booth and charge modest fees which the pupil paid him monthly (see *Two Centuries of Roman Poetry*, pages 54–55, Horace's Education, and notes there). In another letter (2, 18, 3) Pliny undertakes to look for a tutor for a friend's brother's children, and visits various schools for the purpose, 'going back to school', as he puts it, 'and reliving, as it were, the happiest days of my life' (*illam dulcissimam aetatem quasi resumo*). Hiring of teachers by local authorities (see § 6 below) was rare. **in habitationes,** 'for lodgings'. There were no boarding schools in ancient times (apart from the military training establishments of Sparta) and parents had to make their own arrangements for children at school away from home. **in ea quae peregre emuntur (omnia autem peregre emuntur),** 'for all things that cost money away from home — and that means everything', lit. moreover everything is bought away from home. **adicere mercedibus,** 'add to their (the teachers') salaries'. The object of this verb is the whole clause *quod . . . impenditis*, 'add to their salaries what you spend on . . .'.

5. **atque adeo,** 'and what is more . . .', a common use of the adverb *adeo*. **qui nondum liberos habeo,** this letter was written soon after Pliny married his third wife, Calpurnia; in fact he never had any children of his own. **quasi pro filia vel parente,**

'as though for a daughter or mother'. Pliny often expresses affection for his native Como in strong terms such as this. **tertiam partem . . . dare,** 'to contribute a third of whatever sum you decide (lit. it shall please you) to collect'. By this public-spirited act, and the obvious interest he intends to show in the proposed school, Pliny places himself on record as one of the first school benefactors and governors. This pattern for schools, owing their existence partly to the donations of founders and other benefactors, partly to fees paid by parents, remained the basis of British education at primary, secondary, and university level until well into the nineteenth century, when the State gradually and often reluctantly became involved. It still survives in independent schools, including the so-called 'public schools' and direct grant schools, today.

6. **totum etiam pollicerer, nisi timerem . . . ,** 'I should even promise the whole amount, were I not afraid . . .', a present unfulfilled conditional sentence. **ne hoc . . . corrumperetur,** 'that this gift of mine would at some time be abused for selfish purposes'. Pliny's fear is that, if the parents are not themselves involved by paying part of the fees, they would not trouble to ensure that the best choice of teachers is made. Instead it would be left to the municipal officials, who might be tempted to favouritism or other reasons for appointing teachers on non-educational grounds. Pliny's distrust of local officials appears in another letter (7, 18) where he advised a friend who wanted to leave a bequest to provide a local feast not to hand over the money direct to the town for fear it would be dissipated (*verendum est ne dilabatur*), but to make other arrangements, as he himself had done when making a benefaction of 500,000 sesterces for the maintenance of some free-born boys and girls. Whether or not Pliny is being fair to local officials, it is certainly true that, in the matter of education, parents who pay fees for their children's education (as Pliny is here insisting that they should do) are generally more determined to have their money's worth than those who receive their education 'free' (i.e. out of rates and taxes) from the State. **ut,** 'as'. **in quibus praeceptores publice conducuntur,** 'where teachers are engaged at public expense'. This does not seem to have been common practice. We hear of a *grammaticus* (elementary school teacher) being hired from Rome by the city of Brundisium after he had given a trial lecture (Aulus Gellius, *Noctes Atticae* 16, 6, 2), and of a school for the sons of the Gallic aristocracy at Augustodunum (Tacitus, *Annals III*, 43). Vespasian encouraged such schools by

exempting the teachers from taxation.   But private enterprise in
education was much commoner, and Pliny's action to encourage
it by personal benefaction seems to have been the first of its
kind.

7. **huic vitio . . . potest,** 'there is only one safeguard against
this abuse', lit. this abuse can be met by one remedy. *occurri,*
being a dative verb, is used impersonally in the passive with what
would have been the subject, *huic remedio,* retained in the dative
case.   **potest si . . . relinquatur . . . addatur,** though this is a
hypothetical future conditional clause — this abuse *could* be met
if the right *were to be* left to parents etc. — the indicative is used in
the main clause with *potest* because it is not the *possibility* of
preventing the abuse, but the actual prevention that depends on
the *si*-clause.   In effect Pliny is saying 'the abuse can be met, and
would be met if . . .' .   **ius conducendi,** 'the right of engaging
(teachers)'.   **isdemque . . . addatur,** 'and they also would have a
conscience about the right choice when it touches their pockets',
lit. to the same people a conscience about choosing rightly would
be added by the necessity of a contribution.   *isdem,* 'and they also',
a common idiom with *idem.   religio* in Latin has a different sense
from 'religion' in English.   In some respects it is more restricted,
emphasising the limitations and taboos of 'religion' rather than its
more inspiring and positive qualities — the 'thou shalt not' of the
Ten Commandments rather than 'thou shalt' of the Sermon on the
Mount — but it is also wider in its application (choosing a teacher
has little to do with 'religion') and has two elements: (a) the feeling
of obligation which makes a person do what is right; (b) the
scruples which prevent him from doing what is wrong.   Our
nearest equivalent in this context is 'conscience', the scrupulous
care that will make parents ensure they choose good teachers and
avoid choosing bad ones.

8. **qui . . . negligentes,** *qui = ei qui,* 'those who', and supply
sunt or *erunt* as the verb of this relative clause.   **de alieno,** 'about
other people's money', supply *aere,* lit. copper (coins).   **de suo,**
supply *aere* again.   **dabuntque operam ne . . . non nisi dignus
accipiat,** 'they will see to it that only a suitable person receives . . .',
lit. that nobody unless a worthy man.   *nisi* often has the meaning
'only', 'not . . . except'.   **si . . . accepturus erit,** 'if he is going to
receive money from themselves as well'.   The compound future
is more definite than the simple, as if Pliny's project were already
in hand.   Note that the main verb of this conditional sentence is

dabunt operam, not *accipiat*, which is the verb of the purpose clause
ne . . . accipiat.

9. **proinde . . . sumite**, 'so agree together, make a common
plan and increase your determination from my own'. Note the
'asyndeton' (omission of *et*), suggesting urgency. **meo**, supply
animo. **qui cupio . . . conferre**, 'for I want my own contribution
to be as large as possible'. *qui* has causal force, though in this
sense it would normally be followed by a subjunctive. *quam
plurimum*, the normal idiom with a superlative for 'as . . . as
possible'. **quod debeam conferre**, generic subjunctive, 'the
sort of amount I must contribute', i.e. my own contribution.
nihil honestius, 'nothing more worthwhile', i.e. that will bring
them more credit in the end. **educentur . . . nascuntur**, 'those
who are born here should be brought up here'. Note the emphatic
position of *educentur*, jussive subjunctive of *educāre*, to 'rear' or
'nourish' — not the future indicative of *educere*, 'to bring out',
from which the word 'education' is sometimes quite wrongly
derived. **amare frequentare**, note the 'asyndeton' (omission of
et) and assonance of *-are*. We can convey something of the effect
by translating 'love and live with'. **utinam . . . inducatis**, 'I hope
you will introduce . . .', present subjunctive as a wish for the future
with *utinam*. **ut . . . studia . . . petantur**, 'that . . . education (lit.
studies) . . . may be obtained (lit. sought). **ut . . . utque**, note the
different uses of *ut* here. The first introduces a double result
clause, with the verbs *petantur* and *confluant*, linked by the *-que* of
utque. The second *ut* is comparative, correlative to *ita*, 'and (that)
as now . . . so soon'. **confluant**, a strong metaphor. Pliny hopes
for a flood of registrations at his new school. As Sherwin-White
points out in his large commentary (*The Letters of Pliny*, OUP
1966) this whole letter underlines the ease of communications in Italy,
whether from Comum to Mediolanum, or to Rome, in Pliny's times

15 (*b*). Convalescence of a Sick Slave (5, 19)

s, abbreviated for SALUTEM, supply DAT, 'sends greetings'.
1. **quam . . . habeas**, 'how kindly you treat your dependents',
i.e. slaves and freedmen. *habeas* is subjunctive in a dependent
(indirect) question. **quo simplicius**, 'all the more frankly', lit.
by how much. . . . *quo* is a connecting relative and ablative of
measure of difference.

2. **est mihi,** 'I have . . .'. **hoc nostrum, 'pater familiae',** 'this expression of ours "father of the household" '. From earliest times the Roman father had wide powers, both religious and secular, even powers of life and death. Pliny is stressing that these powers carry responsibilities to slaves no less than to wife and children. **quod si essem,** 'but even if I were more harsh and unfeeling by nature' (than I am). *quod* is accusative of respect, lit. with regard to which, i.e. 'but'. *essem* and *frangeret* are imperfect subjunctives in a present unfulfilled conditional clause. **frangeret me,** 'would soften my heart', lit. break. **cui tanto maior . . . magis eget,** 'to whom even greater kindness should be shown now that he needs it more', lit. greater by so much . . . by how much. *exhibenda,* gerundive of obligation from *exhibere.* **illa,** supply *humanitate,* ablative after *eget.*

3. **homo . . . litteratus,** '(he is) an honest fellow, obliging and educated'. Note the 'asyndeton' (omission of *et*). **ars . . . comoedus,** 'his talent and label, as it were, is for acting comedy', lit. to be a comic actor, *esse* understood. Slaves in the slave-market had their particulars and price inscribed on a label (*inscriptio* or *titulus*), and it is to this practice that Pliny's simile refers. **in qua plurimum facit,** 'in which he is a great success', lit. does very much. **nam pronuntiat . . . etiam,** 'for his delivery is clear (lit. he recites clearly) and intelligent, his acting correct and indeed graceful'. *pronuntiare* means both 'to recite' and 'to perform on the stage'. The first two adverbs apply naturally to the former meaning, the second pair to the latter. **utitur,** 'he plays'. **ultra quam . . . est,** 'better than an actor need do'. The reciting and acting of comedy was a specialist talent, and to offer instrumental expertise as well was a pure bonus, especially when combined with a flair for reading speeches aloud, and history and poetry, as is mentioned in the next sentence. **idem,** 'he also', lit. the same man, a common idiomatic use of *idem.* **tam commode . . . ut . . . videatur,** 'so well that he appears to have specialised in this art', lit. learned this alone.

4. **quo magis scires,** 'so that you can better realise'. *quo* for *ut* in a purpose clause containing a comparative is the rule. **quam multa,** for the more usual *quot,* perhaps to balance *quam iucunda* and give more emphasis. **unus,** emphatic, 'Zosimus and nobody else.'

5. **accedit,** 'I have moreover . . .', lit. there is added. **caritas hominis,** 'affection for the man'. *hominis* is objective genitive.

est enim ita natura comparatum ut, 'for it is a law of nature that . . .', lit. so ordained by nature that. **aeque . . . quam carendi metus,** 'so much as a fear of losing the person one loves', lit. fear of being without. **quem,** 'this fear . . .'.

6. **ante aliquot annos,** 'some years before', a mainly Silver Latin use; Cicero might have written *aliquot ante annis*, lit. before by several years. **dum intente instanterque pronuntiat,** 'while he was exerting himself in an impassioned performance', lit. reciting earnestly and vigorously. **sanguinem reiecit,** 'he spat blood', a common symptom of tuberculosis, for which a sea-cruise, a warmer climate like that in Egypt, milk and fresh air (see § 7 below) were the usual palliatives. The disease was subject to relapses and usually fatal even until comparatively recently; the fate of Little Nell in Dickens' *Old Curiosity Shop* and Ralph Tuckett in Henry James' *Portrait of a Lady* is a grim reminder in fiction of a tragic medical reality. Early warning of the disease through X-rays and more sophisticated treatment have now robbed it of much of its terror in more favoured parts of the world, though by no means everywhere. **confirmatus redit nuper,** 'he returned with his health restored just recently'. *redit* is a contracted form of *rediit*, or it may be historic present. *nuper* here gains emphasis by assuming the normal position of the verb. **per continuos dies,** 'for several days on end'. **nimis imperat voci,** 'demanded too much of his voice', lit. ordered voice too much. **veteris . . . admonitus,** 'warned of (the return of) his old complaint by a slight cough'. *tussicula* is a diminutive of *tussis* (French *toux*).

7. **qua ex causa,** 'for this reason', connecting relative. **Foro Iulii,** the modern Fréjus, in Gallia Narbonensis (Provence), an important Roman colony in which the remains of a Roman amphi-theatre can still be seen. *Foro* is ablative of 'place where', without a preposition, for the more usual locative (with names of towns). Perhaps Pliny felt the double genitive ending of the locative (*Fori Iulli*) would be confusing. **referentem esse . . . aera,** 'saying both that the air there is . . . and . . .'. **eiusmodi curationibus accommodatissium,** 'well suited to cures of this kind'.

8. **rogo . . . scribas,** *ut* omitted in a dependent request, as commonly in conversational Latin, especially when another dependent request follows, *ut . . . pateat, offerant . . . etiam*. **ut illi . . . pateat,** 'to offer him the hospitality of the estate and house', lit. that the estate . . . should be open to him. **si quid opus erit** is the object of *offerant*, 'and contribute anything

necessary (lit. if anything will be necessary) to his expenses'. Note that the phrase *opus erit* can take either the nominative or the ablative of the 'thing needed'. Here it is the former; in the next sentence the ablative *modico*.

9. **opus . . . modico,** 'his needs will be small', lit. there will be need of a small thing. Note the 'chiastic' (crossed over like the Greek letter χ) and balanced word order, with three corresponding words in reversed sequence:

$$
\begin{array}{ccc}
1 & 2 & 3
\end{array}
$$
(*si*) *quid opus erit,*

$$
\begin{array}{ccc}
3 & 2 & 1
\end{array}
$$
erit (*autem*) *opus modico.*

See also No. 9 (Cicero) (*d*), 2, 2, for another example. **ut . . . restringat,** 'that he frugally (lit. with frugality) denies himself not only the delicacies but also the essentials for his health', **proficiscenti . . . in tua,** 'when he sets off I will give him sufficient travelling money for his journey to your estates', lit. I will give to him setting out so much of travel money how much to be sufficient for him going to your (estates — supply *praedia*). *eunti* is dative of advantage with *sufficiat*, a subjunctive in a relative clause of purpose or perhaps generic. Pliny is not being mean or distrustful of Zosimus in restricting the amount of the *viaticum*. Those who travelled with a large sum of money risked the attentions of highway or local robbers. Cicero tells the story (*De Invent.* 2, 4, 14) of an innkeeper who murdered a guest for his money, and Pliny (6, 25) records the mysterious disappearance of a wealthy traveller and how this reminded him of the unexplained death of a centurion on the road from Comum to Rome when he was carrying 40,000 sesterces.

TACITUS

16. A Murder Ship Miscarries (*Annals* XIV, 3–5)

I.

1. **vitare,** historic infinitive, like *laudare* later. **secretos eius congressus,** 'being alone with her' (Agrippina), lit. her secret meetings. **(eam) abscedentem in . . . ,** 'her when she was leaving for . . .', object of *laudare*. **hortos,** 'her park' (at Rome), perhaps

the gardens of Lucullus, appropriated for the imperial family by
Messalina, wife of Claudius, in A.D. 47. **Tusculanum ... in agrum,**
'her country estates at Tusculum or Antium'.   These were south-
east of Rome, the former inland (modern Frascati), the latter on
the coast (Anzio);   Cicero had estates at both places.   **quod ...
capesseret,** 'for taking a holiday'.   *capesseret* is subjunctive of
virtual *oratio obliqua*, 'because (as Nero said) . . .', not the real
reason, which was, as the next sentence implies, that she was out
of his way.

2. **ubicumque haberetur,** 'wherever she was', lit. was kept.
haberetur is subjunctive in a subordinate clause inside a dependent
statement with *ratus*.   **praegravem,** 'more than he could stand',
lit. excessively burdensome; supply *eam* before and *esse* after, in
the dependent statement with *ratus*.   **hactenus consultans,** 'de-
bating only (thus far)'.   **veneno . . . vi,** 'whether (he should kill
her) by poison . . .', supply *utrum* before *veneno* and *interficeret*
(deliberative subjunctive) at the end.   **vel qua alia vi,** 'or perhaps
by violence of some other kind'.   *qua =aliqua*.   The pronoun *quis*
and adjective *qui* is regularly used for *aliquis* after *si, nisi, num*
and *ne* and sometimes elsewhere, perhaps here to avoid the jingle
aliqua alia.

3. **placuit primo venenum,** 'poison was the first choice', lit.
first pleased (him).   **inter epulas principis,** 'at the emperor's
table', lit. during a banquet.   **si daretur,** imperfect subjunctive
because Nero's thoughts are being reported: he said to himself
si dabitur (or *detur*).   **referri ad casum non poterat,** 'it
could not be put down to chance'.   **tali iam Britannici exitio,**
'since Britannicus had already met such a fate', ablative of cause.
Britannicus was the son of the previous emperor Claudius, who
had also been poisoned, and Messalina.   Agrippina had intrigued
to rob him of the succession in favour of Nero, whom she then
provoked, through jealousy, to poison him.   A third death by
poisoning would be too much!   **ministros temptare, arduum
videbatur,** 'to try to corrupt the servants seemed hard', i.e.
persuade them to poison her or at least turn a blind eye to a
poisoner at work in the kitchen.   **mulieris . . . intentae,** 'of a
woman who was alert to (*adversus*) plots through experience of
crime'.   **atque,** 'and in any case', emphatic here, introducing a
short sharp sentence which delivers a knockout blow to these
hopes.   **praesumendo remedia,** 'by taking antidotes beforehand,' *praesumendo* is an instrumental gerund in the ablative.

4. **ferrum et caedes,** 'murder by the sword', a 'hendiadys', where two words, loosely linked by *et*, form a single concept, as we say 'nice and warm' or 'bread and butter'. Either word would have sufficed but Tacitus, by using both, gains emphasis which he increases both by extracting the subject from its clause (*quomodo . . . occultaretur*) and by placing this indirect deliberative question before the main clause (*nemo reperiebat*) on which it depends. The normal order would be *nemo reperiebat quonam modo ferrum et . . .*, but to write this is to spell out the reason why Tacitus changed it; for thus the second item on Nero's shopping-list of murder-weapons is highlighted. **et ne quis . . . sperneret, metuebat,** again the normal order would be *metuebat ne . . . sperneret*. But Tacitus produces a horrific effect by placing the paradoxical fear (for few fear, as Nero did, that someone would *fail to kill* their mother) before the verb of fearing on which it depends. **illi tanto facinori delectus,** 'the man selected for such a shocking crime', lit. for that so great crime.

5. **obtulit ingenium Anicetus,** 'it was Anicetus who put forward a (brilliant) scheme'. Note the inverted word order, with subject and verb each given emphasis by being interchanged. So the entry of Anicetus, the *deus ex machina*, as it were, who solves Nero's dilemma, is dramatised. **libertus,** ex-slaves frequently rose to high positions in the Roman Empire; but there is a touch of irony here too, for Agrippina employed a freedman, Pallas, in her intrigues, and there is a hint that she was being hoist with her own petard. **Misenum,** the important naval base at the north-west end of the Bay of Naples (see map on page 129). **pueritiae Neronis educator,** 'Nero's tutor in boyhood', lit. tutor of Nero's boyhood. **mutuis odiis Agrippinae invisus,** 'loathed by Agrippina (lit. hateful to Agrippina) with a hatred which he reciprocated', or more simply 'he and Agrippina loathed each other'. Note how Tacitus, having dramatically introduced Anicetus, proceeds to list his sinister qualifications: he was a freedman — a suitable agent for revenge; a naval man, with the necessary expertise and authority to organise the scheme; a tutor to Nero, someone he could trust and yet, by a grim twist, not altogether to be trusted (it had been Britannicus' tutors who had administered his first abortive dose of poison, *Annals* XIII, 15, 6); and he loathed his victim.

6. **navem posse componi docet,** 'a ship could be put together, he said'. Again the dependent clause anticipates its verb with

telling effect. So Tacitus teases the reader along: conventional murder weapons, poison and cold steel, have been dismissed; Anicetus had been 'built up' to make us agog to know what the *ingenium* is. A piece of shipbuilding, we are told; who, at this point, could fail to read on? **cuius pars . . . ignaram,** 'of which part would come loose by design while actually at sea and throw an unsuspecting female passenger overboard'. Note two things here: we are not told now or later the exact mechanics of the 'accident', and this adds to the sinister suspense; also, though most editors and translators supply 'Agrippina' with *ignaram* it seems that, had Tacitus meant this, he would have written *effunderet eam ignaram*. Perhaps he is being more subtle: Anicetus is offering Nero a device to dispose of *any* unsuspecting female passenger — it is for Nero to decide who she is to be. But perhaps the editor is being too subtle! **effunderet** is subjunctive in a relative clause either of purpose or of result ('of such a kind that . . .').

7. **nihil tam capax fortuitorum quam mare,** 'nothing was so capable of causing surprises as the sea', supply *esse*, continuing the reported speech. So Anicetus persuasively argues his case. Very ingenious, Nero might say, but will it be detected? Anicetus reassures him. **et si naufragio intercepta sit, quem adeo iniquum . . . ,** 'and if she had been disposed of by shipwreck, who would be so unfair . . .'. The original words of Anicetus would have been *si . . . intercepta erit, quis adeo iniquus erit . . .*; but the reporting is made more vivid in two ways: (*a*) after *docet*, a historic present is used which could be treated either as primary or historic. Tacitus, having treated it as historic by using *effunderet* in the previous sentence, now shifts to primary by using the perfect subjunctive *intercepta sit* for the pluperfect *intercepta esset*, the normal tense in reported speech to represent an original future perfect; (*b*) *quem adeo iniquum (fore)* is called a 'rhetorical question'. What Anicetus meant was *nemo adeo iniquus erit*, 'nobody will be so unfair', but he phrased it as a question for effect. When this becomes reported speech Latin sometimes compromises over what is both a question and tantamount to a statement by phrasing it as a question and using the construction (accusative and infinitive) of a statement. **ut . . . deliquerint,** 'as to read crime into the shortcomings of wind and wave', lit. assign to crime what winds and waves have done wrong. Note that the verbs in the result clause (*adsignet*) and dependent relative clause (*deliquerint*) are also primary, in line with *intercepta sit*. **additurum principem . . .**

ostentandae pietati, 'the emperor would allot to the deceased . . . and other tokens to display his affection'. *additurum* represents *addes*, future indicative for a polite imperative; *defunctae* is a dative indirect object of *additurum* and refers to Agrippina, still not mentioned by name but by the end of the sentence Anicetus, warming to his task, leaves no doubt who is meant; *ostentandae pietati* is a dative gerundive phrase of purpose, frequently used by Tacitus for what in earlier Latin would have been *ad ostentandam pietatem*. This sentence is masterly: Tacitus often rounds off a chapter with an epigram in case it should end 'not with a bang but a whimper'. But this is so much more — a profound study of the psychology of an unscrupulous freedman. There, Anicetus seems to say, I have taken care of the mechanics of the plot and reassured you about the risk of detection; but just in case you have a conscience about matricide you can make it good to her posthumously by exceptional memorial arrangements. With Anicetus the right impression was enough. He could not grasp the ramifications of Nero's twisted conscience. In fact Nero had his mother cremated on a dining-room couch and given a mean funeral the same night. It was left to household slaves to raise a small mound to her beside the Misenum road 'near the villa of Caesar the dictator' (*Annals*, XIV, 9).

2.

1. **placuit sollertia,** 'the ingenious plan found favour', lit. the ingenuity (of the plan) pleased (him). **tempore etiam iuta,** 'the date, too, was in its favour', lit. helped also by the time, *iuta* with *sollertia*. **quando Quinquatruum festos dies . . . frequentabat,** 'since Nero habitually attended the festival of Minerva'. The *Quinquatrus* was an annual feast of Minerva, the goddess of wisdom, from 19 to 23 March and observed as a school holiday. Its name originated from its date, five days (*quinque*) after the Ides of March (15th) by inclusive reckoning. By misinterpretation of its name the festival was later prolonged to five days. **Baias,** a holiday resort at the north-west end of the Bay of Naples, a convenient four miles or so from Misenum (see map on page 129).

2. **ferendas . . . dictitans,** 'observing repeatedly that parents' outbursts of temper must be endured and their feelings humoured'. **placandum animum,** lit. spirit must be appeased, though often referred to Nero's own feelings, makes better sense, as Professor Woodcock argues, when applied to Agrippina's. Nero's pose is

all concern for his mother; his own feelings do not matter. **quo rumorem reconciliationis efficeret,** 'his aim was to start a rumour of reconciliation', lit. in order that thereby (*quo* =*ut eo* in a relative clause of purpose) . . . , but it is easier to start a new sentence here. **acciperetque . . . ad gaudia,** 'and that Agrippina should believe (lit. accept) it with the ready credulity of women towards welcome news (lit. joys)'; *credulitate* is ablative of manner or cause.

3. **venientem dehinc obvius in litora . . . excepit,** 'in due course she came, and he went down to the beach to meet her . . .', with *venientem* supply *Agrippinam*, object of *excepit*. Note how the focus of interest, shifted to Agrippina in the last sentence, is adroitly kept there by placing the object participle first. **Antio,** 'from Antium'. **(excepit) manu et complexu,** 'took her hand and embraced her', lit. (welcomed her when coming) by hand and embrace. **Baulos,** another holiday resort on the Bay of Naples (see map on page 129) a couple of miles from Baiae.

4. **Misenum inter et Baianum lacum,** 'between Misenum and the Baian (=Lucrine) lake'. *inter*, like many two-syllable prepositions, may follow its case; here it is 'sandwiched' neatly between the two place-names it governs. **flexo mari adluitur,** 'is washed by the waters of the bay', lit. by the curved sea.

5. **stabat,** 'there stood . . .'. Note the striking effect of the verb placed first, dramatically introducing another 'character', as it were, in this macabre tragi-comedy. **ornatior,** 'more handsomely appointed', an adroit dual-purpose comparative, for *ornare* is the standard word for 'equipping a ship' but also means 'to adorn', so that this vessel is both more 'shipshape' than usual and also attractively 'dressed overall' — fitting bait for a queen mother. **alias** =*ceteras*, 'the others'. **tamquam id . . . daretur,** 'apparently another compliment to his mother', lit. as if this also was being offered as an honour to his mother. *honori* is a predicative dative, and the subjunctive *daretur* signifies an unreal comparison, but with a subtler innuendo for the perceptive: for it *indeed was* being offered as a compliment to her, yet not just that alone — the *real motive* was more sinister. **quippe . . . vehi,** 'for, to be sure, she had been accustomed to travel in a warship manned by imperial marines', lit. by a trireme and rowing (or crew) of marines. This was a special privilege, for normally ships were rowed by slaves. The pluperfect *sueverat* suggests a privilege granted before her estrangement from Nero and now magnanimously restored.

6. **ut occultando . . . nox adhiberetur,** 'so that night could be enlisted (lit. used) to cover up the crime'. **occultando facinori,** like *ostentandae pietati* in 1. 7, is a dative gerundive phrase of purpose. **satis constitit** (from *constat*). . . **proditorem,** 'but it has been well established that an informer emerged'. **auditis insidiis,** ablative absolute. **an crederet ambiguam,** 'wondering (lit. doubtful) whether to believe it'; *an* for *num* is not uncommon in Tacitus. **gestamine sellae,** 'with a litter as her conveyance', lit. by the conveyance of a litter. *sellae* is defining genitive with its meaning extended from 'chair' to 'travelling-chair', i.e. sedan-chair or litter. Or it may be that the whole phrase is simply a variant on *lectica*, 'litter', lit. a carrying device consisting of a chair. If so translate 'by a litter (or sedan-chair)'. On the litter as a mode of transport see *Two Centuries of Roman Poetry*, page 81 and Plate 9. **pervectam,** supply *esse*, perfect infinitive continuing the dependent statement after *constitit*. The exact details of the plot are somewhat obscure. Originally Agrippina had been invited from Bauli, where the ship was, to a late banquet at Nero's villa at Baiae, and was presumably intended to travel in the 'murder ship' to it, when the 'accident' would be staged. But the informer frightened her into making the journey from Bauli to Baiae by road. So there must have been a last-minute change of plan: the ship would have been moved from Bauli to Baiae, where Nero coaxed her to make the return journey after the banquet. It was then that the 'accident' occurred. Perhaps the detailed timetable, like the precise mechanics of the collapsible ship, are deliberately left hazy to focus the reader's attention on the leading characters. Fussiness over detail can spoil a good story.

7. **blandimentum,** '(Nero's) flattering attentions'. **superque ipsum collocata (est),** 'and she was given a place of honour above himself'. The normal positions of diners at table, reclining on couches on their left elbows, was as shown overleaf. The guest of honour would recline at position 6 on the 'middle couch' (*lectus medius*), the host at 7 on the 'lowest couch' (*lectus imus*). In their positions at the right-angle between couches they could more easily face one another and thereby Nero exercise, and Agrippina succumb to, his charms the better.

8. **iam pluribus sermonibus . . . tracto in longum convictu,** 'then Nero prolonged the entertainment with numerous topics of conversation, now with youthful intimacy, again with a serious air, as if he were communicating important matters'. This passage is

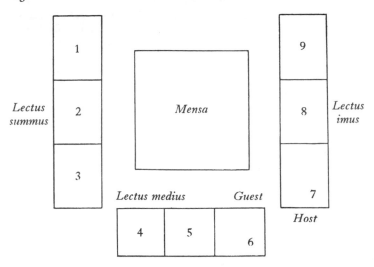

made difficult by Tacitus' love of variety of expression. The backbone of it is the ablative absolute **tracto . . . convictu,** lit. the entertainment being prolonged, with an ablative of instrument added, *pluribus sermonibus*, lit. by many conversations. But in the middle, as subject of *prosequitur*, Nero is 'sandwiched' and his manner characterised first by an ablative of description, *familiaritate iuvenili*, then by the adjective *adductus*, 'serious', lit. drawn tight, tensed. This varied manner of description is further complicated by indicating the alternation in Nero's moods first by *modo*, then *rursus*. It would have been easier written *modo familiaritate iuvenili Nero, modo adducto vultu*, but this would not have been Tacitus. With *tracto in longum* supply *tempus*, lit. dragged out into a long time. *quasi . . . consociaret*, subjunctive of unreal comparison. **prosequitur abeuntem,** 'saw her off as she left'. **oculis et pectori haerens,** 'reluctant to leave her sight and clinging to her breast', lit. clinging to her eyes and breast, an example of the figure called 'zeugma' or 'syllepsis', where a verb is used with two nouns in a slightly different sense with each (there is a similar example in Part I, No. 1 (Cicero), 1. 3). Here *haerens* is first metaphorical with *oculis*, then literal with *pectori*. *oculis haerens* could also mean 'kissing her eyes'; Dio Cassius (LXI, 3) says as much, and he and Tacitus may have used a common source here. **sive explenda simulatione,** 'whether as a final piece of hypocrisy', lit. whether in fulfilling the pretence, a gerundival ablative of manner, almost equivalent to a present participle *sive simulationem explens*. **seu periturae . . . retinebat,** 'or whether the last sight of his mother going to her death (lit. about to perish) was clutching at (lit. holding back) his heart, brutalised though it was'. *quamvis* goes closely with *ferum*, not with *retinebat*, which is the finite verb with *seu*. Again Tacitus' love of variety of expression gives us *sive . . . seu*, which normally take parallel constructions (usually finite verbs), followed first by a gerundive phrase, then a finite verb (there is a similar example, but with an ablative absolute instead of the gerundive phrase, in Part I, No. 8 (Tacitus), 2. 3.). This study of the psychology of a monster's final farewell to his mother is penetrating: was this physical show of affection the crowning pretence in a callous act, or an involuntary flush of real feeling?

3.

1. **noctem . . . praebuere,** 'a quiet, star-lit night with a calm sea, as if to afford proof of guilt, was sent by heaven'. The word order here is masterly: first the scene is set, with *noctem* dominant to shake the reader from the tenderness of the last sentence, whether sham or sincere, to the grim reality of what was afoot; then the malign influence of the gods, at work behind the scenes, as it were, at the end of the sentence, hinting at failure or detection. Tacitus does not, on the whole, see the gods active in history, but where he does their operation is mainly malevolent — *ira deum* — aggravating the retribution men suffer for their follies. **quasi convincendum ad scelus,** gerundive of purpose. Note the inverted order, perhaps to bring *scelus* and *di* closer together.

2. **duobus . . . comitantibus,** ablative absolute, lit. two accompanying, i.e. 'while two . . . accompanied . . .'. **ex quis** = *ex quibus*. **Crepereius Gallus,** is not elsewhere mentioned in Tacitus, his appearance is something of a record even there, for he is both introduced and dispatched in a single sentence. **Acerronia,** who lasts a little longer, and at least has partly herself to blame, may have been the daughter of Cn. Acerronius Proculus, consul in the last year of Tiberius' reign (*Ann.* VI, 45). The fate of this man and woman is dramatic; they shift the focus of interest momentarily from Agrippina and make her escape, reserved for the end of the chapter, seem all the more miraculous. **super pedes**

cubitantis reclinis, 'bending over the feet of her mistress who was lying down'. Supply *Agrippinae* with *cubitantis*, *Acerronia* with *reclinis*. The assonant endings of *cubitantis reclinis*, whether by accident or design, suggest touching feminine intimacy. Presumably Agrippina was lying on the couch, Acerronia sitting on a lower stool and leaning back across her feet. **reciperatam matris gratiam,** 'the recovery of his mother's influence', lit. a mother's influence recovered. **per gaudium,** 'joyfully'. **cum dato signo ruere tectum loci,** 'when the signal was given and the cabin roof fell in'. The climax is brilliantly contrived: a long main clause of quiet social activity, Agrippina among her friends, and then the crash; the unexpectedness of it all carries the conviction of how accidents happen. And the syntax helps: an 'inverted' *cum*-clause, where the indicative is used in what is in effect the main clause while the grammatical main clause merely gives the time and circumstances, and the effect of this 'inverted' *cum*-clause accentuated by its containing a historic infinitive (*ruere*) as well as a finite verb. This use of a historic infinitive in a *subordinate* clause is limited, and reserved by Tacitus for dramatic moments such as this. **loci,** lit. of the place, i.e. the place where the ladies were relaxing, either a covered cabin or perhaps a large wooden canopy, for Crepereius, though standing near the tiller at the stern, seems to have been underneath it as he too was crushed (*pressus* later in the sentence) by its collapse.

multo plumbo grave, this, one of the most teasing examples of Tacitean brevity and understatement, is the chief clue to the nature of the 'accident'. As it stands the phrase means 'heavy' or 'weighed down with much lead'. Presumably the cabin/canopy carried a load of lead too much for the supports (perhaps deliberately weakened) when even a gentle swell out to sea set the ship rolling; or perhaps lead weights of some sort were dropped on it from above. Furneaux suggests that the collapse of the cabin roof was an alternative plan when the sea proved too calm (*placido mari*, 3, 1) to make the shipwreck implied in *naufragio intercepta* (1, 7) look plausible. But, as Professor Woodcock points out, a rough sea, just as much as an informer, could have frightened Agrippina into returning by land as well. Woodcock's own view is that the falling of a weight was intended to knock a hole in the hull and scuttle the ship. But this does not explain why the cabin was wrecked in the process unless the weight was intended to rebound off the cabin roof into the hull with enough force to hole it — surely a daunting ballistic problem — or something went wrong. Perhaps too much importance has been given to *naufragio intercepta* (1, 7). The word *naufragium* means 'breaking a ship' (*navem — frangere*) usually, but perhaps not necessarily by actual shipwreck. Could it be that the wreck of the cabin — a little local 'ship-breaking' — was all Anicetus intended? Why should an admiral waste a perfectly good trireme if the collapse of a cabin/ canopy was enough to dispose of the dowager empress? He had not reckoned on the projecting sides of the couch (§ 3 below). Whatever his somewhat evasive words to Nero in 1, 6–7, — *pars per artem soluta* (could *pars* mean the cabin/canopy only?), *effunderet* and *naufragio* — were meant to convey, the collapse of the *whole* ship oddly enough did not occur — *nec dissolutio navigii sequebatur* (§ 4 below). The *conscii* ('accomplices') do not seem to have been trying very hard, for someone really determined to scuttle a ship properly prepared for the purpose would not have been frustrated by a mere crowd. And the crew, in their attempt to capsize the ship, may have exceeded their orders (*visum* in § 5 suggests an initiative) through an exaggerated rumour of what was intended to happen. It is noteworthy that the one failure that must not occur — the survival of Agrippina suggested by the ill-advised screams of Acerronia — was speedily averted with unerring thoroughness *contis et remis et quae fors obtulerat navalibus telis* (§ 6 below). For Agrippina, recollecting the events afterwards in comparative tranquillity, one thing stood out clearly; (*Annals* XIV, 6, 1) *litus iuxta non ventis acta, non saxis impulsa navis summa sui parte veluti terrestre machinamentum concidisset*, 'near the shore a vessel, driven by no gale, striking no reef, had collapsed from the top like an artificial structure on land'. We are not even told whether the ship actually sank. Perhaps all that happened was that the cabin or canopy collapsed; perhaps that was all Anicetus meant to happen. We shall probably never know, but it is some comfort that the art of Tacitus does not require us to know. He may not even have known himself, or cared.

3. **eminentibus . . . protectae sunt,** 'were sheltered by the projecting sides of the couch which, as it happened, were too solid to give way under the pressure', lit. yield to the burden. *cederent* is subjunctive in a result clause following a comparative (*validioribus*) with *quam ut*, the usual Latin idiom. Acerronia, who was leaning back over Agrippina's feet, would have shared the protection of the couch sides.

4. **turbatis omnibus et quod . . .** 'because there was general confusion and because . . .'. *turbatis omnibus* is ablative absolute of cause, lit. all having been thrown into confusion, and is used as a parallel variant to the causal clause that follows: another example of Tacitus' love of variety of expression. **etiam conscios impediebant,** 'were hindering even those in the know'. Note the imperfect tense, describing the scene as actually in progress before the reader's eyes.

5. **visum (est) dehinc remigibus,** 'the crew then decided. . .', lit. it seemed good to the oarsmen to. . . . **sed neque ipsis . . . consensus,** 'even by them there was no quick concerted action for this emergency', or 'to meet this emergency', lit. there was not to themselves. . . . The suggestion here that the 'emergency plan' to capsize the ship was the crew's initiative, or even that there was no emergency plan, only an emergency, lends colour to the view expressed above (note on § 2) that Anicetus was not exactly hell-bent on scuttling his ship. **et alii . . . iactus,** 'and a counter-effort by others made possible a gentler fall overboard into the sea', lit. and others leaning in the opposite direction gave a chance of . . . *iactus,* often used of jettisoning cargo, here applies to a human one.

6. **imprudentia,** 'foolishly', lit. through foolishness, causal ablative. Note its extraction from its clause *dum . . . clamitat* to give emphasis. We might almost translate 'silly girl!' **dum . . . clamitat,** 'in (lit. while) shouting that she was Agrippina and demanding help for the emperor's mother'. *clamitat* here has two constructions, first a dependent statement (*se . . . esse*), then a dependent command (*ut . . . subveniretur*). **subveniretur matri,** lit. that there should be help for the mother . . . , impersonal passive with the subject retained in the dative, the regular construction when a verb governing the dative is used in the passive. **quae fors obtulerat,** 'that came to hand', lit. that chance had offered. The relative clause, as often in Tacitus, anticipates its antecedent *navalibus telis* (probably 'nautical gear' or 'implements' rather than 'weapons' here).

7. **eoque minus agnita,** 'and for that reason not recognised', lit. less recognised. But how can one be 'less recognised'? By fewer people? Or uncertainly? Probably Tacitus here uses *minus* as poets did for *non*. For the speedy despatch of Acerronia suggests that if Agrippina had been even half-recognised by one of the *conscii* she would have gone the same way. The wound in her shoulder (*unum tamen vulnus umero excepit*) was perhaps

caused by the collapse of the cabin/canopy or in the fracas which followed. **nando,** 'by swimming', ablative gerund of manner. **deinde occursu,** 'then she was met by', lit. by meeting of. **Lucrinum in lacum . . . infertur,** '(and) was conveyed to the Lucrine lake and carried to her villa'. There is no evidence that she had a villa by the Lucrine lake, so we must assume that, on landing there, she was carried overland, once more *gestamine sellae* as in 2, 6, to Bauli. Note the carefully contrived calm of the last few words: after the tension and terror of the rest of the chapter the murder victim, wet and slightly wounded but otherwise unscathed, slips unobtrusively home. One is reminded of Pepys' 'and so to bed'; or, more aptly, of Regulus, in Horace's *Ode* (III, 5, 55–56), returning to his death in Carthage like a lawyer leaving for a weekend break in the country or by the sea:

> *tendens Venafranos in agros*
> *aut Lacedaemonium Tarentum.*

With Agrippina, too, it was only the calm before the final storm.

VOCABULARY

ABBREVIATIONS

1, 2, 3, 4, 5 after a noun means that it is a regular noun declined like *mensa, dominus* or *bellum, cīvis, gradus* or *cornu, rēs*, feminine in the first and fifth declensions and masculine or neuter in the second, third, and fourth. Exceptions and irregularities are given, and the genitive singular and gender of third declension nouns other than those ending in *-is*. 2 or 3 after an adjective means that it is declined like *bonus, -a, -um* or *tristis, -e.* 1, 2, 3, 4 after a verb means that it is conjugated like *amō, moneō, regō, audiō.* For other verbs the perfect and supine (when there is one) are given. All long syllables are marked, and unmarked syllables are short, except that diphthongs are always long. Second declension nouns ending in *-ius* and *-ium* have their genitive singular in *-iī* or *-ī*, e.g. *imperium,* genitive *imperiī* or *imperī.*

abl.	ablative	*impers.*	impersonal
acc.	accusative	*indecl.*	indeclinable
adj.	adjective	*intr.*	intransitive
adv.	adverb	*m.*	masculine
c.	common	*n.*	neuter
	also circā, about	*part.*	present participle
comp.	comparative	*perf.*	perfect
conj.	conjunction	*pl.*	plural
dat.	dative	*p.p.*	past participle deponent
d.	died	*p.p.p.*	past participle passive
defect.	defective	*prep.*	preposition
dep.	deponent	*reflex.*	reflexive
f.	feminine	*sing.*	singular
gen.	genitive	*superl.*	superlative
imperat.	imperative	*tr.*	transitive

A

ā, ab, *prep. with abl.,* by, from.

abdō, 3, **-didī, -ditum,** hide.

abduco, 3, lead away, take away.

abeō, -īre, -iī, -itum, depart.

abhinc, ago, from this time (*with acc.*).

abiciō, 3, **-iēcī, -iectum,** throw away, put down.

abigō, 3, **-ēgī, -āctum,** drive away.

Aborīginēs, -um, *m. pl.,* Aborigines, original inhabitants.

abrumpō, 3, **-rūpī, -ruptum,** break off.

abscēdō, 3, **-cessī, -cessum,** depart.

absolvō, 3, **-solvī, -solūtum,** acquit, vote for the acquittal of.

abstergeō, 2, **-tersī, -tersum,** wipe away.

abstinentia, 1, honesty, integrity, self-denial, avoidance of wrong.

absum, -esse, abfuī, be away, be absent, keep away, be lacking.

absūmō, 3, **-sumpsī, -sumptum,** destroy; *pass.*, perish.

absurdus, 2, foolish, incongruous, uncalled for; *adv.* **absurdē,** in an uncalled for manner.

abunde, in abundance, quite enough.

abūtor, 3, **-ūsus,** *dep. with abl.,* use up.

ac, *conj.,* and, and moreover.

Acadēmicus, 2, of the *Academica, a philosophical work by Cicero.*

accēdō, 3, **-cessī, -cessum,** approach, be added.

accidō, 3, **-cidī,** happen.

accendō, 3, **-cendī, -cēnsum,** kindle, inspire.

acciō, 4, summon, call, invite.

accipiō, 3, **-cēpī, -ceptum,** receive, hear, learn by tradition, suffer (*gerundive in Sallust* **accipiundus**).

accūsō, 1, accuse.

acclīvis, 3, sloping.

accola, 1, *c.,* inhabitant.

accurātē, *adv.,* in detail.

ācer, ācris, ācre, fierce; *adv.* **ācriter.**

acerbus, 2, harsh, strident.

Acerrōnia, 1, Acerronia, *a friend of Agrippina.*

acētum, 2, vinegar.

aciēs, 5, line of battle.

ācriter, *adv. of* **ācer,** sharply, clearly.

ad, *prep. with acc.,* to, up to, against, near, at.

adcrēscō, 3, **-crēvī, -crētum,** *intr.,* increase, flow.

addō, 3, **-didī, -ditum,** add, allot to.

addūcō, 3, bring to, contract;

vultum addūcere, frown; *p.p.p.,* **adductus,** with a serious air.

adeō, so much, to such an extent, indeed.

adfectiō, -ōnis, *f.,* feeling.

adfectus, 4, emotion.

adferō, -ferre, -attulī, allātum, bring.

adficiō, 3, **-fēcī, -fectum,** affect.

adfirmō, 1, declare, prove.

adflīgō, 3, **-flīxī, -flictum,** throw down, trouble.

adhibeō, 2, use.

adhūc, *adv.,* still.

adiaceō, 2, lie near, stand near.

adiciō, 3, **-iēcī, -iectum,** add, join, attach.

adipīscor, 3, **adeptus,** *dep.,* obtain, reach (*p.p. in Sallust, pass.*).

adiungō, 3, **-iunxī, -iunctum,** join, attach.

adiūtō, 1, *with dat.,* help.

adiūvō, 1, **-iūvī, -iūtum,** help.

adloquor, 3, **-locūtus,** *dep.,* address.

adluō, 3, **-luī,** bathe, make wet, wash, flow over.

adminiculum, 2, prop, support.

admodum, *adv.,* quite, fully.

admoneō, 2, warn, remind.

adnumerō, 1, count.

adorior, 4, **-ortus,** *dep.,* attack.

adrīdeō, 2, **-rīsī, -rīsum,** smile, laugh.

adsēverō, 1, proclaim, point to.

adsiduus, 2, endless.

adsignō, 1, ascribe, attribute.

adsimulō, 1, liken to.

adstō, 1, **-stitī,** stand near, stand by.

adsurgō, 3, **-surrexī, -surrectum,** rise up, flow.

adulēscēns, -entis, young man, youth.

advectus, 2, immigrant (*p.p.p. of* **adveho**).

advena, 1, *m.*, stranger, foreigner.
adveniō, 4, **-vēnī, -ventum,** arrive.
adventō, 1, approach.
adversārius, 2, opponent.
adversor, 1, *dep.*, oppose; *part.* **adversāns,** contrary.
adversus, 2, opposite, contrary, hostile, in the opposite direction.
adversus, *adv. and prep. with acc.,* against.
Aeacus, 2, Aeacus, *son of Jupiter, a judge in the Underworld.*
aedēs, -is, *f.,* temple; *pl.* house.
aedificium, 2, building.
aedificātiuncula, 1, small building.
aedificō, 1, build.
aegrē, with difficulty; *superl.,* **agerrimē,** with very great difficulty.
Aegyptus, 2, *f.,* Egypt.
Aenēās, -ae, *m.,* Aeneas, *son of Anchises and Venus, Trojan prince who settled in Italy.*
aēneus, 2, made of bronze.
aequālis, 3, of the same age, contemporary, equally matched.
aequitās, -ātis, *f.,* fairness, uprightness, justice, calmness.
aequus, 2, equal; *adv.* **aequē.**
āēr, āeris, acc. **āera,** *m.,* air.
aerārium, 2, treasury.
aes, aeris, *n.,* copper, money.
aestimō, 1, reckon the value of, think worth, consider (*a question*).
aestus, 4, tide.
aetās, -ātis, *f.,* age, time of life.
aeternus, 2, eternal; *n.* that which is everlasting.
Agamemnōn, -nonis, *m.,* Agamemnon, *a teacher of rhetoric in Petronius.*
ager, agrī, 2, field, estate; *pl.* territory.

agglūtinō, 1, *tr.,* stick, fasten.
aggredior, 3, **-gressus,** *dep.,* attack.
agilis, 3, fast, nimble.
aginō, 1, plan.
agitō, 1, keep on doing; **imperium agitāre,** govern, rule.
agmen, -inis, *n.,* column, army.
agō, 3, **ēgī, āctum,** do, plot, spend (*time*), live (*one's life*); **āctum est,** it is all up.
agrestis, 3, rustic, of the country.
Agrippīna, 1, Agrippina, *mother of Nero.*
Aiāx, -ācis, Ajax, *Greek hero who went mad and killed himself at Troy.*
āiō, ait, āiunt, *defect.,* say.
alacer, -cris, -cre, eager, willing.
alacritās, -ātis, *f.,* cheerfulness, good spirits.
aliās, at another time.
aliēnus, 2, belonging to another, from elsewhere.
aliōqui, aliōquin, otherwise.
aliquandō, sometimes, one day, ever.
aliquis, -quid, someone; **aliquī, -qua, -quod,** some.
aliquot, *indecl. pl.,* several, some.
alius, -a, -ud, other, another; **alii . . . alii,** some . . . others; **alius alium,** one another.
alō, 3, **aluī, altum,** feed, bring up.
Alpēs, -ium, *f. pl.,* the Alps.
Alpīnus, 2, of the Alps, Alpine.
alsus, 2, cold, cool.
alternus, 2, alternate.
altitūdō, -dinis, *f.,* height, depth.
altus, 2, high, deep, profound; *adv.* **altē,** deeply.
ambiguus, 2, doubtful.
ambiō, -īre, make one's way round.
ambitus, 4, detour, ambition, selfish purposes.

ambō, -ae, -ō, both.
ambulātiō, -ōnis, *f.*, promenade, cloister.
ambulō, 1, walk.
amīcitia, 1, friendship, alliance.
amictus, 2 (*p.p.p.* of **amīciō**), dressed in.
amīcus, 2, friend; **amīca,** 1, girl-friend, sweetheart.
āmittō, 3, **āmīsī, āmissum,** lose.
amnis, 3, river.
amō, 1, love, fall in love with.
amoenitās, -ātis, *f.,* beauty, beautiful scenery.
amor, -ōris, *m.*, love; *pl.* loved one, darling.
amphora, 1, jar.
amplus, 2, large, spacious, deep; *comp. adv.* **amplius,** more, some more, any longer.
ampulla, 1, bottle.
an, *conj.*, or, whether.
Ancus, 2, Ancus Martius, *fourth king of Rome.*
anfractus, 4, zigzag, winding path.
angulus, 2, corner.
angustiae, 1, *pl.*, difficulties.
angustus, 2, narrow.
Anicētus, 2, Anicetus, *a freedman of Nero.*
anima, 1, breath, air, life.
animus, 2, mind, spirit, senses, courage; **bonō animō es,** be of good cheer.
annus, 2, year; *pl.* age.
annuus, 2, annual, yearly.
ante, *adv. and prep. with acc.*, before.
anteā, *adv.*, before.
antecēdō, 3, **-cessī, -cessum,** go before.
antepōnō, 3, **-posuī, -positum,** prefer, put before.
antestō, 1, **-stetī,** be superior to, *with dat.*
Antiās, -ātis, *adj.*, at Antium, *where Agrippina had a villa.*

Antiochus, 2, Antiochus, *king of Syria.*
Antipater, -tris, Antipater, *a Stoic philosopher.*
antīquus, 2, ancient.
Antium, 2, Antium, *a seaside town in Latium.*
Antōnius, 2, Mark Antony.
ānulus, 2, ring.
aperiō, 4, **-uī, apertum,** open, reveal; *p.p.p.,* **apertus,** open, in the open.
apoculō, 1, *reflex.*, get oneself off.
apodȳterium, 2, changing room.
appāreō, 2, appear, turn up.
appāritor, -ōris, attendant.
appellō, 1, call, call upon, name.
appetō, 3, **-petīvī, -petītum,** approach, take to.
applicō, 1, attach; *reflex.*, join.
aprīcus, 2, sunny.
aptus, 2, suitable, fit; *adv.*, **aptē,** correctly.
apud, *prep. with acc.*, at, before, in the presence of, with, among, in the opinion of.
aqua, 1, water.
Aquīnum, 2, Aquinum, *a town in Latium.*
āra, 1, altar.
arbiter, -trī, eye-witness.
arbitrium, 2, decision.
arbitror, 1, *dep.*, think.
arbor, arboris, *f.*, tree.
Arcānum, 2, Cicero's estate near Arcae.
arceō, 2, **arcuī,** ward off, repel, prevent.
ārdeō, 2, **ārsī, ārsum,** catch fire, burst into flames.
arduus, 2, steep, difficult.
argentum, 2, silver.
argūmentum, 2, argument, conclusion.
argūtō, 1, chatter.

Aristīdēs, -is, Aristides, *Athenian soldier and statesman, famed for his integrity.*

arma, 2, *pl.,* arms, weapons.

armō, 1, arm; *p.p.p.,* **armātus,** armed.

Arpīnās, -ātis, *m.,* Cicero's estate at Arpinum.

arrectus, 2, steep.

ars, artis, *f.,* art, skill, accomplishment, talent, device.

artificium, 2, trade.

artē, *adv.,* closely, tightly.

artūs, 4, *pl.,* limbs.

arx, arcis, *f.,* citadel.

as, assis, *m.,* as, *a bronze coin, one-tenth of a denarius.*

ascendo, 3, **-cendī, -cēnsum,** climb.

ascēnsus, 4, ascent.

aspectus, 4, appearance.

asper, -pera, -perum, rough, sharp, difficult, rude; *adv.,* **asperē.**

asperitās, -ātis, *f.,* harshness, excess.

aspiciō, 3, aspexī, aspectum, see.

assa, 2, *pl.,* hot room, Turkish bath.

at, but.

atque, and, and moreover.

Athēnae, 1, *pl.,* Athens.

Athēniēnsis, 3, Athenian.

athlēta, 1, *m.,* athlete.

ātriolum, 2, small entrance-hall.

ātrium, 2, entrance-hall.

attollō, 3, —, raise up, disturb.

Attica, 1, Attica, *daughter of Atticus.*

Atticus, 2, T. Pomponius Atticus, *an Athenian, friend of Cicero.*

attingō, 3, -tigī, -tactum, touch.

auctor, -ōris, author, writer.

auctus, 4, increase.

audācia, 1, boldness.

audeō, 2, ausus, *semi-dep.,* dare.

audiō, 4, hear, hear of; **dictō audiēns esse,** obey, *with dat.*

auferō, -ferre, abstulī, ablātūm, take away.

augeō, 2, auxī, auctum, *tr.,* increase, increase the power of.

auguror, 1, *dep.,* foretell.

Augustus, 2, Augustus, *first Roman emperor,* 63 B.C.–A.D. 14.

aurīga, 1, *m.,* charioteer.

auris, 3, *f.,* ear.

aurum, 2, gold.

aut, or, either . . . or.

autem, however, moreover, now.

auxilium, 2, help; **auxiliō esse,** to help, *with dat.*

avāritia, 1, avarice, greed for money.

āvellō, 3, āvellī, āvulsum, tear away.

āvertō, 3, āvertī, āversum, turn away.

aviārium, 2, aviary, bird sanctuary.

avidus, 2, eager, eager for, *with gen.*

āvocātiō, -ōnis, *f.,* distraction.

āvocō, 1, distract.

B

bacciballum, 2, *perhaps* a peach of a girl.

Bāiae, 1, *pl., abl.* **Bāis,** Baiae, *a seaside resort near Naples;* **Bāiānus, 2,** of Baiae.

balineum, balneum, 2, public bath.

balneāria, 2, *pl.,* baths.

bāsis, 3, *f.,* base, foundation wall.

barbarus, 2, a barbarian, non-Greek; *in Nepos,* Persian.

Baulī, 2, *pl.,* Bauli, *town between Baiae and Misenum.*

beātus, 2, happy.

bellicōsus, 2, warlike.

bellum, 2, war.

bellus, 2, beautiful; *adv.,* **bellē,**
nicely, delightfully; **bellē erit,**
it will be nice.

bene, *adv. of* **bonus,** well.

beneficium, 2, favour, kindness.

biberārius, 2, drink-seller.

bīduum, 2, two days.

bīnī, 2, *pl.,* two each; two each
year.

bipennis, 3, *f.,* axe.

Bīthȳnius, 2, of Bithynia, *in Asia
Minor.*

blandīmentum, 2, flattery, charm.

blandior, 4, *dep.,* flatter.

bonus, 2, good; *n.* **bonum,**
goodness, the good.

botulārius, 2, sausage-maker,
sausage seller.

bovis, 3, *c., ante- and post-classical
form of* **bos, bovis,** ox, cow.

brevis, 3, short; *abl.* **brevī,** soon.

Britannī, 2, *pl.,* the British,
Britons.

Britannia, 1, Britain.

Britannicus, 2, Britannicus, *son
of the emperor Claudius and
Messalina.*

C

C., Gāius, 2, Gaius, *a Roman
praenomen (first name).*

cacūmen, -minis, *n.,* mountain
top.

cadō, 3, **cecidī, cāsum,** fall

cadūceus, 2, herald's staff.

caecus, 2, concealed, out of sight.

caedēs, -is, *f.,* murder.

caedō, 3, **cecīdī, caesum,** strike,
kill, cut.

caelestis, 3, heavenly.

caelum, 2, sky, heaven, geographical position.

Caesar, -aris, Julius Caesar.

Caesius, Caesius, *a clerk of works
at Quintus Cicero's villa.*

calculus, 2, pebble.

Calēdonia, 1, Caledonia, *the
highlands of Scotland.*

calidus, 2, warm.

cālīgō, -inis, *f.,* darkness.

cālīgō, 1, become dizzy.

callidus, 2, clever.

calx, calcis, *f.,* kick.

camera, 1, ceiling.

cantābundus, 2, *adj.,* singing.

cantō, 1, sing, play an instrument.

capax, -ācis, capable of (*causing*),
with gen.

capessō, 3, **-īvī, -ītum,** take,
engage in.

capiō, 3, **cēpī, captum,** capture,
take, deceive.

captīva, 1, female prisoner.

Capua, 1, Capua, *town in S. Italy.*

caput, capitis, *n.,* head, source,
capital; **capitis damnāre,** condemn to death.

carcer, -eris, *m.,* prison.

cardēlis, 3, *f.,* goldfinch.

careō, 2, be without, *with abl.*

cāritās, -ātis, *f.,* affection.

castra, 2, *pl.,* camp.

casula, 1, little hut.

cāsus, 4, fall.

Catilīna, 1, *m.,* Catiline, *revolutionary leader.*

Catō, -ōnis, 1, Cato 'the Censor',
*d. 149 B.C., famed for his old-
fashioned sternness;* 2, Cato
'Uticensis', *d. 45 B.C., Stoic
philosopher, hostile to Caesar.*

caupō, -ōnis, 1, inn-keeper.

causa, 1, cause, reason.

causidicus, 2, lawyer.

cēdō, 3, **cessī, cessum,** retreat,
give way, withdraw; **locō
cēdere,** give ground.

celebrō, 1, honour, celebrate.

cēlō, 1, conceal.

cenātiuncula, 1, little dining-
room.

centēsimus, 2, hundredth.

cernō, 3, crēvī, crētum, perceive.

cērōma, -atis, n., ointment, oil-massage.

certāmen,-inis, n., contest, rivalry.

certātim, in rivalry.

certō, 1, contend, rival.

certus, 2, sure, certain, fixed; adv., certē, surely, at any rate; certum habēre, be sure of.

cēterī, 2, pl., the others, the rest (of); adv., cēterum, but.

Chrȳsippus, 2, Chrysippus, Stoic philosopher.

cicarō, -ōnis, lad.

Cicerō, -ōnis, Cicero; 1, Marcus, the famous orator; 2, Quintus, his brother.

circā, circum, adv. and prep. with acc., around, about.

circumdūnō, 3, lead round.

circumferō, -ferre, -tulī, -lātum, carry round.

circumfundō, 3, -fūdī, -fūsum, pour round.

Circumpādānus, 2, around the River Po.

circumsonō, 1, -sonuī, -sonitum, echo round.

circumstrepō, 3, -strepuī, make a noise round.

circumvehō, 3, carry round; pass. sail round.

circumveniō, 4, -vēnī, -ventum, surround, ruin, overthrow.

cithara, 1, lyre.

cito, adv., quickly.

citrā, prep. with acc., on this side of, south of.

cīvis, 3, citizen.

cīvitās, -ātis, f., state, city-state.

clāmitō, 1, keep shouting.

clāmō, 1, shout, cry.

clāmor, -ōris, m., shouting up-roar, din.

clārus 2, bright, clear, famous, distinguished.

classiārius, 2, marine.

classis, 3, f., fleet.

claudō, 3, clausī, clausum, close, shut up.

cliēns, -entis, client, dependant.

Clītumnus, 2, the River Clitum-nus, in Umbria.

clīvus, 2, hill, slope.

coalēscō, 3, coaluī, -alitum, be mingled into one.

coepī, -isse, defect., began.

coerceō, 2, restrain.

cōgitō, 1, think, think about.

cognōmen, -inis, n., name, sur-name.

cognōscō, 3, -nōvī, -nitum, find out, realise, perceive, recognise.

cōgō, 3, coēgī, -āctum, compel.

cohortātiō, -ōnis, f., encourage-ment.

collabefacio, 3, -fēcī, -factum, ruin, overthrow.

collātiō, -ōnis, f., contribution.

colligō, 3, -lēgī, -lectum, gather, collect, accumulate.

collis, 3, hill.

collocō, 1, place, give in marriage.

colloquium, 2, conversation, parley.

colloquor, 3, -locūtus, dep., con-verse.

collum, 2, neck.

colō, 3, coluī, cultum, cultivate, practise, live in.

color, -ōris, m., colour, brightness, complexion.

colōrātus, 2, coloured, swarthy.

columna, 1, pillar, column.

coma, 1, hair.

comedō, 3, -ēdī, -ēsum, eat up.

comes, comitis, companion.

cōmiter, courteously.

comitor, 1, dep., accompany.

commemorō, 1, mention, quote examples of.

committō, 3, **-mīsī, -missum,**
do; **proelium committere,**
join battle.
commodus, 2, convenient, adaptable; *adv.,* **commodē,** well.
commoveō, 2, **-mōvī, -mōtum,**
stir up, upset.
commūnis, 3, common, general,
public, combined; **in commūne,** for the common good.
cōmoedus, 2, comic actor.
comparātio,-ōnis,f., comparison.
comparō, 1, prepare, get ready,
equip, establish, ordain.
comperiō, 4, **-perī, -pertum,** discover.
compilō, 1, rob, defraud.
complector, 3, **-plexus,** *dep.,*
embrace, include.
compleō, 2, **-plēvī, -plētum,** fill.
complexus, 4, embrace.
complōrātiō, -ōnis, *f.,* lamentation.
complūrēs, 3, very many, several.
compōnō, 3, **-posuī, -positum,**
put together; *p.p.p.* **compositus,** calm, composed; *n.* **compositum,** previous agreement.
comprehendō, -prehendī, -prehēnsum, *and* **comprēndō,
-prēndī,-prēnsum,**seize, arrest.
concavus, 2, hollow.
concēdō, 3, **-cessī, -cessum,**
allow, let.
conciliō, 1, win over.
concinnus, 2, harmonious, well
matched.
concipiō, 3, **-cēpī, -ceptum,**
absorb.
concitō, 1, rouse, stir up, cause.
concordia, 1, harmony.
concrētus, 2, frozen hard.
concurrō, 3, **-currī, -cursum,**
make a concerted attack.
concursus, 4, rush, clash.
condemnō, 1, condemn.

condō, 3, **-didī, -ditum,** found.
condūcō, 3, hire, engage.
conductor, -ōris, contractor.
cōnferō, -ferre, -tulī, collātum,
convey, collect, contribute, compare; **sē cōnferre,** betake oneself, go.
cōnficiō, 3, **-fēcī, -fectum,** finish
off, kill.
cōnfīdō, 3, **-fīsus,** *semi-dep.,* trust,
be confident.
cōnfirmō, 1, strengthen; *p.p.p.*
cōnfirmātus, recovered (*in
health*).
cōnfiteor, 2, **-fessus,** *dep.,* admit.
cōnfluō, 3, **-fluxi,** flow together,
flood.
congressus, 4, meeting.
cōniciō, 3, **-iēcī, -iectum,** throw,
hurl in.
coniectō, 1, guess.
cōnitor, 3, **-nīsus (nīxus),** *semi-dep.,* struggle up.
cōnor, 1, *dep.,* try.
cōnscius, 2, in the know, accessory
to the plot.
cōnscriptus, see **pater.**
cōnsēnsus, 4, agreement, concerted action.
cōnsentiō, 4, **-sēnsī, -sēnsum,**
agree together.
cōnsequor, 3, **-secūtus,** *dep.,*
follow, pursue, overtake, ensue,
achieve.
cōnservō, 1, keep safe, preserve.
cōnsīderō, 1, reflect on, consider.
cōnsilium, 2, plan, counsel.
cōnsistō, 3, **-stitī,** *intr.,* halt, stop.
cōnsociō, 1, share, communicate.
cōnspectus, 4, sight.
cōnspiciō, 3, **-spexī, -spectum,**
see.
cōnspīrō, 1, make a common plan.
cōnstantia, 1, resolution.
cōnstō, 1, **-stitī,** stand firm; *impers.*
cōnstat, it is agreed.

cōnsuēscō, 3, -suēvī, -suētum,
grow accustomed; cōnsuētus,
2, accustomed.

cōnsulāris, 3, ex-consul.

cōnsulō, 3, -suluī, -sultum, consult, take counsel; *with dat.*,
take thought for, consider.

cōnsultō, 1, consult; *with dat.*,
take thought for.

cōnstituō, 3, -uī, -ūtum, decide,
determine, establish; *p.p.p.*
cōnstitūtus, when placed, when
standing.

cōnsūmō, 3, -sumpsī, -sump-
tum, spend.

contemnō, 3, -tempsī, -temp-
tum, despise.

contendō, 3, -tendī, -tentum,
struggle, compete.

contentus, 2, satisfied.

continēns, -entis, temperate,
moderate.

contineō, 2, -tinuī, -tentum, keep,
control, have within oneself.

continuus, 2, unbroken, continual,
successive.

contrā, *prep. with acc.*, opposite,
facing, against, contrary to;
adv., on the other hand.

contrārius, 2, different, opposite,
in conflict with.

contubernālis, 3, husband (of a
slave).

contumēlia, 1, insult, disgrace.

contus, 2, pole, boathook.

conveniō, 4, -vēnī, -ventum,
come together, be united; *with
acc.*, meet.

conventus, 4, agreement, combination.

convertō (*in Sallust* -vortō), 3,
-vertī, -versum, turn, attract
the attention of; *reflex. with* in,
become, turn into.

convestiō, 4, clothe, cover.

convīcium, 2, noise, din.

convīctus, 4, entertainment,
banquet.

convincō, -vīcī, -victum, show
up, reveal, prove.

convīvium, 2, banquet.

convocō, 1, call together.

coorior, 4, -ortus, *dep.*, rise, blow
up.

cōpia, 1, plenty; *pl.*, forces.

cōpo, -ōnis (*same as* caupo), innkeeper.

cor, cordis, *n.*, heart; cordi est,
it is pleasing.

Corniculum, 2, Corniculum, *in
Latium, home of Servius Tullius'
mother.*

corpus, -poris, *n.*, body.

corrumpō, 3, -rūpī, -ruptum,
corrupt, abuse.

corruō, 3, -ruī, -rutum, fall down.

cotidiē, daily, every day.

crēber, -bra, -brum, frequent.

crēdibilis, 3, credible, believable.

crēdō, 3, -didī, -ditum, *with dat.*,
believe; *with acc.*, entrust.

crēdulitās, -ātis, *f.*, credulity,
readiness to believe.

Crepereius, 2, Crepereius Gallus,
a friend of Agrippina.

crepīdō, -inis, *f.*, edge.

crepitus, 4, clatter, sound.

crēscō, 3, crēvī, crētum, increase,
become strong, blow hard.

Crēta, 1, Crete.

Crētēnsis, 3, Cretan.

crinis, 3, hair.

Critiās, -ae, Critias, *Athenian
statesman, leader of the oligarchs,
d. 403 B.C.*

cruor, -ōris, *m.*, blood.

crustulārius, 2, confectioner.

crypta, 1, tunnel.

cubiculum, 2, bedroom.

cubitō, 1, lie down.

cultus, 4, cultivation, pursuit,
style, way of life.

cum, *conj.*, when, since, although; **cum . . . tum,** not only . . . but also.
cum, *prep. with abl.*, with.
cuneus, 2, wedge.
cupidē, *adv.*, eagerly, particularly.
cupiditās, -ātis, *f.*, greed.
cupīdō, -inis, *f.*, desire, thirst.
cupiō, 3, -**īvī,** -**ītum,** desire.
cupressus, 4, *f.*, cypress tree.
cūr, *conj.*, why?
cūra, 1, care, trouble, duties.
cūrātiō, -ōnis *f.*, treatment
cūrātus, 4, treatment, cure.
cūriōsus, 2, conscientious.
Cūrius, 2, Curius, *a banker friend of Cicero at Patras.*
cūrō, 1, take care of, guard, attend to, heal.
currus, 4, chariot.
cursus, 4, course, direction.
custōdiō, 4, guard.

D
damnō, 1, condemn.
dē, *prep. with abl.*, about, concerning, out of, from, for.
dēbeō, 2, ought, have to.
dēcēdō, 3, -**cessī,** -**cessum,** depart, die.
decem, *indecl.*, ten.
decenter, gracefully.
dēcernō, 3, -**crēvī,** -**crētum,** judge, decide.
dēcidō, 3, -**cidī,** fall down.
dēclārō, 1, make clear.
decōrus, 2, handsome.
dēcrēscō, 3, -**crēvī,** -**crētum,** ebb, fall.
dēcurrō, 3, -**(cu)currī,** -**cursum,** run down, travel.
decus, decoris, *n.*, glory, renown, propriety.
dēdō, 3, -**didī,** -**ditum,** surrender.
dēdūcō, 3, lead down, lead forth, conduct.

dēfendō, 3, -**fendī,** -**fēnsum,** defend.
dēferō, -**ferre,** -**tulī,** -**lātum,** carry down; *pass.*, flow down.
dēfungor, 3, -**functus,** *dep.*, die.
dehinc, from here, next, in due course.
dēiciō, 3, -**iēcī,** -**iectum,** throw down, bring down, fell.
dēiectus, 4, fall.
deinde, then, next.
dēlābor, 3, -**lapsus,** *dep.*, melt away, be crushed.
dēlectātiō, -ōnis, *f.*, delight, pleasure.
dēlectō, 1, delight, give pleasure to.
dēliciae, 1, *pl.*, delight, darling, delicacies.
dēligō, 3, -**lēgī,** -**lēctum,** choose; *p.p.p.*, **dēlēctī,** picked men.
dēlinquō, 3, -**līquī,** -**lictum,** fall short, commit a fault.
Dēlos, -i, *f.*, *acc.* **Dēlon,** the island of Delos.
dēmandō, 1, put, place.
dēminūtiō, -ōnis, *f.*, decrease.
dēmittō, 3, -**mīsī,** -**missum,** lower.
dēmōlior, 4, *dep.*, pull down.
dēmum, *adv.*, at last.
dēnegō, 1, refuse.
dēnique, at last, in fact.
dēpōnō, 3, -**posuī,** -**positum,** put down.
dēposcō, 3, -**poposcī,** demand, wish to face.
dēprehendō (-prēndō), 3, -**prehendī (-prēndī),** -**prehēnsum (-prēnsum),** catch, find, observe.
dērīdeō, 2, -**rīsī,** -**rīsum,** laugh at.
dēscendō, 3, -**scendī,** -**scēnsum,** descend, sink, come down (upon), invade.

dēsecō, 1, -secuī, -sectum, cut out.

dēserō, 3, -seruī, -sertum, abandon, desert, leave high and dry.

dēsistō, 3, -stitī, -stitum, cease, *with infin.*

dēspērātiō, -ōnis, *f.*, despair.

dēspiciō, 3, -spexī, -spectum, look down at.

dēspondeō, 2, -spondī, -spōnsum, betroth, promise in marriage.

dēstinō, 1, decide.

dēstituo, 3, -uī, -ūtum, be false.

dēsum, -esse, -fuī, be lacking.

dētegō, 3, reveal.

dētrectō, 1, avoid.

dētruncō, 1, lop off, lop.

deus, a, god.

dēvexitās, -ātis, *f.*, slope.

dextra, 1, right hand.

dī, diī, deum, dīs, *pl. of* deus.

Diāna, 1, Diana, *goddess of the moon and of hunting.*

dīcō, 3, say, speak, tell; *n.* dictum, word, saying; dictō audiēns, obedient.

dictitō, 1, say repeatedly.

diēs, 5, *c.*, day.

difficilis, 3, difficult.

dignitās, -ātis, distinction, splendour.

dignus, 2, worthy, worthy of, *with abl.*

dīgredior, 3, -gressus, *dep.*, go aside.

dīligēns, -entis, careful; *adv.* dīligenter, carefully, thoroughly.

dīligō, 3, -lēxī, -lēctum, love.

dīmēnsus, 2, measured (*p.p.p. of dep.* dīmētior).

Diogenēs, -is, Diogenes, *Stoic philosopher.*

Diphilus, 2, Diphilus, *an architect at Q. Cicero's Manilian estate.*

discēdo, 3, -cessī, -cessum, depart.

disciplīna, 1, training, discipline.

discipulus, 2, pupil.

discō, 3, didicī, learn.

discordia, 1, discord.

discumbō, 3, -cubuī, -cubitum, recline at table.

disparpaliō, 1, scatter, make havoc of.

dispiciō, 3, -spexī, -spectum, see at a distance.

discrētus, 2, separated (*p.p.p. of* discernō).

discrīmen, -inis, *n.*, difference, interval.

dispar, -paris, different.

dispersus, 2, scattered (*p.p.p. of* dispergō).

dissideō, 2, -sēdī, -sessum, be opposed to, *with ab.*

dissimilis, 3, unlike, dissimilar.

dissimulō, 1, hide, keep secret.

dissolūtiō, -ōnis, *f.*, break up.

dissolvō, 3, -solvī, -solūtum, pay a penalty.

dissonus, 2, discordant.

distrahō, 3, draw apart, split.

diū, for a long time; *comp.* diūtius.

dīversus (*in Sallust* dīvorsus), 2, different, opposite; in dīversa, in opposite directions.

dīves, dīvitis, rich.

dīvīnus, 2, divine.

dīvitiae, 1, *pl.*, riches, wealth.

dīvus, 2, divine; *of emperors,* deified, 'the late . . .'.

dō, 1, dedī, datum, give.

doceō, 2, -uī, doctum, teach, tell.

documentum, 2, proof.

doleō, 2, feel pain.

dolor, -ōris, *m.*, pain, grief, indignation, resentment.

dolus, 2, deceit, trick.

domesticus, 2, private, in the family.

dominātio, -ōnis, *f.,* tyranny.
dominor, 1, *dep.,* hold sway, rule.
dominus, 2, master, owner.
domō, 1, **-uī, -itum,** overcome, subdue.
domus, 2 *and* 4, *f.,* house, home, palace; **domī,** at home, in domestic affairs.
domūsiō, -ōnis, *f.,* home use.
dōnec, *conj.,* until, as long as.
dōnum, 2, gift, giving; **dōnō dare,** give as a present.
dormiō, 4, sleep.
dōs, dōtis, *f.,* dowry.
dubitō, 1, hesitate.
dubius, 2, doubtful; *n.* **dubium,** doubt.
dūcō, 3, lead, consider, take (away).
dulcis, 3, sweet, considerate.
dum, *conj.,* while, until.
duo, duae, duo, two.
duodēquadrāgēsimus, 2, thirty-eighth.
dūrō, 1, *intr.,* persist, endure; *tr.,* harden.
dūrus, 2, hard, hardy.
dux, ducis, leader, general.

E

ē, ex, *prep. with abl.,* from, out of.
ēbulliō, 4, cause to boil over; **animam ēbullīre,** be at one's last gasp.
Echīōn, -onis, *m.,* Echion, *a rag-collector or blanket-maker (in Petronius).*
ecce, behold, see.
ecquis, -quid, is anyone, is there anyone.
ēdō, 3, **ēdidī, ēditum,** give birth to.
ēducātor, -ōris, tutor.
ēducō, 1, bring up.
ēdūcō, 3, bring up, rear.
effectus, 4, result, change.

efferō, -ferre, extulī, ēlātum, raise, lift, carry out for burial.
efficiō, 3, **-fēcī, -fectum,** bring about, cause, make up; *pass.,* happen.
effugiō, 3, **-fūgī,** escape, avoid.
effundō, 3, **-fūdī, -fūsum,** pour out, throw out, eject.
egeō, 2, **eguī,** need, *with abl.*
ēgerō, 3, **ēgessī, ēgestum,** drive forward, carry out, cause to flow.
ego, meī, I.
ēgredior, 3, **ēgressus,** *dep.,* go out.
ēiciō, 3, **ēiēcī, ēiectum,** throw out, send out, eject; *reflex.* rush out.
ēiusmodī, of that kind.
ēlabōrō, 1, take pains.
elephantus, 2, elephant.
ēlātus, 2, lofty (*p.p.p. of* **efferō**).
ēliciō, 3, **-uī, -icitum,** entice out, lure forth, set in motion.
ēligō, 3, **ēlēgī, ēlectum,** choose, select.
ēloquēns, -entis, eloquent.
ēloquentia, 1, eloquence.
ēluctor, 1, *dep.,* force one's way out of.
ēmineō, 2, **-uī,** be conspicuous, project.
ēmolliō, 4, enervate, enfeeble.
ēmorior, 3, **ēmortuus,** *dep.,* die.
emptor, -ōris, purchaser, buyer.
ēn, behold, see.
enim, for.
ēnitēscō, 3, **ēnituī,** shine forth.
ēnitor, 3, **ēnīsus (ēnīxus),** *dep.,* struggle up.
ēnormis, 3, shapeless.
eō, īre, īvī (iī), itum, go.
eōdem, to the same place.
ephorus, 2, ephor, *one of the five chief magistrates at Sparta.*
epistula, 1, letter.

epulae, 1, *pl.*, feast, banquet.
eques, equitis, horseman, member of the middle class Equestrian Order.
equidem, indeed.
equus, 2, horse.
ērigō, 3, **ērēxī, ērēctum,** rouse, raise, throw up, cause to flow.
ergā, *prep. with acc.*, towards, in relation to.
ergō, therefore.
errō, 1, be wrong, wander, lose one's way.
errātum, 2, mistake, error.
error, -ōris, *m.*, mistake, loss of way, roundabout route.
ērudiō, 4, train.
ērudītiō, -ōnis, *f.*, learning.
esseda, 1, chariot.
et, and, also, even, too; **et . . . et,** both . . . and.
etenim, for, for indeed.
etiam, even, also.
etiamnunc, furthermore.
etsī, although, even though.
Eumenēs, -is, Eumenes *king of Pergamum in Asia Minor.*
ēvādō, 3, **ēvāsī, ēvāsum,** escape, turn out to be.
ēveniō, 4, **ēvēnī, eventum,** come to pass, happen, ensue, come, befall.
ēventus, 4, outcome, result.
ex, ē, *prep. with abl.*, from, out of.
exanimō, 1, kill.
exarō, 1, hack out, write.
excēdō, 3, **-cessī, -cessum,** withdraw, depart; **ē vītā excēdere,** die.
excello, 3, **-uī, -celsum,** be superior.
exceptiō, -ōnis, *f.*, exception.
exciō, 4, awake, arouse.
excipiō, 3, **-cēpī, -ceptum,** receive, catch, catch up, welcome.
excitō, 1, stir up, spur on, encourage.

exclāmātiō, -ōnis, *f.*, shout, cry.
exclāmō, 1, shout, blare, blast.
excursus, 4, outflow.
excutiō, 3, **-cussī, -cussum,** shake out.
exeō, -īre, -iī, -itum, go away, emerge, go out, leak out.
exerceō, 2, carry on, practise, exercise, train.
exercitus, 4, army.
exhauriō, 4, **-hausī, -haustum,** discharge.
exhibeō, 2, offer, show.
exiguus, 2, small, very small.
exināniō, 4, empty, discharge.
exīstimō, 1, think, consider.
exitium, 2, destruction, death.
exitus, 4, way out, outlet, means of departing.
exopīnissō, 1, —, think.
exoptō, 1, long for.
expediō, 4, set free, look after; *p.p.p.* **expedītus,** unencumbered.
expellō, 3, **-pulī, -pulsum,** drive out, banish, exile, throw up.
expergīscor, 3, **-perrēctus,** *dep., intr.*, awake.
experior, 4, **-pertus,** *dep.*, test, make trial of, experience, endure, tune.
expetō, 3, **-īvī, ītum,** aim at.
expleō, 2, **-plēvī, -plētum,** complete.
expōnō, 3, **-posuī, -positum,** explain.
exprimō, 3, **-pressī, -pressum,** describe, point out; *pass.* gush forth.
exquīrō, 3, **-quisīvī, -quisītum,** ask, question.
exsanguis, 3, lifeless.
exsecrātiō, -ōnis, *f.*, cursing.
exsilium, 2, exile, banishment.
exspīrō, 1, breathe one's last, die.
exstinguō, 3, **-stinxī, -stinctum,** extinguish, destroy, obliterate.

exstō, 1, **-stitī,** emerge, come forth.
exsulō, 1, live in exile.
exsurgō, 3, **-surrexī, -surrectum,** arise, rise.
externus, 2, external, outside.
extendō, 3, **-tendī, -tentum,** extend; *reflex.*, measure up to.
exterō, 3, **-trīvī, -trītum,** crush.
extollō, 3, —, raise up, distinguish.
extrēmus, 2, last, furthest, extremity of, most northerly, in the end.
exuō, 3, **-uī, -ūtum,** strip.

F

faber, fabrī, carpenter.
Fābius, 2, Fabius, *name of a Roman gens.*
faciēs, 5, shape, appearance.
facilis, 3, easy; *adv.,* **facile.**
facilitās, -ātis, *f.,* good nature.
facinus, -oris, *n.,* deed, crime, outrage.
faciō, 3, **fēcī, factum,** do, make, cause, commit, bring it about (that), fight (*a battle*), represent, make for (*with* **ad**).
factiō, -ōnis, *f.,* faction, political party, intrigue, party strife.
factiōsus, 2, partisan, intriguer.
factum, 2, deed, exploit.
facultās, -ātis, opportunity.
fallō, 3, **fefellī, falsum** (*in Petronius* **fefellitum**), cheat, take in.
fāma, 1, report, rumour, reputation.
famēs, -is, *f.,* hunger.
familiāris, 3, member of a household, servant, friend.
familiāritās, -ātis, *f.,* friendship, intimacy.
fascia, 1, bundle, rank, class.
fateor, 2, **fassus,** *dep.,* admit.
fātidicus, 2, prophetic.
fatīgō, 1, fatigue, wear out.

fātum, 2, fate.
fatuus, 2, foolish.
faucēs, -um, *f. pl.,* jaws, outlet.
fax, facis, *f.,* torch.
fēcundus, 2, fruitful, rich, rich in, providing food for (*with gen.*).
fēmina, 1, woman.
fenestra, 1, window.
ferē, *adv.,* almost, about, practically.
feriō, 4, —, strike, strike down, fill (with excitement).
feriātus, 2, festive, on holiday.
fermē, *adv.,* about.
ferō, ferre, tulī, lātum, bear, produce, flow; **ferunt,** men say.
ferōcia, 1, boldness, spirit.
ferōx, -ōcis, fierce, desperate.
ferrāmentum, 2, tool, implement.
ferreus, 2, made of iron, ironhearted.
ferrum, 2, iron, sword.
ferus, 2, cruel, brutal.
fessus, 2, weary, exhausted.
festīnō, 1, make haste, hurry.
fēstus, 2, festive, festal.
fictilis, 3, made of earthenware.
fidēlis, 3, loyal.
fidēs, 5, faith, trust, honour, protection; **fidem facere,** make one believe, **cum fidē,** honourably.
fīlia, 1, daughter.
fīlius, 2, son.
fīlum, 2, thread.
fīnis, 3, end; *pl.,* boundaries.
fīnitimus (*in Sallust* **fīnitumus**), 2, neighbouring.
fīō, fierī, factus, *semi-dep.,* be made, happen, become; **fierī potest,** it is possible.
firmō, 1, strengthen.
flamma, 1, flame.
flectō, 3, **flexī, flexum,** bend, change; **flexum mare,** bay, cove, inlet.

fleō, 2, flēvī, flētum, weep, weep for, mourn.

flōreō, 2, flōruī, be powerful.

flŭctus, 4, wave.

fluitō, 1, float up and down, boat.

flŭmen, -inis, n., river, ocean-tide.

fluō, 3, flŭxi, flŭxum, flow, run.

fodiō, 3, fōdī, fossum, dig.

foedĭtās, -ātis, f., unpleasantness.

foedus, 2, gloomy.

fōns, fontis, m., spring, source.

forās, out of doors.

forēnsis, 3, in the law courts.

fōrma, 1, shape.

forĭs, outside.

formĭdō, -inis, f., fear, cowardice.

formĭdulōsus, 2, causing fear, fearful.

fortasse, perhaps.

fors, fortis, f., chance; abl. as adv., forte, by chance.

fortis, 2, brave, strong.

fortuĭtus, 2, accidental; adv. fortuĭtō.

fortŭna, 1, fortune; pl., possessions.

Forum Iūliī, 2, Forum Iulii, a town in Narbonese Gaul (Provence), now Fréjus.

fragor, -ōris, m., crash, noise.

frangō, 3, frēgī, frāctum, break, crush.

frāter, -tris, brother.

fraus, fraudis, f., treachery, deceit, crime, loss.

fraxinus, 2, f., ash tree.

fremitus, 4, din.

fremō, 3, -uī, -itum, be in an uproar.

frequentō, 1, associate with, keep in touch with, celebrate habitually.

frigidus, 2, adj., cold.

frigus, -oris, n., also pl., cold.

fuga, 1, flight.

fugiō, 3, fūgī, fūgitum, flee.

fugō, 1, rout, put to flight.

fulgor, -ōris, m., glow.

fundō, 3, fūdī, fūsum, pour, shed, rout, put to flight.

fundus, 2, farm.

fungor, 3, functus, dep. with abl., discharge, perform.

fūr, fūris, thief.

Fūrīna, 1, Furina, an Italian goddess.

fūrtum, 2, raid, secret attack.

futūrus, 2, coming, future (fut. part. of sum).

G

Gāius, 2, Gaius, a Roman praenomen (first name), abbreviated to C.

Gallī, pl., the Gauls.

Gallus, 2, Gallus Crepereius, a friend of Agrippina.

gallicinium, 2, also pl., cock-crow, the fourth watch of the night.

gaudium, 2, joy; pl. good news; per gaudium, joyfully.

Gāvilla, 1, Gavilla, a woman mentioned by Petronius.

gemitus, 4, groan, grunt.

gener, -ī, son-in-law.

genius, 2, guardian spirit.

gēns, gentis, f., tribe, family.

genū, 4, knee.

genus, -eris, n., race, kind, birth, way.

Germānī, 2, pl., the Germans.

Germānia, 1, Germany.

Germānicus, 2, German.

gerō, 3, gessī, gestum, do, perform, fight (a war).

gestāmen, -inis, n., means of conveyance; gestāmen sellae, sedan-chair, litter.

gignō, 3, genuī, -itum, produce, give birth to.

glaciēs, 5, ice.

gladius, 2, sword, sword-stroke.

glārea, 1, gravel.
glōria, 1, fame, glory.
glōrior, 1, *dep.*, boast.
Gortȳnī, 2, *pl.*, the Gortynians, *a people of Crete.*
Graecia, 1, Greece.
Graeculus and Graecus, 2, Greek; *pl.*, the Greeks.
grātia, 1, favour, influence, gratitude; grātiās habēre, be grateful, thank.
grātus, 2, welcome, pleasant.
gravidus, 2, heavy; *f.*, pregnant.
gravis, 3, heavy, severe, oppressive; *adv.*, graviter, violently.
gremium, 2, lap, expanse.
gubernācula, 2, *pl.*, tiller.
gubernātor, -ōris, helmsman.
gurges, -itis, *m.*, eddy.
gustō, 1, taste, eat.

H
habeō, 2, have, hold, possess, consider, reckon, take, bestow, inhabit; grātiās habēre, be grateful, thank.
habitātiō, -ōnis, *f.*, lodging.
habitō, 1, live, live in.
habitus, 4, appearance; habitus corporum, physical characteristics.
hāctenus, as far as this, so far, only.
haereō, 2, haesī, haesum, stick, cling, keep one's footing.
Hannibal, -is, Hannibal, *famous Carthaginian general.*
haphē, -ēs, *f.*, sand-sprinkling.
haud, *adv.*, not.
hedera, 1, ivy.
hērēs, -ēdis, heir.
Hēsiodus, 2, Hesiod, *seventh-century Greek poet of country life.*
Hibērī, 2, *pl.*, Spaniards.
hibernus, 2, wintry, of winter.
hīc, haec, hoc, this; *pron.* he, she, it.

hīc, *adv.*, here.
hiemō, 1, spend the winter.
hiems, hiemis, *f.*, winter.
hilaris, 3, cheerful.
hinc, from here.
hiō, 1, gape open; *part.* hiāns, wide.
Hispānia, 1, Spain.
Hispellātēs, -um, *pl.*, inhabitants of Hispellum, *12 miles north of the source of the Clitumnus.*
historia, 1, history.
Homērus, 2, Homer, *eighth-century Greek epic poet.*
homō, -inis, *c.*, human being, *m.* man; *pl.*, mankind.
honestus, 2, of high birth, honourable, worthwhile, honourably won.
honor and honōs, -ōris, *m.*, honour, compliment.
hortor, 1, *dep.*, encourage.
hortus, 2, garden.
hospes, -itis, stranger, guest.
hospita, 1, stranger, visitor.
hospitium, 2, inn.
hostis, 3, enemy.
HS., *abbreviation for* sestertius, sesterce, *a small silver coin originally worth* 2½ asses; *a bar above the figure following means that it is in units of 1000 sesterces, so that* HS. X̄V̄Ī *means* 16,000 sesterces.
hūc, *adv.*, hither, to this place.
hūmānitās, -ātis, *f.*, good nature, kindness.
hūmānus, 2, human, of man; *adv.*, hūmānē, kindly, pleasurably.
humilis, 3, low, lowly, humble, poor.
hūmor, -ōris, *m.*, water, a body of water.

I
iaceō, 2, lie.

iaciō, *3*, **iēcī, iactum,** throw, throw in.

iactō, 1, throw about.

iactus, 4, throwing overboard.

iaculum, 2, javelin.

iam, *adv.*, already.

ibi, *adv.*, there.

ictus, 4, blow; **ictus animī,** excitement, thrill.

idcircō, *adv.*, for that reason.

īdem, eadem, idem, the same.

ideō, *adv.*, therefore.

Īdūs, 4, *f. pl.*, the Ides, *the 13th of the month, except in March, May, July, October, when they were the 15th.*

igitur, therefore.

ignārus, 2, unawares, unsuspecting.

ignis, 3, fire.

ignōrō, 1, know not, be unacquainted with.

ignōscō, 3, **-nōvī, -nōtum,** *with dat.*, pardon.

illā, in that direction.

ille, illa, illud, that; he, she, it.

illīc, there.

illīdō, 3, **-līsī, -līsum,** strike, smash.

illūc, thither, to that place.

illūdō, -lūsī, -lūsum, ridicule.

illūstris, 3, bright, famous.

imāgō, -inis, *f.*, reflection.

imber, -bris, *m.*, shower, rain

imitor, 1, *dep.*, imitate.

immātūrus, 2, premature.

immēnsus, 2, huge.

immortālis, 3, immortal.

immortālitās, -ātis, *f.*, immortality.

immūtō, 1, change, alter.

impār, -is, unequal, of unequal sides.

impediō, 4, hinder.

impellō, 3, **-pulī, -pulsum,** drive forward, set in motion, strike against.

impendō, 3, **-pendī, -pēnsum,** spend.

impēnsius, *comp. adv.*, more greatly.

imperātor, -ōris, general, magistrate.

imperium, 2, command, rule, empire, government, authority, magistracy, order; **imperium maritimum,** naval forces.

imperō, 1, order, make demands on, *with dat.*

impetus, 4, attack, pushing.

impingō, 3, **-pēgī, -pactum,** strike, implant, **calcem impingere,** give a kick.

impleō, 2, **-plēvi, -plētum,** fill.

improbē, evilly, wickedly.

imprūdentia, 1, lack of foresight

in, *prep. with acc.*, into, to, towards, against; *with abl.*, in, on, at, upon, in the case of.

inānis, 3, empty.

incēdō, 3, **-cessī, -cessum,** advance, approach, ensue, come upon.

incendium, 2, fire.

inceptum, 2, undertaking, subject.

incertus, 2, uncertain, not settled.

incessus, 4, trampling.

incidō, 3, **-cidī, -cāsum,** fall upon, light upon.

incitō, 1, rouse, stimulate.

inclīnō, 1, throw one's weight.

inclūdō, -clūsī, -clūsum, shut, close, enclose.

incōgitātus, 2, unexpected.

incognitus, 2, unknown, unexpected, unexplored.

incola, 1, *c.*, inhabitant.

incommodum, 2, disadvantage, inconvenience.

incrēdibilis, 3, unbelievable.

incurrō, 3, **-(cu)currī, -cursum,** run into, fall into.

inde, *adv.*, then, from there, after that.

indicium, 2, proof.

indicō, 1, prove, testify.

indigena, 1, *c.*, native.

indignitās, -ātis, *f.*, indignation, anger.

indignus, 2, unworthy, disgraceful; **prō indignissimō,** as the greatest outrage.

indolēs, -is, *f.*, natural character.

indūcō, 3, lead on, persuade, bring in, introduce.

indulgentia, 1, care, gentleness, indulgence.

ineō, -īre, -iī, -itum, enter, make (a plan).

ineptē, *adv.*, foolishly.

iners, -ertis, idle.

inexpugnābilis, 3, not to be overcome.

infantia, 1, infancy, childhood.

inferior, -ius, lower.

inferō, -ferre, -tulī, illātum, bring in, bring to, force in.

īnfimus, 2, lowest.

īnfirmitās, -ātis, ill health, weakness.

īnfirmus, 2, weak, enfeebled.

īnfluō, 3, **-fluxī,** flow into.

īnfrā, *adv. and prep. with acc.*, below.

īnfundō, 3, **-fūdī, -fūsum,** pour on.

ingeniōsus, 2, gifted, clever.

ingenium, 2, character, mind, ability, abilities, clever plan; *pl.* men of ability.

ingēns, -entis, huge, great, unbounded.

ingredior, 3, **-gressus,** *dep.*, tread on.

inhorrēscō, 3, **-horruī,** shudder.

inhūmānus, 2, unkind.

iniciō, 3, **-iēcī, -iectum,** throw on.

inimīcus, 2, private enemy, enemy.

inīquus, 2, unjust, unfair, unfavourable.

initium, 2, beginning; *abl.* **initiō,** originally.

iniūria, 1, wrong, injury.

iniussū, *abl.*, without the orders (of.)

iniussus, 2, unbidden.

iniustē, *adv.*, unjustly, wrongly.

innocēns, -entis, innocent, blameless, undeserved.

innocentia, 1, uprightness, integrity.

innumerābilis, 3, countless.

inquam, inquit, *defect.*, I said, he said.

inquilīnus, 2, lodger, one living in same building.

inquinō, 1, stain; *pass.*, dabble in.

īnsānia, 1, madness, folly.

īnsciēns, -entis, unaware, not knowing.

īnscrībō, 3, **-scrīpsī, -scrīptum,** write upon, inscribe.

īnscriptiō, -ōnis, *f.*, title, label.

īnserō, 3, **-seruī, -sertum,** force in; *pass.*, force one's way among.

īnsidiae, 1, *pl.*, trap, plot, secret attack, ambush.

īnsignītus, 2, distinctive.

īnsistō, 3, **-stitī,** keep a foothold, stand on, be built on, *with dat.*

īnsolēscō, 3, —, become arrogant.

īnsolitus, 2, unfamiliar, unusual.

īnspectiō, -ōnis, *f.*, viewing, looking at, sight.

īnspiciō, 3, **-spexī, -spectum,** examine, see.

īnstanter, vigorously.

īnstitor, -ōris, hawker, pedlar.

īnstituō, 3, **-uī, -ūtum,** undertake, begin.

īnsula, 1, island.

īnsuperābilis, 3, unsurmountable.

intactus, 2, untouched.

integritās, -ātis, *f.*, honesty, innocence.

intellegō, 3, -lēxī, -lēctum, realise, understand.

intemperantia, 1, arrogance, lack of self-control.

intentus, 2, alert, intent, actively engaged, eager, absorbed in; *adv.* intentē, earnestly.

inter, *prep. with acc.*, among, between, during; inter sē, with one another.

intercipiō, 3, -cēpī, -ceptum, cut off, do away with.

intercolumnium, 2, space between pillars.

interdum, sometimes.

intereā, meanwhile.

interficiō, 3, -fēcī, -fectum, kill.

interim, meanwhile.

intermittō, 3, -mīsī, -missum, interrupt; *pass.* be intermittent.

internōscō, 3, -nōvī, -nōtum, distinguish between.

intersum, -esse, -fuī, take part in, *with dat.*; *impers.*, interest, it matters, it is important, it makes a difference.

intrā, *prep. with acc.*, within, among, to.

intrō, 1, enter, come over.

intus, *adv.*, within.

inultus, 2, unpunished, unavenged.

inveniō, 4, -vēnī, -ventum, find, discover the truth of.

invīsus, 2, hateful.

invītō, 1, invite.

invius, 2, pathless.

iocor, 1, *dep.*, joke, jest.

iocus, 2, joke, amusement.

ipse, ipsa, ipsum, himself.

īrācundia, 1, anger, bad temper.

īrātus, 2, angry.

irrīdeō, 2, -rīsī, -rīsum, mock, make fun of.

is, ea, id, that; he, she, it.

iste, ista, istud, that of yours, your.

istic, istaec, istuc, *stronger form of* iste.

ita, *adv.*, so, thus.

itaque, *conj.*, and so, therefore.

Italia, 1, Italy.

Italicus, 2, Italian.

item, *adv.*, likewise, also.

iter, itineris, *n.*, road, journey.

iterum, again, a second time.

iubeō, 2, iussī, iussum, order.

iūcundus, 2, pleasant, enjoyable; *adv.*, iūcundē.

iūdex, iudicis, judge.

iūdicium, 2, judgment, decision, sentence, proof.

iūdicō, 1, judge, consider.

iugum, 2, ridge, hill summit; *pl.* the Highlands.

iūmentum, 2, baggage-animal, mule.

Iuppiter, Iovis, Jupiter, *father and king of the gods.*

iūrgium, 2, enmity.

iūs, iūris, *n.*, right, law, justice, power; iūra reddere, administer justice.

iūs, iūris, *n.*, soup, broth.

iussum, 2, order.

iussū, *abl.*, by order (of).

iūstitia, 1, justice.

iūstus, 2, just; *adv.* iustē.

iuvenīlis, 3, youthful.

iuvenis, 3, young man.

iuventūs, -ūtis, time of youth, young men.

iuvō, 1, iūvī, iūtum, help.

iūxtā, *adv.*, close by.

K

kakostomachus (κακοστό-μαχος), 2, indisposed, sick.

L

labor, -ōris, *m.*, work, toil, hardship.

labōrō, 1, work, exert oneself, struggle (with), suffer (from).

labrum, 2, lip.

lac, lactis, n., milk.

Lacaena, 1, Spartan woman.

Lacaedaemonii, 2, pl., Lacedaemonians, Spartans, living at Lacedaemon in southern Greece.

lacus, 4, lake.

laetus, 2, happy, joyful.

lancea, 1, spear, lance.

lanius, 2, butcher.

lapideus, 2, made of stone; lapideum facere, turn to stone, petrify.

lapidōsus, 2, made of stone.

lāpsus, 4, falling.

largior, 4, dep., bribe.

Larius, 2, Larian; Larius lacus, the Larian Lake, now Lake Como in north Italy.

larva, 1, ghost.

lateō, 2, lie hid; part. latēns, hidden.

Laterium, 2, Laterium, a property of Q. Cicero near Arpinum.

Latīnus, 2, Latin.

lātus, 2, broad; adv. lātē, broadly, far and wide; comp. lātius, more widely.

laudō, 1, praise, approve of.

laus, laudis, f., praise, glory.

laxō, 1, open.

lectus, 2, couch, bed.

legiō, -ōnis, f., legion (4000-6000 men).

lēgitimus (in Sallust lēgitumus), 2, legal, founded on law.

legō, 3, lēgī, lēctum, gather, read.

lēnis, 3, gentle, polite.

lēnunculus, 2, small boat, fishing-vessel.

lēvis, 3, smooth.

lex, lēgis, f., law.

libenter, gladly, willingly; superl. libentissimē.

liber (in Petronius also lībrum), 2, book.

līber, -era, -erum, free; m. pl., līberī, gen. also līberum, children.

līberālis, 3, generous with, with gen.

līberō, 1, set free.

lībertās, -ātis, f., liberty.

lībertus, 2, freedman, former slave.

libīdō (in Sallust lubīdō), -inis, f., pleasure, desire.

lībrāmentum, 2, counterpoise, force of water, water level.

licentia, 1, unbounded freedom, licence.

licet, 2, impers., it is permitted; as conj. with subj., although.

lictor, -ōris, 2, lictor, attendant.

lignum, 2, wood, log.

linea, 1, measuring line.

lingua, 1, tongue, speech.

linquo, 3, līquī, leave; pass. linquī animō, faint.

liquēscō, 3, licuī, melt.

littera, 1, letter (of the alphabet); pl. a letter, literature.

litterātus, 2, educated.

litus, -oris, n., shore, coast.

līvēns, -entis, dark.

līvidus, 2, dark.

Līvius, 2, Titus, the historian Livy.

locus, 2, place ground; pl., loca, n., regions.

longus, 2, long, long standing; adv., longē, far, by far; comp. adv. longius, too far.

loquor, 3, locūtus, dep. (in Petronius also loquō), speak, discuss.

lūbricus, 2, slippery.

lūceo, 2, lūxī, shine.

Lūcīlius, 2, Lucilius, the friend to whom Seneca wrote his letters.

Lucrīnus, 2, the Lucrine lake, near Baiae.

lucrum, 2, gain.

luctātiō, -ōnis, f., struggle.

Lucusta, 1, m., Lucusta, owner of an estate near Q. Cicero's.

lūdibrium, 2, laughing-stock.

lūdō, 3, lūsī, lūsum, play, jest.

lūdus, 2, game, school.

lūmen, -inis, n., light, glory.

lūna, 1, moon.

lupus, 2, wolf.

lutum, 2, mud.

lūx, lūcis, f., light, day; prīmā lūce, at dawn.

lūxuria, 1, luxury.

Lycūrgus, 2, Lycurgus, a seventh-century legendary law-giver at Sparta.

Lysimachus, 2, Lysimachus, father of Aristides.

Lysō, -ōnis, Lyso, a friend of Cicero living at Patras.

M

M., Marcus, 2, Marcus, a Roman praenomen (first name).

magister, -trī, master.

magnificus, 2, lavish.

magnitūdō, -inis, f., greatness.

magnus, 2, great, large, high; comp. māior; adv., magis, more; superl. maximus (in Sallust maxumus).

mālō, mālle, māluī, prefer.

malus, 2, bad, wicked; n. malum, an evil; adv., male, badly; non male, quite well.

mandō, 1, order, give instructions.

manducō, 1, eat.

māne, adv., in the morning.

maneō, 2, mānsī, mānsum, remain.

mansuētūdō, -inis, f., gentleness.

manus, 4, f., hand, band of men, troops; manū factus, artificial; in manūs venīre, fall into the hands (of).

Mardonius, 2, Mardonius, Persian general killed at Plataea, 479 B.C.

mare, -is, n., sea; abl. marī, by sea.

margarīta, 1, pearl.

mārgō, -inis, c., edge, bank.

maritimus, 2, naval, maritime; imperium maritimum, naval forces.

māter, -tris, mother.

māteria, 1, cause, origin.

māteriātūs, 2, timbered.

mātūrē, early, soon.

maximē, superl. adv., of magnus, very much, especially.

mēcum, with me.

medicus, 2, doctor.

mediocris, 3, ordinary.

Mediolānum, 2, Mediolanum, now Milan.

mehercule and mehercules, interj., by Hercules.

melior, -ōris, better (comp. of bonus).

Melissa, 1, Melissa, wife of Terentius in Petronius.

membrum, 2, limb, room.

meminī, -isse, defect., remember.

memoria, 1, memory, record, history.

memorō, 1, describe, relate, say.

mēns, mentis, f., mind.

mēnsa, 1, table.

mēnsis, 3, month.

mēnsūra, 1, length (of days), amount (of water).

mentiō, -ōnis, f., mention.

mentior, 4, dep., tell lies.

mercēs, -ēdis, f., pay, wages.

mereor, 2, dep., deserve.

mergō, 3, -sī, -sum, tr., sink.

merīdiēs, 5, m., midday, the south.

merx, mercis, f., goods, wares.

Mescinius, 2, Mescinius, Cicero's quaestor in Cilicia.

Mēta Sūdāns, Mētae Sūdantis, *f.,* the Trickling Fountain, *near which Seneca lodged in Rome.*

metallum, 2, metal.

mētior, 4, **mēnsus,** *dep.,* measure.

metus, 4, fear.

metuō, 3, **-uī, -ūtum,** fear.

meus, 2, my.

migrātiō, -ōnis, *f.,* change of abode.

migrō, 1, change one's abode, depart.

mīles, -itis, soldier.

mīliārium, 2, mile-stone.

mīlitāris, 3, military, trained for war; **rēs mīlitāris,** warfare; **equus mīlitāris,** warhorse.

mīlitia, 1, warfare, military service; **mīlitiae,** on active service.

mīlle, *indecl.,* a thousand; *pl.* **mīlia,** 3.

minister, -trī, agent, perpetrator.

ministerium, 2, service.

minor, -ōris, smaller, less (*comp. of* **parvus**); *adv.* **minus;** *superl.* **minimus** (*in Sallust* **minumus**), least, very little; *adv.* **minimē.**

Minōs, -ōis, Minos, *son of Jupiter, king of Crete, and later judge in the Underworld.*

mīrābilis, 3, wonderful, marvellous.

mīrāclum, 2, miracle, marvellous event.

mīror, 1, *dep.,* wonder (at), be surprised.

mīrus, 2, remarkable.

misceō, 2, **-cuī, mixtum,** mingle with, *with acc. and dat.; pass. intr.*

Mīsēnum, 2, Misenum, *promontory near Naples.*

miser, -era, -erum, wretched.

miserābiliter, pitifully, in a way that arouses pity.

misericordia, 1, pity.

mītēscō, 3, —, ripen.

mītis, 3, gentle, kind.

mittō, 3, **mīsī, missum,** send, let (blood).

modestia, 1, self-control.

modestus, 2, orderly, restrained.

modicus, 2, small, moderate, gentle.

modo, only, just, at one time; **modo ... modo,** at one time ... at another time.

modulātiō, -ōnis, *f.,* intonation.

modus, 2, way, manner, stroke; *abl.,* **modō** *with gen.,* like.

moenia, 3, *pl.,* walls, town-walls, city.

mōlēs, -is, *f.,* mass.

molestus, 2, disagreeable, unpleasant, troublesome; *m.,* a bore.

mōlior, 4, *dep.,* devise.

molliō, 4, soften, ease.

mollis, 3, soft; *adv.* **molliter,** kindly.

mōmentum, 2, short time, interval.

monimentum, 2, tombstone, tomb.

mōns, montis, *m.,* mountain, hill.

mōnstrō, 1, show.

mora, 1, delay, stoppage.

morbōsus, 2, sick, crazy (about).

moribundus, 2, dying, about to die.

morior, 3, **mortuus,** *dep.,* die.

moror, 1, *dep.,* delay, check.

mors, mortis, *f.,* death.

mortālis, 3, mortal, human; *m. pl.* **mortālēs,** men; *n. pl.* **mortālia,** human affairs.

mortālitās, -ātis, *f.,* mortality.

mortifer, -era, -erum, deadly.

mortuus, 2, lifeless; *m.,* a dead man (*p.p. of* **morior**).

mōs, mōris, *m.,* way, manner, form, constitution; *pl.* civilisation, culture; **bonī mōrēs,** good morals, virtue.

moveō, 2, mōvī, mōtum, move, disturb.

mulier, -eris, woman.

multitūdō, -inis, f., large number, mob, people.

multō, 1, punish; morte multāre, condemn to death.

multus, 2, much, many; abl. multō, (by) much; adv. multum, much, very.

mūnia, 2, pl., duties.

mūniceps, -cipis, fellow-townsman.

mūnificentia, 1, generosity.

mūniō, 4, fortify, build, protect, make up (a road).

mūnus, -eris, n., gift.

mūnusculum, 2, little gift.

mūrus, 2, wall.

Mūsacus, 2, Musaeus, a legendary Greek poet.

muscōsus, 2, mossy.

mūstella, 1, weasel.

mūtātiō, -ōnis, f., change, mental change.

mūtō, 1, change, tr.; pass., intr.

mūtuātiō, -ōnis, f., borrowing.

mūtuus, 2, mutual, shared.

N

nam, namque, conj., for.

nancīscor, 3, nactus, dep., obtain, find.

nārrō, 1, relate, tell.

nāscor 3, nātus, dep., be born; p.p. nātus, with abl., son of, sprung from.

nāsus, 4, nose.

nātālis, 3, of birth, native.

nātiō, -ōnis, f., tribe.

natō, 1, swim.

nātūra, 1, nature, natural characteristics, quality; abl. naturally.

nātūrālis, 3, natural.

naufragium, 2, shipwreck.

nauticus, 2, naval.

nāvālis, 3, naval.

nāvigātiō, -ōnis, f., sailing.

nāvigō, 1, sail, boat, make a voyage, go by sea.

nāvis, 3, f., ship, boat.

nē, conj. with subj., that . . . not, lest; conj., nē . . . quidem, not even.

Neāpolis, 3, acc., -im, f., Naples.

Neāpolitānus, 2, of Naples, Neapolitan.

nebula, 1, fog, mist.

nec, neque, neither, nor, and . . . not.

necessārius, 2, necessary.

necesse, indecl., necessary.

necessitās, -ātis, f., need, necessity; pl. essentials.

nēdum, much more; still less.

neglegentia, 1, carelessness.

neglegō, 3, disregard, neglect; part., neglegēns, careless.

negō, 1, deny, say . . . not, refuse.

negōtium, 2, business, affair.

nēmō, defect., nobody; as adj. no.

nemorōsus, 2, densely wooded, thick.

nēnia, 1, song; hobby.

neque, nec, neither, nor, and . . . not.

nēquiquam, in vain.

Nerō, -ōnis, the Roman emperor Nero.

nesciō, 4, not know; nescio quis, someone or other; nescio qui, some.

nī, nisi, unless, if . . . not; nisi quod, except that.

Nicēphorus, 2, Nicephorus, Q. Cicero's bailiff.

nihil, indecl., nothing.

nihilōminus, none the less.

Nīlus, 2, the River Nile.

nimis, too much.

nisi, nī, unless, if . . . not; nisi quod, except that.

nīsus, 4, effort, hard work.
nītor, 3, **nīsus (nīxus)**, *dep.*, lean, apply weight.
nix, nivis, *f.*, *also pl.*, snow.
nō, 1, swim.
nōbilitās, -ātis, *f.*, nobility, high birth, noble appearance.
noceō, 2, injure, hurt, *with dat.*
nōlō, nolle, nōluī, be unwilling; **nōlī, nōlīte**, *with infin.*, do not. . . .
nōmen, -inis, *n.*, name.
nōminō, 1, name.
nōn, not.
nōndum, not yet.
nōnnullī, 2, *pl.*, some.
nōnnunquam, sometimes.
nōnus, 2, ninth.
Norbānus, 2, Norbanus, *a popular magistrate in Petronius.*
nōs, nostrī (nostrum), we; *sometimes* I.
nōscō, 3, **nōvī, nōtum**, get to know; **nōvisse**, know (a person); **nōveram**, I remember.
noster, -tra, -trum, our, my, Roman; *m. pl.* **nostrī**, the Romans.
nōtitia, 1, knowledge.
novitās, -ātis, *f.*, strangeness.
novus, 2, new, newly inflicted, remote; *superl. adv.* **novissimē**, finally.
nox, noctis, *f.*, night.
noxius, 2, harmful, injurious.
nūbēs, -is, *f.*, cloud.
nūdus, 2, bare.
nūllus, 2, *gen.* **nūllius**, no, none.
nūmen, -inis, *n.*, deity, god.
numerō, 1, count.
numerus, 2, number.
numquam (nunquam), never.
nunc, now.
nūntiō, 1, report.
nūper, lately.
nusquam, nowhere.

nūtrio, 4, bring up, rear.

O

ob, *prep. with acc.*, on account of; **quam ob rem**, wherefore.
obdūcō, 3, swallow, drink.
obeō, -īre, -iī, -itum, perform, discharge, meet (death).
obiurgō, 1, reprove.
oblongus, 2, elongated.
obloquor, 3, **-locūtus**, *dep.*, interrupt.
obluctor, 1, *dep.*, struggle against; *part.* **obluctāns**, opposing.
obruō, 3, **-ruī, -rutum**, cover, bury.
obscūritās, -ātis, *f.*, darkness.
obscūrus, 2, dark.
obsequor, 3, **-secūtus**, *dep.*, obey, *with dat.*
observō, 1, watch.
obstrepō, 3, **-uī, -itum**, shout down, *with dat.*
obtendō, 3, **-tendī, -tentum**, stretch; *pass.* face, *with dat.*
obterō, 3, **-trīvī, -trītum**, crush.
obtrectō, 1, be at variance, rival, contend.
obvius, 2, meeting, opposing; **obviam īre**, meet, *with dat.*
occāsiō, -ōnis, *f.*, opportunity, chance.
occīdō, 3, **-cīdī, -cīsum**, kill.
occidō, 3, **-cidī, -cāsum**, fall, die, set; **occidēns (sōl)**, the west.
occultō, 1, hide.
occultus, 2, hidden.
occumbō, 3, **-cubuī, -cubitum**, fall down; *with* **mortem**, meet death, die.
occupō, 1, occupy, settle in.
occurrō, 3, **-(cu)currī, -cursum**, meet, block the way, *with dat.*
occursus, 4, meeting, encounter.
Ōceanus, 2, ocean, Atlantic Ocean, sea.

ocrea, 1, greave (*leg armour*); per scūtum per ocream, by hook or by crook.

oculus, 2, eye.

odium, 2, hatred.

offendō, 3, -fendī, -fēnsum, meet, come upon.

offēnsio, -ōnis, *f.*, offence.

offerō, -ferre, obtulī, oblātum, offer, bring to notice.

officiō, 3, -fēcī, -fectum, be in the way, block the view.

officiōsus, 2, obliging.

officium, 2, duty, sense of duty.

ōlim, formerly, in days gone by, some time ago.

olīva, 1, olive.

omittō, 3, -mīsī, -missum, give up, let drop.

omnīnō, altogether.

omnis, 3, all, the whole; *n. pl.* omnia, everything.

onus, oneris, *n.*, weight, burden.

opācus, 2, shady.

opem, opis, *f.* (*no nom.*), help, power; *pl.* opēs, wealth, resources, position.

opera, 1, effort, attention; operam dare, see to it (that).

opīnor, 1, *dep.*, suppose.

opperiō, 4, -peruī, -pertum, shut, keep shut, cover.

oppidum, 2, town.

oppleō, 2, -plēvī, -plētum, fill.

opportūnē, conveniently, suitably.

opprimō, 3, -pressī, -pressum, crush, overpower.

optō, 1, wish, desire, pray for.

opulentia, 1, wealth.

opus, operis, *n.*, work; tantō opere, so much; opus esse, be useful, opus est, there is need of, *with abl.*

ōra, 1, district, region, seashore.

ōrātiō, -ōnis, *f.*, speech.

orbis, 3, world, part of the world.

Orcades, 3, *f. pl.*, Orcades, the Orkneys.

Orcus, 2, Orcus, the Underworld, hell, death.

ōrdior, 4, orsus, *dep.*, begin, begin to state.

orīgō, -inis, *f.*, origin.

orior, 4, ortus, *dep.*, rise, arise, grow, spring from; *part. as noun, m.*, oriēns, the east.

ōrnō, 1, equip, adorn, dress; *p.p.p.* ōrnātus, fully equipped.

ōrō, 1, beg, pray.

Orpheūs, -eī, Orpheus, *mythical Greek musician and poet.*

ortus, 2, *p.p. of* orior.

ōs, ōris, *n.*, mouth, face.

ostendō, 3, -tendī, -tentum, show, point to.

ostento, 1, display.

ōtium, 2, calmness, leisure, peace, holiday.

ōvum, 2, egg.

P

pābulum, 2, fodder.

paene, almost.

paenitentia, 1, remorse, change of heart.

paenitet, 2, *impers.*, it makes one repent; mē paenitet, I repent, I regret.

pāgina, 1, page.

palam, openly, plainly; palam factum est, the truth was revealed.

Palamēdēs, -is, Palamedes, *a Greek killed at Troy on a false charge laid by Ulysses.*

pandō, 3, pandī, passum, open a way through, lay open.

pānis, 3, bread, food.

pār, paris, equal, similar; *adv.*, pariter, at the same time.

parcō, 3, pepercī, parsum, spare, *with dat.*

parcus, 2, frugal, economical.

parēns, -entis, *c.,* parent, father, mother.

pāreō, 2, obey, *with dat.*

pariēs, -etis, *m.,* wall (of a room), side.

pariō, 3, **peperī, partum,** produce, bring to birth.

parō, 1, prepare, make preparations, win, make; *p.p.p.* **parātus,** ready, prepared.

pars, partis, *f.,* part.

parturiō, 4, be pregnant with, be in travail with.

partus, 4, child.

parum, too little, not fully.

parvus, 2, small; **ā parvō,** from childhood.

passus, 4, pace.

pāstor, -ōris, shepherd.

pateō, 2, lie open, be open, be revealed; *part.* **patēns,** open.

pater, patris, father, Senator; **patrēs cōnscrīptī,** Senators, members of the Senate.

patēscō, 3, **patuī,** broaden out.

patior, 3, **passus,** *dep.,* suffer, allow; *part.* **patiēns,** able to endure, *with gen.*

patria, 1, native land.

patrimōnium, 2, inheritance, property, fortune.

patrius, 2, of one's father.

paucī, 2, *pl.,* few, a few.

paulātim, gradually, little by little.

paulum, a little, for a short time.

pauper, -eris (*in Petronius,* **-erī**), *m.,* poor.

paupertās, -ātis, *f.,* poverty.

Pausaniās, -ae, Pausanias, *Spartan regent, commander of the Greeks at Plataea in 479* B.C.

pausārius, 2, boatswain.

pavīmentātus, 2, paved.

pavīmentum, 2, pavement.

pāx, pācis, *f.,* peace.

pectus, -oris, *n.,* chest, heart.

pecūnia, 1, money.

pecus, -oris, *n.,* flock, herd; *pl.* sheep.

pedes, -itis, foot-soldier; *pl.* infantry.

pedester, -tris, -tre, *adj.,* infantry.

pedica, 1, snare, trap.

pellō, 3, **pepulī, pulsum,** drive, drive out, banish; *p.p.p.* **pulsus,** hard pressed.

penitus, entirely, far in, deep inland.

per, *prep. with acc.,* through, throughout, over, by means of.

percellō, 3, **-culī, -culsum,** smite (with fear), worry, thrill; *p.p.p.* **perculsus metū,** panic-stricken.

percolō, 3, **-coluī, -cultum,** adorn.

perdō, 3, **-didī, -ditum,** lose.

perdomō, 1, **-domuī, -domitum,** conquer completely.

perdūcō, 3, bring to.

peregrē, away from home.

peregrīnātiō, -ōnis, *f.,* journey abroad, journey, stay abroad.

peregrīnus, 2, foreigner.

pereō, -īre, -iī, -itum, perish, die.

perfectus, 2, perfect, faultless.

perferō, -ferre, -tulī, -lātum, endure, suffer, send on one's way.

perficiō, 3, **-fēcī, -fectum,** finish, perform.

perfringō, 3, **-frēgī, -frāctum,** break through.

perfugium, 2, refuge.

perfungor, 3, **-functus,** *dep.,* perform, accomplish, *with abl.*

Pergamēnus, 2, of Pergamum, *in N.W. Asia Minor.*

pergō, 3, **-rēxī, -rēctum,** proceed, come forward.

perhibeō, 2, say.

perīculum, 2, danger.

perinde, as much.

perītē, skilfully.

permaneō, 2, **-mānsī, -mānsum,** remain, remain in existence.

perniciēs, 5, ruin.

perpendiculum, 2, plumb-line.

perpetior, 3, **-pessus,** *dep.,* endure.

perpetuitās, -ātis, *f.,* eternity.

persequor, 3, **-secūtus,** *dep.,* punish, take vengeance on.

Persēs (Persa), -ae, *m.,* a Persian; *also as adj.*

perspiciō, 3, **-spexī, -spectum,** inspect, examine.

perspicuus, 2, very clear, translucent.

persuādeō, 2, **-suāsī, -suāsum,** persuade, *with dat. (acc. in Petronius).*

persuāsiō, -ōnis, *f.,* belief.

perterreō, 2, terrify.

pertimēscō, 3, **-timuī,** dread.

pertineō, 2, **-tinuī, -tentum,** concern, reach.

perturbātiō, -ōnis, *f.,* disturbance (of mind).

perturbō, 1, upset, provoke.

pervehō, 3, convey, transport.

perveniō, 4, **-vēnī, -ventum,** arrive; *with* **ad,** reach.

pes, pedis, *m.,* foot.

pessimus, 2, very bad (*superl. of* **malus**).

pestilēns, -entis, unhealthy, insanitary.

petō, 3, **petīvī (-iī), -ītum,** ask for, look for, make for.

Philerō, -ōnis, Philero, *a successful lawyer in Petronius.*

philosophus, 2, philosopher; *also adj.,* philosophical.

pietās, -ātis, *f.,* righteousness, filial love.

piger, -gra, -grum, slow, sluggish.

pigritia, 1, listlessness, reluctance.

pila, 1, ball.

Pilia, 1, Pilia, *wife of Atticus.*

pilicrepus, 2, ball-player.

pingō, 3, **pinxī, pinctum,** paint.

piscīna, 1, fish-pond.

placeō, 2, please, seem good, *with dat.,* **mihi placuit,** I have decided.

placidus, 2, calm.

plācō, 1, appease, calm; *p.p.p.* **plācātus,** calm, peaceful, conciliatory.

plānus, 2, level, flat; *adv.,* **plānē,** absolutely; **nōn plānē,** not at all.

Plataeae, 1, *pl.,* Plataea, *town in Boeotia where the Greeks defeated the Persians in 479 B.C.*

Platō, -ōnis, Plato, *Greek philosopher (429–348 B.C.), follower of Socrates.*

plēbēius, 2, plebeian, cheap.

plēbēs, -eī (-ī) *and* **plēbs, -is,** *f.,* the people, common people.

plērīque, -aeque, -aque, *pl.,* most; *adv.* **plērumque,** generally.

plumbum, 2, lead.

plūrimus, 2, most, very many, very great (*superl. of* **multus**).

plūs, plūris, *adj. and adv.,* more, several; *gen.* **plūris,** at a higher price (*comp. of* **multus**).

pōculum, 2, cup.

poena, 1, punishment, penalty.

Poenus, 2, Punic, Carthaginian.

poliō, 4, polish, smooth.

pollēns, -entis, powerful.

polliceor, 2, *dep.,* promise.

Pōmētia, 1, Suessa Pometia, *a town of the Volsci.*

Pompōnia, 1, Pomponia, *wife of Q. Cicero.*

pondus, -eris, *n.,* weight.

pōnō, 3, **posuī, -itum,** place, put down.

pōns, pontis, *m.,* bridge.

ponticulus, 2, small bridge.

Pontus, 2, Pontus, *a kingdom south of the Black Sea.*

popīna, 1, cook-shop, eating-house.

populus, 2, people, tribe.

pōpulus, 2, *f.*, poplar.

porrō, onwards.

portendō, 3, -tendī, -tentum, foretell.

porticus, 4, *f.*, colonnade, cloister.

portō, 1, carry, bring.

positiō, -ōnis, *f.*, position.

possideō, 2, -sēdī, -sessum, possess, win.

possum, posse, potuī, be able.

post, *prep. with acc.,* after.

post, posteā, *adv.,* after, afterwards.

posterus, 2, next, later.

postquam, *conj.,* after.

postrēmō, finally.

postrīdiē, on the next day.

potestās, -ātis, *f.*, power.

potissimum, *superl. adv.,* especially.

pōtō, 1, drink.

prae, *prep. with abl. (acc. in Petronius),* before, on account of.

praealtus, 2, very deep.

praebeō, 2, provide.

praebibō, 3, -bibī, drink to the health of, *with acc. and dat.* ·

praeceps, -cipitis, headlong, steep.

praeceptor, -ōris, *c.*, teacher.

praecipiō, 3, -cēpī, -ceptum, order, *with dat.*

praecipuē, particularly, especially.

praecō, -ōnis, auctioneer.

praecordia, 2, *pl.*, heart, vitals.

praedicō, 1, publish, proclaim.

praedium, 2, estate.

praefectus, 2, commander.

praeferō, -ferre, -tulī, -lātum, show, display.

praegravis, 3, intolerable.

praegredior, 3, -gressus, *dep.*, go ahead.

praemium, 2, reward.

praesēns, -entis, present, at hand.

praesertim, especially.

praesidium, 2, defence, means of defence, garrison, guard.

praestō, 1, -stitī, -stitum, *intr.*, be outstanding; *tr.*, show, make good, perform (a service), cause, make it possible; *part.* **praestāns,** outstanding.

praesum, -esse, -fuī, be in control of, *with dat.*

praesūmō, 3, -sūmpsī, -sūmptum, take beforehand, provide.

praeter, *prep. with acc.,* beyond, besides, except, more than.

praetereō, -īre, -iī, -itum, go past, leave unmentioned.

praetexta toga, 1, toga with an embroidered purple edge, *worn by higher magistrates at Rome.*

praetextātus, 2, wearing the **toga praetexta.**

praetor, -ōris, praetor, judge, general.

prandeō, 2, -dī, -sum, have lunch.

prandium, 2, lunch.

premō, 3, pressī, pressum, press, crush.

pretium, 2, price, reward.

Prīmigenius, 2, Primigenius, *son of Echion in Petronius.*

prīmitus, at first.

prīmus, 2, first; **in prīmīs,** in particular; *adv.* **prīmō, prīmum,** at first; **quam prīmum,** as soon as possible.

prīnceps, -ipis, leader, emperor, chieftain, principal man.

prīncipātus, 4, leadership.

prior, -ōris, *comp. adj.*, former, first; *m. pl.* **priōrēs,** predecessors.

prīscus, 2, ancient.

Prīscus, 2, Tarquinius Priscus, *fifth king of Rome.*

priusquam (prius quam), *conj.*, before.

prīvātim, privately, for one's family.

prīvātus, 2, *adj.*, private; *m.*, private individual.

prō, *prep. with abl.*, for, on behalf of, as.

probō, 1, approve.

probus, 2, honest; *adv.* **probē**, properly.

prōclīvis, 3, sloping, downhill.

procul, at a distance, far from.

prōcurrō, 3, -(cu)currī, -cursum, project, jut out.

prōdeō, -īre, -iī, -itum, go forward

prōdigium, 2, portent, omen.

prōdō, 3, -didī, -ditum, hand down.

prōditor, -ōris, *m.*, traitor, informer.

proelior, 1, *dep.*, fight.

proelium, 2, battle.

profānus, 2, open to the public, ordinary.

prōferō, -ferre, -tulī, -lātum, carry forward; *pass.* gush out.

proficīscor, 3, -fectus, *dep.*, set out, march.

profiteor, 2, -fessus, *dep.*, declare, speak out.

profugus, 2, exiled, in exile.

profundus, 2, deep.

prōgnātus, 2, descended from; *m.*, son of, *with abl.*

progredior, 3, -gressus, *dep.*, advance.

prohibeō, 2, prevent, rescue from.

prohoemium, 2, preface.

proinde, therefore.

prōlabor, 3, -lapsus, *dep.*, fall.

prōmittō, 3, -mīsī, -missum, promise.

prōmoveō, 2, -mōvī, -mōtum, move forward, shift.

prōmptū, *abl. sing., only in* **in promptu**, in readiness.

prōmptus, 2, ready, quick.

promunturium, 2, promontory, projecting ridge, vantage point.

prōnuntiō, 1, recite, perform (on stage).

prōnus, 2, face downwards, tilted, downhill.

prōpatulum, 2, forecourt.

prope, *adv. and prep. with acc.*, near, nearly; **propediem**, soon.

prōpellō, -pulī, -pulsum, repel, avert.

properē, hastily.

properō, 1, hurry, hurry on.

propīnō, 1, drink to the health of, *with acc. and dat.*

prōpōnō, 3, -posuī, -positum, imagine, picture.

propter, *prep. with acc.*, on account of; **proptereā quod**, on account of the fact that, because.

prōpugnō, 1, fight for.

prōpulsō, 1, repel, avert.

prōscrībō, 3, -scrīpsī, -scrīptum, advertise.

prōsequor, 3, -secūtus, *dep.*, escort, see off.

prōspectus, 4, view.

prosperus, 2, prosperous, flourishing.

prōsum, prōdesse, prōfuī, help, benefit, *with dat.*

prōtego, 1, protect, save.

prout, just as.

prōveniō, 4, -vēnī, -ventum, grow, spring up.

prōvideō, 2, -vīdī, -vīsum, foresee, take precautions.

prōvinciālis, 3, provincial, living in the provinces.

proximus, 2, *superl. of* **prope**, nearest, next; *adv.* **proximē**, lately, quite recently.

prūdentia, 1, wisdom.

Prūsiās, -ae, Prusias, *king of Bithynia in Asia Minor.*

pūblicus, 2, public; **rēs pūblica,** the state; *adv.* **pūblicē,** publicly, at the public expense.

pudicē, strictly.

pudor, -ōris, *m.*, sense of shame, decency.

puer, -ī, boy.

pueritia, 1, boyhood.

pugna, 1, battle, fight.

pugnō, 1, fight, attack.

pulcher, -chra, -chrum, handsome, pretty.

pullus. 2, chicken.

pulsō, 1, beat, wash.

pulvis, -veris, *m.*, dust, earth.

puppis, 3, *f.*, stern, ship.

pūrgo, 1, clear.

purulentus, 2, festering.

pūrus, 2, clean.

putō, 1, think.

putrefaciō, 3, **-fēcī -factum,** cause to crumble.

Q

quā, by which way, where; **quā . . . quā,** not only . . . but also.

quadriduum, 2, four days.

quadringēnī, 2, *pl.*, 400 each, 400.

quaerō, 3, **quaesīvī, -sītum,** ask, ask for, look for, inquire into *or* after.

quaesō, 3, **quaesīvī,** beg.

quaestiō, -ōnis, *f.*, problem, inquiry.

quaestor, -ōris, quaestor, *Roman official.*

quālis, 3, of what sort, as.

quam, *adv.*, how, how much, than.

quamquam, although.

quamvīs, although; *with adj.*, however.

quandō, since.

quandōque, at some time.

quantulus, 2, how little, how small.

quantus, 2, how great; *acc.* as far as; *gen.* at what price; *abl.* (by) how much.

quāre, why?, for what reason?

quārtus, 2, fourth.

quasi, as if, as it were.

quattuor, *indecl.*, four.

-que, *enclitic*, and.

quemadmodum, how?

quī, quae quod, *relative pron.*, who, which; *old abl.* **quī,** whereby; **quodsī,** but if; *also interrog. pron.*, which?

quia, because.

quīcumque, quaecumque, quodcumque, whoever, whatever.

quīdam, quaedam, quoddam (quiddam), a certain one, someone; *adj.* a certain.

quidem, indeed, at least; **nē . . . quidem,** not even.

quiēs, -ētis, *f.*, rest, peace.

quīn, *conj. with subj.*, but that; *adv.* **quīn etiam,** on the contrary.

quīnam, quaenam, quodnam, who?, what?

Quīnquatrūs, 4, *f. pl.*, Quinquatrus, *festival of Minerva, held in March.*

quīntus, 2, fifth.

quippe, of course, to be sure.

quis, quid, who?, what?; **quid,** why?

quis, quid, *after* **sī, nē,** anyone.

quisquam, quaequam, quidquam (quicquam), anyone, *in a negative sentence.*

quisque, quaeque, quidque, each, each one.

quisquis, quaequae, quidquid, whoever, whichever.

quō, whither, to what place.

quoad, as long as.

quod, because, that.
quōmodō, how? as.
quondam, at some time, once, one day.
quoniam, because, since.
quoque, also, too, even.
quotannīs, every year, yearly.
quotiēns, quotiēs, whenever.

R

rādix, -icis, *f.,* root.
rārus, 2, rare, scarce.
ratiō, -ōnis, *f.,* reason, method, way, plan, account.
recēns, -entis, recent, fresh.
recidō, 3, -cidī, fall back.
reciperō, 1, recover, win back.
recipiō, 3, -cēpī, -ceptum, receive, afford *reflex.,* **sē recipero,** retire, retreat.
reclīnis, 3, reclining, bending over.
reconciliātiō, -ōnis, *f.,* reconciliation.
recreō, 1, refresh, revive, encourage.
rēctus, 2, upright, perpendicular; *adv.* **rēctē,** rightly, properly.
recumbō, 3, -cubuī, recline (*at a meal*).
reddō, 3, -didī, -ditum, give back, restore, make (*a noise*), administer (*justice*), bring up (*blood*).
redeō, -īre, -iī, -itum, return, revert.
referō, -ferre, rettulī, relātum, describe, relate; *reflex.* withdraw.
reficiō, 3, -fēcī, -fectum, *tr.* revive; *pass. intr.,* recover.
rēgia, 1, palace.
rēgīna, 1, queen.
regiō, -ōnis, *f.,* district, direction; **ā regiōne,** in a straight line, equidistant.
rēgius, 2, royal, of the king.

rēgnō, 1, reign, be king.
rēgnum, 2, kingdom, royal power.
rēiciō, 3, -iēcī, -iectum, refuse, spit.
religiō, -ōnis, *f.,* scruple, conscience.
religiōsus, 2, venerable.
relinquō, 3, -līquī, -lictum, leave, abandon.
reliquus, 2, the rest, the other, the remainder; *n.* the dregs.
relūceō, 2, -lūxī, shine, gleam.
remaneō, 2, -mānsī, -mānsum, remain.
remedium, 2, remedy, cure, antidote.
rēmex, -igis, rower, oarsman.
rēmigium, 2, rowing, crew.
rēmigō, 1, row.
remittō, 3, -mīsī, -missum, send back, let go.
removeō, 2, -mōvī, -mōtum, remove, get rid of.
rēmus, 2, oar.
renovō, 1, renew.
reor, 2, **ratus,** *dep.,* think.
repellō, 3, reppulī, repulsum, repulse, drive back.
repente, suddenly.
repercutiō, 3, -cussī, -cussum, drive back.
reperiō, 4, repperī, repertum, find.
repetō, 3, -petīvī (-iī), -petītum, return to
repleō, 2, -plēvī, -plētum, fill, fill up.
repraesentō, 1, imagine, redeem.
reprimō, 3, -pressī, -pressum, check.
reputō, 1, consider.
rēs, 5, thing, matter, affair, project, case, fact; **rēs pūblica,** the state.
rescrībō, 3, -scrīpsī, -scrīptum, write back.
resiliō, 4, -siluī, resist.

resonō, 1, —, make a noise, echo.
resorbeō, 2, —, suck back; *pass.*
ebb.
respectō, 1, —, look back.
respiciō, 3, -spexi, -spectum,
look back at, consider, care for.
respirātiō, -onis, *f.*, breathing,
gasp.
respondeō, 2, -spondī, -spōn-
sum, reply.
restinguō, 3, -stinxī, -stinctum,
quench, put out.
restituō, 3, -uī, -ūtum, restore,
recall.
restō, 1, -stitī, remain.
restringō, 3, -strinxī, -strictum,
restrict, deny oneself.
retineō, 2, -tinuī, -tentum, check,
stop, hold back, give pause to,
cling to.
retorqueō, 2, -torsī, -tortum,
force back.
revocō, 1, recall.
rēx, rēgis, king.
Rhadamanthus, 2, Rhadamanthus, *son of Jupiter, king of
Lycia, later judge in the Underworld.*
rideō, 2, rīsī, rīsum, laugh, smile
at.
rigor, -ōris, *m.*, coldness.
rīpa, 1, river-bank.
rīsus, 4, laughter.
rīvus, 2, stream, flow.
rīxa, 1, quarrel.
rixor, 1, *dep.*, quarrel.
rōbur, rōboris, *n.*, main strength.
rōbustus, 2, strong.
rogō, 1, ask.
Rōma, 1, Rome.
Rōmānus, 2, Roman; *m. pl.* the
Romans.
ruber, -bra, -brum, red; **rub-
rum mare**, the Red Sea, Indian
Ocean, *or* Persian Gulf.
rubrïcātus, 2, with headings in red.

ruïna, catastrophe, ruin.
ruïnōsus, 2, dilapidated, falling
into ruin.
rūmor, -ōris, *m.*, rumour, report.
ruō, 3, ruī, rutum, rush, fall
down, fall in, rush into ruin.
rūpēs, -is, *f.*, rock, cliff, crag.
rūrsus, again.
Rūsticus, 2, Fabius Rusticus,
Roman historian, c. A.D. *50.*
rutilus, 2, red.

S
sacellum, 2, little shrine.
sacer, -cra, -crum, sacred; *n.*
what is sacred; *n. pl.* sacred
rites.
saepe, often; *comp.* **saepius.**
sagitta, 1, arrow.
Salamis, -inis, *acc.* -ina, *f.*,
Salamis, *near Athens, where the
Greeks defeated the Persians at
sea in 480 B.C.*
saliō, 4, saluī, leap.
saltem, at least.
saluber, -bris, -bre, healthy,
favourable.
salūs, -ūtis, *f.*, health, safety;
salūtem dicere, send greetings.
salutātiō, -ōnis, *f.*, greeting.
salūtō, 1, greet.
salvus, 2, safe, alive, in good
health.
sanciō, 4, sanxī, sanctum, forbid
under penalty.
sanctus, 2, sacred.
sānē, indeed.
sanguis, -guinis, *m.*, blood.
sapientia, 1, wisdom.
sapienter, wisely, intelligently.
satis, enough, fairly, quite, clearly.
Satricum, 2, Satricum, *a small
town on the Appian Way.*
satur, -ura, -urum, well fed.
saxum, 2, rock, stone.

scapha, 1, boat, skiff.

scapula, 1, shoulder-blade.

scelus, sceleris, n., crime, wicked verdict.

scilicet, in fact, of course.

scio, 4, know.

scitum, 2, decree.

scitus, 2, elegant.

scordalus, 2, brawler, rowdy.

scortum, 2, n., woman.

scribo, 3, scripsi, scriptum, write.

scriptor, -oris, writer.

scrutor, 1, dep., examine.

scutum, 2, shield; per scutum per ocream, by hook or by crook.

scyphus, 2, cup

se (sese), sui, reflex. pron., himself, herself, themselves.

seco, 1, secui, sectum, cut.

secundum, prep. with acc., beside.

secretus, 2, secret, private; n., a private place.

securis, 3, acc. -im, f., axe.

sed, but, now.

sedeo, 2, sedi, sessum, sit down, sit.

sedes, 3, f., seat, chair, throne, home, abode, district.

sedulo, carefully, earnestly.

segniter, slowly.

segnitia, 1, lack of spirit.

sella, 1, chair, sedan-chair, litter.

semel, once.

semis, -issis, f., a half.

semper, always.

Seneca, -ae, m., Seneca, Stoic philosopher and writer, tutor of Nero.

senex, senis, old man.

sensim, gradually.

sensus, 4, sensation, feeling.

sententia, 1, opinion, way of thinking.

sentio, 4, sensi, -sum, feel, perceive.

sepono, 3, -posui, -positum, shut away.

September, -bris, of September.

septentrionalis, 3, northern; n. pl. northern regions.

sequor, 3, secutus, dep., follow.

Ser., Servius, 2, Servius, a Roman proper name; Servius Tullius, the sixth king of Rome.

serius, 2, serious, important.

sermo, -onis, m., speech, talk, conversation; pl. languages.

sero, adv., late.

serpens, -entis, snake, worm; pl. vermin.

serrarius, 2, sawyer, one who saws.

serva, 1, female slave.

servio, 4, be a slave.

servitium, 2, slavery, a slave.

servulus, 2, young slave.

servus, 2, slave.

sestertius, 2, (HS), a sesterce, a Roman coin worth about 10 new pence (see note under HS).

seu, whether, or if.

severitas, -atis, f., sternness.

sexageni, 2, pl., 60 each, 60.

si, if.

sibilus, 2, hissing.

sic, so, thus, in such a way.

siccus, 2, dry.

sicut, sicuti, as, just as.

sidus, -eris, n., star, constellation.

signum, 2, sign, signal, standard.

silentium, 2, silence.

sileo, 2, -ui, be silent.

Silures, 3, pl., the Silures, a British people living in South Wales.

silva, 1, wood, forest.

similis, 3, like, similar to.

similitudo, -inis, f., similarity.

Simonides, -is, Simonides of Ceos, Greek lyric poet, d. c. 468 B.C.

simplicitas, -atis, f., frankness.

simul, at the same time; simul ac, conj. as soon as.

simulātiō, -ōnis, *f.,* pretence, hypocrisy.

simulō, 1, pretend.

simultās, -ātis, *f.,* quarrel, strife.

sīn, but if.

sine, *prep. with abl.,* without.

singulī, 2, *pl.,* single, as individuals.

singultus, 4, sob, gurgling sound.

sinō, 3, **sīvī, situm,** allow.

sinus, 4, fold (in a garment), pocket.

Sīrēnes, -um, *f. pl.,* the Sirens.

sistō, 3, **stitī, statum,** hold back.

Sīsyphus, 2, Sisyphus, *legendary king of Corinth famed for his cunning.*

sitiō, 4, be thirsty.

situs, 4, geographical position.

sīve, seu, whether, or if.

socer, -erī, father-in-law.

societās, -ātis, *f.,* alliance.

socius, 2, ally, comrade.

Sōcratēs, -is, Socrates, *famous Athenian philosopher, executed 399 B.C.*

socrus, 4, *f.,* mother-in-law.

sōl, sōlis, *m.,* sun.

soleō, 2, **solitus,** *semi-dep.,* be accustomed.

sollertia, 1, ingenuity, cunning.

solum, 2, ground, soil.

sōlum, *adv.,* only.

solvō, 3, **solvī, -ūtum,** loose, open; *pass.* come loose; *p.p.p.* **solūtus,** unrestrained.

somnium, 2, dream.

somnus, 2, sleep.

sonitus, 4, noise.

sonus, 2, sound.

sōpiō, 4, stun.

soror, -ōris, sister.

sors, sortis, *f.,* lot, oracular reply, *also pl.*

spargō, 3, **sparsī, sparsum,** scatter, destroy.

Sparta, 1, Sparta, *capital of Laconia in southern Greece, also called Lacedaemon.*

Spartiātēs, -ae, *m.,* a Spartan.

spatium, 2, space, extent, length, district.

speciēs, 5, appearance, pretence.

spectō, 1, look at, consider.

spernō, 3, **sprēvī, sprētum,** despise, reject.

spērō, 1, hope.

spēs, 5, hope.

spīrāmentum, 2, passage for ventilation, air-hole.

spīritus, 4, breath, current of air.

spīrō, 1, breathe.

sponte, *abl. f.,* of one's own accord.

statim, immediately.

Stātius, 2, Statius, *a slave of Cicero.*

statīva (castra), 2, *pl.,* permanent camp.

Stator, -ōris, *m.,* the Stayer (of flight), *a name given to Jupiter.*

statua, 1, statue.

status, 2, fixed, regular.

stēla, 1, tombstone, epitaph.

stimulō, 1, urge on, spur on.

stips, stipis, *f.,* a small coin.

stirps, stirpis, *f.,* root, stock, race, children.

stō, 1, **stetī, statum,** stand.

Stōicus, 2, a Stoic philosopher.

stomachus, 2, anger.

strangulō, 1, block.

strēnuus, 2, energetic.

stringō, 3, **strinxī, strictum,** draw (a sword).

struēs, -is, *f.,* heap, pile.

studeō, 2, study (*with dat.*), research, be at a secondary school.

studiōsus, 2, keen, interested.

studium, 2, study, rivalry, taste; *pl.,* education.

suāvis, 3, charming.

subfuscus, 2, discoloured.

subgrandis, 3, fair sized.

subiciō, 3, **-iēci**, **-iectum**, place under; *p.p.p.* **subiectus**, lying below.

subinde, repeatedly.

subitus, 2, sudden, unexpected; *n. pl.* **subita**, sudden apparitions; *adv.* **subitō**, suddenly.

sublevō, 1, help, diminish.

submergō, 3, **-mersī**, **-mersum**, *tr.*, sink, capsize; *pass. intr.*

subsum, -esse, —, be present.

subter, *prep. with acc. or abl.*, at the foot of.

subtrahō, 3, **-trāxi**, **-tractum**, withdraw; *pass.* ebb.

subveniō, 4, **-vēnī**, **-ventum**, come to the help of, *with dat.*

succendō, 3, **-cēnsi**, **-cēnsum**, kindle.

succēnseō, 2, **-uī**, be angry with, *with dat.*

succidō, 3, **-cidī**, fall down.

sūdor, **-ōris**, *m.*, sweat.

suēsco, 3, **suēvī**, **suētum**, become accustomed, *p.p.*, **suētus**, accustomed.

Suessa Pōmētia, 1, Suessa Pometia, *a town of the Volsci.*

sufficiō, 3, **-fēcī**, **-fectum**, be enough for.

sum, esse, fuī, be.

summa, 1, chief command; **in summā**, in brief.

summus, 2, *superl.*, greatest, highest, top of, supreme.

sūmō, 3, **sūmpsī**, **sūmptum**, take, derive.

sūmptus, 4, expense, expenditure.

superbia, 1, pride, arrogance.

superior, **-ōris**, *comp.*, higher, upper.

superō, 1, overcome.

superstes, **-stitis**, surviving; **superstes esse**, to survive.

superstitiō, **-ōnis**, *f.*, *also pl.*, religion.

supersum, -esse, -fuī, survive.

superveniō, 4, **-vēnī**, **-ventum**, come on the scene.

supplicium, 2, prayer, offering to the gods, punishment.

supprimō, 3, **-pressī**, **-pressum**, check, cause to ebb.

suprā, *prep. with acc.* over, above, upon.

suprēmus, 2, *superl.*, last.

surdus, 2, deaf.

suscitō, 1, stir up, start.

suspectus, 2, suspected; *comp.* **suspectior.**

sustineō, 2, **-tinuī**, **-tentum**, withstand, keep from.

suus, 2, his, her, its, their.

syngramma (σύγγραμμα), *n.*, composition.

T

tabellārius, 2, letter-carrier.

tābēs, **-is**, *f.*, slush.

tābidus, 2, thawing, melting.

tabula, 1, writing-tablet.

taedium, 2, weariness, strain.

taeter, **-tra**, **-trum**, foul, horrible, disgraceful, hostile; *superl.*, **taeterrimus.**

talentum, 2, talent, *a sum of money in Athens, 60 minae or 6000 drachmae.*

tālis, 3, such.

tam, so.

tamen, however, nevertheless.

tamquam, as though, as if, like, as.

Tanaquil, **-is**, *f.*, Tanaquil, *wife of Tarquinius Priscus.*

tandem, at length.

tantus, 2, so great, so much, so important; **tantō opere**, so much; *adv.* **tantum**, only.

tarditās, **-ātis**, *f.*, lateness, slowness.

tardus, 2, slow; *adv.* **tardē.**

Tarentinus, 2, of Tarentum.

Tarentum, 2, Tarentum, *town in S.W. Italy.*

Tarquinius, 2, Tarquinius Priscus, *the fifth king of Rome.*

Taurus, 2, M. Taurus, *owner of an estate near Q. Cicero's.*

tectōrium, 2, plaster, stucco.

tectum, 2, roof.

tēcum, with you.

tegō, 3, defend.

tēlum, 2, weapon, implement; *pl.* gear.

temere, rashly, blindly, suddenly.

tempestās, -ātis, *f.*, storm, weather, time.

templum, 2, temple.

temptābundus, 2, feeling one's way.

temptō, 1, test, attempt, assault, try to corrupt.

tempus, -oris, *n.*, time, date.

tendō, 3, **tetendī, tentum (tēnsum),** make one's way, move (into).

tenebrae, 1, *pl.*, darkness.

teneō, 2, **tenuī,** hold; **spēs me tenet,** I am hopeful.

tenuō, 1, lessen; *pass.* taper off.

tenus, *prep. following abl.*, as far as.

ter, three times, thrice.

Terentius, 2, Terentius, *a slave innkeeper in Petronius.*

terminus, 2, limit.

terō, 3, **trīvī, trītum,** tread.

terra, 1, land, earth, *also pl.*

terror, -ōris, *m.*, terror.

tertius, 2, third; *adv.* **tertiō,** for a third time.

testula, 1, potsherd, vote written on a potsherd.

Themistoclēs, -i, Themistocles, *famous Athenian general and statesman, d. c. 458* B.C.

Theramenēs, -is, Theramenes, *Athenian statesman and general, d. 404* B.C.

Thermopylae, 1, *pl.*, Thermopylae, *a narrow pass in N. Greece held by Leonidas against the Persians in 490* B.C.

thēsaurus, 2 (*n.*, *in Petronius*), treasure.

Thūlē, -ēs, *f.*, Thule, *an island north of Scotland, perhaps one of the Shetlands.*

tībia, 1, flute.

timeō, 2, fear.

timōr, -ōris, *m.*, fear.

Tīrō, -ōnis, Tiro, *Cicero's secretary.*

titubō, 1, stumble, lose one's way.

tolerābilis, 3, endurable, average.

tollō, 3, **sustulī, sublātum,** raise, pick up, remove.

tōnstrēinus, 2, barber.

tōpiāria, 1, landscape gardening.

tōpiārius, 2, landscape gardener.

torpeō, 2, **-uī,** be numb, be inactive.

torqueō, 2, **torsī, tortum,** twist, torture.

torridus, 2, scorching, heated.

tortus, 2, curly.

tot, totidem, *indecl.*, so many, as many.

tōtus, 2, the whole, all, entirely.

trabēa, 1, robe of state.

tractātiō, -ōnis, *f.*, handling.

tractō, 1, handle.

trādō, 3, **-didī, -ditum,** hand on, relate, describe.

trahō, 3, **trāxi, tractum,** draw, draw apart, draw out, prolong, distract.

trāiciō, 3, **-iēcī, -iectum,** pierce, run through, cross over.

trānscendō, 3, **-cendī, -cēnsum,** cross.

trānscurrō, 3, **-currī, -cursum,** run across, run over, run past.

trānseō, -īre, -iī, -itum, cross, pass along the horizon.

trānsferō (trāferō), -ferre, -tulī, -lātum, transfer, move over.

trānsgredior, 3, -gressus, *dep.*, cross, cross over.

trānsmittō, 3, -mīsī, -missum, span, cross, allow to pass.

trēs, tria, *pl.*, three.

trīduum, 2, three days.

trīgintā, *indecl.*, *pl.*, thirty.

Triptolemus, 2, Triptolemus, *mythical king of Eleusis and later judge in the Underworld.*

trirēmis, 3, *f.*, trireme, *Greek warship with three banks of oars.*

tristis, 3, sad; *n. pl.* sad news.

trītūs, 2, trodden (*p.p.p.* of **terō**).

Trōia, 1, Troy, *in N.W. Asia Minor.*

Trōiānī, 2, *pl.*, the Trojans.

tū, tuī, you (*sing.*).

tubula, 1, horn, trumpet.

Tullius, 2, Servius Tullius, *sixth king of Rome.*

tum, then, at that time, after that, moreover.

tumultuōsē, noisily, with an uproar.

tumultus, 4, disturbance, uproar.

turbō, 1, throw into confusion.

Tusculānum, 2, Cicero's estate at Tusculum, *near Rome*; *also* Agrippina's.

tussicula, 1, slight cough.

tūtor, -ōris, *m.*, guardian.

tuus, 2, your (*sing.*); **tuum est**, it is your duty.

tyrannus, 2, tyrant, king.

U

ubi, when, where.

Ulixēs, -is, Ulysses (*in Greek Odysseus*), *of Ithaca, most cunning of the Greek leaders at Troy.*

ūllus, 2, any.

ultor, -ōris, avenger, punisher.

ultrā, *adv. and prep. with acc.*, beyond; **ultrā esse**, exceed.

ululō, 1, howl.

umbra, 1, shade, shadow.

umerus, 2, shoulder.

ūmor, -ōris, *m.*, wetness, moistness, water.

umquam, ever.

ūnā, *adv.*, together, at one place.

unctiō, -ōnis, *f.*, massage.

unde, whence, from where, from which.

undique, from all sides.

ungula, 1, hoof.

ūnicus, 2, unique, remarkable.

ūniversus, 2, whole, as a whole, in a body; **in ūniversum**, as a whole.

ūnus, 2, one, alone; *adv.* **ūnā**, together.

urbānus, 2, of a city, of a town.

urbs, urbis, *f.*, city.

ūsus, 4, practice, experience.

ut, as, when, whenever; *with subj.*, that, in order that, with the result that.

utcumque, whenever.

uter, utra, utrum, which of the two.

uterque, utraque, utrumque, each of the two, both.

ūtilis, 3, useful, advantageous.

utinam, would that, *with subj.*

ūtor, 3, ūsus, *dep.*, use, make (a speech), *with abl.*

utrōbīque, on both sides, in both places.

utrum, whether (*in a double question*).

uxor, uxōris, wife.

V

vacō, 1, be free.

vādō, 3, —, go.

vagor, 1, *dep.*, wander about.

vagus, 2, wandering, roaming.

valdē, very much.

valeō, 2, be well, flourish, prevail, be powerful; *imper.* **valē,** farewell.

validus, 2, powerful, strong.

vallis, 3, *f.*, valley.

vānus, 2, empty, useless.

vapōrārium, 2, chimney.

variō, 1, alternate, take in turn.

varius, 2, different, of a different kind, various, varied; *adv.* **variē,** differently.

Varrō, -ōnis, Varro, *owner of an estate near Q. Cicero's.*

vās, vāsis, *n.*, vessel, jar.

vāstus, 2, great, enormous.

-ve, *enclitic,* or.

vehementer, extremely.

vehō, 3, **vēxi, vectum,** carry, convey; *pass.* sail.

velut, as though, as if, just as.

vēna, 1, channel.

vēnālis, 3, for sale.

vēnditor, -ōris, *m.*, seller.

vēndō, 3, **-didī, -ditum,** sell, display.

venēnātus, 2, poisonous.

venēnum, 2, poison.

venerātiō, -ōnis, *f.*, worship, cult.

veniō, 4, **vēnī, ventum,** come.

ventus, 2, wind.

verbum, 2, word.

verberō, 1, beat, batter.

verbum, 2, word.

vergēns, -entis, leaning, upsidedown.

Vergiliae, 1, *pl.,* the constellation of the Pleiades.

versipellis, 3, changing one's shape; *m.* a werewolf.

versūra, 1, loan, taking a loan.

vertō, 3, **vertī, versum,** turn; *p.p.p.,* **versus,** facing.

versus, *adv.,* in the direction of.

vērus, 2, true; *n.* **vērum,** the truth; *adv.* **vērē,** truly; **vērum,** but; **vērō,** indeed, but.

vescor, 3, —, *dep.,* take a meal.

vester, -tra, -trum, your (*pl.*).

vēstibulum, 2, entrance court.

vēstigium, 2, footprint, trace, track.

vestimentum, 2, clothing.

vestio, 4, clothe, cover.

vetō, 1, **-uī, -itum,** forbid, order . . . not.

vetus, veteris, old, prehistoric; *m. pl.* **veterēs,** old writers.

vexō, 1, trouble, annoy.

via, 1, road, way, street.

viāticum, 2, journey-money.

vicem, -is, *f.* (*no nom.*), turn, duty; **in vicem,** in turn; **alternīs vicibus,** alternately.

vicīnus, 2, neighbouring.

victōria, 1, victory.

vīcus, 2, street.

videō, 2, **vīdī, vīsum,** see, look at; *pass.,* seem; **vidēn = vidēsne.**

vigilārium, 2, watch-tower.

vīgintī, *indecl. pl.,* twenty.

vīlicus, 2, farm bailiff.

vīlla, 1, country house, inn (on an estate).

vincō, 3, **vīcī, victum,** conquer, overcome.

vindicō, 1, inflict punishment (on).

vir, virī, man, husband.

virgultum, 2, bush, thicket.

viridis, 3, green.

virīlis, 3, manly.

virtūs, -ūtis, *f.,* courage, virtue, merit, worth.

vīs, *abl.,* **vī,** *f.,* force, power; *pl.,* **vīrēs, vīrium,** strength.

vīsō, 3, **vīsī, vīsum,** visit, go to see.

vīsum, 2, a vision.

vīsus, 4, appearance.

vīta, 1, life.

vītis, 3, *f.,* vine, vine tree.

vitium, 2, fault, flaw.

vītō, 1, avoid.

vitreus, 2, glassy.

vīvō, 3, vīxi, vīctum, live.

vīvus, 2, alive.

vix, scarcely.

vōciferor, 1, *dep.*, raise one's voice, shout.

vocō, 1, call, summon.

volō, 1, fly, flow, run down.

volō, velle, voluī, want, wish.

voluntās, -ātis, *f.*, wish, will, consent.

voluptās, -ātis, *f.*, pleasure.

volūtō, 1, *tr.*, roll; *pass. intr.*

vōs, vestrum (vestrī), you (*pl.*).

vōx, vōcis, *f.*, voice, word.

vulnus, -eris, *n.*, wound.

vultus, 4, face.

X

X, decem, ten.

Xerxēs, -is, Xerxes, *king of Persia, who invaded Greece in 480 B.C.*

Z

Zōsimus, 2, Zosimus, *a freed slave of Pliny.*